Prentice Hall Mathematics

ALGEBRA READINESS

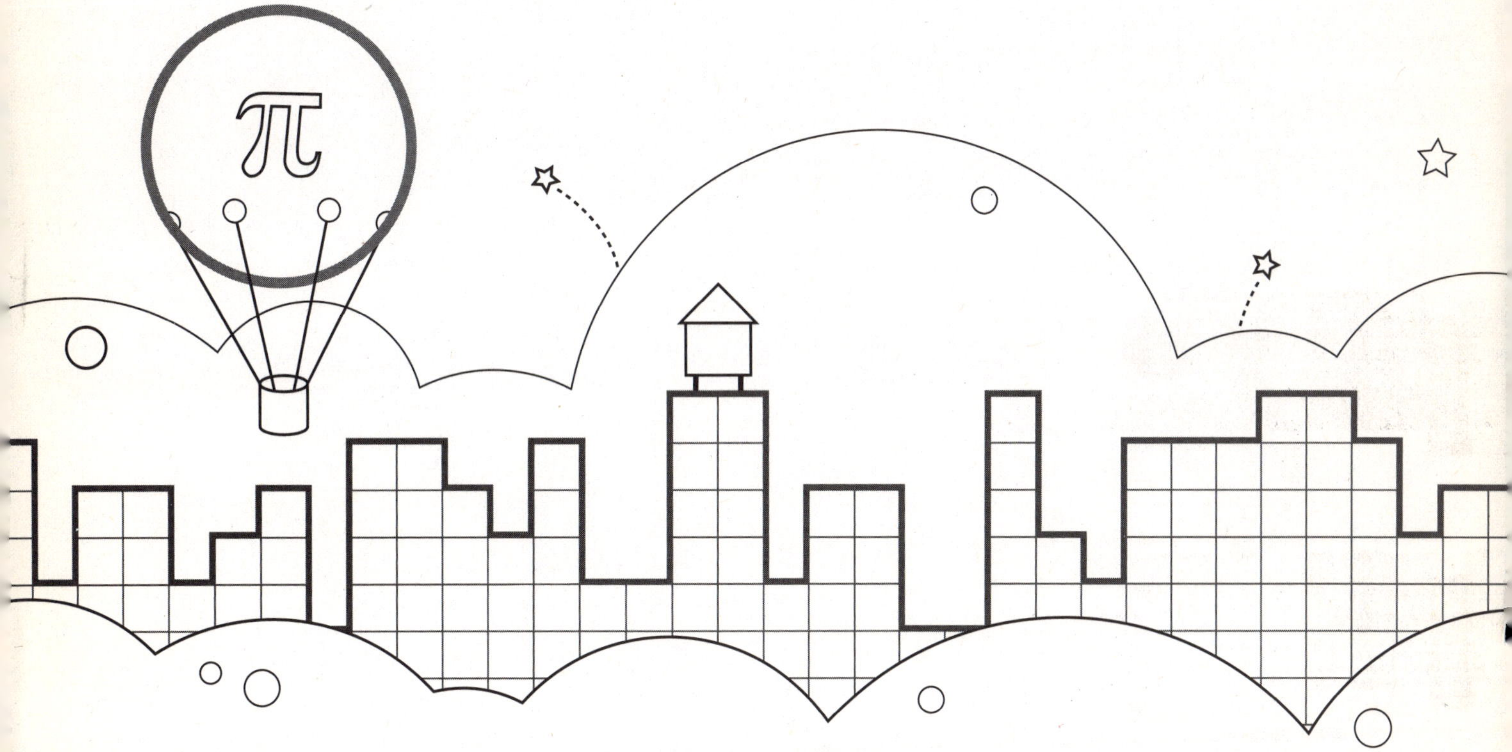

ALL-IN-ONE
Student Workbook
VERSION B

PEARSON

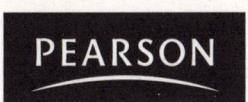

Boston, Massachusetts • Chandler, Arizona • Glenview, Illinois • Upper Saddle River, New Jersey

Copyright © 2010 Pearson Education, Inc., or its affiliates. All rights reserved. Printed in the United States of America. This publication is protected by copyright, and permission should be obtained from the publisher prior to any prohibited reproduction, storage in a retrieval system, or transmission in any form or by any means, electronic, mechanical, photo-copying, recording, or likewise. The publisher hereby grants permission to reproduce these pages, in part or in whole, for classroom use only, the number not to exceed the number of students in each class. Notice of copyright must appear on all copies. For information regarding permissions, write to Pearson Curriculum Group, Rights and Permissions, One Lake Street, Upper Saddle River, New Jersey 07458.

Pearson, Prentice Hall, and Pearson Prentice Hall are trademarks in the U.S. and / or other countries, of Pearson Education, Inc., or its affiliates.

ISBN-13: 978-0-13-372150-8
ISBN-10: 0-13-372150-7

1 2 3 4 5 6 7 8 9 10   13 12 11 10 09

Daily Notetaking Guide

Lesson 1-1 2
Lesson 1-2 4
Lesson 1-3 6
Lesson 1-4 8
Lesson 1-5 10
Lesson 1-6 12
Lesson 1-7 14
Lesson 1-8 16
Lesson 1-9 18
Lesson 1-10 20
Lesson 2-1 22
Lesson 2-2 24
Lesson 2-3 26
Lesson 2-4 28
Lesson 2-5 30
Lesson 2-6 32
Lesson 2-7 34
Lesson 2-8 36
Lesson 2-9 38
Lesson 2-10 40
Lesson 3-1 42
Lesson 3-2 44
Lesson 3-3 46
Lesson 3-4 48
Lesson 3-5 50
Lesson 3-6 52
Lesson 3-7 54
Lesson 4-1 56
Lesson 4-2 58
Lesson 4-3 60
Lesson 4-4 62
Lesson 4-5 64
Lesson 4-6 66
Lesson 4-7 68
Lesson 4-8 70
Lesson 4-9 72
Lesson 5-1 74
Lesson 5-2 76
Lesson 5-3 78
Lesson 5-4 80
Lesson 5-5 82
Lesson 5-6 84
Lesson 5-7 86
Lesson 5-8 88
Lesson 5-9 90
Lesson 6-1 92
Lesson 6-2 94
Lesson 6-3 96
Lesson 6-4 98
Lesson 6-5 100
Lesson 6-6 102
Lesson 6-7 104
Lesson 6-8 106
Lesson 6-9 108
Lesson 6-10 110

Lesson 7-1 112
Lesson 7-2 114
Lesson 7-3 116
Lesson 7-4 118
Lesson 7-5 120
Lesson 7-6 122
Lesson 7-7 124
Lesson 8-1 126
Lesson 8-2 128
Lesson 8-3 130
Lesson 8-4 132
Lesson 8-5 134
Lesson 8-6 136
Lesson 8-7 138
Lesson 9-1 140
Lesson 9-2 142
Lesson 9-3 144
Lesson 9-4 146
Lesson 9-5 148
Lesson 9-6 150
Lesson 9-7 152
Lesson 9-8 154
Lesson 9-9 156
Lesson 9-10 158
Lesson 10-1 160
Lesson 10-2 162
Lesson 10-3 164
Lesson 10-4 166
Lesson 10-5 168
Lesson 10-6 170
Lesson 10-7 172
Lesson 10-8 174
Lesson 10-9 176
Lesson 10-10 178
Lesson 11-1 180
Lesson 11-2 182
Lesson 11-3 184
Lesson 11-4 186
Lesson 11-5 188
Lesson 12-1 190
Lesson 12-2 192
Lesson 12-3 194
Lesson 12-4 196
Lesson 12-5 198
Lesson 12-6 200

Practice, Guided Problem Solving, Vocabulary

Chapter 1 Algebraic Expressions and Integers

Practice 1-1	205
Guided Problem Solving 1-1	206
Practice 1-2	207
Guided Problem Solving 1-2	208
Practice 1-3	209
Guided Problem Solving 1-3	210
Practice 1-4	211
Guided Problem Solving 1-4	212
Practice 1-5	213
Guided Problem Solving 1-5	214
Practice 1-6	215
Guided Problem Solving 1-6	216
Practice 1-7	217
Guided Problem Solving 1-7	218
Practice 1-8	219
Guided Problem Solving 1-8	220
Practice 1-9	221
Guided Problem Solving 1-9	222
Practice 1-10	223
Guided Problem Solving 1-10	224
Vocabulary 1A: Graphic Organizer	225
Vocabulary 1B: Reading Comprehension	226
Vocabulary 1C: Reading/Writing Math Symbols	227
Vocabulary 1D: Visual Vocabulary Practice	228
Vocabulary 1E: Vocabulary Check	229
Vocabulary 1F: Vocabulary Review Puzzle	231

Chapter 2 Solving One-Step Equations and Inequalities

Practice 2-1	233
Guided Problem Solving 2-1	234
Practice 2-2	235
Guided Problem Solving 2-2	236
Practice 2-3	237
Guided Problem Solving 2-3	238
Practice 2-4	239
Guided Problem Solving 2-4	240
Practice 2-5	241
Guided Problem Solving 2-5	242
Practice 2-6	243
Guided Problem Solving 2-6	244
Practice 2-7	245
Guided Problem Solving 2-7	246
Practice 2-8	247
Guided Problem Solving 2-8	248
Practice 2-9	249
Guided Problem Solving 2-9	250
Practice 2-10	251
Guided Problem Solving 2-10	252
Vocabulary 2A: Graphic Organizer	253
Vocabulary 2B: Reading Comprehension	254
Vocabulary 2C: Reading/Writing Math Symbols	255
Vocabulary 2D: Visual Vocabulary Practice	256
Vocabulary 2E: Vocabulary Check	257
Vocabulary 2F: Vocabulary Review	259

Chapter 3 Decimals and Equations

Practice 3-1 261
Guided Problem Solving 3-1 262
Practice 3-2 263
Guided Problem Solving 3-2 264
Practice 3-3 265
Guided Problem Solving 3-3 266
Practice 3-4 267
Guided Problem Solving 3-4 268
Practice 3-5 269
Guided Problem Solving 3-5 270
Practice 3-6 271
Guided Problem Solving 3-6 272
Practice 3-7 273
Guided Problem Solving 3-7 274
Vocabulary 3A: Graphic Organizer 275
Vocabulary 3B: Reading Comprehension 276
Vocabulary 3C: Reading/Writing Math Symbols 277
Vocabulary 3D: Visual Vocabulary Practice 278
Vocabulary 3E: Vocabulary Check 279
Vocabulary 3F: Vocabulary Review Puzzle 281

Chapter 4 Factors, Fractions, and Exponents

Practice 4-1 283
Guided Problem Solving 4-1 284
Practice 4-2 285
Guided Problem Solving 4-2 286
Practice 4-3 287
Guided Problem Solving 4-3 288
Practice 4-4 289
Guided Problem Solving 4-4 290
Practice 4-5 291
Guided Problem Solving 4-5 292
Practice 4-6 293
Guided Problem Solving 4-6 294
Practice 4-7 295
Guided Problem Solving 4-7 296
Practice 4-8 297
Guided Problem Solving 4-8 298
Practice 4-9 299
Guided Problem Solving 4-9 300
Vocabulary 4A: Graphic Organizer 301
Vocabulary 4B: Reading Comprehension 302
Vocabulary 4C: Reading/Writing Math Symbols 303
Vocabulary 4D: Visual Vocabulary Practice 304
Vocabulary 4E: Vocabulary Check 305
Vocabulary 4F: Vocabulary Review 307

Chapter 5 Operations With Fractions

Practice 5-1 309
Guided Problem Solving 5-1 310
Practice 5-2 311
Guided Problem Solving 5-2 312
Practice 5-3 313
Guided Problem Solving 5-3 314

Practice 5-4 315
Guided Problem Solving 5-4 316
Practice 5-5 317
Guided Problem Solving 5-5 318
Practice 5-6 319
Guided Problem Solving 5-6 320
Practice 5-7 321
Guided Problem Solving 5-7 322
Practice 5-8 323
Guided Problem Solving 5-8 324
Practice 5-9 325
Guided Problem Solving 5-9 326
Vocabulary 5A: Graphic Organizer 327
Vocabulary 5B: Reading Comprehension 328
Vocabulary 5C: Reading/Writing Math Symbols ... 329
Vocabulary 5D: Visual Vocabulary Practice 330
Vocabulary 5E: Vocabulary Check 331
Vocabulary 5F: Vocabulary Review Puzzle 333

Chapter 6 Ratios, Proportions, and Percents

Practice 6-1 335
Guided Problem Solving 6-1 336
Practice 6-2 337
Guided Problem Solving 6-2 338
Practice 6-3 339
Guided Problem Solving 6-3 340
Practice 6-4 341
Guided Problem Solving 6-4 342
Practice 6-5 343
Guided Problem Solving 6-5 344
Practice 6-6 345
Guided Problem Solving 6-6 346
Practice 6-7 347
Guided Problem Solving 6-7 348
Practice 6-8 349
Guided Problem Solving 6-8 350
Practice 6-9 351
Guided Problem Solving 6-9 352
Practice 6-10 353
Guided Problem Solving 6-10 354
Vocabulary 6A: Graphic Organizer 355
Vocabulary 6B: Reading Comprehension 356
Vocabulary 6C: Reading/Writing Math Symbols ... 357
Vocabulary 6D: Visual Vocabulary Practice 358
Vocabulary 6E: Vocabulary Check 359
Vocabulary 6F: Vocabulary Review Puzzle 361

Chapter 7 Solving Equations and Inequalities

Practice 7-1 363
Guided Problem Solving 7-1 364
Practice 7-2 365
Guided Problem Solving 7-2 366
Practice 7-3 367
Guided Problem Solving 7-3 368
Practice 7-4 369
Guided Problem Solving 7-4 370
Practice 7-5 371

Guided Problem Solving 7-5 372
Practice 7-6 373
Guided Problem Solving 7-6 374
Practice 7-7 375
Guided Problem Solving 7-7 376
Vocabulary 7A: Graphic Organizer 377
Vocabulary 7B: Reading Comprehension 378
Vocabulary 7C: Reading/Writing Math Symbols 379
Vocabulary 7D: Visual Vocabulary Practice 380
Vocabulary 7E: Vocabulary Check 381
Vocabulary 7F: Vocabulary Review 383

Chapter 8 Linear Functions and Graphing

Practice 8-1 385
Guided Problem Solving 8-1 386
Practice 8-2 387
Guided Problem Solving 8-2 388
Practice 8-3 389
Guided Problem Solving 8-3 390
Practice 8-4 391
Guided Problem Solving 8-4 392
Practice 8-5 393
Guided Problem Solving 8-5 394
Practice 8-6 395
Guided Problem Solving 8-6 396
Practice 8-7 397
Guided Problem Solving 8-7 398
Vocabulary 8A: Graphic Organizer 399
Vocabulary 8B: Reading Comprehension 400
Vocabulary 8C: Reading/Writing Math Symbols 401
Vocabulary 8D: Visual Vocabulary Practice 402
Vocabulary 8E: Vocabulary Check 403
Vocabulary 8F: Vocabulary Review Puzzle 405

Chapter 9 Spatial Thinking

Practice 9-1 407
Guided Problem Solving 9-1 408
Practice 9-2 409
Guided Problem Solving 9-2 410
Practice 9-3 411
Guided Problem Solving 9-3 412
Practice 9-4 413
Guided Problem Solving 9-4 414
Practice 9-5 415
Guided Problem Solving 9-5 416
Practice 9-6 417
Guided Problem Solving 9-6 418
Practice 9-7 419
Guided Problem Solving 9-7 420
Practice 9-8 421
Guided Problem Solving 9-8 422
Practice 9-9 423
Guided Problem Solving 9-9 424

Practice 9-10 425
Guided Problem Solving 9-10 426
Vocabulary 9A: Graphic Organizer 427
Vocabulary 9B: Reading Comprehension 428
Vocabulary 9C: Reading/Writing Math Symbols 429
Vocabulary 9D: Visual Vocabulary Practice 430
Vocabulary 9E: Vocabulary Check 431
Vocabulary 9F: Vocabulary Review 433

Chapter 10 Area and Volume

Practice 10-1 435
Guided Problem Solving 10-1 436
Practice 10-2 437
Guided Problem Solving 10-2 438
Practice 10-3 439
Guided Problem Solving 10-3 440
Practice 10-4 441
Guided Problem Solving 10-4 442
Practice 10-5 443
Guided Problem Solving 10-5 444
Practice 10-6 445
Guided Problem Solving 10-6 446
Practice 10-7 447
Guided Problem Solving 10-7 448
Practice 10-8 449
Guided Problem Solving 10-8 450
Practice 10-9 451
Guided Problem Solving 10-9 452
Practice 10-10 453
Guided Problem Solving 10-10 454
Vocabulary 10A: Graphic Organizer 455
Vocabulary 10B: Reading Comprehension 456
Vocabulary 10C: Reading/Writing Math Symbols 457
Vocabulary 10D: Visual Vocabulary Practice 458
Vocabulary 10E: Vocabulary Check 459
Vocabulary 10F: Vocabulary Review 461

Chapter 11 Irrational Numbers and Nonlinear Functions

Practice 11-1 463
Guided Problem Solving 11-1 464
Practice 11-2 465
Guided Problem Solving 11-2 466
Practice 11-3 467
Guided Problem Solving 11-3 468
Practice 11-4 469
Guided Problem Solving 11-4 470
Practice 11-5 471
Guided Problem Solving 11-5 472
Vocabulary 11A: Graphic Organizer 473
Vocabulary 11B: Reading Comprehension 474
Vocabulary 11C: Reading/Writing Math Symbols 475
Vocabulary 11D: Visual Vocabulary Practice 476
Vocabulary 11E: Vocabulary Check 477
Vocabulary 11F: Vocabulary Review Puzzle 479

Chapter 12 Data Analysis and Probability

Practice 12-1 481
Guided Problem Solving 12-1 482
Practice 12-2 483
Guided Problem Solving 12-2 484
Practice 12-3 485
Guided Problem Solving 12-3 486
Practice 12-4 487
Guided Problem Solving 12-4 488
Practice 12-5 489
Guided Problem Solving 12-5 490
Practice 12-6 491
Guided Problem Solving 12-6 492
Vocabulary 12A: Graphic Organizer 493
Vocabulary 12B: Reading Comprehension 494
Vocabulary 12C: Reading/Writing Math Symbols 495
Vocabulary 12D: Visual Vocabulary Practice 496
Vocabulary 12E: Vocabulary Check 497
Vocabulary 12F: Vocabulary Review Puzzle 499

A Note to the Student:

This section of your workbook contains notetaking pages for each lesson in your student edition. They are structured to help you take effective notes in class. They will also serve as a study guide as you prepare for tests and quizzes.

Daily Notetaking Guide

Name_____ Class_____ Date_____

Lesson 1-1   Variables and Expressions

Lesson Objectives
- Identify variables, numerical expressions, and algebraic expressions
- Write algebraic expressions for word phrases

Vocabulary

A _____ is a letter that stands for a number.

An algebraic expression is _____

_____

$$\text{variable} \rightarrow m \leftarrow \text{miles on 10 gallons}$$
$$\text{algebraic expression} \rightarrow m \div 10 \leftarrow \text{miles per gallon}$$

Examples

❶ Identifying Expressions Identify each expression as a *numerical expression* or an *algebraic expression*.

a. 7×3

[   ] expression

b. $4t$

[   ] expression

[ ] is the variable.

❷ Writing an Algebraic Expression Write an algebraic expression for the cost in cents of p pens priced at 29¢ each.

Words   [29¢] times [number of pens]

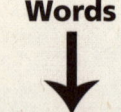

Let [p] = number of pens.

Expression [   ] · [   ]

The algebraic expression $29 \cdot p$ describes the [   ] of p pens.

2 Algebra Readiness Lesson 1-1   Daily Notetaking Guide L1

Name_____ Class_____ Date _____

Quick Check

1. Identify each expression as a *numerical expression* or an *algebraic expression*. For an algebraic expression, name the variable.

   a. $8 \div x$

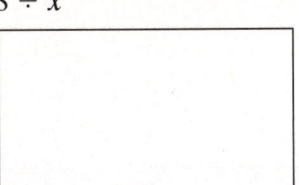

   b. 100×6

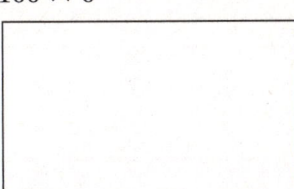

   c. $d + 43 - 9$

2. a. Bagels cost $.50 each. Write an algebraic expression for the cost of b bagels.

   b. **Measurement** Write an algebraic expression for the number of hours in m minutes.

3. Write an algebraic expression for each word phrase.

Word Phrase	Algebraic Expression
Nine more than a number y	
4 less than a number n	
A number z times three	
A number a divided by 12	

Daily Notetaking Guide — Algebra Readiness Lesson 1-1

Name_____ Class_____ Date_____

Lesson 1-2

The Order of Operations

Lesson Objectives
- Use the order of operations
- Use grouping symbols

Take Note

Order of Operations
1. Work inside ☐ symbols.
2. Multiply and ☐ in order from left to right.
3. ☐ and subtract in order from left to right.

Examples

❶ **Simplifying Expressions** Simplify $8 - 2 \cdot 2$.

$8 - 2 \cdot 2$

$8 -$ First multiply.

☐   Then subtract.

❷ **Using the Order of Operations** Simplify $12 \div 3 - 1 \cdot 2 + 1$.

$12 \div 3 - 1 \cdot 2 + 1$

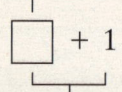 $+ 1$ Multiply and divide from left to right.

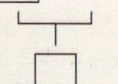 $+ 1$ Add and subtract from left to right.

☐   Add.

Quick Check

1. Simplify each expression.

   a. $2 + 5 \times 3$

   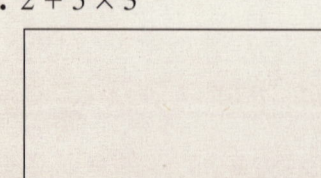

   b. $12 \div 3 - 1$

   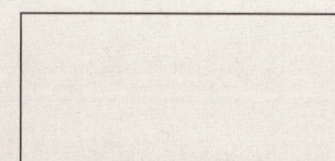

   c. $10 - 1 \cdot 7$

   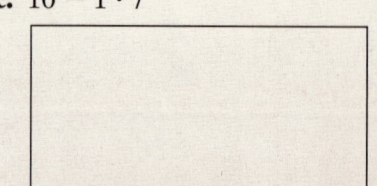

4 Algebra Readiness Lesson 1-2   Daily Notetaking Guide L1

❸ **Simplifying With Grouping Symbols** Simplify $20 - 3[(5 + 2) - 1]$.

$20 - 3[(5 + 2) - 1]$

$20 - 3[\square - 1]$ Add within parentheses.

$20 - 3[\square]$ Subtract within brackets.

$20 - \square$ Multiply.

$\square$ Subtract.

Quick Check

2. Simplify each expression.

   a. $4 - 1 \cdot 2 + 6 \div 3$

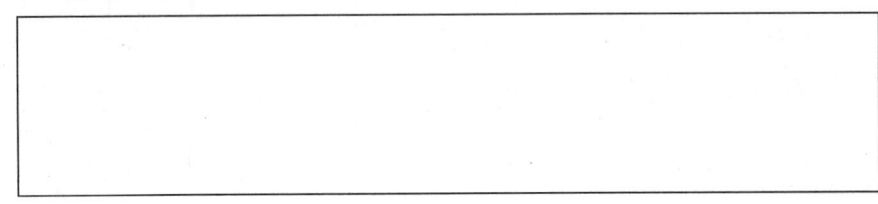

   b. $5 + 6 \cdot 4 \div 3 - 1$

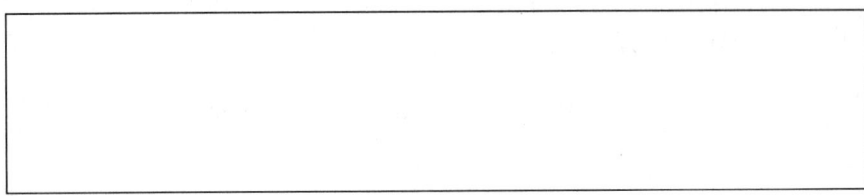

3. Simplify the expression.
   $1 + \dfrac{10 - 2}{4}$

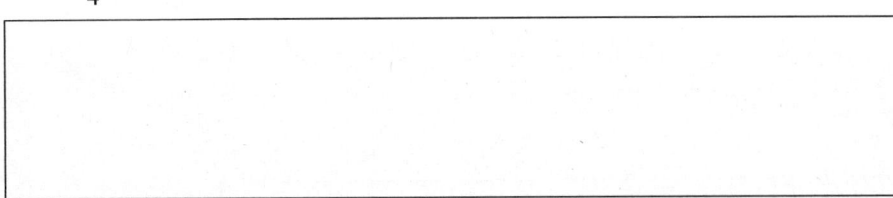

Name_____ Class_____ Date_____

Lesson 1-3

Writing and Evaluating Expressions

Lesson Objectives
- Evaluate algebraic expressions
- Solve problems by evaluating expressions

Vocabulary

To _____ is to replace each variable in an expression with a number, and then follow the order of operations.

Examples

1 **Evaluating an Expression** Evaluate $18 + 2g$ for $g = 3$.

$18 + 2g = 18 + 2(\boxed{})$ Replace $\boxed{}$ with $\boxed{}$.

$ = 18 + \boxed{}$ Multiply.

$ = \boxed{}$ Add.

2 **Replacing More Than One Variable** Evaluate $2ab - \frac{c}{3}$ for $a = 3, b = 4,$ and $c = 9$.

$2ab - \frac{c}{3} = 2 \cdot \boxed{} \cdot \boxed{} - \frac{\boxed{}}{3}$ Replace the variables.

$\phantom{2ab - \frac{c}{3}} = 2 \cdot 3 \cdot 4 - \boxed{}$ Work within grouping symbols.

$\phantom{2ab - \frac{c}{3}} = \boxed{} \cdot 4 - 3$ Multiply from left to right.

$\phantom{2ab - \frac{c}{3}} = \boxed{} - 3$ Multiply.

$\phantom{2ab - \frac{c}{3}} = \boxed{}$ Subtract.

Quick Check

1. Evaluate each expression.

   a. $63 - 5x$, for $x = 7$

   b. $6(g + h)$, for $g = 8$ and $h = 7$

   c. $2xy - z$, for $x = 4, y = 3,$ and $z = 1$

   d. $\frac{r + s}{2}$, for $r = 13$ and $s = 11$

Name_____ Class_____ Date_____

Examples

3 **Evaluating an Expression** The Omelet Café buys cartons of 36 eggs.

a. Write an algebraic expression for the number of cartons the café should buy for x eggs.

An expression for x eggs is ☐.

b. Evaluate the expression for 180 eggs.

$\dfrac{x}{36} = \dfrac{\Box}{36}$ **Evaluate for $x = 180$.**

$= \Box$ **Divide.**

The Omelet Café should buy ☐ cartons to get 180 eggs.

4 **Evaluating an Expression** The One Pizza restaurant makes only one kind of pizza, which costs $16. The delivery charge is $2. Write an algebraic expression for the cost of having pizzas delivered. Evaluate the expression to find the cost of having five pizzas delivered.

Table

Number of Pizzas	Cost of Pizza	Delivery	Total Cost
1	1 · 16	2	1 · ☐ + ☐
2	2 · ☐	☐	2 · ☐ + ☐
4	4 · ☐	☐	4 · ☐ + ☐

Expression ☐ · ☐ + ☐

Evaluate the expression for $p = 5$.

$16 \cdot p + 2 = 16 \cdot \Box + 2$ **Replace p with ☐.**

$= \Box + 2$ **Multiply.**

$= \Box$ **Add.**

It costs ☐ to have five pizzas delivered.

Quick Check

3. The café in Example 3 pays $21 for each case of bottled water. Write an algebraic expression for the cost of c cases. Evaluate the expression to find the cost of 5 cases.

Daily Notetaking Guide — Algebra Readiness Lesson 1-3

Name_____ Class_____ Date_____

Lesson 1-4

Integers and Absolute Value

Lesson Objectives
- Graph and order integers
- Find opposites and absolute values

Vocabulary

_____ are numbers that are the same distance from zero on a number line but in opposite directions.

Integers are _____
_____

An _____ is a number's distance from zero on the number line.

Example

1 **Graphing on a Number Line** Graph 2, −2, and −3 on a number line. Compare the numbers and order them from least to greatest.

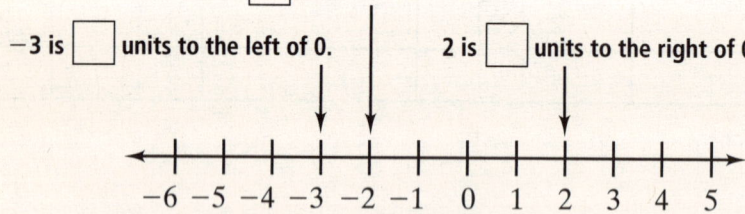

−3 is to the left of −2, and −2 is to the left of 2, so −3 < −2 < 2.

The numbers from least to greatest are ☐, ☐, ☐.

Quick Check

1. Graph 0, 2, and −6 on a number line. Compare the numbers and order the numbers from least to greatest.

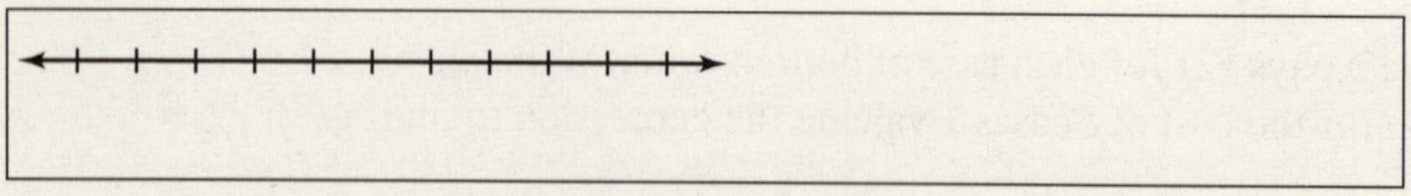

The numbers from least to greatest are ☐, ☐, ☐.

8 Algebra Readiness Lesson 1-4   Daily Notetaking Guide L1

Name _____ Class _____ Date _____

Examples

❷ Finding Absolute Value Use a number line to find |−5| and |5|.

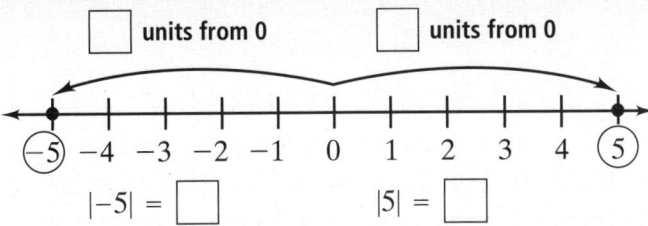

☐ units from 0   ☐ units from 0

|−5| = ☐ |5| = ☐

❸ Simplifying an Expression Simplify 9 − |11 − 7|.

9 − |11 − 7| = 9 − |☐| Work within grouping symbols.

= 9 − ☐   Find the absolute value.

= ☐   Simplify.

Quick Check

2. Find |−10|.

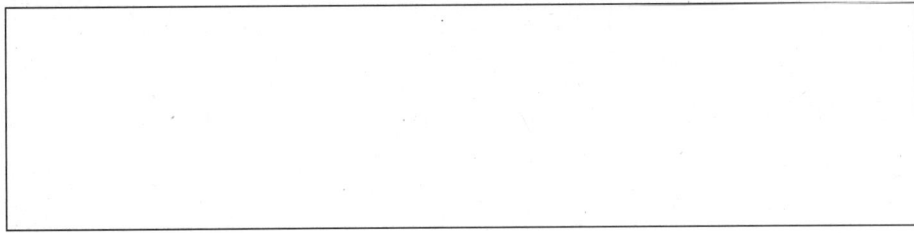

3. Simplify 5|−4|.

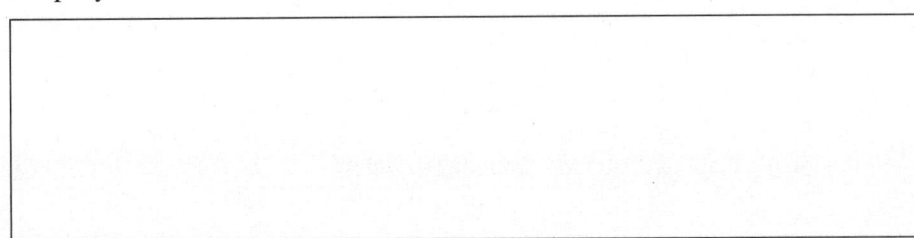

L1 Daily Notetaking Guide   Algebra Readiness Lesson 1-4

Name_____ Class_____ Date_____

Lesson 1-5 — Adding Integers

Lesson Objectives
- Use models to add integers
- Use rules to add integers

Take Note

Inverse Property of Addition

The sum of an integer and its additive inverse is ☐.

Arithmetic

$1 + (-1) = $ ☐

$-1 + 1 = $ ☐

Algebra

$x + (-x) = $ ☐

$-x + x = $ ☐

Adding Integers

Same Sign The sum of two positive integers is ☐. The sum of two negative integers is ☐.

Different Signs To add two integers with different signs, find the difference of their ☐. The sum has the sign of the integer with the ☐ absolute value.

Example

① **Using Models to Add Integers** Use models to find $(-7) + 3$.

 Model the sum.

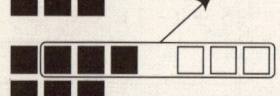 Group and remove zero pairs.

The integer that represents the simplified model is ☐.

$(-7) + 3 = $ ☐

Quick Check

1. Use models to find each sum.

   a. $-1 + 4$
   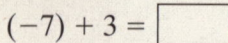

   b. $7 + (-3)$

   c. $-2 + (-2)$
   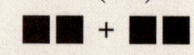

10 Algebra Readiness Lesson 1-5

Name________________________ Class________________________ Date ____________

Examples

❷ Using a Number Line From the surface, a diver goes down 20 feet and then comes back up 4 feet. Find $-20 + 4$ to find where the diver is.

−20 −16 −12 −8 −4 0

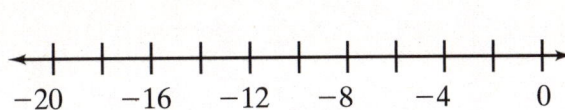

Start at 0. To represent −20, move left ☐ units. To add positive 4, move right ☐ units to ☐.

$-20 + 4 =$ ☐

The diver is ☐ feet below the surface.

❸ Using the Order of Operations Find $-7 + (-4) + 13 + (-5)$.

$-7 + (-4) + 13 + (-5)$ **Add from left to right.**

☐ $+ 13 + (-5)$ **The sum of the two negative integers is** ☐.

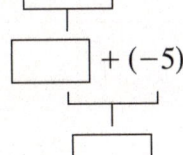

☐ $+ (-5)$ **$|13| - |11| =$ ☐. Since 13 has the greater absolute value, the sum is** ☐.

☐ **$|5| - |2| =$ ☐. Since −5 has the greater absolute value, the sum is** ☐.

$-7 + (-4) + 13 + (-5) =$ ☐.

Quick Check

2. Use this number line to find each sum.

−10 −8 −6 −4 −2 0 2 4 6 8 10

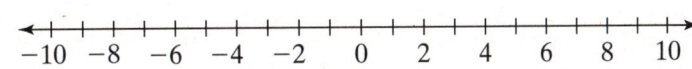

a. $2 + (-6)$ ☐ **b.** $-4 + 9$ ☐ **c.** $-5 + (-1)$ ☐

3. a. $1 + (-3) + 2 + (-10)$ ☐ **b.** $-250 + 200 + (-100) + 220$ ☐

Name_____ Class_____ Date_____

Lesson 1-6

Subtracting Integers

Lesson Objectives
- Use models to subtract integers
- Use a rule to subtract integers

Take Note

Subtracting Integers

To subtract an integer, add its ☐.

Arithmetic

$2 - 5 = 2 + (\boxed{}) = -3$

$2 - (\boxed{}) = 2 + 5 = 7$

Algebra

$a - b = a + (\boxed{})$

$a - (\boxed{}) = a + b$

Examples

❶ **Using Models to Subtract Integers** Find $-7 - (-5)$.

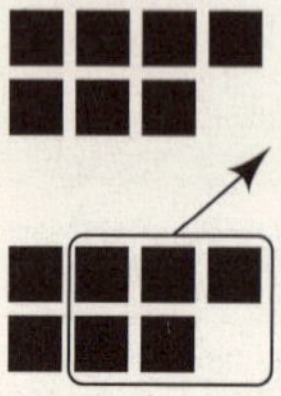

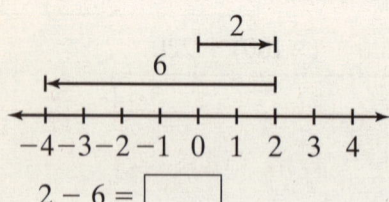

Draw a model of -7.

Subtract -5. The resulting model represents ☐.

$-7 - (-5) = \boxed{}$

❷ **Using a Number Line to Subtract Integers** Find $2 - 6$.

Start at 0. To represent 2, move right ☐ units. To subtract 6, move left ☐ units to ☐.

$2 - 6 = \boxed{}$

12 Algebra Readiness Lesson 1-6 — Daily Notetaking Guide L1

Name_____ Class_____ Date _____

❸ Using a Rule to Subtract Integers An airplane left Houston, Texas, where the temperature was 42°F. When the airplane landed in Anchorage, Alaska, the temperature was 50°F lower. What was the temperature in Anchorage?

42 − 50   Write an expression.

42 − 50 = 42 + (☐)   To subtract 50, add its ☐.

    = ☐   Simplify.

The temperature in Anchorage was ☐.

Quick Check

1. Use models to find each difference.

   a. −7 − (−2)   **b.** −4 − (−3)   **c.** −8 − (−5)

   −7 − (−2) = ☐   −4 − (−3) = ☐   −8 − (−5) = ☐

2. Use a number line to find each difference.

   a. 4 − 8   **b.** −1 − 5

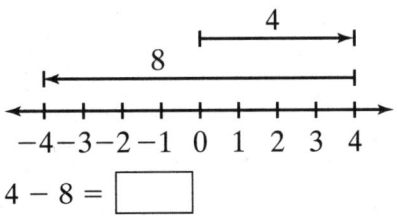   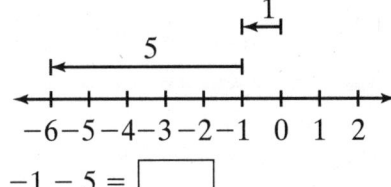

   4 − 8 = ☐   −1 − 5 = ☐

3. **Weather** The lowest temperature ever recorded on the moon was about −170°C. The lowest temperature ever recorded in Antarctica was −89°C. Find the difference in the temperatures.

☐

Name_____ Class_____ Date_____

Lesson 1-7 Inductive Reasoning

Lesson Objectives
- Write rules for patterns
- Make predictions and test conjectures

Vocabulary

_____ is making conclusions based on patterns you observe.

A conjecture is _____

A _____ is an example that proves a statement false.

Examples

1 Reasoning Inductively Use inductive reasoning. Make a conjecture about the next figure in the pattern. Then draw the figure.

  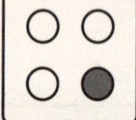

Observation: The circles are rotating _____ within the square.

Conjecture: The next figure will have a shaded circle at the _____.

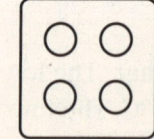

2 Writing Rules for Patterns Write a rule for each number pattern.

a. 0, −4, −8, −12, …   Start with 0 and _____ repeatedly.

b. 4, −4, 4, −4, …   Alternate ☐ and its _____.

c. 1, 2, 4, 8, 10, …   Start with ☐. Alternate _____ and _____.

14 Algebra Readiness Lesson 1-7

Name _____ Class _____ Date _____

❸ Extending a Pattern Write a rule for the number pattern 110, 100, 90, 80, ...
Find the next two numbers in the pattern.

110, 100, 90, 80,   The first number is 110.
 −10 −10 −10   The next numbers are found by subtracting 10.

The rule is *Start with* ☐ *and* ☐ *repeatedly*. The next two

numbers in the pattern are 80 − ☐ = ☐ and ☐ − ☐ = ☐.

❹ Analyzing Conjectures Is the conjecture correct or incorrect? If it is incorrect, give a counterexample.

Every triangle has three sides of equal length.

The conjecture is ☐. The figure to the right is a triangle but

☐

Quick Check

1. Make a conjecture about the next figure in the pattern at the right. Then draw the figure.

2. Write a rule for the pattern 4, 9, 14, 19, ...

3. Write a rule for the pattern 1, 3, 5, 7, ... Find the next two numbers in the pattern.

4. Is each conjecture correct or incorrect? If it is incorrect, give a counterexample.

   a. A number and its absolute value are always opposites.

   b. The next figure in the pattern has 25 dots.

   1   4   9   16

Name_____ Class_____ Date_____

Lesson 1-8

Reasoning Strategy: Look for a Pattern

Lesson Objective
- Find number patterns

Example

1 Finding a Number Pattern Each student on a committee of five students shakes hands with every other committee member. How many handshakes will there be in all?

Understand the Problem How many hands does each committee member shake?

Make and Carry Out a Plan Make a table to organize the numbers. Then look for a pattern.

The pattern is to add the number of new handshakes to the number of handshakes already made.

☐   the number of handshakes by 1 student

4 + ☐ = ☐   the number of handshakes by 2 students

Make a table to extend the pattern to 5 students.

Student	1	2	3	4	5
Number of original handshakes	4	3	2	☐	☐
Total number of handshakes	4	4 + ☐ = ☐	7 + ☐ = ☐	9 + ☐ = ☐	10 + ☐ = ☐

There will be ☐ handshakes in all.

Check the Answer One way to check a solution is to solve the problem by another method. You can use a diagram to show the pattern visually.

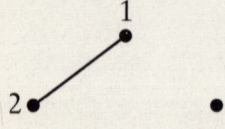

There are ☐ diagonals in the pentagon, so there will be ☐ handshakes in all.

Name _____ Class _____ Date _____

Quick Check

1. Suppose that the committee is made up of six people. How many handshakes would there be?

2. a. News spreads quickly at Riverdell High. Each student who hears a story repeats it 15 minutes later to two students who have not heard it yet and then tells no one else. Suppose one student hears some news at 8:00 A.M. How many students will know the news at 9:00 A.M.?

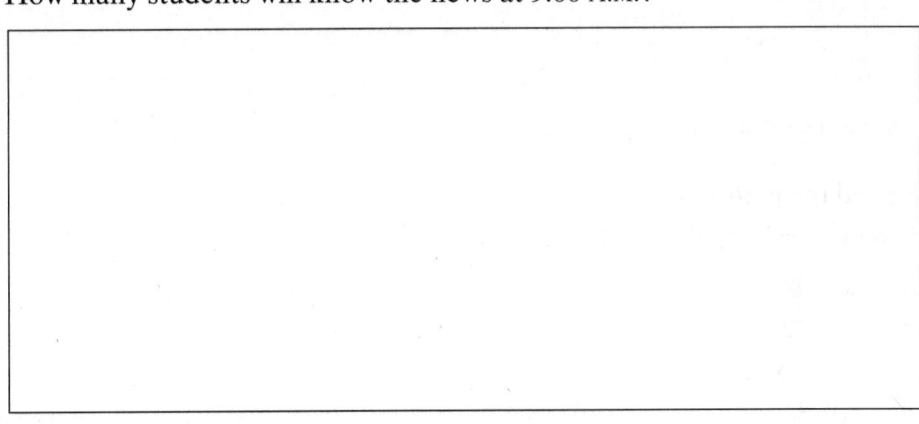

   b. Suppose each student who hears the story repeats it in 10 minutes. How many students will know the news at 9:00 A.M.?

Name_____ Class_____ Date_____

Lesson 1-9   Multiplying and Dividing Integers

Lesson Objectives
- Multiply integers using repeated addition, patterns, and rules
- Divide integers using rules

Take Note

Multiplying Integers

The product of two integers with the same sign is ☐.

The product of two integers with different signs is ☐.

The product of zero and any integer is ☐.

Examples   3(4) = ☐   3(−4) = ☐

−3(−4) = ☐   −3(4) = ☐

3(0) = ☐   −4(0) = ☐

Dividing Integers

The quotient of two integers with the same sign is ☐.

The quotient of two integers with different signs is ☐.

Remember that division by zero is ☐.

Examples   12 ÷ 3 = ☐   12 ÷ (−3) = ☐

−12 ÷ (−3) = ☐   −12 ÷ 3 = ☐

Examples

1 Using Patterns to Multiply Integers Use a pattern to find each product.

a. −2(7)

2(7) = ☐   ← Start with products you know. →   2(−7) = ☐

1(7) = ☐   1(−7) = ☐

0(7) = ☐   0(−7) = ☐

−1(7) = ☐   ←   Continue the pattern.   →   −1(−7) = ☐

−2(7) = ☐   −2(−7) = ☐

b. −2(−7)

Algebra Readiness Lesson 1-9   Daily Notetaking Guide L1

Name_____ Class_____ Date_____

❷ Using Rules to Multiply Integers Multiply $(6)(-2)(-3)$.

$6(-2)(-3) = (\boxed{})(-3)$ Multiply from left to right. The product of a positive integer and a negative integer is $\boxed{}$.

$= \boxed{}$ Multiply. The product of two negative integers is $\boxed{}$.

❸ Find the average of $-7, 5, -6,$ and -8.

$$\frac{-7 + (-6) + (-8) + \boxed{}}{4}$$ Write an expression for the average.

$$= \frac{\boxed{}}{4}$$ Use the order of operations. The fraction bar acts as a $\boxed{}$ symbol.

$$= \boxed{}$$ The quotient of a negative integer and a positive integer is $\boxed{}$.

The average is $\boxed{}$.

Quick Check

1. Patterns Use a pattern to simplify $-3(-4)$.

$\boxed{}$

2. Simplify each product.

   a. $-4 \cdot 8 (-2) = \boxed{}$

   b. $6(-3)(5) = \boxed{}$

3. Simplify each quotient.

   a. $-32 \div 8 = \boxed{}$

   b. $-48 \div (-6) = \boxed{}$

   c. Find the average of $4, -3, -5, 2,$ and -8.

$\boxed{}$

Daily Notetaking Guide   Algebra Readiness Lesson 1-9

Lesson 1-10

The Coordinate Plane

Lesson Objectives
- Name coordinates and quadrants in the coordinate plane
- Graph points in the coordinate plane

Vocabulary

A _____ is formed by the intersection of two number lines.

The x-axis is _____

The _____ is the vertical number line.

Quadrants are _____

The _____ is where the axes intersect on the coordinate plane.

An ordered pair is _____

An _____ is a number that shows the position right or left of the y-axis.

A y-coordinate is _____

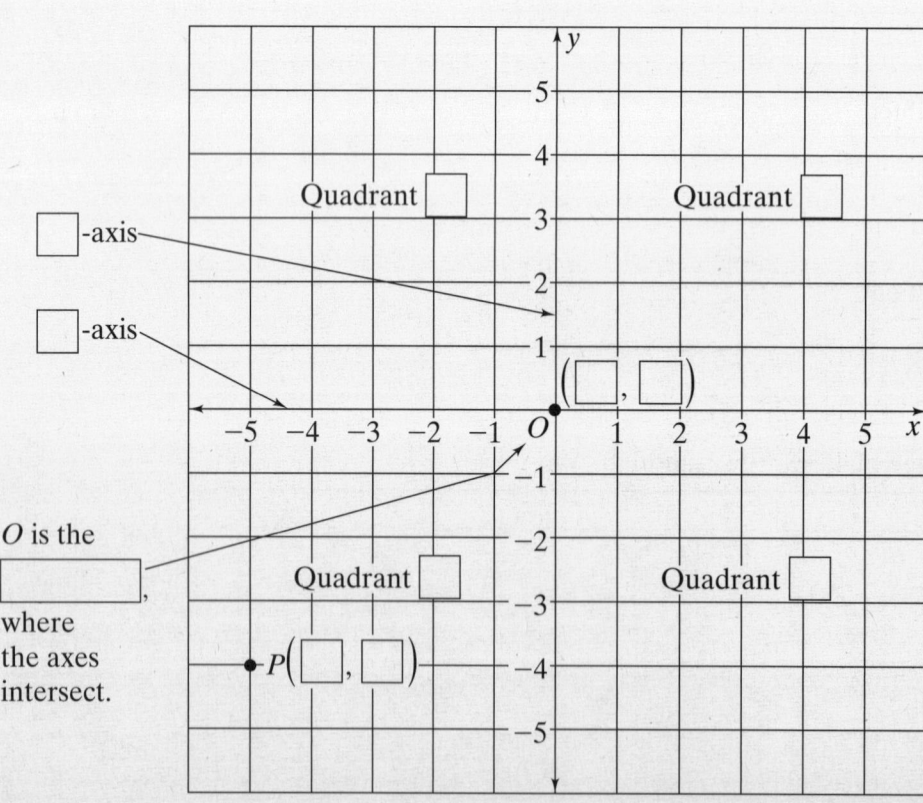

Name_____ Class_____ Date_____

Examples

① Naming Coordinates and Quadrants Write the coordinates of point G. In which quadrant is point G located?

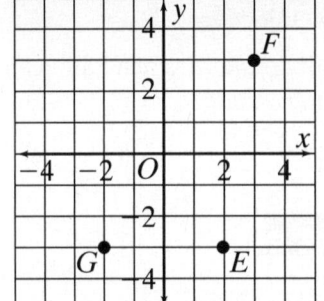

Point G is located ☐ units to the left of the y-axis. So the x-coordinate is ☐. The point is ☐ units below the x-axis. So the y-coordinate is ☐.

The coordinates of point G are (☐, ☐). Point G is located in Quadrant ☐.

② Graphing Points Graph point $M(-3, 3)$.

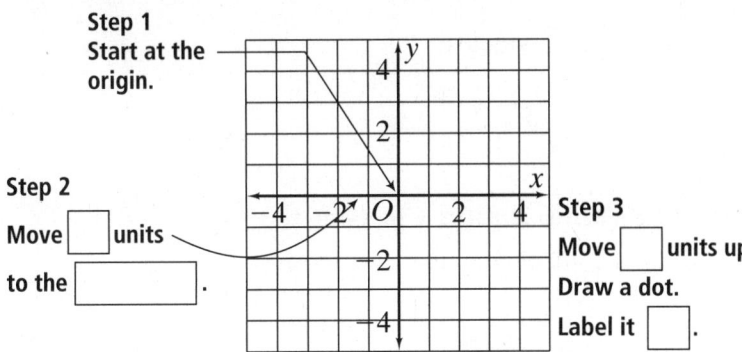

Step 1 Start at the origin.

Step 2 Move ☐ units to the ☐.

Step 3 Move ☐ units up. Draw a dot. Label it ☐.

Quick Check

1. Use the graph in Example 1. Write the coordinates of E and F.

2. Graph these points on one coordinate plane: $K(3, 1)$, $L(-2, 1)$, and $M(-2, -4)$. Connect points K, L, and M.

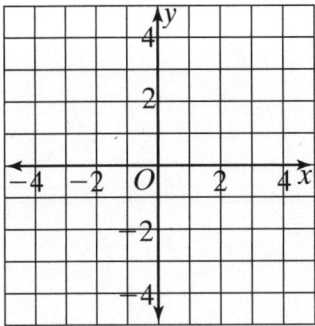

Name_____ Class_____ Date_____

Lesson 2-1 — Properties of Numbers

Lesson Objectives
- Identify properties of addition and multiplication
- Use properties to solve problems

Take Note

Properties of Addition and Multiplication

Commutative Properties of Addition and Multiplication Changing the ☐ of the values you are adding or multiplying does not change the sum or product.

Arithmetic

$6 + 4 = □ + □$

$9 \cdot 5 = □ \cdot □$

Algebra

$a + b = □ + □$

$a \cdot b = □ \cdot □$

Associative Properties of Addition and Multiplication Changing the ☐ of the values you are adding or multiplying does not change the sum or product.

Arithmetic

$(2 + 7) + 3 = 2 + □$

$(9 \cdot 4)5 = 9 □$

Algebra

$(a + b) + c = a + □$

$(ab)c = a □$

Identity Properties of Addition and Multiplication The sum of any number and ☐ is the original number. The product of any number and ☐ is the original number.

Arithmetic

$12 + □ = 12$

$10 \cdot □ = 10$

Algebra

$a + □ = a$

$a \cdot □ = a$

The additive identity is ☐. The multiplicative identity is ☐.

22 Algebra Readiness Lesson 2-1   Daily Notetaking Guide L1

Name_____ Class_____ Date_____

Examples

❶ Using the Associative Property of Addition Suppose you buy school supplies costing $0.45, $0.65, and $1.55. Find the cost of these supplies.

$0.45 + 0.65 + 1.55$

$= 0.65 + 0.45 + 1.55$ Use the [　　　] Property of Addition.

$= 0.65 + (0.45 + 1.55)$ Use the [　　　] Property of Addition.

$= 0.65 +$ [　　　]   Add within parentheses.

$= 2.65$ Add.

The cost of the school supplies is [　　　].

❷ Identifying Properties Name each property shown.

a. $17 + x + 3 = 17 + 3 + x$ [　　　] Property of Addition

b. $(36 \times 2)10 = 36(2 \times 10)$ [　　　] Property of Multiplication

c. $km = km \cdot 1$ [　　　] Property of Multiplication

❸ Using Mental Math With Multiplication Use mental math to simplify $(20 \cdot 13) \cdot 5$.

$(20 \cdot 13) \cdot 5 = (13 \cdot 20) \cdot 5$ Use the [　　　] Property of Multiplication.

$= 13 \cdot (20 \cdot 5)$ Use the [　　　] Property of Multiplication.

$= 13 \cdot$ [　　　]   Multiply within parentheses.

$=$ [　　　]   Multiply.

Quick Check

1. You spend $6 for dinner, $8 for a movie, and $4 for popcorn. Find your total cost. Explain which property or properties you used.

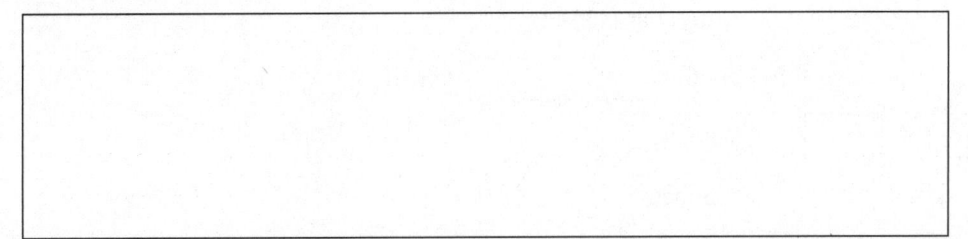

2. Name each property shown.

a. $3 + 6 = 6 + 3$ b. $8 = 1 \cdot 8$ c. $(3z)m = (3zm)$

Name_____ Class_____ Date_____

Lesson 2-2 — The Distributive Property

Lesson Objectives
- Use the Distributive Property with numerical expressions
- Use the Distributive Property with algebraic expressions

Take Note

Distributive Property

To multiply a sum or difference, multiply each number within the parentheses by the number outside the parentheses.

Arithmetic

$3(2 + 6) = 3(\square) + 3(\square)$
$(2 + 6)3 = 2(\square) + 6(\square)$
$6(7 - 4) = 6(\square) - 6(\square)$
$(7 - 4)6 = 7(\square) - 4(\square)$

Algebra

$a(b + c) = a(\square) + a(\square)$
$(b + c)a = b(\square) + c(\square)$
$a(b - c) = a(\square) - a(\square)$
$(b - c)a = b(\square) - c(\square)$

Examples

1 **Using the Distributive Property I** Find 15(110) mentally.

$15(110) = 15(\boxed{} + \boxed{})$ Write 110 as (100 + 10).

$ = 15 \cdot \boxed{} + 15 \cdot \boxed{}$ Use the \boxed{} Property.

$ = \boxed{} + \boxed{}$ Multiply.

$ = \boxed{}$ Add.

2 Ms. Thomas gave 5 pencils to each of her 37 students. What is the total number of pencils she gave to the students?

$(37)5 = (\boxed{} - \boxed{})5$ Write 37 as (40 − 3).

$ = \boxed{} \cdot 5 - \boxed{} \cdot 5$ Use the \boxed{} Property.

$ = \boxed{} - \boxed{}$ Multiply.

$ = \boxed{}$ Subtract.

Ms. Thomas gave the students \boxed{} pencils.

Quick Check

1. Find the product 9 · 201 mentally. \boxed{}

Name_____ Class_____ Date_____

Examples

③ Using the Distributive Property III Simplify 11(23) − 11(3).

11(23) − 11(7) = 11(☐ − ☐) Use the ☐ Property.

= 11(☐) Work within grouping symbols.

= ☐ Multiply.

④ Using Models to Multiply Use a model to multiply 2(3x + 4).

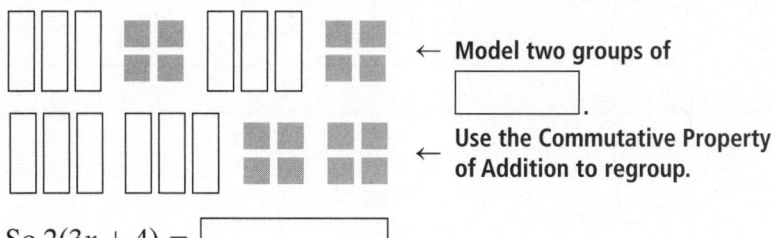

← Model two groups of ☐ .

← Use the Commutative Property of Addition to regroup.

So 2(3x + 4) = ☐ .

⑤ Using the Distributive Property IV Multiply.

a. −9(2 − 8y) = −9(☐) − (−9)(☐) Use the ☐ Property.

= ☐ − (☐) Multiply.

= ☐ + ☐ Simplify.

b. (5m + 6)11 = (☐)11 + (☐)11 Use the ☐ Property.

= ☐ + ☐ Multiply.

Quick Check

2. Your club sold calendars for $7. Club members sold 204 calendars. How much money did they raise?
   ☐

3. Simplify each expression.
   a. 12(52) − 12(62) = ☐   b. (16)7 − (11)7 = ☐

4. Use models to multiply.
   a. 4(2x − 3)   b. 3(x + 4)

   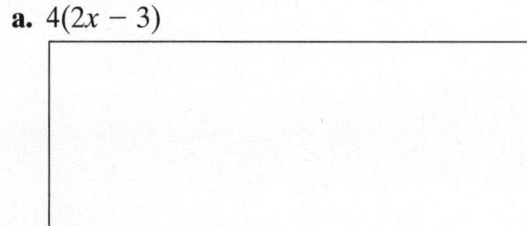

5. Multiply.
   a. 2(7 − 3d) = ☐   b. −3(5t − 2) = ☐

L1 Daily Notetaking Guide   Algebra Readiness Lesson 2-2   25

Name_____ Class_____ Date_____

Lesson 2-3

Simplifying Algebraic Expressions

Lesson Objectives
- Identify parts of an algebraic expression
- Simplify expressions

Vocabulary

A ____ is a number or the product of a number and variable(s).

A constant is _____

_____

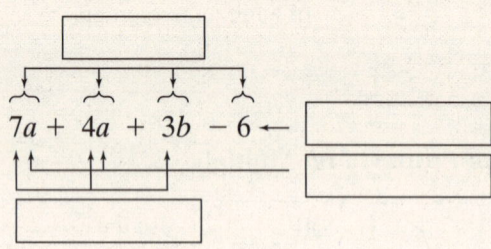

_____ have identical variables.

_____

A coefficient is _____

_____

You simplify an _____ by replacing it with an equivalent expression that has as few terms as possible.

Deductive reasoning is _____

_____

Examples

1 **Identifying Parts of an Expression** Name the coefficients, the like terms, and the constants in $7x + y - 2x - 7$.

Coefficients: 7, ☐ , ☐

Like terms: $7x$, ☐

Constant: ☐

26 Algebra Readiness Lesson 2-3   Daily Notetaking Guide L1

Name _____ Class _____ Date _____

❷ **Using Models to Simplify** Simplify $9 + 4f + 3 + 2f$.

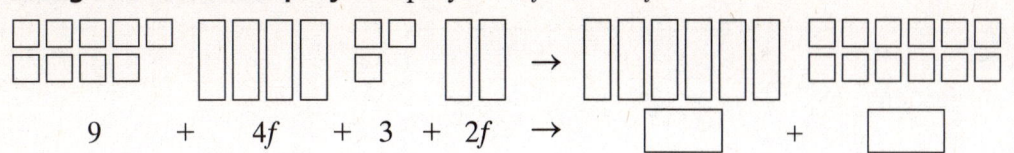

$9 \quad + \quad 4f \quad + \quad 3 \quad + \quad 2f \quad \rightarrow \quad \boxed{} \quad + \quad \boxed{}$

❸ **Combining Like Terms** Simplify $2b + b - 4$.

$2b + b - 4 = \boxed{}b + \boxed{}b - 4$ Use the Identity Property of Multiplication.

$ = (\boxed{} + \boxed{})b - 4$ Use the Distributive Property.

$ = \boxed{}b - 4$ Simplify.

❹ **Using Deductive Reasoning** Evaluate $(7 - 3x)5 + 20x$.

$(7 - 3x)5 + 20x = 35 - 15x + 20x$ Use the $\boxed{}$ Property.

$ = 35 + (\boxed{}x + \boxed{}x)$ Use the $\boxed{}$ Property of Addition.

$ = 35 + (\boxed{} + \boxed{})x$ Use the $\boxed{}$ Property to combine like terms.

$ = 35 + \boxed{}x$ Simplify.

Quick Check

1. Name the coefficients, the like terms, and the constants.

   a. $6 + 2s + 4s$ _____

   b. $-4x$ _____

   c. $9m + 2r - 2m + r$ _____

2. Use a model to simplify $3a + 2 + 4a - 1$.

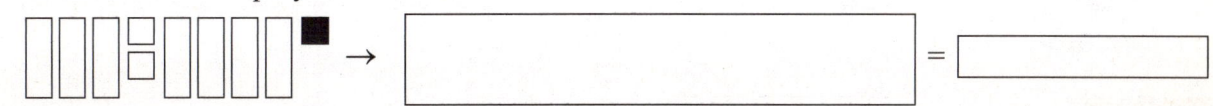

   _____ = _____

3. Simplify each expression.

   a. $3b - b$

   b. $-4m - 9m$

   c. $p + 6p - 4p$

Daily Notetaking Guide — Algebra Readiness Lesson 2-3 — 27

Name_____ Class_____ Date_____

Lesson 2-4　　　　　　　　　　　　　　　　　　　　　　Variables and Equations

Lesson Objectives
- Classify types of equations
- Check equations using substitution

Vocabulary

An _____ is a mathematical sentence with an equal sign.

An open sentence is _____

_____

A _____ is a value for a variable that makes an equation true.

Examples

1 Classifying Equations State whether each equation is *true*, *false*, or an *open sentence*. Explain.

   a. $3(b - 8) = 12$

   [_____], because there is a variable.

   b. $7 - (-6) = 1$

   [_____], because $13 \neq 1$.

   c. $-9 + 5 = -4$

   [_____], because $-4 = -4$.

2 Writing an Equation Write an equation for *Six times a number added to the number is the opposite of forty-two*. State whether the equation is *true*, *false*, or an *open sentence*. Explain.

Words	six times the number	added to	the number	is	the opposite of 42.
	[ ]	added to	[ ]	is	[ ]
Equation	[ ]	+	[ ]	=	[ ]

The equation is [_____], because there is a variable.

Quick Check

1. Explain whether each equation is *true*, *false*, or an *open sentence*.

   a. $9 - 7 = 3$　　　　　**b.** $8 + x = 2$　　　　　**c.** $4 \cdot 5 = 20$

   [_____]　　　　　　　　[_____]　　　　　　　[_____]

Name_____ Class_____ Date _____

Examples

❸ Substituting to Check Is 45 a solution of the equation $120 + x = 75$?

$120 + x = 75$

$120 + \boxed{} \stackrel{?}{=} 75$ Substitute $\boxed{}$ for x.

$\boxed{} \neq 75$

$\boxed{}$, 45 $\boxed{}$ a solution of the equation.

❹ Substituting to Check A gift pack must hold 20 lb of food. Apples weigh 9 lb and cheese weighs 5 lb. Can the jar of jam that completes the package weigh 7 lb?

Words   weight of apples plus weight of cheese plus weight of jam is 20 lb

Let $\boxed{j}$ = weight of jam.

Equation $\boxed{}$ + $\boxed{}$ + $\boxed{}$ = $\boxed{}$

$9 + 5 + j = 20$

$14 + j = 20$ Add.

$14 + \boxed{} \stackrel{?}{=} 20$ Substitute $\boxed{}$ for the variable.

$21 \boxed{} 20$

$\boxed{}$, the jar of jam cannot weigh 7 lb.

Quick Check

2. Write an equation for *Twenty minus x is three*. Is the equation *true*, *false*, or an *open sentence*? Explain.

   $\boxed{}$

3. Is the given number a solution of the equation?

   a. $8 + t = 2t; 1$ **b.** $9 - m = 3; 6$

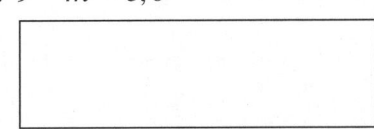

   $\boxed{}$ $\boxed{}$

4. A tent weighs 6 lb. Your backpack and the tent together weigh 33 lb. Use an equation to find whether the backpack weighs 27 lb.

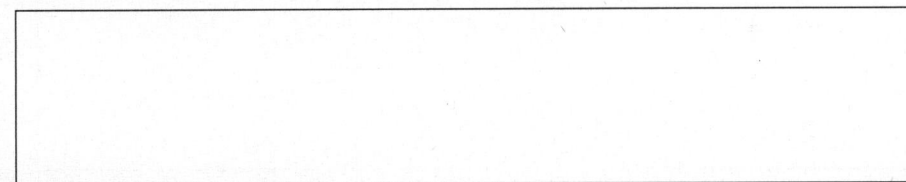

   $\boxed{}$

Daily Notetaking Guide   Algebra Readiness Lesson 2-4   29

Name_____ Class_____ Date_____

Lesson 2-5 — Solving Equations by Adding or Subtracting

Lesson Objectives
- Solve one-step equations using subtraction
- Solve one-step equations using addition

Take Note

Subtraction Property of Equality
You can subtract the same number from each side of an equation.

Arithmetic	Algebra
$10 = 2(5)$	If $a = b$,
$10 - 5 = 2(5) - \Box$	then $a - c = b - \Box$

Addition Property of Equality
You can add the same number to each side of an equation.

Arithmetic	Algebra
$8 = 2(4)$	If $a = b$,
$8 + 3 = 2(4) + \Box$	then $a + c = b + \Box$

_____ are operations that undo each other.

Example

1. Subtracting to Solve an Equation Solve $y + 5 = 13$.

Method 1
$y + 5 = 13$
$y + 5 - \Box = 13 - \Box$ ← Subtract $\Box$ from each side. →
$y = \Box$ ← Simplify. →

Method 2
$y + 5 = 13$
$-\Box = -\Box$
$y = \Box$

Quick Check

1. Solve each equation.

   a. $x + 8 = 3$

   b. $5 = d + 1$

30 Algebra Readiness Lesson 2-5

Name_____ Class_____ Date _____

Example

2 Larissa wants to increase the number of books in her collection to 327 books. She has 250 books now. Find the number of books she needs to buy.

Words [target number] is [250] plus [number to buy]

Let x = number to buy.

Equation [ ] = [ ] + [ ]

$327 = 250 + x$
$327 = x + 250$ Use the [ ] Property of Addition.
$327 - [\ ] = x + 250 - [\ ]$ Subtract [ ] from each side.
$[\ ] = x$ Simplify.

Larissa needs to buy [ ] more books.

3 **Adding to Solve an Equation** Solve $c - 23 = 30$.

$c - 23 = 30$
$c - 23 + [\ ] = 30 + [\ ]$ Add [ ] to each side.
$c = [\ ]$ Simplify.

4 Marcy's CD player cost $113 less than her DVD player. Her CD player cost $78. About how much did her DVD player cost?

Round to numbers that are easy to compute.

$113 \approx 110$
$78 \approx 80$

$80 = t - 110$ Write an equation.
$80 + [\ ] = t - 110 + [\ ]$ Add [ ] to each side.
$[\ ] = t$ Simplify.

Marcy's DVD player cost about [ ].

Quick Check

2. Cora measures her heart rate at 123 beats per minute. This is 55 beats more than her resting heart rate r. Write and solve an equation to find Cora's resting heart rate.

[ ]

3. a. $y - 5 = 8$ **b.** $p - 30 = 42$

[ ]   [ ]

Daily Notetaking Guide   Algebra Readiness Lesson 2-5

Name_____ Class_____ Date_____

Lesson 2-6   Solving Equations by Multiplying or Dividing

Lesson Objectives
- Solve one-step equations using division
- Solve one-step equations using multiplication

Take Note

Division Property of Equality

If you divide each side of an equation by the same nonzero number, the two sides remain equal.

Arithmetic
$6 = 3(2)$
$\dfrac{6}{3} = \dfrac{3(2)}{\Box}$

Algebra
If $a = b$ and $c \neq 0$,
$\dfrac{a}{c} = \dfrac{b}{\Box}$

Multiplication Property of Equality

You can multiply each side of an equation by the same number.

Arithmetic
$12 = 3(4)$
$12 \cdot 2 = 3(4) \cdot \Box$

Algebra
If $a = b$,
then $ac = \Box$.

Examples

❶ Dividing to Solve an Equation I A total of 288 pens are boxed by the dozen. How many boxes are needed?

Words ⬇ number of pens | is | 12 | times | number of boxes

Let $\boxed{b}$ = number of boxes

Equation $\Box$ = $\Box \cdot \Box$

$288 = 12b$

$\dfrac{288}{\Box} = \dfrac{12b}{\Box}$ Divide each side by $\Box$.

$\Box = b$ Simplify.

$\Box$ boxes are needed.

Check Is the answer reasonable?

$\Box$ times the number of boxes is the number of pens.

Since $12 \times 24 = \Box$, the answer is reasonable.

Name_____ Class_____ Date_____

❷ Dividing to Solve an Equation II Solve $-2v = -24$.

$$-2v = -24$$

$$\frac{-2v}{\boxed{}} = \frac{-24}{\boxed{}} \quad \text{Divide each side by } \boxed{}.$$

$$v = \boxed{} \quad \text{Simplify.}$$

Check $\quad -2v = -24$

$$-2(\boxed{}) \stackrel{?}{=} -24 \quad \text{Replace } v \text{ with } \boxed{}.$$

$$\boxed{} = -24 \checkmark$$

❸ Multiplying to Solve an Equation Solve $\frac{x}{8} = -5$.

$$\frac{x}{8} = -5$$

$$\boxed{}\frac{x}{8} = \boxed{}(-5) \quad \text{Multiply each side by } \boxed{}.$$

$$x = \boxed{} \quad \text{Simplify.}$$

Quick Check

Solve each equation.

1. a. $4x = 84$

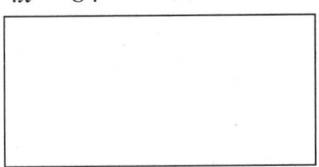

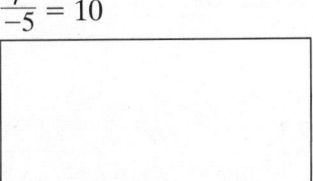

b. $63 = 7y$

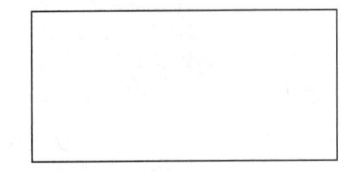

c. $-3b = 24$

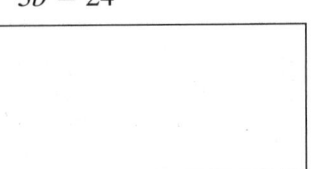

d. $-4d = -56$

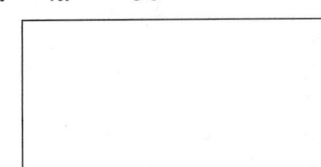

e. $\frac{r}{-5} = 10$

f. $-30 = \frac{t}{20}$

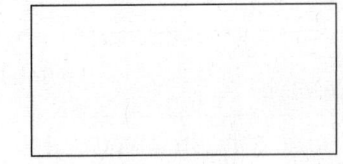

Daily Notetaking Guide — Algebra Readiness Lesson 2-6

Name_____ Class_____ Date_____

Lesson 2-7

Reasoning Strategy: Try, Test, Revise

Lesson Objective
- Solve a problem using the Try, Test, Revise strategy

Example

❶ During the intermission of a play, the Theater Club sold cups of popcorn and soda. The club sold 79 cups of popcorn and 96 sodas for a total of $271. If the selling prices for popcorn and soda were in whole dollars, what was the selling price of a cup of popcorn? Of a soda?

Understand the Problem

Look at the information given to make an informed conjecture.

1. How many cups of [ ] and [ ] did the club sell? [ ]

2. How much money did the club raise from sales of [ ] and [ ]? [ ]

Make and Carry Out a Plan Make a conjecture and then test it. Use what you learn from your conjecture to make a better second conjecture.

3. When you make a conjecture for the selling prices of a cup of popcorn and a cup of soda, how can you use your conjecture to find the actual selling prices of a cup of popcorn and a cup of soda?
   [ ]

4. By what numbers do you multiply your conjecture for the selling prices of a cup of popcorn and a cup of soda to find the amount of money the club would have raised by selling popcorn and soda at those selling prices?
   [ ]

Make and Carry Out a Plan

You can organize conjectures in a table. As a first conjecture, try both with a price of $1.

Popcorn Price	Soda Price	Total Price	
$1	$1	$79(\ ) + 96(\ ) = \ + \ $ $= \ $	The total is too [ ]. Increase the price of the popcorn only.
$2	$1	$79(\ ) + 96(\ ) = \ + \ $ $= \ $	The total is too [ ]. Increase the price of the soda.

Continue your table until the total is correct.

34 Algebra Readiness Lesson 2-7

Name_____ Class_____ Date_____

Popcorn Price	Soda Price	Total Price	
$2	$2	79(☐) + 96(☐) = ☐ + ☐ = ☐	The total is too ☐. Decrease the price of the popcorn only.
$1	$2	79(☐) + 96(☐) = ☐ + ☐ = ☐	The total is correct.

The popcorn price was ☐, and the soda price was ☐.

Check Your Answer To check the answer for reasonableness, solve the problem another way. Consider using logical reasoning.

- We know the prices must be in whole dollars. Since $271 \div 96 \approx 2.8229$, the soda would cost at most $2.
- If the price of the soda were $2, then the theater club would earn $96 \cdot \$2$, or $192, from the sale of sodas.
- At a cost of $2 per soda, that would leave $271 − $192, or $79, for sales from popcorn.
- Since 79 cups of popcorn were sold, the price of a cup of popcorn could be $1.
- Therefore, the solution of $2 for soda and $1 for a cup of popcorn is correct.

Quick Check

1. Suppose the club sold the same number of cups of popcorn and soda as in Example 1, but raised $446. What would have been the selling prices of a cup of popcorn and a cup of soda?

Popcorn Price	Soda Price	Total Price
☐	☐	79(☐) + 96(☐) = ☐ + ☐ = ☐
☐	☐	79(☐) + 96(☐) = ☐ + ☐ = ☐
☐	☐	79(☐) + 96(☐) = ☐ + ☐ = ☐
☐	☐	79(☐) + 96(☐) = ☐ + ☐ = ☐

The popcorn price would have been ☐, and the soda price would have been ☐.

Daily Notetaking Guide — Algebra Readiness Lesson 2-7

Name_____ Class_____ Date_____

Lesson 2-8

Inequalities and Their Graphs

Lesson Objectives
- Graph inequalities
- Write inequalities

Vocabulary

An _____ is a mathematical sentence that contains $>, <, \geq, \leq$ or $\neq$.

A solution of an inequality is _____

_____

Examples

1 Graphing Solutions of Inequalities Graph the solutions of each inequality on a number line.

a. $x > -2$

An [ ] dot shows that -2 is not a solution.

<-+-+-+-+-+-+-+-+-+-+->
 -4 -2 0 2 4 6

Shade all points to the [ ] of -2.

b. $w \geq -5$

A [ ] dot shows that -5 is a solution.

<-+-+-+-+-+-+-+-+-+-+->
 -4 -2 0 2 4 6

Shade all points to the [ ] of -5.

c. $k \leq 4$

A [ ] dot shows that 4 is a solution.

<-+-+-+-+-+-+-+-+-+-+->
 -4 -2 0 2 4 6

Shade all points to the [ ] of 4.

d. $y < 6$

An [ ] dot shows that 6 is not a solution.

<-+-+-+-+-+-+-+-+-+-+->
 -4 -2 0 2 4 6

Shade all points to the [ ] of 6.

36 Algebra Readiness Lesson 2-8   Daily Notetaking Guide L1

Name_____ Class_____ Date_____

② Writing Inequalities to Describe Graphs Write the inequality shown in each graph.

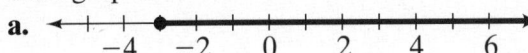

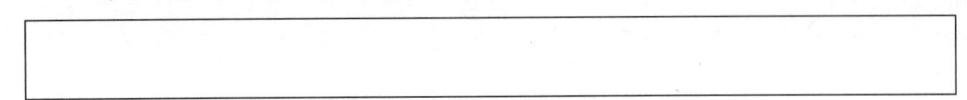

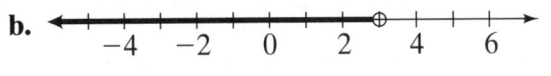

a. [number line with closed dot at −3, shaded right]

b. [number line with open circle at 3, shaded left]

③ Writing an Inequality Food can be labeled *very low sodium* only if it meets the requirements established by the federal government. Use the table to write an inequality for this requirement.

Label	Definition
Sodium-free food	Less than 5 mg per serving
Very low sodium food	At most 35 mg per serving
Low-sodium food	At most 140 mg per serving

Words: a serving of very low sodium | has at most | 35 mg sodium

Let v = the number of milligrams of sodium in a serving of very low sodium food.

Inequality ☐ ☐ ☐

Quick Check

1. Graph the solutions of each inequality.

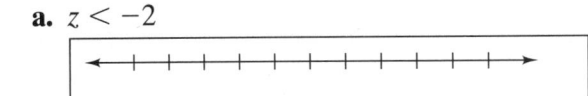

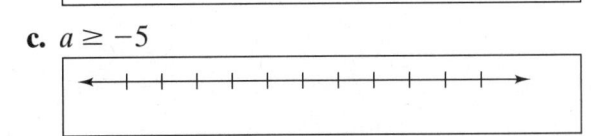

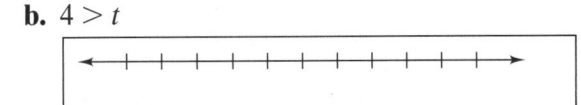

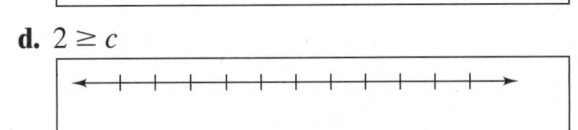

   a. $z < -2$

   b. $4 > t$

   c. $a \geq -5$

   d. $2 \geq c$

2. Write an inequality for the graph.
   [number line from −3 to 5 with closed dot at 3, shaded left]

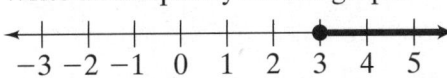

3. Use the table from Example 3. A certain food is labeled sodium-free. Write an inequality for n, the number of milligrams of sodium in a serving of this sodium-free food.

Name_____ Class_____ Date_____

Lesson 2-9

Solving One-Step Inequalities by Adding or Subtracting

Lesson Objectives
- Solve one-step inequalities using subtraction
- Solve one-step inequalities using addition

Take Note

Subtraction Property of Inequality

You can subtract the same number from each side of an inequality.

Arithmetic

$7 > 4$, so $7 - 3 > 4 - \square$

$6 < 9$, so $6 - 2 < 9 - \square$

Algebra

If $a > b$, then $a - c > b - \square$.

If $a < b$, then $a - c < b - \square$.

Addition Property of Inequality

You can add the same number to each side of an inequality.

Arithmetic

$7 > 3$, so $7 + 4 > 3 + \square$

$2 < 5$, so $2 + 6 < 5 + \square$

Algebra

If $a > b$, then $a + c > b + \square$.

If $a < b$, then $a + c < b + \square$.

Examples

1 Subtracting to Solve an Inequality Solve each inequality. Graph the solutions.

a. $4 + s < 12$

$$4 + s < 12$$
$$4 - \square + s < 12 - \square \quad \text{Subtract 4 from each side.}$$
$$s < \square \quad \text{Simplify.}$$

←—+—+—+—+—+—+—+—+—+—+—+—→
 −1 0 1 2 3 4 5 6 7 8 9 10

b. $-16 \geq y - 14$

$$-16 \geq y - 14$$
$$-16 + \square \geq y - 14 + \square \quad \text{Add 14 to each side.}$$
$$\square \geq y \text{ or } y \leq \square \quad \text{Simplify.}$$

←—+—+—+—+—+—+—+—+—+—+—+—→
 −5 −4 −3 −2 −1 0 1 2 3 4 5 6

38 Algebra Readiness Lesson 2-9

② Subtracting to Solve an Inequality Suppose your computer's hard drive has a capacity of 6 gigabytes (GB). The files you have stored on the hard drive occupy at least 2 GB. How much storage space is left for other files?

Words storage space for your files plus storage space left is less than or equal to total space

Let s = storage space left.

Inequality □ + □ ≤ □

$2 + s \leq 6$

$2 - □ + s \leq 6 - □$ Subtract □ from each side.

$s \leq □$ Simplify.

No more than □ GB are left.

③ Adding to Solve an Inequality Solve $-10 < -13 - q$.

$-10 < -13 + q$

$-10 + □ < -13 + □ + q$ Add □ to each side.

$□ < q$ Simplify.

Quick Check

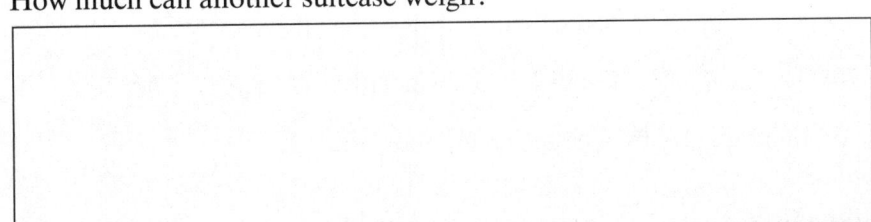

1. Solve each inequality. Graph the solutions.

    a. $8 + t < 15$ □

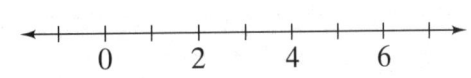

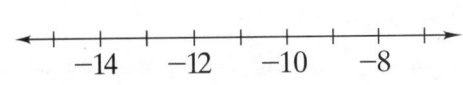

    b. $-3 \leq x + 7$ □

2. An airline lets you check up to 65 lb. of luggage. One suitcase weighs 37 lb. How much can another suitcase weigh?

3. Solve each inequality. Graph the solutions.

    a. $m - 13 > 29$ □

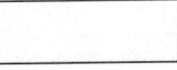

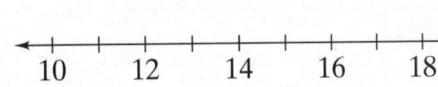

    b. $t - 5 \geq 11$ □

Name_____ Class_____ Date_____

Lesson 2-10

Solving One-Step Inequalities by Multiplying or Dividing

Lesson Objectives
- Solve one-step inequalities using division
- Solve one-step inequalities using multiplication

Take Note

Division Properties of Inequality

If you divide each side of an inequality by a positive number, you leave the inequality symbol unchanged.

Arithmetic

$3 < 6$, so $\dfrac{3}{3}$ ☐ $\dfrac{6}{3}$

$8 > 2$, so $\dfrac{8}{2}$ ☐ $\dfrac{2}{2}$

Algebra

If $a < b$ and c is positive, then $\dfrac{a}{c}$ ☐ $\dfrac{b}{c}$.

If $a > b$ and c is positive, then $\dfrac{a}{c}$ ☐ $\dfrac{b}{c}$.

If you divide each side of an inequality by a negative number, you *reverse the inequality symbol*.

Arithmetic

$6 < 12$, so $\dfrac{6}{-3}$ ☐ $\dfrac{12}{-3}$

$16 > 8$, so $\dfrac{16}{-4}$ ☐ $\dfrac{8}{-4}$

Algebra

If $a < b$ and c is negative, then $\dfrac{a}{c}$ ☐ $\dfrac{b}{c}$.

If $a > b$ and c is negative, then $\dfrac{a}{c}$ ☐ $\dfrac{b}{c}$.

Multiplication Properties of Inequality

If you multiply each side of an inequality by a positive number, you leave the inequality symbol unchanged.

Arithmetic

$3 < 4$, so $3(5)$ ☐ $4(5)$

$7 > 2$, so $7(6)$ ☐ $2(6)$

Algebra

If $a < b$ and c is positive, then ac ☐ bc.

If $a > b$ and c is positive, then ac ☐ bc.

If you multiply each side of an inequality by a negative number, you *reverse the inequality symbol*.

Arithmetic

$6 < 9$, so $6(-2)$ ☐ $9(-2)$

$7 > 5$, so $7(-3)$ ☐ $5(-3)$

Algebra

If $a < b$ and c is negative, then ac ☐ bc.

If $a > b$ and c is negative, then ac ☐ bc.

Name_____ Class_____ Date_____

Examples

1 Using Division to Solve an Inequality A 1-ton truck has the ability to haul 1 ton, or 2,000 lb. At most, how many television sets can the truck carry if each TV set weighs 225 lb?

Words [number of televisions] times [225 lb] is less than or equal to [2,000 lb]

Let $\boxed{x}$ = number of televisions.

Inequality $\boxed{} \cdot \boxed{} \leq \boxed{}$

$255x \leq 2{,}000$

$\dfrac{255x}{\boxed{}} \leq \dfrac{2{,}000}{\boxed{}}$ Divide each side by $\boxed{}$.

$x \leq \boxed{}$ Simplify.

At most, the truck can carry $\boxed{}$ television sets.

Check Is the answer reasonable?
The total weight of 8 television sets is $8(\boxed{}) = \boxed{}$ lbs, which is less than 2,000 lb but so close that another television set could not be carried. The answer is reasonable.

2 Multiplying to Solve an Inequality Solve $\dfrac{z}{-8} \leq -2$.

$\dfrac{z}{-8} \leq -2$

$\boxed{}\left(\dfrac{z}{-8}\right) \geq \boxed{}(-2)$ Multiply each side by $\boxed{}$ and reverse the inequality symbol.

$z \geq \boxed{}$ Simplify.

Quick Check

1. Solve each inequality.

   a. $4x > 40$

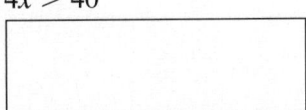

   b. $21 > 3m$

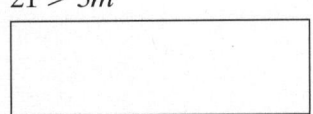

   c. $36 > -9t$

2. Solve each inequality.

   a. $\dfrac{m}{4} \geq 2$

   b. $\dfrac{t}{-3} > 7$

   c. $5 < \dfrac{r}{7}$

Daily Notetaking Guide   Algebra Readiness Lesson 2-10   41

Name_____ Class_____ Date_____

Lesson 3-1

Rounding and Estimating

Lesson Objectives	
• Round decimals • Estimate sums and differences	

Examples

① Rounding Decimals

a. Round 8.7398 to the nearest tenth.

tenths place
8.7398
☐ than 5
☐ to ☐.
☐

b. Round 8.7398 to the nearest one.

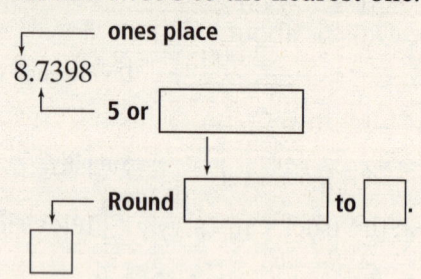

ones place
8.7398
5 or ☐
Round ☐ to ☐.
☐

② Rounding to Estimate Estimate to find whether each answer is reasonable.

Calculation	Estimate		Calculation	Estimate
$115.67	≈ $ ☐		$176.48	≈ $ ☐
$ 83.21	≈ $ ☐		− $ 39.34	≈ − $ ☐
+ $ 59.98	≈ + $ ☐		$107.14	$ ☐
$258.86	$ ☐			

The answer ☐ close to the estimate. It is ☐.

The answer ☐ close to the estimate. It is ☐.

Quick Check

1. Identify the underlined place. Then round each number to that place.

   a. <u>0</u>.7772

   ☐

   b. 7,098.<u>5</u>6

   ☐

   c. 274.94<u>3</u>4

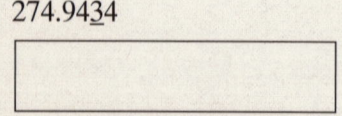

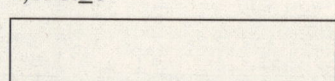

   ☐

   d. 9.8<u>5</u>1

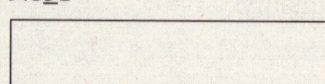

   ☐

2. Estimate by rounding.

   a. 355.302 + 204.889

   ☐

   b. 453.56 − 230.07

   ☐

Name _____ Class _____ Date _____

Examples

❸ Using Front-End Estimation You are buying some fruit. The bananas cost $1.32, the apples cost $2.19, and the avocados cost $1.63. Use front-end estimation to estimate the total cost of the fruit.

Add the front-end digits.
$$1.32 \rightarrow \quad .30$$
$$2.19 \rightarrow \quad \boxed{}$$
$$+1.63 \rightarrow \quad \boxed{}$$

Estimate by rounding.

$$\boxed{} + \boxed{} = \boxed{}$$

The total cost is about $\boxed{}$.

❹ Using Clustering Estimate the total electricity cost: March $81.75; April: $79.56; May: $80.89.

3 Months

The values cluster around $80 → $\boxed{} \cdot 3 = \boxed{}$

The total electricity cost is about $\boxed{}$.

Quick Check

3. Estimate using front-end estimation.

   a. $6.75 + 2.2 + 9.58$

   b. $\$1.07 + \$2.49 + \$7.40$

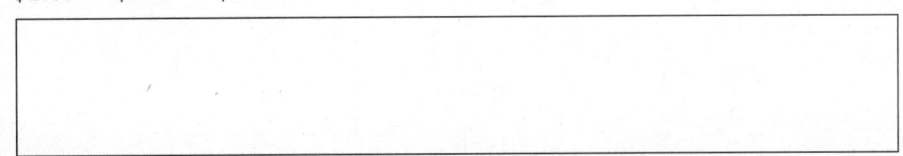

4. Estimate using clustering.
   $26.7 + 26.2 + 24.52 + 25.25 + 23.9$

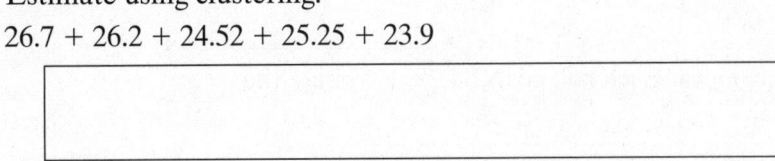

Daily Notetaking Guide   Algebra Readiness Lesson 3-1

Name_____ Class_____ Date_____

Lesson 3-2

Estimating Decimal Products and Quotients

Lesson Objectives
- Estimate products
- Estimate quotients

Vocabulary

_____ are numbers that are easy to compute mentally.

Examples

1 **Estimating the Product** Estimate 6.43 · 4.7.

6.43 ≈ ☐   4.7 ≈ ☐   Round to the nearest one.

☐ · ☐ = ☐   Multiply.

6.43 · 4.7 ≈ ☐

2 **Checking Calculations** Joshua bought 3 yd of fabric to make a flag. The fabric cost $5.35/yd. The clerk said his total was $14.95 before tax. Did the clerk make a mistake? Explain.

5.35 ≈ ☐   Round to the nearest dollar.

5 · 3 = ☐   Multiply ☐ times ☐, the number of yards of fabric.

The sales clerk ☐_____☐. Since 5.35 ☐ 5, the actual cost should be more than the estimate.

Quick Check

1. Estimate each product.
   a. 4.72 · 1.8

   b. 17.02 · 3.78

2. You buy 8 rolls of film for your camera. Each roll costs $4.79. Estimate the cost of the film before tax.

44 *Algebra Readiness* Lesson 3-2

Name _____ Class _____ Date _____

❸ Using Compatible Numbers The cost to ship one yearbook is $3.12. The total cost for a shipment was $62.40. How many books were in the shipment? Estimate 62.40 ÷ 3.12.

$3.12 \approx$ ☐   Round the divisor.

$62.40 \approx$ ☐   Round the dividend to a multiple of ☐ that is close to 62.40.

$60 \div 3 =$ ☐   Divide.

The shipment is made up of about ☐ books.

❹ Estimating to Determine Reasonableness Is 3.29 a reasonable quotient for 31.423 ÷ 5.94?

$5.94 \approx$ ☐   Round the divisor.

$31.423 \approx$ ☐   Round the dividend to a multiple of ☐ that is close to 31.423.

$30 \div 6 =$ ☐   Divide.

Since 3.29 is not close to ☐, it is not reasonable.

Quick Check

3. Estimate each quotient.

   a. $38.9 \div 1.79$

   b. $11.95 \div 2.1$

4. Use estimation. Is each quotient reasonable? Explain.

   a. $1.564 \div 2.3 = 0.68$

   b. $26.0454 \div 4.98 = 10.12$

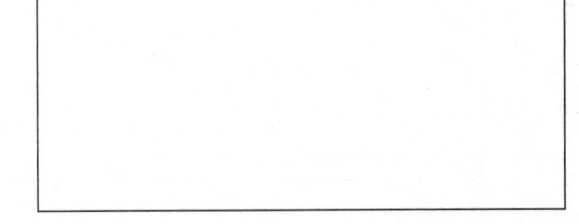

Daily Notetaking Guide   Algebra Readiness Lesson 3-2   45

Lesson 3-3

Using Formulas

Lesson Objectives
- Substitute into formulas
- Use the formula for the perimeter of a rectangle

Vocabulary

A _____ is an equation that shows a relationship between quantities that are represented by variables.

Perimeter is _____

_____

Example

1 Using the Rate Formula Suppose you ride your bike 18 miles in 3 hours. The distance formula is $d = rt$, where d is the distance, r is the speed, and t is the time. Use this formula to find your average speed.

$d = rt$ Write the formula.

☐ $= (r)($☐$)$ Substitute ☐ for d and ☐ for t.

$\dfrac{18}{☐} = \dfrac{3r}{☐}$ Divide each side by ☐.

☐ $= r$ Simplify.

Your average speed is ☐ mi/h.

Quick Check

1. Use the formula $d = rt$. Find d, r, or t.

   a. $d = 273$ mi, $t = 9.75$ h

   b. $d = 540.75$ in., $r = 10.5$ in./yr

46 Algebra Readiness Lesson 3-3

Name _____ Class _____ Date _____

Examples

❷ Substituting Into a Formula Use the formula $F = \frac{n}{4} + 37$, where n is the number of times a cricket chirps in one minute, and F is the temperature in degrees Fahrenheit. Estimate the temperature when a cricket chirps 76 times in a minute.

$F = \frac{n}{4} + 37$ Write the formula.

$F = \frac{\boxed{}}{4} + 37$ Replace n with $\boxed{}$.

$F = \boxed{} + 37$ Divide.

$F = \boxed{}$ Add.

The temperature is $\boxed{}$.

❸ Finding Perimeter Find the perimeter of a rectangular tabletop with a length of 14.5 in. and width of 8.5 in. Use the formula for the perimeter of a rectangle, $P = 2\ell + 2w$.

$P = 2\ell + 2w$ Write the formula.

$P = 2(\boxed{}) + 2(\boxed{})$ Replace ℓ with $\boxed{}$ and w with $\boxed{}$.

$P = \boxed{} + \boxed{}$ Multiply.

$P = \boxed{}$ Add.

The perimeter of the tabletop is $\boxed{}$ in.

Quick Check

2. Use the formula $F = \frac{n}{4} + 37$ to estimate the temperature in degrees Fahrenheit for each situation.

   a. 96 chirps/min

   b. 88 chirps/min

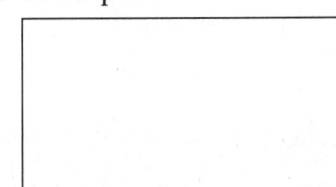

3. Find the perimeter of each rectangle.

   a. 16.8 cm, 27.3 cm

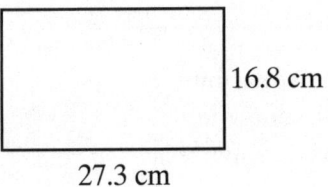

   b. 8.6 in., 17.4 in.

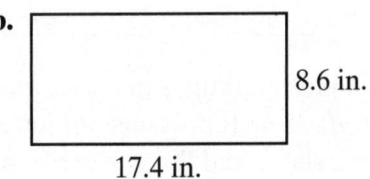

Daily Notetaking Guide — Algebra Readiness Lesson 3-3

Lesson 3-4

Solving Equations by Adding or Subtracting Decimals

Lesson Objectives
- Solve one-step decimal equations involving addition
- Solve one-step decimal equations involving subtraction

Examples

1 **Subtracting to Solve an Equation** Solve $6.8 + p = -9.7$.

$6.8 + p = -9.7$

$6.8 - \boxed{} + p = -9.7 - \boxed{}$ Subtract $\boxed{}$ from each side.

$p = \boxed{}$ Simplify.

Check $6.8 + p = -9.7$

$6.8 + \left(\boxed{}\right) \stackrel{?}{=} -9.7$ Replace p with $\boxed{}$.

$\boxed{} = -9.7$ ✓

2 **Solving a One-Step Equation by Subtracting** Ping has a board that is 14.5 ft long. She saws off a piece that is 8.75 ft long. Find the length left over.

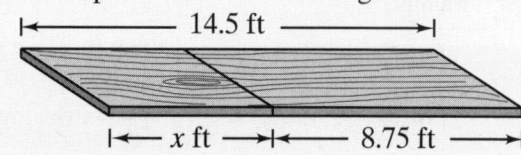

[Diagram: board of length 14.5 ft, divided into x ft and 8.75 ft]

$x + 8.75 = 14.5$

$x + 8.75 - \boxed{} = 14.5 - \boxed{}$ Subtract $\boxed{}$ from each side.

$x = \boxed{}$ Simplify.

The length of the piece that is left is $\boxed{}$ ft.

Quick Check

1. Solve each equation.
   a. $x + 4.9 = 18.8$
   b. $14.73 = -24.23 + b$

2. A store's cost plus markup is the price you pay for an item. In the equation $35.98 + m = 70$, 35.48 represents the store's cost of shoes, m represents the markup on the shoes, and 70 represents the price the customer pays. Solve this equation to find the markup.

Name _____ Class _____ Date _____

Examples

❸ Adding to Solve an Equation Solve $-23.34 = q - 16.99$.

$-23.34 = q - 16.99$

$-23.34 + \boxed{} = q - 16.99 + \boxed{}$ Add $\boxed{}$ to each side.

$\boxed{} = q$ Simplify.

❹ Adding to Solve an Equation Alejandro wrote a check for $49.98. His new account balance is $169.45. What was his previous balance?

Words | previous balance | minus | check | is | new balance |

Let $\boxed{p}$ = previous balance.

Equation $\boxed{p}$ − $\boxed{}$ = $\boxed{}$

$p - 49.98 = 169.45$

$p - 49.98 + \boxed{} = 169.45 + \boxed{}$ Add $\boxed{}$ to each side.

$p = \boxed{}$ Simplify.

Alejandro's previous balance was $\boxed{}$.

Quick Check

3. Solve each equation.

    a. $n - 5.85 = 15.25$ **b.** $-10 = c - 2.6$

4. You spent $14.95 for a new shirt. You now have $12.48. Write and solve an equation to find how much money you had before you bought the shirt.

Daily Notetaking Guide   *Algebra Readiness* Lesson 3-4

Name_____ Class_____ Date_____

Lesson 3-5

Solving Equations by Multiplying or Dividing Decimals

Lesson Objectives
- Solve one-step decimal equations involving multiplication
- Solve one-step decimal equations involving division

Examples

❶ **Dividing to Solve an Equation** Every day the school cafeteria uses about 85.8 gallons of milk. About how many days will it take for the cafeteria to use the 250 gallons in the refrigerator?

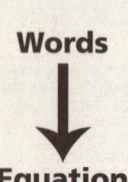

Words → daily milk use times number of days equals 250 gallons

Let x = number of days.

Equation [ ] · x = [ ]

$85.8x = 250$

$\dfrac{85.8x}{\boxed{}} = \dfrac{250}{\boxed{}}$ Divide each side by [ ].

$x = \boxed{}$ Simplify.

$x \approx \boxed{}$ Round to the nearest whole number.

The school will take about [ ] days to use 250 gallons of milk.

❷ **Multiplying to Solve an Equation** Solve $-37.5 = \dfrac{c}{-1.2}$.

$-37.5 = \dfrac{c}{-1.2}$

$-37.5\left(\boxed{}\right) = \dfrac{c}{-1.2}\left(\boxed{}\right)$ Multiply each side by [ ].

$\boxed{} = c$ Simplify.

Check $-37.5 = \dfrac{c}{-1.2}$

$-37.5 \stackrel{?}{=} \dfrac{\boxed{}}{-1.2}$ Replace c with [ ].

$-37.5 = -37.5$ ✔   Simplify.

50 *Algebra Readiness* Lesson 3-5

Name_____ Class_____ Date _____

❸ **Multiplying to Solve an Equation** A little league player was at bat 15 times and had a batting average of 0.133, rounded to the nearest thousandth. The batting average formula is $a = \frac{h}{n}$, where a is the batting average, h is the number of hits, and n is the number of times at bat. Use the formula to find the number of hits the little league player made.

$a = \dfrac{h}{n}$

☐ $= \dfrac{h}{\boxed{}}$ Replace a with ☐ and n with ☐.

$0.133\left(\boxed{}\right) = \dfrac{h}{15}\left(\boxed{}\right)$ Multiply each side by ☐.

☐ $= h$ Simplify.

☐ $\approx h$ Since h (hits) represents an integer, round to the nearest integer.

The little league player made ☐ hits.

Quick Check

1. You paid $7.70 to mail a package that weighed 5.5 lb. In the equation $5.5p = 7.70$, 5.5 represents the weight of the package, p represents the cost per pound, and 7.70 represents the price you paid. Solve this equation to find the cost per pound.

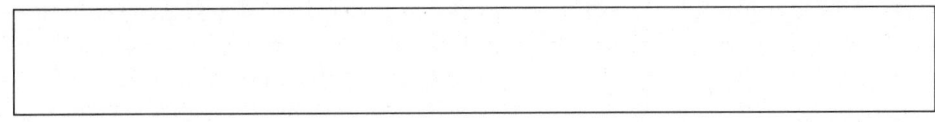

2. Solve each equation. Check the solution.
    a. $0.8x = 1.6$ **b.** $\dfrac{s}{2.5} = 5$

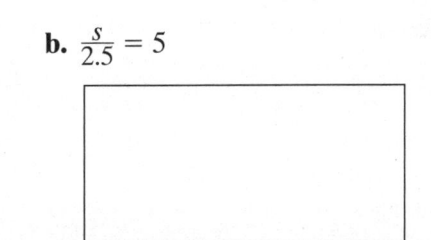

3. Suppose your batting average is 0.222. You have batted 54 times. How many hits do you have?

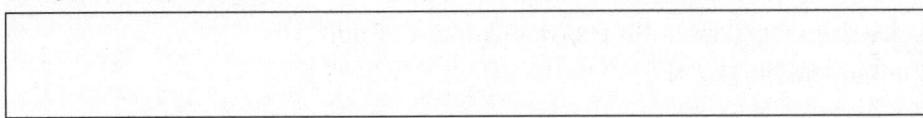

Daily Notetaking Guide   Algebra Readiness Lesson 3-5   51

Name_____ Class_____ Date_____

Lesson 3-6

Using the Metric System

Lesson Objectives
- Identify appropriate metric measures
- Convert metric units

Take Note

Metric Units of Measurement

	Unit	Reference Example
	millimeter ( )	about the thickness of a dime
	centimeter ( )	about the width of a thumbnail
	meter ( )	about the distance from a doorknob to the floor
	kilometer ( )	a little more than one half mile
	milliliter ( )	about 5 drops of water
	liter ( )	a little more than a quart of milk
	milligram ( )	about the mass of a speck of sawdust
	gram ( )	about the mass of a paper clip
	kilogram ( )	about one half the mass of your math book

Examples

1 Estimating With Metric Units Choose a reasonable estimate. Explain your choice.

a. capacity of a drinking glass: 500 L or 500 mL

_____ ; a drinking glass holds less than a quart of milk.

b. mass of a pair of hiking boots: 1kg or 1g

_____ ; the mass is about one half the mass of your math book.

52 *Algebra Readiness* Lesson 3-6

Name _____ Class _____ Date _____

❷ **Converting Between Metric Units** Complete each statement.
   a. 7,603 mL = ▢ L
      7,603 ÷ ▢ = ▢   To convert milliliters to liters, divide by 1,000.
      7,603 mL = ▢

   b. 4.57 m = ▢ cm
      4.57 × ▢ = ▢ cm   To convert meters to centimeters, multiply by 100.
      4.57 m = ▢

❸ **Converting Between Metric Units** A blue whale caught in 1931 was about 2,900 cm long. What was its length in meters?

   Words [length in centimeters] ÷ [centimeters per meter] = [length in meters]

   Equation ▢ ÷ ▢ = ▢

   The whale was about ▢ m long.

Quick Check

1. Choose a reasonable estimate.
   a. distance between two cities: 50 mm or 50 km

   ▢

   b. amount of liquid that an eyedropper holds: 10 mL or 10 L

   ▢

2. Complete each statement.
   a. 35 mL = ▢ L   b. ▢ cm = 60 m

3. a. The record for the highest a kite has flown is 3.8 km. Find the height of the kite in meters.

   ▢

   b. You have a recipe that requires 0.25 L of milk. Your measuring cup is marked only in milliliters. How many milliliters of milk do you need?

   ▢

Daily Notetaking Guide — Algebra Readiness Lesson 3-6   53

Name_____ Class_____ Date_____

Lesson 3-7 Reasoning Strategy: Act It Out

Lesson Objective
- Solve problems by acting them out

Example

1 Using Act It Out Marta gives her sister one penny on the first day of October, two pennies on the second day, and four pennies on the third day. She continues to double the number of pennies each day. On what date will Marta give her sister $10.24 in pennies?

Understand the Problem Marta needs to give her sister pennies worth $ ☐ . Marta gives her ☐ penny on the first day. She ☐ the number of pennies every day.

1. How many pennies does Marta's sister get on the first day? ☐
2. How many pennies does Marta's sister get on the second day? ☐
3. How many pennies does Marta's sister get on the third day? ☐

Make and Carry Out a Plan Act out the problem. Keep track of the amount given each day in a chart.

Days After the First	Number of Pennies	Amount
0	1	$.01
1	2	$.02
2	2 · 2 = ☐	
3	4 · 2 = ☐	
4	8 · 2 = ☐	
5	16 · 2 = ☐	

You can tell from the pattern in the chart that you just need to count the number of 2's multiplied until you reach ☐ , which is $ ☐ in pennies.

2 · 2 · 2 · 2 · 2 · 2 · 2 · 2 · 2 · 2 = ☐

☐ twos = ☐ days after the first penny is given.

Marta will give her sister $10.24 in pennies on ☐ .

54 Algebra Readiness Lesson 3-7

Name_____ Class_____ Date _____

Quick Check

1. Complete the chart to check your answer to Example 1.

Days After the First	Number of Pennies	Amount
0	1	$.01
1	2	$.02
2	2 · 2 = ☐	
3	4 · 2 = ☐	
4	8 · 2 = ☐	
5	16 · 2 = ☐	

Daily Notetaking Guide — Algebra Readiness Lesson 3-7

Name_____ Class_____ Date_____

Lesson 4-1   Divisibility and Factors

Lesson Objectives
- Use divisibility tests
- Find factors

Take Note

Divisibility Rules for 2, 5, and 10

An integer is divisible by

- ☐ if it ends in 0, 2, 4, 6, or 8.
- ☐ if it ends in 0 or 5.
- ☐ if it ends in 0.

☐ numbers end in 0, 2, 4, 6, or 8 and are divisible by 2.

☐ numbers end in 1, 3, 5, 7, or 9 and are not divisible by 2.

Divisibility Rules for 3 and 9

An integer is divisible by

- ☐ if the sum of its digits is divisible by 3.
- ☐ if the sum of its digits is divisible by 9.

One integer is divisible by another if the remainder is __ when you divide.

One integer is a factor of another integer if it divides the integer with a remainder of __.

Examples

❶ **Divisibility by 2, 5, and 10** Is the first number divisible by the second?

   a. 1,028 by 2

      ☐ ; 1,028 ends in ☐ .

   b. 572 by 5

      ☐ ; 572 doesn't end in ☐ or ☐ .

   c. 275 by 10

      ☐ ; 275 doesn't end in ☐ .

Name_____ Class_____ Date _____

❷ **Divisibility by 3 and 9** Is the first number divisible by the second?
   a. 1,028 by 3   ▢ ; 1 + 0 + 2 + 8 = 11; 11 is not divisible by ▢ .
   b. 522 by 9   ▢ ; 5 + 2 + 2 = 9; 9 is divisible by ▢ .

❸ **Finding Factors** Ms. Washington's class is having a class photo taken. Each row must have the same number of students. There are 35 students in the class. How can Ms. Washington arrange the students in rows if there must be at least 5 students, but no more than 10 students, in each row?

Find pairs of factors of 35: 1 · ▢ , 5 · ▢

There can be 5 rows of ▢ students, or 7 rows of ▢ students.

Quick Check

1. Is the first number divisible by the second? Explain.
   a. 160 by 5

   b. 56 by 10

   c. 53 by 2

   d. 174 by 3

   e. 43,542 by 9

2. List the positive factors of each integer.
   a. 10   b. 21
   c. 24   d. 31

3. What are the possible arrangements for Example 3 if there are 36 students in Ms. Washington's class?

Name_____ Class_____ Date_____

Lesson 4-2   Exponents

Lesson Objectives
- Use exponents
- Use the order of operations with exponents

Take Note

Order of Operations

1. Work inside [   ] symbols.
2. Simplify any terms with [   ].
3. [   ] and [   ] in order from left to right.
4. [   ] and [   ] in order from left to right.

_____ are used to show repeated multiplication.

A *power* has two parts, a [   ] and an [   ].

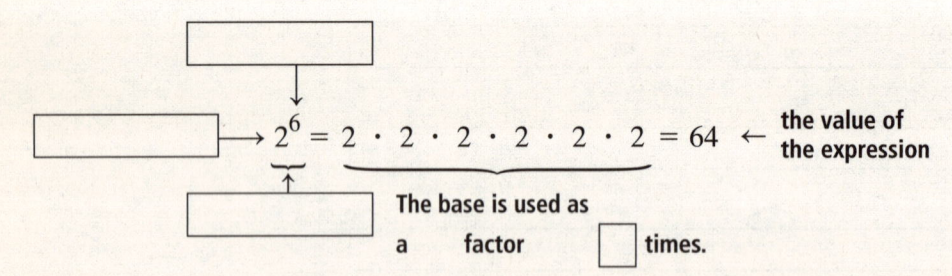

[   ] → 2^6 = 2 · 2 · 2 · 2 · 2 · 2 = 64 ← the value of the expression

[   ] The base is used as a factor [ ] times.

Examples

1 Using an Exponent Write the expression using an exponent.

a. $(-11)(-11)(-11)(-11)$

   $([])^{[]}$ Include the negative sign within parentheses.

b. $-5 \cdot x \cdot x \cdot y \cdot y \cdot x$

   $-5 \cdot x \cdot x \cdot x \cdot y \cdot y$ Rewrite the expression using the [   ] and [   ] Properties.

   $-5x^{[]}y^{[]}$ Write $x \cdot x \cdot x$ and $y \cdot y$ using exponents.

58 Algebra Readiness Lesson 4-2   Daily Notetaking Guide L1

Name _____ Class _____ Date _____

② Simplifying a Power Suppose a certain star is 10^4 light-years from Earth. How many light-years is that?

$10^4 = $ ☐   The exponent indicates that the base ☐ is used as a factor ☐ times.

= ☐ light-years   Multiply.

③ Using the Order of Operations

a. Simplify $3(1 + 4)^3$.

$3(1 + 4)^3 = 3(\boxed{})^3$ Work within parentheses first.

$= 3 \cdot \boxed{}$ Simplify 5^3.

$= \boxed{}$ Multiply.

Quick Check

1. Write using exponents.

   a. $4 \cdot y \cdot x \cdot y$

   b. $(-3)(-3)(-3)(-3)$

2. a. Simplify 7^2.

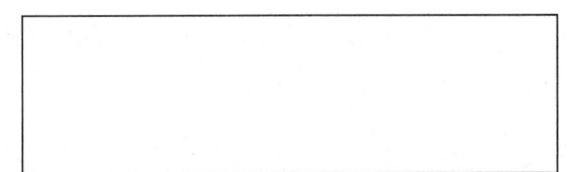

   b. Evaluate $-a^4$ and $(-a)^4$, for $a = 2$.

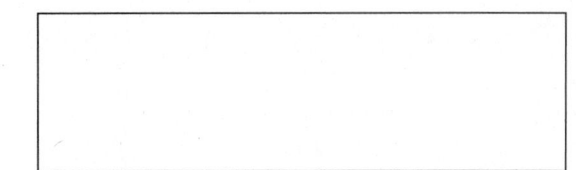

3. a. Simplify $2 \cdot 5^2 + 4 \cdot (-3)^3$.

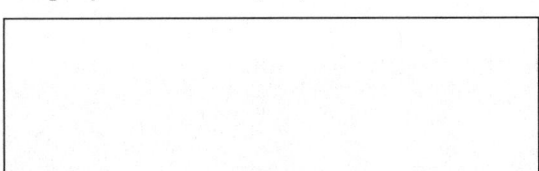

   b. Evaluate $3a^2 + 6$, for $a = -5$.

Daily Notetaking Guide   Algebra Readiness Lesson 4-2

Name_____ Class_____ Date_____

Lesson 4-3

Prime Factorization and Greatest Common Divisor

Lesson Objectives
- Find the prime factorization of a number
- Find the greatest common divisor (GCD) of two or more numbers

Vocabulary

A _____ is a positive integer greater than 1 with exactly two factors, 1 and the number itself.

A composite number is _____

_____

The _____ of a number is a written form of a number as the products of its prime factors.

The greatest common divisor (GCD) is _____

_____

Examples

1 Prime or Composite? State whether each number is *prime* or *composite*. Explain.

a. 46

☐☐☐☐ ; 46 has ☐☐☐☐ two factors, 1, ☐ , ☐ , and ☐ .

b. 13

☐☐☐☐ ; 13 has ☐☐☐☐ two factors, 1 and ☐ .

2 Writing the Prime Factorizations Use a factor tree to write the prime factorization of 273.

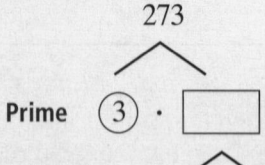

```
        273
        / \
Prime  ③ · ☐     Start with a prime factor.
           / \   Continue branching.
Primes  ☐ · ☐    Stop when all factors
                 are prime.

273 = ☐ · ☐ · ☐    Write the prime factorization.
```

Algebra Readiness Lesson 4-3 — Daily Notetaking Guide

Name _____ Class _____ Date _____

❸ **Finding the Greatest Common Divisor** Find the GCD of each pair of numbers and expressions.

24 and 30

24 = ☐³ · ☐   **Write the prime factorizations.**

30 = ☐ · ☐ · ☐

GCD = ☐ · ☐   **Find the common factors. Use the lesser power of the common factors.**

= ☐

The GCD of 24 and 30 is ☐.

Quick Check

1. a. Which numbers from 10 to 20 are prime?

   b. Which are composite?

2. Write the prime factorization of each number.

   a. 72

   b. 121

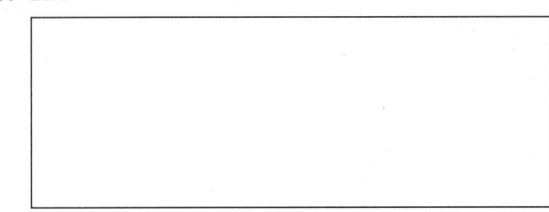

3. Use prime factorizations to find each GCD.

   a. 8, 20

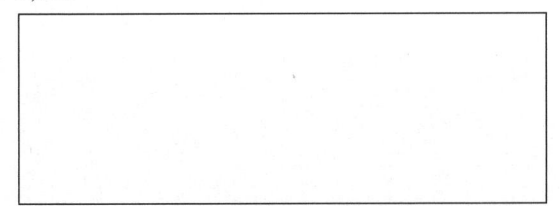

   b. 12, 87

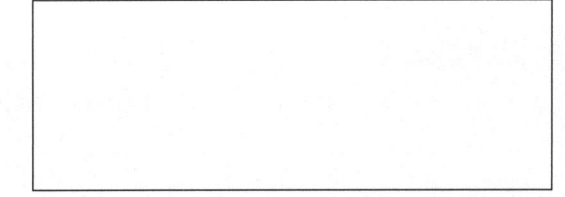

Name _____ Class _____ Date _____

Lesson 4-4

Simplifying Fractions

Lesson Objectives
- Find equivalent fractions
- Write fractions in simplest form

Vocabulary

Two fractions are _____ if they describe the same part of a whole.

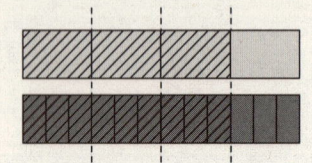

$\frac{3}{4}$ of the model is shaded.

$\frac{9}{12}$ of the model is shaded.

$\frac{3}{4} = \frac{3 \cdot \boxed{}}{4 \cdot \boxed{}} = \frac{9}{12}$

A fraction is in simplest form when _____

Example

1 **Finding an Equivalent Fraction** Find two fractions equivalent to $\frac{18}{21}$.

a. $\frac{18}{21} = \frac{18 \cdot 2}{21 \cdot \boxed{}}$

$= \dfrac{\boxed{}}{\boxed{}}$

b. $\frac{18}{21} = \frac{18 \div \boxed{}}{21 \div 3}$

$= \dfrac{\boxed{}}{\boxed{}}$

The fractions $\dfrac{\boxed{}}{\boxed{}}$ and $\dfrac{\boxed{}}{\boxed{}}$ are both equivalent to $\frac{18}{21}$.

Quick Check

1. Find two fractions equivalent to each fraction.

a. $\frac{5}{15}$

b. $\frac{10}{12}$

c. $\frac{14}{20}$

Name_____ Class_____ Date_____

Examples

② Simplifying a Fraction You learn that 21 out of the 28 students in a class, or $\frac{21}{28}$, buy their lunches in the cafeteria. Write this fraction in simplest form.

$\frac{21}{28} = \frac{21 \div \square}{28 \div \square}$ Divide the numerator and denominator by the GCD, $\square$.

$= \frac{\square}{\square}$ Simplify.

$\frac{\square}{\square}$ of the students in the class buy their lunches in the cafeteria.

③ Simplifying a Fraction With a Variable Write in simplest form.

a. $\frac{p}{2p} = \frac{p\square}{2p\square}$ Divide the numerator and denominator by the common factor, $\square$.

$= \frac{\square}{\square}$ Simplify.

b. $\frac{14q^2r}{8qr} = \frac{2 \cdot 7 \cdot q \cdot q \cdot r}{2 \cdot 2 \cdot 2 \cdot q \cdot r}$ Write as a product of prime factors.

$= \frac{2^{\square} \cdot 7 \cdot q^{\square} \cdot q \cdot r^{\square}}{2^{\square} \cdot 2 \cdot 2 \cdot q^{\square} \cdot r^{\square}}$ Divide the numerator and denominator by the common factors.

$= \frac{\square \cdot \square}{\square \cdot \square}$ Simplify.

$= \boxed{}$ Simplify.

Quick Check

2. Write each fraction in simplest form.

a. $\frac{6}{8} = \frac{6 \div \square}{8 \div \square} = \frac{\square}{\square}$ b. $\frac{9}{12} = \frac{9 \div \square}{12 \div \square} = \frac{\square}{\square}$

c. $\frac{b}{abc} = \frac{\square}{\square}$ d. $\frac{2mn}{6m} = \frac{\square}{\square}$

Name_____ Class_____ Date_____

Lesson 4-5

Reasoning Strategy: Solve a Simpler Problem

Lesson Objective	
• Solve complex problems by first solving simpler cases	

Example

1 Solving a Simpler Problem Aaron, Chris, Maria, Sonia, and Ling are on a class committee. They want to choose two members to present their conclusions to the class. How many different groups of two members can they form?

Understand the Problem

1. What do you need to find?
   ☐

2. How many people are there in all?
   ☐

3. How many people will present their conclusions?
   ☐

Make and Carry Out a Plan

To make sure that you account for every pair of committee members, make an organized list.

Solve a simpler problem. Change the problem to a simpler one based on three committee members, and then try four members to see if there is a pattern.

Three Members
(Aaron, Chris, Maria)

Aaron ⟨ ☐
         ☐

Chris —— Maria

(Chris has already been paired with ☐.)

Four Members
(Aaron, Chris, Maria, Sonia)

Aaron ⟨ ☐
         ☐
         ☐

Chris ⟨ ☐
         ☐

Maria —— ☐

(Maria has already been paired with ☐ and ☐.)

64 Algebra Readiness Lesson 4-5   Daily Notetaking Guide L1

Name_____ Class_____ Date _____

Example

4. What pattern do you see?

   [   ]

5. How many different groups of two committee members are there?

   [   ]

Check the Answer

Another way to solve this problem is to use a diagram. Draw line segments to represent the number of different groups of two members that can be formed.

Aaron

Maria •   • Chris

•   •
Sonia   Ling

There are [   ] line segments. The answer checks. ✔

Quick Check

1. Suppose there were eight people on the committee. How many different groups of two committee members would there be?

[   ]

Daily Notetaking Guide   Algebra Readiness Lesson 4-5

Name_____ Class_____ Date_____

Lesson 4-6   Rational Numbers

Lesson Objectives
- Identify and graph rational numbers
- Evaluate fractions containing variables

Vocabulary

A _____ is any number you can write as a quotient $\frac{a}{b}$ of two integers, where b is not zero.

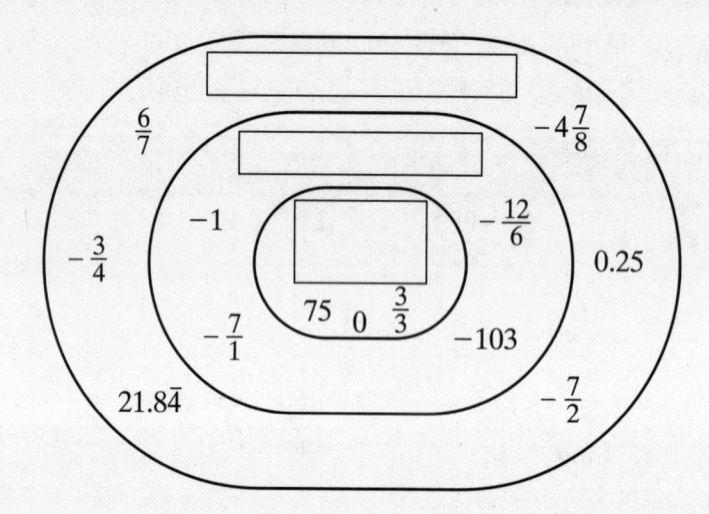

(Diagram with nested ovals containing: $\frac{6}{7}$, $-4\frac{7}{8}$, -1, $-\frac{12}{6}$, $-\frac{3}{4}$, 0.25, 75, 0, $\frac{3}{3}$, $-\frac{7}{1}$, -103, $21.8\overline{4}$, $-\frac{7}{2}$)

Example

1 Writing Equivalent Fractions Write two lists of fractions equivalent to $\frac{2}{3}$.

$\frac{2}{3} = \frac{\square}{6} = \frac{\square}{9} = \cdots$ **Numerators and denominators are positive.**

$\frac{2}{3} = \frac{\square}{-3} = \frac{\square}{-6} = \cdots$ **Numerators and denominators are negative.**

Quick Check

1. Write two fractions equivalent to each fraction.

    a. $\frac{1}{3} = \square = \square$ b. $\frac{5}{8} = \square = \square$

    c. $-\frac{4}{5} = \square = \square$ d. $-\frac{1}{2} = \square = \square$

Name _____ Class _____ Date _____

Examples

② Comparing and Ordering Rational Numbers Use a number line to order the numbers $-\frac{3}{4}, 0.5,$ and $\frac{1}{3}$ from least to greatest.

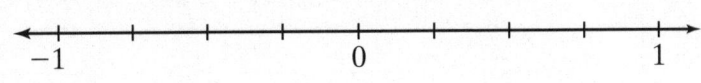

The order of the numbers from least to greatest is ☐ , ☐ , ☐ .

③ Evaluating Fractions With Variables A fast sports car can accelerate from a stop to 90 ft/s in 5 seconds. What is its acceleration in feet per second per second (ft/s²)? Use the formula $a = \frac{f - i}{t}$, where a is acceleration, f is final speed, i is initial speed, and t is time.

$a = \dfrac{f - i}{t}$ Use the acceleration formula.

$= \dfrac{\Box - \Box}{\Box}$ Substitute for the variables.

$= \dfrac{\Box}{\Box}$ Subtract.

$= \Box$ Write in simplest form.

The car's acceleration is ☐ ft/s².

Quick Check

2. Use a number line to order the numbers $-\frac{1}{2}, -2,$ and 0.9 from least to greatest.

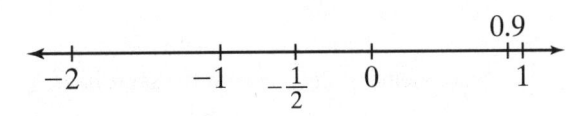

The order of the numbers from least to greatest is ☐ , ☐ , ☐ .

3. Evaluate each expression for $a = 6$ and $b = -5$. Write in simplest form.

a. $\dfrac{a + b}{-3}$

b. $\dfrac{7 - b}{3a}$

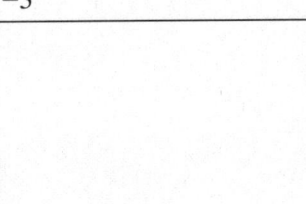

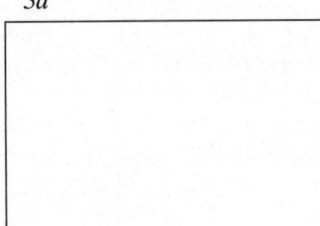

c. $\dfrac{a + 9}{b}$

Name_____ Class_____ Date_____

Lesson 4-7

Exponents and Multiplication

Lesson Objectives
- Multiply powers with the same base
- Find a power of a power

Take Note

Multiplying Powers With the Same Base

To multiply numbers or variables with the same base, ☐ the exponents.

Arithmetic

$2^3 \cdot 2^4 = 2^{\square + \square} = 2^{\square}$

Algebra

$a^{\square} \cdot a^{\square} = a^{\square + \square}$, for positive integers m and n.

Finding a Power of a Power

To find a power of a power, ☐ the exponents.

Arithmetic

$(2^3)^4 = 2^{\square \cdot \square} = 2^{\square}$

Algebra

$(a^m)^n = a^{\square \cdot \square}$, for positive integers m and n.

Example

1 Multiplying Powers Simplify each expression.

a. $5^2 \cdot 5^3 = 5^{\square + \square}$ ☐ the exponents of powers with the same base.

$\quad = 5^{\square}$ Simplify the exponent.

$\quad = \square$ Simplify.

b. $x^5 \cdot x^7 \cdot y^2 \cdot y = x^{\square + \square} \cdot y^{\square + \square}$ ☐ the exponents of powers with the same base.

$\quad = x^{\square} y^{\square}$ Simplify.

Quick Check

1. Simplify each expression.

   a. $(0.2)^2 \cdot (0.2)^3$

   b. $m^5 \cdot m^7$

Name _____ Class _____ Date _____

Examples

❷ **Using the Commutative Property** Simplify $3a^3 \cdot (-5a^4)$.

$3a^3 \cdot (-5a^4) = 3 \cdot (-5) \cdot a^3 \cdot a^4$ Use the [ ] Property of Multiplication.

$= -15a^{\Box + \Box}$ [ ] the exponents.

$= $ [ ]   Simplify.

❸ **Simplifying Powers of Powers** Simplify each expression.

a. $(2^3)^3 = (2)^{\Box \cdot \Box}$ [ ] the exponents.

$= (2)^{\Box}$ Simplify the exponent.

$= $ [ ]   Simplify.

b. $(g^5)^4 = g^{\Box \cdot \Box}$ [ ] the exponents.

$= (g)^{\Box}$ Simplify the exponent.

Quick Check

2. Simplify each expression.
   a. $6a^3 \cdot 3a$
   b. $-5c^2 \cdot (-3c^7)$

3. Simplify each expression.
   a. $(2^4)^2$
   b. $(c^5)^4$

Daily Notetaking Guide   Algebra Readiness Lesson 4-7   69

Name_____ Class_____ Date_____

Lesson 4-8 — Exponents and Division

Lesson Objectives
- Divide expressions containing exponents
- Simplify expressions with integer exponents

Take Note

Dividing Powers With the Same Base

To divide numbers or variables *with the same nonzero base*, ☐ the exponents.

Arithmetic

$\dfrac{4^5}{4^2} = 4^{\boxed{} - \boxed{}} = 4^{\boxed{}}$

Algebra

$\dfrac{a^m}{a^n} = a^{\boxed{} - \boxed{}}$, for $a \neq 0$ and positive integers m and n.

Zero as an Exponent

Arithmetic   Algebra

$3^0 = \boxed{}$ $a^0 = \boxed{}$, for $a \neq 0$.

Negative Exponents

Arithmetic   Algebra

$3^{-2} = \dfrac{1}{3^2}$ $a^{-n} = \dfrac{1}{a^n}$, for $a \neq 0$.

Example

1 **Dividing a Power by a Power** Simplify each expression.

a. $\dfrac{4^{12}}{4^8} = 4^{\boxed{} - \boxed{}}$ ☐ the exponents.

 $= 4^{\boxed{}}$ Simplify the exponent.

 $= \boxed{}$ Simplify.

b. $\dfrac{w^{18}}{w^{13}} = w^{\boxed{} - \boxed{}}$ ☐ the exponents.

 $= w^{\boxed{}}$ Simplify the exponent.

Quick Check

1. Simplify each expression.

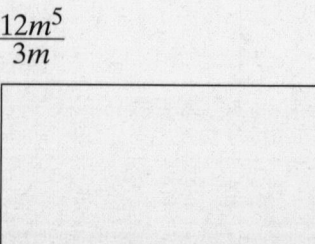

 a. $\dfrac{10^7}{10^4}$

 b. $\dfrac{12m^5}{3m}$

70 Algebra Readiness Lesson 4-8   Daily Notetaking Guide L1

Name_____ Class_____ Date_____

Examples

② Simplifying When Zero Is an Exponent Simplify each expression.

a. $\dfrac{(-12)^{73}}{(-12)^{73}} = (-12)^{\boxed{} - \boxed{}}$ $\boxed{}$ the exponents.

$= (-12)^{\boxed{}}$ Simplify.

$= \boxed{}$ Simplify.

③ Using Positive Exponents Simplify $\dfrac{z^4}{z^{15}}$.

$\dfrac{z^4}{z^{15}} = z^{\boxed{} - \boxed{}}$ Subtract the exponents.

$= z^{\boxed{}}$

$= \dfrac{1}{z^{\boxed{}}}$ Write with a positive exponent.

④ Using Negative Exponents Write $\dfrac{a^2 b^3}{ab^{15}}$ without a fraction bar.

$\dfrac{a^2 b^3}{ab^{15}} = a^{\boxed{} - \boxed{}} b^{\boxed{} - \boxed{}}$ Use the Rule for Dividing Powers With the Same Base.

$= ab^{\boxed{}}$ Subtract the exponents.

Quick Check

2. Simplify each expression.

2. $\dfrac{5^2 x^6}{5 x^6} = \boxed{} = \boxed{}$ 3. $\dfrac{4^5}{5^7} x^0 = \boxed{} = \boxed{}$

4. Write each fraction without a fraction bar.

a. $\dfrac{b^3}{b^9} = \boxed{}$ b. $\dfrac{m^3 n^2}{m^6 n^8} = \boxed{}$

Daily Notetaking Guide — Algebra Readiness Lesson 4-8

Name_____ Class_____ Date_____

Lesson 4-9

Scientific Notation

Lesson Objectives
- Write and evaluate numbers in scientific notation
- Calculate with scientific notation

Vocabulary

_____ is a way to write numbers using powers of 10. A number written in scientific notation is written as the product of two factors.

$$7,500,000,000,000 = 7.5 \times 10^{\square} \quad \leftarrow \text{Second factor is a power of } \square .$$

First factor is greater than or equal to $\square$, but less than $\square$.

You can change numbers from scientific notation to $\square$ by simplifying the product of the two factors.

Examples

① Writing in Scientific Notation

a. About 6,300,000 people visited the Eiffel Tower in the year 2000. Write this number in scientific notation.

6,300,000   Move the decimal point to get a decimal greater than $\square$ but less than $\square$.

$\square$ places

6.3   Drop the zeros after the 3.

$6.3 \times 10^{\square}$ You moved the decimal point $\square$ places. The number is large. Use $\square$ as the exponent of 10.

b. Write 0.00037 in scientific notation.

0.00037   Move the decimal point to get a decimal greater than $\square$ but less than $\square$.

$\square$ places

3.7   Drop the zeros after the 3.

$3.7 \times 10^{\square}$ You moved the decimal point $\square$ places. The number is small. Use $\square$ as the exponent of 10.

Name_____ Class_____ Date_____

Examples

② Writing in Standard Notation Write each number in standard notation.

a. 3.6×10^4

3.6000 Write zeros while moving the decimal point.

☐   Rewrite in standard notation.

b. 7.2×10^{-3}

007.2

☐

③ Multiplying with Scientific Notation Multiply $(2 \times 10^{-8})(8 \times 10^5)$. Express the result in scientific notation.

$(2 \times 10^{-8})(8 \times 10^5)$

$= 2 \times 8 \times 10^{-8} \times 10^5$ Use the ☐ Property of Multiplication.

$= $ ☐ $\times 10^{-8} \times 10^5$ Multiply 2 and 8.

$= 16 \times 10^{☐}$ ☐ the exponents.

$= 1.6 \times 10^{☐} \times 10^{☐}$ Write 16 as $1.6 \times 10^{☐}$.

$= 1.6 \times 10^{☐}$ ☐ the exponents.

Quick Check

1. Write each number in scientific notation.

   a. 54,500,000

   b. 0.00021

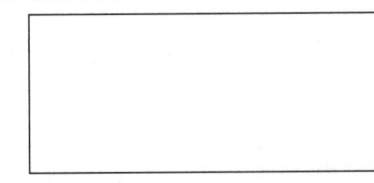

2. Write each number in standard notation.

   a. 3.21×10^7

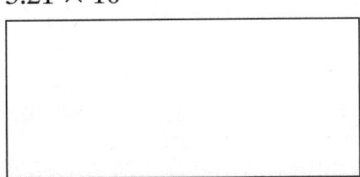

   b. 5.9×10^{-8}

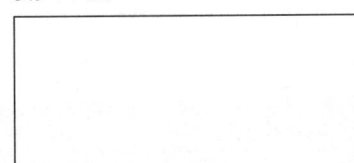

3. Multiply $(7.1 \times 10^{-8})(8 \times 10^4)$. Express the result in scientific notation.

L1 Daily Notetaking Guide   Algebra Readiness Lesson 4-9

Name_____ Class_____ Date_____

Lesson 5-1 Comparing and Ordering Rational Numbers

Lesson Objectives
- Find the least common multiple
- Compare fractions

Vocabulary

A _____ is a product of a number and any nonzero whole number.

A least common multiple (LCM) is _____

_____

A _____ is the least common multiple of the denominators of two or more fractions.

Examples

1 Finding the LCM Today, the school's baseball and soccer teams had games. The baseball team plays every 7 days. The soccer team plays every 3 days. When will the teams have games on the same day again?

7, 14, ☐, ☐, ☐, ☐, ...   List the multiples of 7.

3, 6, ☐, ☐, ☐, ☐, ☐, ...   List the multiples of 3.

The LCM is ☐. In ☐ days both teams will have games on the same day again.

2 Using Prime Factorization Find the LCM of 16 and 36.

16 = ☐   Write the prime factorizations.
36 = ☐ · ☐
LCM = ☐ · ☐   Use the greatest power of each factor.
    = ☐   Multiply.

The LCM of 16 and 36 is ☐.

74 Algebra Readiness Lesson 5-1   Daily Notetaking Guide L1

❸ Ordering Fractions Order $-\frac{3}{7}, -1, \frac{1}{4},$ and $\frac{2}{3}$ from least to greatest.

All ☐ numbers are less than all ☐ numbers, so $-\frac{3}{7}$ and -1 are both less than $\frac{1}{4}$ and $\frac{2}{3}$. Compare each pair.

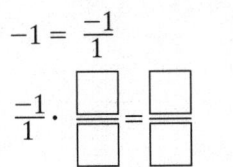

$-1 = \frac{-1}{1}$

$\frac{-1}{1} \cdot \frac{\square}{\square} = \frac{\square}{\square}$

Change -1 to a fraction by using 1 as its denominator. The LCM of 1 and 7 is ☐. Use ☐ as the common denominator.

$\frac{1}{4} = \frac{1 \cdot \square}{4 \cdot \square} = \frac{\square}{\square}$

The LCM of 7, 4, and 3 is ☐. Use ☐ as the common denominator.

$\frac{2}{3} = \frac{2 \cdot \square}{3 \cdot \square} = \frac{\square}{\square}$

$-\frac{7}{7} \square -\frac{3}{7}$ and $\frac{21}{84} \square \frac{56}{84}$, so $-1 \square -\frac{3}{7} \square \frac{1}{4} \square \frac{2}{3}$.

Quick Check

1. Find the LCM.
   a. 3, 4
   b. 3, 4, 5

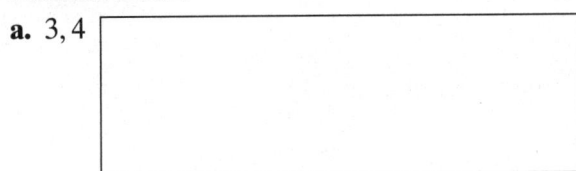

2. Use prime factorization to find the LCM.
   a. 6, 16
   b. 12, 15, 18

3. Compare the fractions in each pair.
   a. $\frac{6}{7} \square \frac{4}{5}$
   b. $\frac{2}{3} \square \frac{3}{4}$
   c. $-\frac{3}{4} \square -\frac{7}{10}$

4. Order from least to greatest.
   a. $\frac{2}{3}, \frac{1}{6}, \frac{5}{12}$
   b. $\frac{3}{10}, \frac{1}{5}, \frac{1}{2}, \frac{7}{12}$

Daily Notetaking Guide — Algebra Readiness Lesson 5-1

Name_____ Class_____ Date_____

Lesson 5-2

Fractions and Decimals

Lesson Objectives
- Write rational numbers as decimals
- Write terminating and repeating decimals as fractions

Vocabulary

A _____ is a decimal with a finite number of digits.

A repeating decimal is _____

Examples

1 Writing a Terminating Decimal A customer at a delicatessen asks for $\frac{1}{2}$ lb of coleslaw. The scale reads 0.5. Is the customer getting the amount of coleslaw she requested? Explain.

Since ☐ = ☐, the customer is getting the ☐ amount of coleslaw.

2 Writing a Decimal as a Fraction Write 1.72 as a mixed number in simplest form.

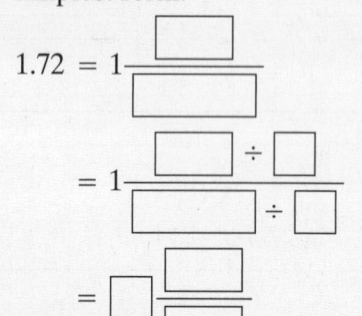

$1.72 = 1\frac{\square}{\square}$ Keep the whole number 1.
Write seventy-two hundredths as a fraction.

$= 1\frac{\square \div \square}{\square \div \square}$ Divide the numerator and denominator of the fraction by the GCF, ☐.

$= \frac{\square}{\square}$ Simplify.

76 *Algebra Readiness* Lesson 5-2   Daily Notetaking Guide

Name _____ Class _____ Date _____

Example

3 **Writing a Repeating Decimal as a Fraction** Write the repeating decimal $0.\overline{18}$ as a fraction in simplest form.

$n = 0.\overline{18}$ Let the variable *n* equal the decimal.

$\boxed{}\, n = \boxed{}$ Multiply each side by 10^2, or $\boxed{}$.

$\boxed{}\, n = \boxed{}$

$-n = -0.\overline{18}$ The Subtraction Property of Equality lets you subtract the same value from each side of the equation. So, subtract to eliminate $0.\overline{18}$.

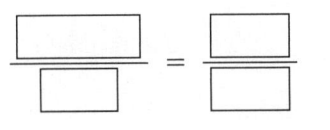

$\boxed{} = \boxed{}$

$\dfrac{\boxed{}}{\boxed{}} = \dfrac{\boxed{}}{\boxed{}}$ Divide each side by $\boxed{}$.

$n = \dfrac{\boxed{} \div \boxed{}}{\boxed{} \div \boxed{}}$ Divide the numerator and denominator by the GCF, $\boxed{}$.

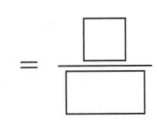

$= \dfrac{\boxed{}}{\boxed{}}$ Simplify.

As a fraction in simplest form, $0.\overline{18} = \dfrac{\boxed{}}{\boxed{}}$.

Quick Check

1. Write each rational number as a decimal. State whether the decimal is *terminating* or *repeating*. If the decimal repeats, state the block of digits that repeats.

    a. $\dfrac{7}{9}$ _____   b. $\dfrac{21}{22}$ _____

    c. $\dfrac{11}{8}$ _____   d. $\dfrac{8}{11}$ _____

2. Write as a fraction or a mixed number in simplest form.

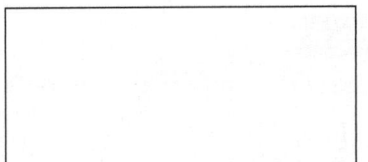

    a. 1.75 _____   b. 0.65 _____

3. Write each decimal as a fraction in simplest form.

    a. $0.\overline{7}$ _____   b. $0.\overline{54}$ _____

Daily Notetaking Guide — Algebra Readiness Lesson 5-2

Name_____ Class_____ Date_____

Lesson 5-3

Adding and Subtracting Fractions

Lesson Objectives
- Add and subtract fractions
- Use factoring to find common denominators

Examples

① Simplifying With Like Denominators Find each sum or difference. Simplify if possible.

a.
$\dfrac{4}{9} + \dfrac{2}{9} = \dfrac{\Box + \Box}{9}$ Add the numerators.

$= \dfrac{\Box}{\Box}$ Simplify.

$= \dfrac{\Box}{\Box}$ Write in simplest form.

b.
$\dfrac{12}{b} - \dfrac{5}{b} = \dfrac{\Box - \Box}{\Box}$ Subtract the numerators.

$= \dfrac{\Box}{\Box}$ Simplify.

② Simplifying With Unlike Denominators Simplify each difference.

a.
$\dfrac{1}{6} - \dfrac{3}{4} = \dfrac{\Box \cdot \Box - \Box \cdot \Box}{\Box \cdot \Box}$ Rewrite using a common denominator.

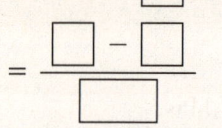

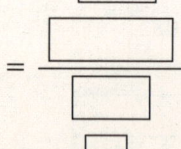

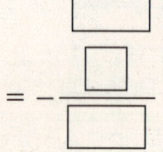

$= \dfrac{\Box - \Box}{\Box}$ Simplify.

$= \dfrac{\Box}{\Box}$ Subtract the numerators.

$= -\dfrac{\Box}{\Box}$ Write in simplest form.

Quick Check

1. Find the sum or difference. Simplify if possible.

a. $\dfrac{3}{7} + \dfrac{1}{7} =$

b. $\dfrac{2}{k} + \dfrac{3}{k} =$

Example

3 **Adding Mixed Numbers** Suppose one day you rode a bicycle for $3\frac{1}{2}$ hours and jogged for $1\frac{1}{4}$ hours. How many hours did you exercise?

$3\frac{1}{2} + 1\frac{1}{4} = \dfrac{\Box}{\Box} + \dfrac{\Box}{\Box}$ Write mixed numbers as improper fractions.

$= \dfrac{\Box \cdot \Box + \Box \cdot \Box}{\Box \cdot \Box}$ Rewrite using a common denominator.

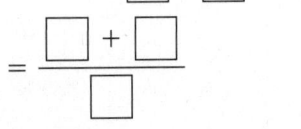

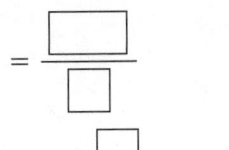

$= \dfrac{\Box + \Box}{\Box}$ Simplify.

$= \dfrac{\Box}{\Box}$ Add the numerators.

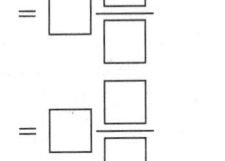

$= \Box\dfrac{\Box}{\Box}$ Write as a mixed number.

$= \Box\dfrac{\Box}{\Box}$ Simplify.

You exercised for ⬚ hours.

Quick Check

2. Find each sum or difference. Simplify, if possible.

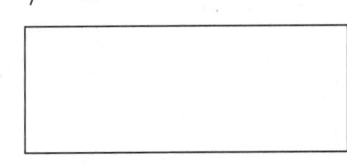

    a. $-\dfrac{7}{8} + \dfrac{3}{4}$

    b. $\dfrac{3}{7} - \dfrac{2}{m}$

    c. $5\dfrac{2}{3} - 3\dfrac{1}{6}$

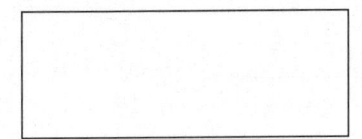

    d. $2\dfrac{3}{8} + \dfrac{7}{8}$

Name_____ Class_____ Date_____

Lesson 5-4

Multiplying and Dividing Fractions

Lesson Objectives
- Multiply fractions
- Divide fractions

Vocabulary

_____ are two numbers with a product of 1.

Example

1 Multiplying Fractions

a. Find $\frac{3}{4} \cdot \frac{2}{3}$.

$\frac{3}{4} \cdot \frac{2}{3} = \frac{\boxed{} \cdot \boxed{}}{\cancel{3} \cdot \cancel{2}} \cdot \frac{\cancel{2}}{\cancel{3}}$ Divide common factors.

$= \dfrac{\boxed{}}{\boxed{}}$ Multiply.

b. Find $\frac{5}{w} \cdot \frac{3w}{17}$.

$\frac{5}{w} \cdot \frac{3w}{17} = \frac{5}{\cancel{w}} \cdot \frac{3\cancel{w}}{17}$ with boxes

$= \dfrac{\boxed{}}{\boxed{}}$

Quick Check

1. Find each product. Simplify if possible.

a. $\frac{2}{3} \cdot \frac{6}{7}$

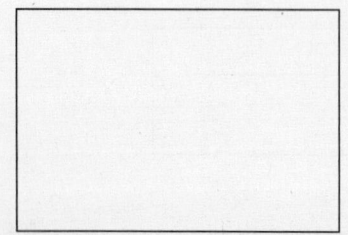

b. $\frac{2x}{9} \cdot \frac{3}{4}$

c. $\frac{2}{3} \cdot \frac{6}{7}$

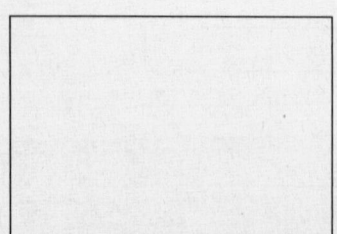

d. $-\frac{5}{15} \cdot \frac{21}{25}$

80 *Algebra Readiness* Lesson 5-4

Name_____ Class_____ Date_____

Examples

② Multiplying Mixed Numbers Find $4\frac{1}{5} \cdot \frac{3}{4}$.

$4\frac{1}{5} \cdot \frac{3}{4} = \frac{\square}{\square} \cdot \frac{3}{4}$ Write $\square\frac{\square}{\square}$ as an improper fraction.

$= \frac{\square}{\square}$ Multiply.

$= \square\frac{\square}{\square}$ Write as a mixed number.

③ Dividing Fractions

a. Find $\frac{3}{5} \div \frac{7}{10}$.

$\frac{3}{5} \div \frac{7}{10} = \frac{3}{5} \cdot \frac{\square}{\square}$ Multiply by the reciprocal of the divisor.

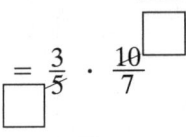

$= \frac{3}{\square} \cdot \frac{10^{\square}}{7}$ Divide the common factors.

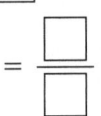

$= \frac{\square}{\square}$ Multiply. Simplify if necessary.

Quick Check

2. Find each product or quotient. Simplify if possible.

a. $3\frac{3}{4} \cdot \frac{2}{5}$

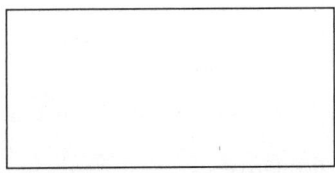

b. $\frac{2}{3} \cdot 1\frac{2}{7}$

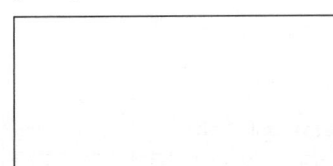

c. $-\frac{1}{4} \div \frac{1}{2}$

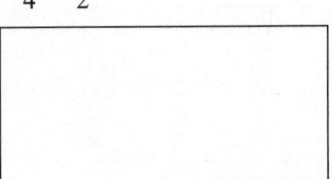

d. $\frac{5a}{8} \div \frac{2}{3}$

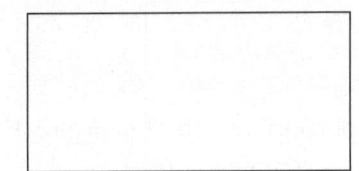

Daily Notetaking Guide — Algebra Readiness Lesson 5-4   81

Name_____ Class_____ Date_____

Lesson 5-5   Using Customary Units of Measurement

Lesson Objectives
- Identify appropriate customary units
- Convert customary units

Vocabulary

_____ is a process of analyzing units to decide which conversion factors to use.

Customary Units of Measure

Type	Length	Capacity	Weight
Unit	Inch (in.) Foot (ft) Yard (yd) Mile (mi)	Fluid ounce (fl oz) Cup (c) Pint (pt) Quart (qt) Gallon (gal)	Ounce (oz) Pound (lb) Ton (t)
Equivalents	1 ft = 12 in. 1 yd = 3 ft 1 mi = 5,280 ft = 1,760 yd	1 c = 8 fl oz 1 pt = 2 c 1 qt = 2 pt 1 gal = 4 qt	1 lb = 16 oz 1 t = 2,000 lb

Example

1 Choosing a Unit of Measure Choose an appropriate unit of measure. Explain your choice.

a. weight of a hummingbird

Measure its weight in [   ] because a hummingbird is very light.

b. length of a soccer field

Measure its length in [   ] because it is too long to measure in [   ] or [   ] and too short to measure in [   ].

Quick Check

1. Choose an appropriate unit of measure. Explain.

a. length of a swimming pool

b. capacity of an eyedropper

Name_____ Class_____ Date _____

Examples

② Using Conversion Factors Convert 68 fluid ounces to cups.

$68 \text{ fl oz.} = \dfrac{68 \text{ fl oz.}}{1} \cdot \dfrac{1 \text{ c}}{\boxed{} \text{ fl oz.}}$ Use a conversion factor that changes fluid ounces to cups.

$= \dfrac{68 \text{ fl oz.} \cdot 1 \text{ c}}{\boxed{}\; \cancel{8 \text{ fl oz.}}}$ Divide the common factors and units.

$= \dfrac{\boxed{}}{\boxed{}} \text{ c}$ Simplify.

$= \boxed{} \dfrac{\boxed{}}{\boxed{}} \text{ c}$ Write as a mixed number.

There are $\boxed{}$ c in 68 fl oz.

③ Comparing Units Fred's fruit stand sells homemade lemonade in $6\frac{1}{2}$-pint bottles for $1.99. Jill's fruit stand sells homemade lemonade in $3\frac{1}{2}$-qt containers for the same price. At which stand do you get more lemonade for your money?

$3\frac{1}{2} \text{ qt} = \dfrac{7}{2} \text{ qt} \cdot \dfrac{\boxed{} \text{ pt}}{1 \text{ qt}}$ Use a conversion factor that changes quarts to pints.

$= \dfrac{7 \cancel{\text{ qt}}}{\cancel{2}} \cdot \dfrac{\overset{\boxed{}}{\cancel{2} \text{ pt}}}{1 \cancel{\text{ qt}}}$ Divide the common factors and units.

$= \boxed{} \text{ pt}$ Multiply.

Since $\boxed{}$ pints $\boxed{}$ $6\frac{1}{2}$ pints, you get more lemonade for your money at $\boxed{}$ stand.

Quick Check

2. Complete each equation.

a. 14 oz = $\boxed{}$

   = $\boxed{}$ lb

b. $3\frac{1}{2}$ yd = $\boxed{}$

   = $\boxed{}$ ft

Name_____ Class_____ Date_____

Lesson 5-6   Work Backward

Lesson Objective
- Solve problems by working backward

Example

1 Your flight leaves the airport at 10:00 A.M. You must arrive 2 hours early to check your luggage. The drive to the airport takes about 90 minutes. A stop for breakfast takes about 30 minutes. It will take about 15 minutes to park and get to the terminal. At what time should you leave home?

Understand the Problem

Think about the information you are given.

1. What do you want to find?

2. What is your arrival time?

3. How much time will you spend driving to the airport?

4. How much time will you spend eating breakfast?

5. How much time will you spend parking and getting to the terminal?

Make and Carry Out a Plan

You know that the series of events must end at 10:00 A.M. Work backward to find when the events must begin.

Carry Out the Plan

Redraw the hands of the clock to find the time you should leave home.

Write the starting time for each event.

    Flight leaves   Arrive at airport   Park

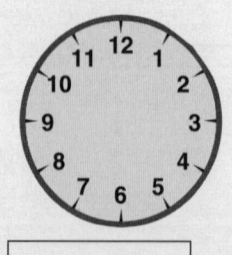

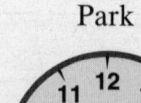

                A.M.   A.M.   A.M.

84   *Algebra Readiness* Lesson 5-6   Daily Notetaking Guide   L1

Name _____ Class _____ Date _____

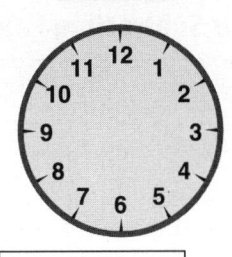

Breakfast   Leave home

[ ] A.M.   [ ] A.M.

You should leave home at [ ]

Check the Answer

Check the departure time. Find the total time needed.

90 min + 30 min + 15 min + 120 min = [ ] min

Add [ ] minutes to your departure time.

5:45 + 0:255 = 5: 300

5: [ ]   [ ] min = [ ] h

5: [ ] = [ ] hours after 5:00, or [ ]

Since your flight leaves at 10:00 A.M., your departure time is correct.

Quick Check

1. Suppose you find out the night before that the flight is delayed until 11:15 A.M. What time should you leave home?

Name_____ Class_____ Date_____

Lesson 5-7   Solving Equations by Adding or Subtracting Fractions

Lesson Objectives
- Solve equations by subtracting fractions
- Solve equations by adding fractions

Example

1 **Subtracting a Fraction to Solve an Equation** One school recycles about $\frac{1}{3}$ of its waste paper. The student council set a goal of recycling $\frac{3}{4}$ of the school's waste paper by the end of the year. By how much does the school need to increase its paper recycling to reach the goal?

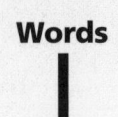

Words   [fraction school recycles] plus [the increase] is [student goal]

Let $\boxed{n}$ = the increase.

Equation $\dfrac{\Box}{\Box} + \boxed{n} = \dfrac{\Box}{\Box}$

$\frac{1}{3} + n = \frac{3}{4}$

$\frac{1}{3} - \dfrac{\Box}{\Box} + n = \frac{3}{4} - \dfrac{\Box}{\Box}$ Subtract $\dfrac{\Box}{\Box}$ from each side.

$n = \dfrac{3 \cdot \Box - \Box \cdot 4}{\Box \cdot \Box}$ Use 3 · 4 as the common denominator.

$n = \dfrac{\Box - \Box}{\Box}$ Use the order of operations.

$n = \dfrac{\Box}{\Box}$ Simplify.

To meet the student council goal, the school needs to recycle $\dfrac{\Box}{\Box}$ more of its waste paper.

Check Is the answer reasonable? The present fraction of paper waste that is recycled plus the increase must equal the goal. Since

$\frac{1}{3} + \frac{5}{12} = \frac{4}{12} + \frac{5}{12} = \boxed{} = \boxed{}$, the answer is reasonable.

86 *Algebra Readiness* Lesson 5-7

Name_____ Class_____ Date _____

Example

② Adding a Fraction to Solve an Equation Solve $q - 6\frac{1}{2} = -1\frac{3}{5}$.

$$q - 6\frac{1}{2} = -1\frac{3}{5}$$

$$q - 6\frac{1}{2} + \boxed{}\frac{\boxed{}}{\boxed{}} = -1\frac{3}{5} + \boxed{}\frac{\boxed{}}{\boxed{}}$$ Add $\boxed{}\frac{\boxed{}}{\boxed{}}$ to each side.

$$q = -\frac{\boxed{}}{\boxed{}} + \frac{\boxed{}}{\boxed{}}$$ Write mixed numbers as improper fractions.

$$q = \frac{-8 \cdot \boxed{} + 5 \cdot \boxed{}}{\boxed{} \cdot \boxed{}}$$ Use $5 \cdot 2$ as the common denominator.

$$q = \frac{\boxed{} + \boxed{}}{\boxed{}}$$ Use the order of operations.

$$q = \frac{\boxed{}}{\boxed{}}$$ Simplify.

$$q = \boxed{}\frac{\boxed{}}{\boxed{}}$$ Write as a mixed number.

Quick Check

1. Solve and check each equation.

   a. $y + \frac{8}{9} = \frac{5}{9}$

   b. $a - \frac{3}{5} = \frac{1}{5}$

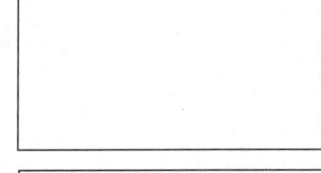

   c. $c - 2\frac{1}{6} = 5\frac{1}{4}$

   d. $3\frac{7}{18} = z + 1\frac{1}{3}$

Name_____ Class_____ Date_____

Lesson 5-8
Solving Equations by Multiplying Fractions

Lesson Objectives
- Solve equations by multiplying fractions
- Solve equations by multiplying mixed numbers

Examples

1 Multiplying by a Reciprocal Solve $7y = \frac{1}{3}$.

$7y = \frac{1}{3}$

$\frac{\square}{\square} \cdot (7y) = \frac{\square}{\square} \cdot \frac{1}{3}$ Multiply each side by $\frac{1}{7}$, the reciprocal of 7.

$y = \frac{\square}{\square}$ Simplify.

2 Multiplying by the Negative Reciprocal Solve $-\frac{20}{27}c = \frac{4}{9}$.

$-\frac{20}{27}c = \frac{4}{9}$

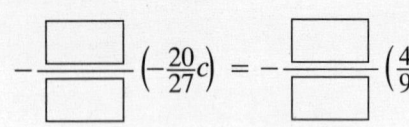

$-\frac{\square}{\square}\left(-\frac{20}{27}c\right) = -\frac{\square}{\square}\left(\frac{4}{9}\right)$ Multiply each side by $-\frac{\square}{\square}$, the reciprocal of $-\frac{20}{27}$.

$c = -\dfrac{\overset{\square\;\square}{27 \cdot 4}}{\underset{\square\;\square}{20 \cdot 9}}$ Divide common factors.

$c = -\frac{\square}{\square}$ Simplify.

Quick Check

1. Solve each equation.

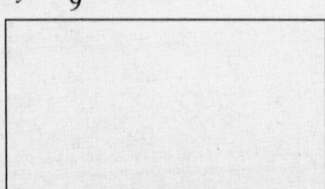

   a. $2y = \frac{7}{9}$ b. $\frac{5}{4} = \frac{5}{4}d$ c. $-\frac{2}{9}t = \frac{5}{6}$

Name _____ Class _____ Date _____

Example

3 **Solving an Equation With Mixed Numbers** How many $2\frac{1}{2}$-t trucks can you place on a rail car that has a carrying capacity of 15 t?

Words $\boxed{\text{weight of each truck}}$ times $\boxed{\text{the number of trucks}}$ is $\boxed{\text{carrying capacity}}$

Let $\boxed{n}$ = the number of trucks.

Equation $\boxed{}\frac{\boxed{}}{\boxed{}} \cdot \boxed{n} = \boxed{}$

$2\frac{1}{2} \cdot n = 15$

$\frac{\boxed{}}{\boxed{}} n = 15$ Write $2\frac{1}{2}$ as improper fraction.

$\frac{\boxed{}}{\boxed{}} \cdot \frac{5}{2} n = \frac{\boxed{}}{\boxed{}} \cdot 15$ Multiply each side by $\frac{\boxed{}}{\boxed{}}$, the reciprocal of $\frac{5}{2}$.

$n = \frac{2 \cdot \cancel{15}^{\boxed{}}}{\cancel{5} \cdot 1}$ Divide common factors.

$n = \boxed{}$ Simplify.

You can place $\boxed{}$ trucks on the rail car.

Quick Check

2. Solve each equation.

   a. $-\frac{6}{7}r = \frac{3}{4}$

   b. $-6n = \frac{3}{7}$

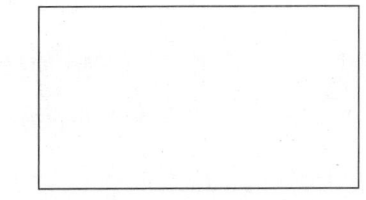

   c. $3\frac{1}{2}n = 28$

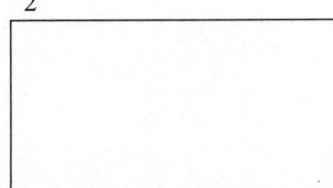

   d. $-\frac{7}{20} = 1\frac{1}{6}r$

Name_____ Class_____ Date_____

Lesson 5-9   Powers of Products and Quotients

Lesson Objectives
- Find powers of products
- Find powers of quotients

Take Note

Rule for Raising a Product to a Power

To raise a product to a power, raise each factor to the power.

Arithmetic

$(5 \cdot 3)^4 = 5^{\square} \cdot 3^{\square}$

Algebra

$(ab)^m = a^{\square} b^{\square}$ for any positive integer m

Rule for Raising a Quotient to a Power

To raise a quotient to a power, raise both the numerator and denominator to the power.

Arithmetic

$\left(\dfrac{2}{3}\right)^4 = \dfrac{2^{\square}}{3^{\square}}$

Algebra

$\left(\dfrac{a}{b}\right)^m = \dfrac{a^{\square}}{b^{\square}}$, for $b \neq 0$ and any positive integer m

Example

1 Simplifying a Power of a Product Simplify $(3z^5)^4$.

$(3z^5)^4 = 3^{\square} \cdot (\square)^{\square}$ Raise each factor to the fourth power.

$= 3^4 \cdot z^{\square \cdot \square}$ Use the Rule for Raising a Power to a Power.

$= 3^4 \cdot \square$ Multiply exponents.

$= \square$ Simplify.

Quick Check

1. Simplify each expression.

   a. $(2(3))^3$

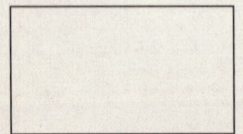

   b. $(2p)^4$

   c. $(5x^3)^2$

90 *Algebra Readiness Lesson 5-9*   Daily Notetaking Guide

Name_____ Class_____ Date _____

Examples

② Working With a Negative Sign

a. Simplify $(-3a)^4$.

$(-3a)^4 = (-3)^{\boxed{}}(a)^{\boxed{}}$

$= \boxed{}$

b. Simplify $-(3a)^4$.

$-(3a)^4 = (-1)(3a)^{\boxed{}}$

$= (-1)(3)^{\boxed{}}(a)^{\boxed{}}$

$= \boxed{}$

Quick Check

2. Simplify each expression.

a. $(-2y)^4$

b. $-(2y)^4$

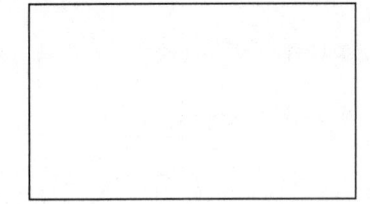

3. Simplify each expression.

a. $\left(-\frac{2}{3}\right)^4$

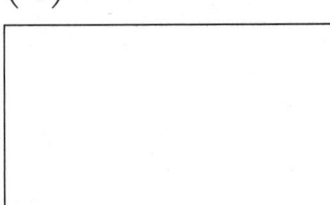

b. $\left(\frac{2x^2}{3}\right)^3$

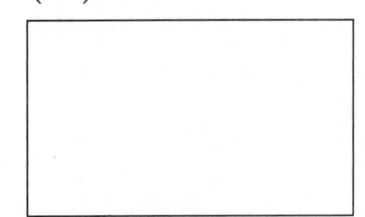

Daily Notetaking Guide — Algebra Readiness Lesson 5-9   91

Name _____ Class _____ Date _____

Lesson 6-1   Ratios and Unit Rates

Lesson Objectives
- Find rates and unit rates
- Use measures expressed as rates and products to solve problems

Take Note

Ratio

A ratio is _____

_____

Arithmetic   **Algebra**

10 to 15   [ ]   [ ]/[ ]   [ ]   [ ] $\frac{a}{b}$, for $b \neq 0$

A ___ is a ratio that compares quantities in different units.

A unit rate is _____

_____

Examples

1 Finding Unit Rates The table shows prices for different packages of index card. What size has the lowest unit cost?

Size (cards)	Price
100	$2.70
50	$1.30
25	$.75

100 cards: $\frac{price}{number\ of\ cards}$ → $\frac{\boxed{}}{100\ cards}$ = $\frac{\boxed{}}{card}$

50 cards: $\frac{price}{number\ of\ cards}$ → $\frac{\boxed{}}{50\ cards}$ = $\frac{\boxed{}}{card}$ Find the unit costs.

25 cards: $\frac{price}{number\ of\ cards}$ → $\frac{\boxed{}}{25\ cards}$ = $\frac{\boxed{}}{card}$

The [ ]-card pack has the lowest unit cost.

Name_____ Class_____ Date _____

❷ Finding Rates Expressed as Products A job takes 280 person-days to complete. How many workers are needed to complete the job in 40 days? It takes 280 workers to complete the job in 1 day. To find the number of workers needed to complete the job in 40 days, divide.

$$\frac{280 \text{ person-days}}{\boxed{} \text{ days}} = \boxed{} \text{ persons}$$ **Divide the number of person-days by the number of days.**

$\boxed{}$ workers are needed to complete the job in 40 days.

Check Since $\dfrac{\text{person-days}}{\boxed{}} = \boxed{}$, the units check.

Quick Check

1. Find each unit rate.

    a. Two liters of spring water cost $1.98.

    b. A car goes 425 mi on 12.5 gal of gas.

2. A contractor has a job that requires 540 person-days. How many workers are needed to complete the job in 60 days?

Daily Notetaking Guide — Algebra Readiness Lesson 6-1

Name_____ Class_____ Date_____

Lesson 6-2
Proportions

Lesson Objectives
- Solve proportions
- Use proportions to solve problems

Take Note

Cross Products

In a proportion, the cross products are ☐.

Arithmetic

$$\frac{6}{9} = \frac{8}{12}$$

$6 \cdot \boxed{} = 9 \cdot \boxed{} = \boxed{}$

Algebra

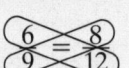

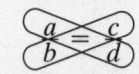

$$\frac{a}{b} = \frac{c}{d}$$

$ad = \boxed{}$

A _____ is an equality of two ratios.

The cross products of the proportion $\frac{a}{b} = \frac{c}{d}$ are ☐ and ☐.

Examples

1 Multiplying to Solve a Proportion Solve $\frac{2}{7} = \frac{y}{14}$.

Cross Products

$$\frac{2}{7} = \frac{y}{14}$$

$2 \cdot \boxed{} = 7 \cdot \boxed{}$ Write cross products.

$28 = 7y$ Multiply.

$\dfrac{28}{\boxed{}} = \dfrac{7y}{\boxed{}}$ Divide each side by ☐.

$\boxed{} = y$ Simplify.

94 Algebra Readiness Lesson 6-2

Name _____ Class _____ Date _____

② Testing for a Proportion Do the ratios $\frac{3}{5}$ and $\frac{21}{35}$ form a proportion? Explain.

$\frac{3}{5} \stackrel{?}{=} \frac{21}{35}$ Test by writing as a proportion.

$3 \cdot \boxed{} \stackrel{?}{=} 5 \cdot \boxed{}$ Write cross products.

$\boxed{} = \boxed{}$ Simplify.

The ratios $\boxed{}$ form a proportion. The $\boxed{}$ are equal.

③ Solving a Problem using a Proportion One hundred rods is about 275 fathoms. To the nearest fathom, how many fathoms is 25 rods?

Let d = distance in fathoms.

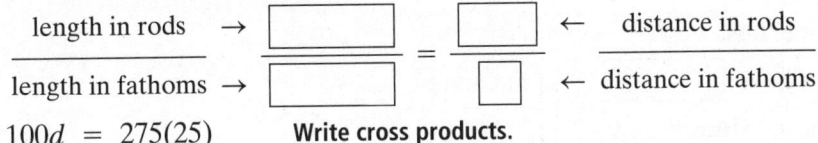

length in rods → $\dfrac{\boxed{}}{\boxed{}} = \dfrac{\boxed{}}{\boxed{}}$ ← distance in rods
length in fathoms → ← distance in fathoms

$100d = 275(25)$ Write cross products.

$d = \dfrac{275(25)}{\boxed{}}$ Divide each side by $\boxed{}$.

$d \approx \boxed{}$ A calculator may be useful.

25 rods is about $\boxed{}$ fathoms.

Quick Check

1. Solve each proportion.

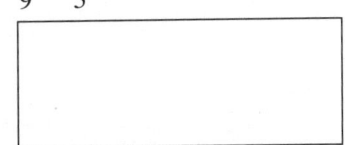

   a. $\frac{h}{9} = \frac{2}{3}$ b. $\frac{4}{5} = \frac{t}{55}$

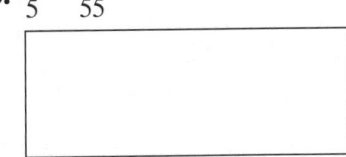

2. Tell whether the two ratios form a proportion. Explain.

   a. $\frac{6}{9}, \frac{4}{6}$ b. $\frac{15}{20}, \frac{5}{7}$

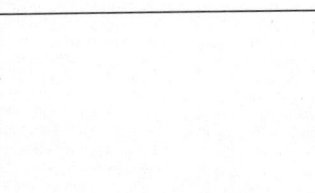

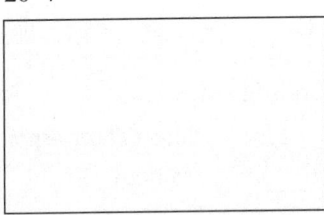

3. To the nearest rod, about how many rods is 100 fathoms?

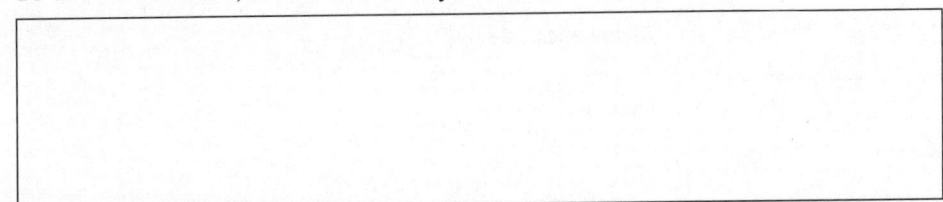

Name_____ Class_____ Date_____

Lesson 6-3

Similar Figures and Scale Drawings

Lesson Objectives
- Solve problems that involve similar figures
- Solve problems that involve scale drawings

Take Note

Similar Figures

Similar figures have two properties:
- The corresponding angles have ☐ measures.
- The lengths of corresponding sides are in ☐.

_____ have the same shape, but not necessarily the same size.

The symbol ~ means _____

Indirect measurement is _____

_____

A _____ is an enlarged or reduced drawing that is similar to an actual object or place.

Examples

❶ Using Similar Figures Trapezoid $ABCD$ ~ trapezoid $EFGH$. Find the value of k.

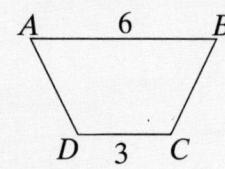

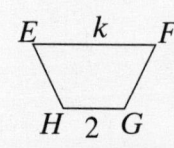

Write a proportion for corresponding sides.

Side $\overline{AB}$ corresponds to side ☐. $\dfrac{6}{☐} = \dfrac{3}{☐}$ Side $\overline{CD}$ corresponds to side ☐.

$6 \cdot ☐ = k \cdot ☐$ Write cross products.

$\dfrac{6 \cdot 2}{☐} = \dfrac{3k}{☐}$ Divide each side by ☐.

☐ $= k$ Simplify.

96 *Algebra Readiness* Lesson 6-3

② Using Scale Drawings The scale of a map is 1 in. : 24 mi. About how far is it between two cities that are 3 in. apart on the map?

$$\frac{\text{map (in.)} \rightarrow}{\text{actual (mi)} \rightarrow} \frac{1}{\boxed{}} = \frac{3}{\boxed{}} \leftarrow \frac{\text{map (in.)}}{\text{actual (mi)}}$$ Write a proportion.

$1 \cdot d = \boxed{} \cdot \boxed{}$ Write cross products.

$d = \boxed{}$ Simplify.

It is about $\boxed{}$ mi between the two cities.

Quick Check

1. Trapezoid *KLMN* is similar to trapezoid *ABCD* in Example 1. Find the value of *y*.

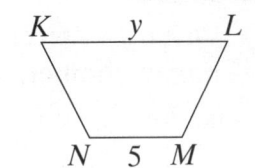

2. The distance from Sacramento to San Diego is about 480 mi. On a map whose scale is the same as the scale in Example 2, what is the approximate map distance between these two cities?

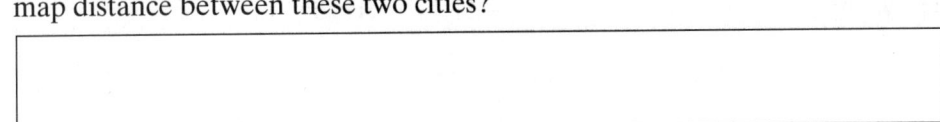

Name_____ Class_____ Date_____

Lesson 6-4

Fractions, Decimals, and Percents

Lesson Objectives
- Write percents as fractions and decimals
- Write decimals and fractions as percents

Vocabulary

A _____ is a ratio that compares a number to 100.

Examples

① **Writing a Percent as a Fraction** Write each percent as a fraction or a mixed number.

a. 30%

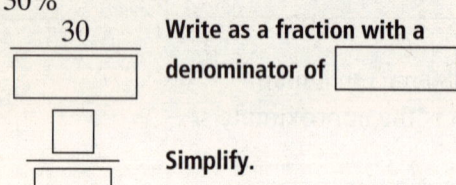

$\dfrac{30}{\boxed{}} = \dfrac{\boxed{}}{\boxed{}}$ Write as a fraction with a denominator of ☐.

Simplify.

b. 175%

$\dfrac{175}{\boxed{}} = \dfrac{\boxed{}}{\boxed{}}$ Write as a fraction with a denominator of ☐.

Simplify.

$= \boxed{}\dfrac{\boxed{}}{\boxed{}}$ Write as a mixed number.

② **Writing a Percent as a Decimal** Express 7.3% as a decimal.

$7.3\% = \dfrac{7.3}{\boxed{}}$ Write as a fraction with a denominator of ☐.

$= 00\underset{\curvearrowleft}{7.3}$ Divide a decimal by 100 by moving the decimal point ☐ places to the left. You may need to write one or more zeros.

$= \boxed{}$

③ **Writing a Decimal as a Percent** Express 0.412 as a percent.

Rewrite as a fraction.

$0.412 = \dfrac{412}{\boxed{}}$

$= \dfrac{412 \div \boxed{}}{1{,}000 \div \boxed{}}$ Divide the numerator and the denominator by ☐ to get a denominator of ☐.

$= \dfrac{\boxed{}}{100}$ Simplify.

$= \boxed{}\%$ Write as a percent.

Algebra Readiness Lesson 6-4

Daily Notetaking Guide

Name_____ Class_____ Date_____

④ Writing a Fraction as a Percent Four out of seven members of the chess club are boys. What percent of the chess club members are boys?

$\dfrac{\boxed{}}{\boxed{}}$ Write a fraction.

$4 \div 7 \approx \boxed{}$ Divide the numerator by the denominator.

$= \boxed{}$ Write as a percent.

About $\boxed{}$ of the chess club members are boys.

Quick Check

1. Write each percent as a fraction or mixed number in simplest form.

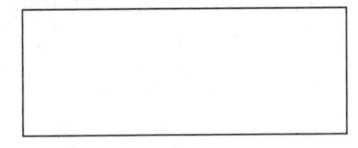

   a. 58%   **b.** 72%

2. a. Write 62.5% as a decimal.

   b. About 45% of the people in the United States have type O blood. Write this percent as a decimal and as a fraction in simplest form.

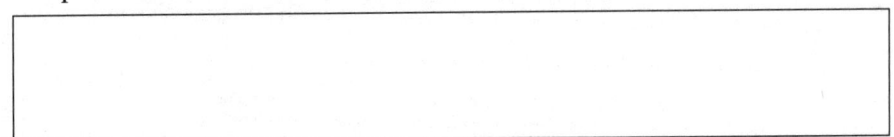

3. Write each decimal as a percent.

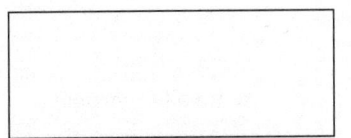

   a. 0.4   **b.** 1.75

4. Three out of eleven families in the United States own cats. To the nearest percent, what percent of families own cats?

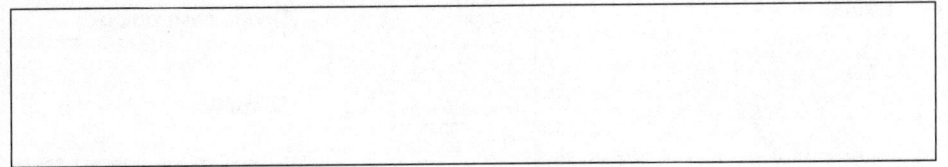

Daily Notetaking Guide   Algebra Readiness Lesson 6-4

Name_____ Class_____ Date_____

Lesson 6-5
Proportions and Percents

Lesson Objectives
- Find a part of a whole
- Find a whole amount

Take Note

Percents and Proportions

Finding the Percent
What percent of 40 is 6?

$\dfrac{n}{100} = \dfrac{\Box \leftarrow \text{part}}{\Box \leftarrow \text{whole}}$

Finding the Part
What number is 15% of 40?

$\dfrac{15}{100} = \dfrac{\Box \leftarrow \text{part}}{\Box \leftarrow \text{whole}}$

Finding the Whole
6 is 15% of what number?

$\dfrac{15}{100} = \dfrac{\Box \leftarrow \text{part}}{\Box \leftarrow \text{whole}}$

Examples

1 Finding Part of a Whole Find 23% of 158.

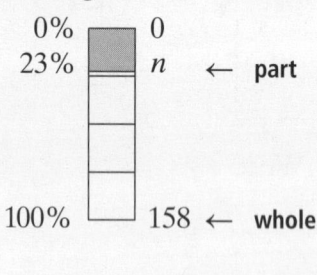

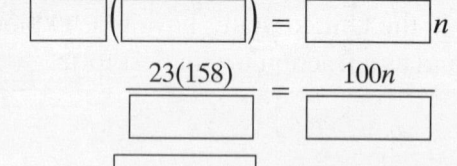

0%   0
23% n ← part

100% 158 ← whole

$\dfrac{23}{100} = \dfrac{\Box}{\Box}$ Write a proportion.

$\Box(\Box) = \Box n$ Write cross products.

$\dfrac{23(158)}{\Box} = \dfrac{100n}{\Box}$ Divide each side by $\Box$.

$\Box = n$ Simplify.

23% of 158 is $\Box$.

2 Finding a Percent What percent of 34 is 28? Round to the nearest tenth of a percent.

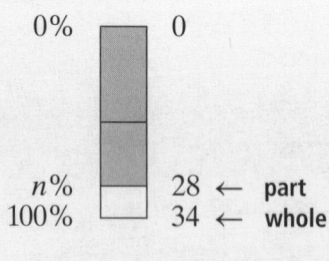

0%   0

n%   28 ← part
100% 34 ← whole

$\dfrac{n}{100} = \dfrac{\Box}{\Box}$ Write a proportion.

$\Box n = \Box(\Box)$ Write cross products.

$\dfrac{34n}{\Box} = \dfrac{100(28)}{\Box}$ Divide each side by $\Box$.

$n = \Box$ Simplify.

$\approx \Box$ Round to the nearest tenth.

28 is approximately $\Box$ % of 34.

100 Algebra Readiness Lesson 6-5

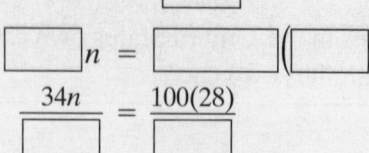

Name_____ Class_____ Date_____

❸ Using Percents to Solve a Problem A tile floor has 90 blue tiles, which is 15% of all the tiles in the floor. How many tiles are in the floor in all?

$\dfrac{15}{100} = \dfrac{\boxed{}}{\boxed{}}$ Write a proportion.

$\boxed{} x = \boxed{} (\boxed{})$ Write cross products.

$\dfrac{15x}{\boxed{}} = \dfrac{100(90)}{\boxed{}}$ Divide each side by $\boxed{}$.

$x = \boxed{}$ Simplify.

The floor has $\boxed{}$ tiles in all.

Check Is the answer reasonable? The problem says the number of blue tiles is 15%. 10% of 600 is $\boxed{}$, so 5% of 600 is $\boxed{}$, and 15% is 60 + 30 = $\boxed{}$. The answer is reasonable.

Quick Check

1. Draw a model and write a proportion. Then solve.

   a. 25% of 124 is $\boxed{}$.   b. 12.5% of 80 is $\boxed{}$.

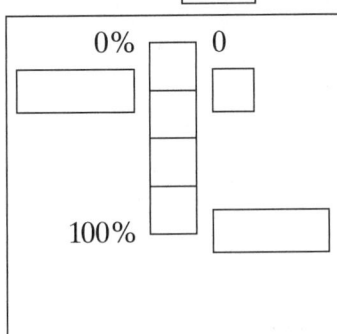

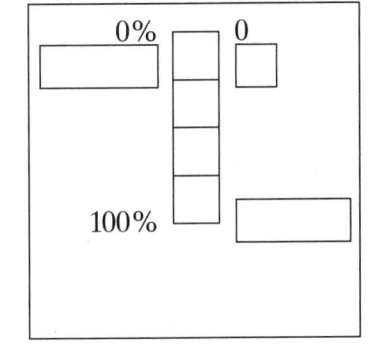

2. Round to the nearest tenth.
   a. What percent of 250 is 138?   b. 14 is what percent of 15?

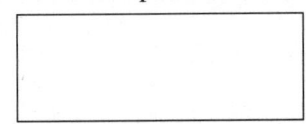

3. In 2000, the number of drive-in movie screens was about 20.1% of the number in 1980. If there were 717 drive-in movie screens in 2000, about how many drive-in movie screens were there in 1980?

Daily Notetaking Guide   Algebra Readiness Lesson 6-5   **101**

Name_____ Class_____ Date_____

Lesson 6-6

Percents and Equations

Lesson Objectives
- Write and solve percent equations
- Use equations to solve percent problems

Take Note

Percent Equations

Finding the Percent	Finding the Part	Finding the Whole
What percent of 40 is 6?	What is 15% of 40?	6 is 15% of what?
$n \cdot 40 = \boxed{}$	$n = \boxed{} \cdot 40$	$\boxed{} = 0.15 \cdot n$

_____ is pay based on an amount sold.

Examples

1 Solving a Percent Equation What is 35% of 84?

$n = \boxed{} \cdot \boxed{}$ Write an equation. Write the percent as a decimal.

$n = \boxed{}$ Simplify.

35% of 84 is $\boxed{}$.

2 Percents Greater Than 100% What percent of 26 is 65?

$n \cdot \boxed{} = \boxed{}$ Write an equation.

$\dfrac{26n}{\boxed{}} = \dfrac{65}{\boxed{}}$ Divide each side by $\boxed{}$.

$n = \boxed{}$ Simplify.

$= \boxed{}$ %   Change the decimal to a percent.

65 is $\boxed{}$% of 26.

Quick Check

Write and solve an equation.

1a. 0.96 is what percent of 10?   **b.** 19.2 is 32% of what?   **2.** What is 145.5% of 20?

Name_____ Class_____ Date _____

Examples

3 **Solving a Commission Problem** A car salesman makes a 6.5% commission on each car he sells. How much does he make on the sale of a car for $35,000?

Words [Amount of commission] is [6.5%] of [$35,000]

Let [c] = amount of commission.

Equation [ ] = [ ] · [ ]

$c = 0.065 \cdot 35{,}000$

= [ ]

The salesman's commission is [ ].

4 **Solving a Percent Problem** During a telephone survey, 414 people, or 46% of those called, said they were watching station RFGT at the time of the call. How many people were called?

Words [414] is [46%] of [people called]

Let [n] = number of people called.

Equation [ ] = [ ] · [ ]

$0.46n = 414$

$\dfrac{0.46n}{[]} = \dfrac{414}{[]}$

$n =$ [ ]

[ ] people were called.

Quick Check

3. A singer receives a 5% royalty on each CD sale. To the nearest cent, find his royalty for a CD that sells for $16.99.

4. In a survey, 952 people, or 68%, preferred smooth peanut butter to crunchy. How many people were surveyed?

Daily Notetaking Guide — Algebra Readiness Lesson 6-6

Name_____ Class_____ Date_____

Lesson 6-7

Percent of Change

Lesson Objectives
- Find percent of increase
- Find percent of decrease

Vocabulary

The _____ is the percent a quantity increases or decreases from its original amount

Example

1 Finding Percent of Increase Find the percent of increase from 8 to 9.6.

amount of increase = ☐ − ☐ = ☐

percent of increase = ☐/☐   Write an equation.

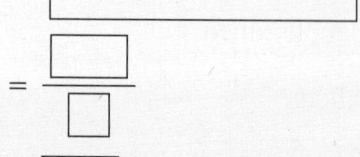

= ☐/☐   Substitute.

= ☐   Simplify.

= ☐ %   Write as a percent.

The percent of increase from 8 to 9.6 is ☐.

Quick Check

1. Find each percent of increase.

   a. from 100 to 114

   b. from 2.0 to 3.2

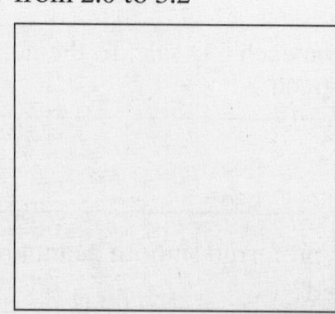

104 Algebra Readiness Lesson 6-7

Name _____ Class _____ Date _____

Examples

2 Finding Percent of Increase In a given year, Hillsboro had a total of 7.5 in. of rain by March 1 and a total of 22.5 in. by July 1. Find the percent of increase from 7.5 to 22.5.

amount of increase = ☐ − ☐ = ☐

percent of increase = ☐ / ☐

= ☐ / ☐

= ☐

= ☐ %

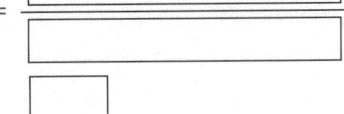

The percent increase from March 1 to July 1 was ☐.

3 Finding Percent of Decrease Find the percent of decrease from 1,250 to 1,120.

amount of decrease = ☐ − ☐ = ☐

percent of decrease = ☐ / ☐

= ☐ / ☐

= ☐

= ☐ %

The percent of decrease from 1,250 to 1,120 is ☐.

Quick Check

2. In the same year as in Example 2 above, Hillsboro had a total of 10.5 inches of rain by April 1. Find the percent of increase from 7.5 to 10.5.

3. Find each percent of decrease. Where necessary, round to the nearest tenth of a percent.

   a. from 9.6 to 4.8   **b.** from 200 to 190

Name_____ Class_____ Date_____

Lesson 6-8 — Markup and Discount

Lesson Objectives
- Find markups
- Find discounts

Vocabulary

_____ is the amount of increase in price.

_____ is the amount of price decrease.

Percent of discount is _____

Examples

1 Finding Markup A grocery store has a 20% markup on a can of soup. The can of soup costs the store $1.25. Find the markup.

markup = [_____] · [_____]

= [___] · [___]

= [_____]

The markup is [___].

2 Finding Selling Price A bookstore pays $4.50 for a novel. The percent markup is 45%. Find the novel's selling price.

[___] · [___] = [___]   Multiply to find the markup.

4.50 + [___] = [___]   store's cost + [_____] = [_____]

The selling price is [___].

3 Finding Discount A camera that regularly sells for $210 is on sale for 30% off. Find the discount.

discount = [_____] · [_____]

= [___] · [___]

= [___]

The discount is [___].

Name_____ Class_____ Date _____

④ **Finding Sale Price** A video game that regularly sells for $39.95 is on sale for 20% off. What is the sale price?
Find the discount. Then find the sale price.

discount = ▢ · ▢

= ▢ · ▢

= ▢

sale price = ▢ − ▢

= 39.95 − ▢

= ▢

The sale price is ▢.

Quick Check

1. A clothing store pays $56 for a jacket. The store's percent markup is 75%. Find the markup for the jacket.

2. A $5 cap has a 70% markup. Find the selling price.

3. Pants priced at $21.99 are marked 15% off. Find the discount.

4. Find the sale price of the video game from Example 4 if the percent discount is 25%. Round to the nearest cent.

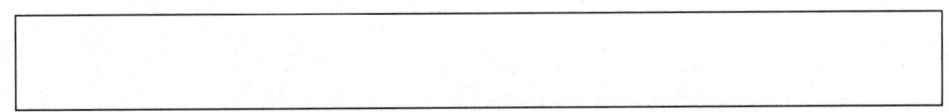

Daily Notetaking Guide — Algebra Readiness Lesson 6-8   107

Name_____ Class_____ Date_____

Lesson 6-9

Applications of Rational Numbers

Lesson Objectives
- Apply rational numbers
- Estimate percents using fractions and decimals

Examples

❶ Comparing Rational Numbers A family drove 900 mi to a vacation spot. They drove $\frac{1}{4}$ of the trip on the first day, 0.3 of the trip on the second day, 20% of the trip on the third day, and 225 mi on the last day. On which day did they drive the farthest?

Method 1 Find the distance traveled each day. Compare.

$\frac{\Box}{\Box}$ · 900 mi = $\Box$ mi   They drove $\frac{1}{4}$ of 900 mi on the first day.

$\Box$ · 900 mi = $\Box$ mi   They drove 0.3 of 900 mi on the second day.

$\Box$ · 900 mi = $\Box$ mi   They drove 20%, or 0.20, of 900 mi on the third day.

$\Box$ mi   They drove 225 mi on the fourth day.

They drove the farthest on the $\Box$ day.

Method 2 Write the parts of the trip in the same form. Compare.

$\frac{\Box}{\Box}$ = $\Box$ Write the fraction for the first day as a decimal.

$\Box$ The part of the trip on the second day is a decimal.

$\Box$% = $\Box$ Write the percent for the third day as a decimal.

$\frac{\Box}{900}$ = $\Box$ Divide $\Box$ by 900 for the fourth day.

Compare the decimals: $\Box$ > $\Box$ > $\Box$. They drove the farthest on the $\Box$ day.

108   Algebra Readiness Lesson 6-9   Daily Notetaking Guide

Name_____ Class_____ Date _____

❷ Estimating Percents Using Decimals A pair of boots is on sale for 35% off the cost of $45.95. After the discount, 7.75% sales tax is added. Is $25 enough money to buy the boots?

Step 1 Estimate the discount on the boots.

35% ≈ ☐   Use a decimal close to 35%.

45.95 ≈ ☐   Round the regular price

35% of 45.95 ≈ ☐ · ☐   Estimate.

= ☐   Multiply.

The discount is about $☐.

Step 2 Subtract to find the sale price of the boots.

$☐ − $☐ = ☐

The sale price of the boots is about $☐.

Step 3 Estimate the amount of tax.

7.75% ≈ ☐   Use a decimal close to 7.75%.

7.75% of ☐ ≈ ☐ · ☐   Estimate.

= ☐   Multiply.

The amount of tax is about $☐.

Step 4 Add the tax to the sale price.

$☐ + $☐ = $☐

The total cost is about $☐. So $25 is ☐ ☐.

Quick Check

1. An event planner has a $2,000 budget for an event. She spends 32% of the budget on chair rentals, 0.4 of the budget on food, 1/5 of the budget on door prizes, and $80 on decorations. On what part of the event does she spend the most money?

2. A computer is on sale for 15% off the regular price of $399.95. After the discount, 8.25% sales tax is added. Is $350 enough money to buy the computer? Justify your answer.

Daily Notetaking Guide — Algebra Readiness Lesson 6-9

Name_____ Class_____ Date_____

Lesson 6-10

Reasoning Strategy: Make a Table

Lesson Objective
- Solve problems by making a table

Example

① Martin had 100 trees in his orchard the first year. Each year after that, he increased the number of trees in his orchard by 10%, rounded to the nearest whole number. How many trees did he have in his orchard in the sixth year?

Understand the Problem   Read the problem carefully.

1. What information are you given?

   Martin had [   ] trees in his orchard the first year. Each year after that, he increased the number of trees in his orchard by [   ].

2. What information are you asked to find?

   [   ]

Make and Carry Out a Plan   Decide on a strategy. You can use the percent of increase to predict the increase in the number of trees in the orchard each year for six years. You can make a table to organize your predictions for each year.

3. How can you find the increase in the number of trees in the orchard from the beginning of the first year to the end of the first year?

   [   ]

4. How can you find the number of trees in the orchard at the beginning of the second year?

   [   ]

5. The percent of increase is the same each year. Does that mean that the increase in the number of trees in the orchard will be the same each year? Explain your reasoning.

   [   ]

Algebra Readiness Lesson 6-10   Daily Notetaking Guide

Complete the table below.

6. Find the numbers for Column 4 by multiplying the numbers in Columns 2 and 3. Round to the nearest whole number.

7. Find the numbers for Column 5 by adding the numbers in Columns 2 and 4.

1	2	3	4	5
Year	Tree Count at Beginning of Year	Rate of Increase (10%)	Increase in Tree Count	Tree Count at Beginning of Next Year
1	100	0.1	10	110
2	110	0.1		
3		0.1		
4		0.1		
5		0.1		

8. What is your prediction for the number of trees in the orchard at the beginning of the sixth year?

Check the Answer Your friend says that she knows a quicker way to find the answer. Simply multiply 100 · 0.1 · 6 to find the increase for the six-year period. Do you agree with your friend's approach? Explain your reasoning.

Quick Check

1. Suppose the annual increase in the number of trees in the orchard is 15%. At that rate, how many trees will Martin have in the orchard at the beginning of the sixth year?

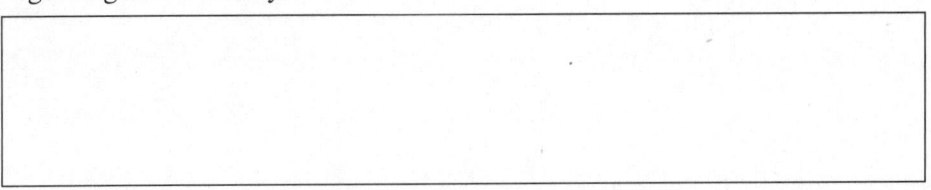

Name_____ Class_____ Date_____

Lesson 7-1

Solving Two-Step Equations

Lesson Objectives
- Solve two-step equations
- Use two-step equations to solve problems

Example

① **Undoing an Operation** Solve $5v - 12 = 8$.

$5v - 12 = 8$

$5v - 12 + \boxed{} = 8 + \boxed{}$ Add $\boxed{}$ to each side.

$5v = \boxed{}$ Simplify.

$\dfrac{5v}{\boxed{}} = \dfrac{\boxed{}}{\boxed{}}$ Divide each side by $\boxed{}$.

$v = \boxed{}$ Simplify.

Check $5v - 12 = 8$

$5(\boxed{}) - 12 \stackrel{?}{=} 8$ Replace v with $\boxed{}$.

$\boxed{} - 12 \stackrel{?}{=} 8$ Multiply.

$\boxed{} = 8$ ✓ Simplify.

Quick Check

1. Solve each equation.

   a. $15x + 3 = 48$

   b. $\dfrac{t}{4} - 10 = -6$

112 *Algebra Readiness* Lesson 7-1 Daily Notetaking Guide L1

Name _____ Class _____ Date _____

Examples

② Negative Coefficients Solve $7 - 3b = 1$.

$7 - 3b = 1$

$\boxed{} + 7 - 3b = \boxed{} + 1$ Add $\boxed{}$ to each side.

$\boxed{} - 3b = \boxed{}$ Simplify.

$-3b = \boxed{}$ $0 - 3b = \boxed{}$

$\dfrac{-3b}{\boxed{}} = \dfrac{\boxed{}}{\boxed{}}$ Divide each side by $\boxed{}$.

$b = \boxed{}$ Simplify.

③ Using Two-Step Equations You borrow $350 to buy a bicycle. You agree to pay $100 the first week, and then $25 each week until the balance is paid off. To find how many weeks w it will take you to pay for the bicycle, solve $100 + 25w = 350$.

$100 + 25w = 350$

$100 + 25w - \boxed{} = 350 - \boxed{}$ Subtract $\boxed{}$ from each side.

$25w = \boxed{}$ Simplify.

$\dfrac{25w}{\boxed{}} = \dfrac{\boxed{}}{\boxed{}}$ Divide each side by $\boxed{}$.

$w = \boxed{}$ Simplify.

It will take you $\boxed{}$ weeks to pay for the bicycle.

Quick Check

2. Solve each equation.

   a. $-a + 6 = 8$

   b. $-9 - \dfrac{y}{7} = -12$

3. Jacob bought four begonias in 6-in. pots and a $19 fern at a fundraiser. He spent a total of $63. Solve the equation $4p + 19 = 63$ to find the price p of each begonia.

Daily Notetaking Guide Algebra Readiness Lesson 7-1 113

Name_____ Class_____ Date_____

Lesson 7-2

Solving Multi-Step Equations

Lesson Objectives
- Combine like terms to simplify an equation
- Use the Distributive Property to simplify an equation

Take Note

Steps for Solving a Multi-Step Equation
- **Step 1** Use the Distributive Property, if necessary.
- **Step 2** Combine like terms.
- **Step 3** Undo addition or subtraction.
- **Step 4** Undo multiplication or division.

_____ are a sequence of integers obtained by counting by ones from any integer.

Example

① **Finding Consecutive Integers** The sum of two consecutive integers is 27. Find the integers.

Words → sum of two consecutive integers is 27

Let $\boxed{n}$ = the least integer.

Then $\boxed{}$ = the second integer.

Equation

$\boxed{} + \boxed{} = \boxed{}$

$\boxed{} + (\boxed{}) = \boxed{}$

$(\boxed{} + \boxed{}) + (\boxed{}) = 27$ Use the $\boxed{}$ and $\boxed{}$ Properties of Addition to group like terms together.

$\boxed{} + \boxed{} = 27$ Combine like terms.

$\boxed{} + \boxed{} - \boxed{} = 27 - \boxed{}$ Subtract $\boxed{}$ from each side.

$2n = \boxed{}$ Simplify.

$\dfrac{2n}{\boxed{}} = \dfrac{\boxed{}}{\boxed{}}$ Divide each side by $\boxed{}$.

$n = \boxed{}$ Simplify.

If $n = \boxed{}$, then $n + 1 = \boxed{}$. The two integers are $\boxed{}$ and $\boxed{}$.

Algebra Readiness Lesson 7-2

❷ Using the Distributive Property Solve $44 = -5(r - 4) - r$.

$44 = -5(r - 4) - r$

$44 = \boxed{} + \boxed{} - r$ Use the $\boxed{}$ Property.

$44 = \boxed{} + 20$ Combine like terms.

$44 - \boxed{} = -6r + 20 - \boxed{}$ Subtract $\boxed{}$ from each side.

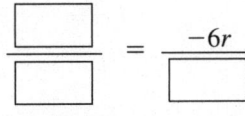

$\boxed{} = -6r$ Simplify.

$\dfrac{\boxed{}}{\boxed{}} = \dfrac{-6r}{\boxed{}}$ Divide each side by $\boxed{}$.

$\boxed{} = r$ Simplify.

Quick Check

1. **Basketball Scores** One basketball team defeated another by 13 points. The total number of points scored by both teams was 171. Solve the equation $p + p - 13 = 171$ to find the number of points p scored by the winning team.

2. For *consecutive even integers*, the first is n, and the second is $n + 2$. Find two consecutive even integers with a sum of 66.

3. Solve the equation.
   $-3(m - 6) = 4$

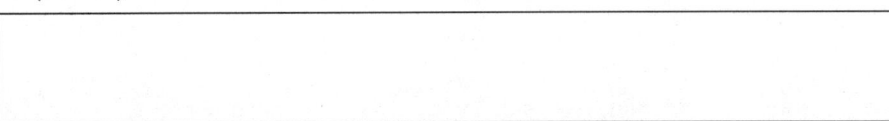

Daily Notetaking Guide   Algebra Readiness Lesson 7-2

Name_____ Class_____ Date_____

Lesson 7-3

Two-Step Equations With Fractions and Decimals

Lesson Objectives
- Solve two-step equations with fractions
- Solve two-step equations with decimals

Examples

1 Using the Reciprocal Solve $\frac{3}{4}p - 7 = 11$.

$\frac{3}{4}p - 7 = 11$

$\frac{3}{4}p - 7 + \boxed{} = 11 + \boxed{}$ Add $\boxed{}$ to each side.

$\frac{3}{4}p = \boxed{}$ Simplify.

$\frac{\boxed{}}{\boxed{}} \cdot \frac{3}{4}p = \boxed{} \cdot \frac{\boxed{}}{\boxed{}}$ Multiply each side by $\frac{\boxed{}}{\boxed{}}$, the reciprocal of $\frac{3}{4}$.

$1p = \frac{4 \cdot 18}{3}^{\boxed{}}$ Divide common factors.

$p = \boxed{}$ Simplify.

Check $\frac{3}{4}p - 7 = 11$

$\frac{3}{4}\left(\boxed{}\right) - 7 \stackrel{?}{=} 11$ Replace p with $\boxed{}$.

$\frac{3 \cdot 24}{4}^{\boxed{}} - 7 \stackrel{?}{=} 11$ Divide common factors.

$\boxed{} - 7 \stackrel{?}{=} 11$ Multiply.

$\boxed{} = 11 \checkmark$

2 Using the LCM Solve $\frac{1}{2}y + 3 = \frac{2}{3}$.

$\frac{1}{2}y + 3 = \frac{2}{3}$

$\boxed{}\left(\frac{1}{2}y + 3\right) = \boxed{}\left(\frac{2}{3}\right)$ Multiply each side by $\boxed{}$, the $\boxed{}$ of 2 and 3.

$\boxed{} \cdot \frac{1}{2}y + \boxed{} \cdot 3 = 6\left(\frac{2}{3}\right)$ Use the $\boxed{}$ Property.

$\boxed{}y + \boxed{} = 4$ Simplify.

$3y = \boxed{}$ Subtract $\boxed{}$ from each side. Simplify.

$\frac{3y}{\boxed{}} = \frac{-14}{\boxed{}}$ Divide each side by $\boxed{}$.

$y = -\frac{\boxed{}}{\boxed{}}$ Simplify.

116   *Algebra Readiness* Lesson 7-3

Name _____ Class _____ Date _____

❸ Using Properties of Equality Suppose your cell phone plan is $30 per month plus $.05 per minute. Your bill is $36.75. Use the equation $30 + 0.05x = 36.75$ to find the number of minutes on your bill.

$30 + 0.05x = 36.75$

$30 - \boxed{} + 0.05x = 36.75 - \boxed{}$ Subtract $\boxed{}$ from each side.

$0.05x = \boxed{}$ Simplify.

$\dfrac{0.05x}{\boxed{}} = \dfrac{6.75}{\boxed{}}$ Divide each side by $\boxed{}$.

$x = \boxed{}$ Simplify.

There are $\boxed{}$ minutes on your bill.

Quick Check

1. Use a reciprocal to solve each equation.

   a. $-\dfrac{7}{10}k + 14 = -21$

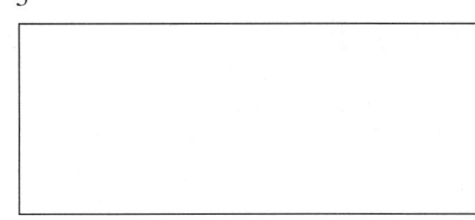

   b. $\dfrac{2}{3}m - 4 = 3$

2. Solve the equation $-\dfrac{7}{12} + y = \dfrac{1}{6}$.

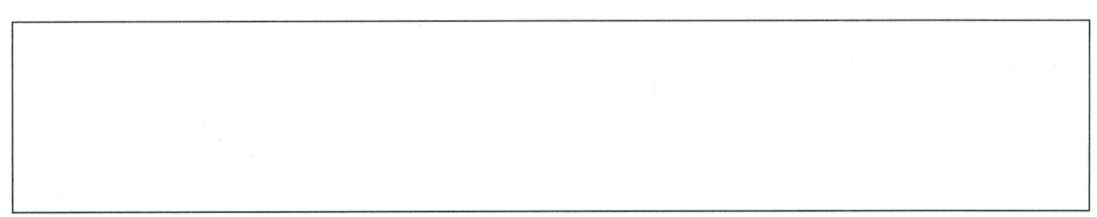

3. Solve $1.5x - 3.6 = 2.4$.

Name_____ Class_____ Date_____

Lesson 7-4

Reasoning Strategy: Write an Equation

Lesson Objective
- Write an equation to solve a problem

Example

1 Writing an Equation A moving van rents for $29.95 a day plus $.12 per mile. Mr. Reynolds's bill was $137.80, and he drove the van 150 mi. For how many days did he have the van?

Understand the Problem

1. What is the goal of this problem?

2. How many miles did Mr. Reynolds drive?

3. What does the van cost without mileage?

4. What is the mileage charge?

Make and Carry Out a Plan

Write an equation.

Words | number of days | · $29.95/d + $.12/mi · | 150 mi | = | $137.80 |

Let | d | = the number of days Mr. Reynolds had the van.

Equation [ ] · 29.95 + 0.12 · [ ] = [ ]

Solve the equation.

$d \cdot 29.95 + 0.12 \cdot 150 = 137.80$

$29.95d + \boxed{} = 137.80$ Multiply 0.12 and 150.

$29.95d + 18 - \boxed{} = 137.80 - \boxed{}$ Subtract [ ] from each side.

$29.95d = \boxed{}$ Simplify.

$\dfrac{29.95d}{\boxed{}} = \dfrac{119.80}{\boxed{}}$ Divide each side by [ ].

$d = \boxed{}$ Simplify.

Mr. Reynolds had the van for [ ] days.

118 *Algebra Readiness* Lesson 7-4

Name_____ Class_____ Date _____

Check the Answer

You can estimate to check the reasonableness of the answer.

$29.95 \approx 30$
$0.12 \approx 0.1$ } **Round each number.**
$137.80 \approx 140$

$4 \cdot 30 + 0.1 \cdot 140 = 120 + 14$
$= 134$

Since $134 \approx 137.80$, 2 days is a reasonable answer.

Quick Check

1. Suppose that Mr. Reynold's bill was $161.80, and he drove the van 350 mi.
   a. How would the equation change?

   b. Solve the new equation to find how many days he rented the van.

   c. Estimate to check the reasonableness of your answer to part (b).

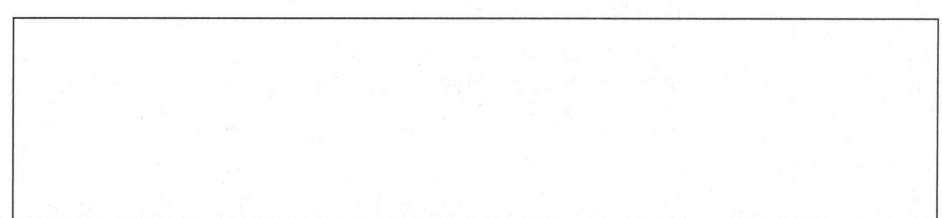

2. Mr. Reynolds rented the van for one day. His bill was $41.95. How many miles did he drive?

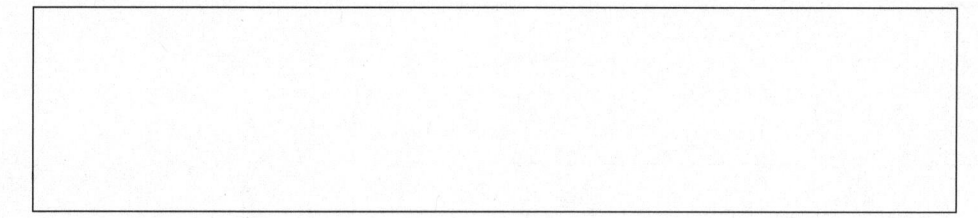

Daily Notetaking Guide — Algebra Readiness Lesson 7-4 — 119

Name_____ Class_____ Date_____

Lesson 7-5

Solving Two-Step Inequalities

Lesson Objectives
- Solve two-step inequalities
- Use two-step inequalities to solve problems

Example

❶ **Undoing Operations** Solve and graph $7g + 11 > 67$.

$$7g + 11 > 67$$

$7g + 11 - \square > 67 - \square$ Subtract $\square$ from each side.

$7g > \square$ Simplify.

$\dfrac{7g}{\square} > \dfrac{56}{\square}$ Divide each side by $\square$.

$g > \square$ Simplify.

<--+--+--+--+--+--+--+--+--+--+-->
 2 3 4 5 6 7 8 9 10 11 12

❷ **Reversing the Inequality Symbol** Solve $6 \leq -\dfrac{2}{3}r - 6$.

$$6 \leq -\dfrac{2}{3}r - 6$$

$6 + \square \leq -\dfrac{2}{3}r - 6 + \square$ Add $\square$ to each side.

$12 \leq -\dfrac{2}{3}r$ Simplify.

$-\dfrac{\square}{\square}(12) \geq -\dfrac{\square}{\square}\left(-\dfrac{2}{3}r\right)$ Multiply each side by $-\dfrac{\square}{\square}$.
Reverse the direction of the inequality symbol.

$\square \geq r$, or $r \leq \square$ Simplify.

Quick Check

1. Solve and graph $-10 \geq \dfrac{1}{2}x - 6$.

<--+--+--+--+--+--+--+--+--+--+-->

Examples

③ Using Two-Step Inequalities Dale has $25 to spend at a carnival. If the admission to the carnival is $4 and the rides cost $1.50 each, what is the greatest number of rides Dale can go on?

Words $4 admission + $\boxed{\$1.50/\text{ride}}$ · $\boxed{\text{number of rides}}$ is less than or equal to $\boxed{\$25}$

Let $\boxed{r}$ = number of rides Dale goes on.

Inequality $\boxed{} + \boxed{} \cdot \boxed{} \leq \boxed{}$

$4 + 1.5r \leq 25$

$4 + 1.5r - \boxed{} \leq 25 - \boxed{}$ Subtract $\boxed{}$ from each side.

$1.5r \leq 21$ Simplify.

$\dfrac{1.5r}{\boxed{}} \leq \dfrac{21}{\boxed{}}$ Divide each side by $\boxed{}$.

$r \leq \boxed{}$ Simplify.

The greatest number of rides Dale can go on is $\boxed{}$.

Quick Check

2. Solve and graph $-2m + 4 \leq 34$.

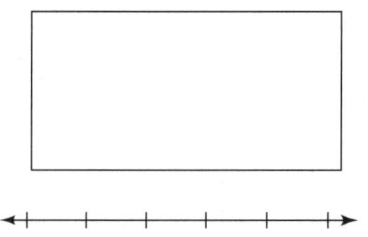

3. A stereo salesperson earns a salary of $1,900 per month, plus a commission of 4% of sales. The salesperson wants to maintain a monthly income of at least $2,200. How much must the salesperson sell each month?

Daily Notetaking Guide — Algebra Readiness Lesson 7-5

Name_____ Class_____ Date_____

Lesson 7-6
Transforming Formulas

Lesson Objectives
- Solve a formula for a given variable
- Use formulas to solve problems

Examples

1 Transforming in One Step Solve the circumference formula $C = 2\pi r$ for r.

$C = 2\pi r$

$\dfrac{C}{\square} = \dfrac{2\pi r}{\square}$ Use the Division Property of Equality.

$\dfrac{\square}{\square} = r$, or $r = \dfrac{\square}{\square}$ Simplify.

2 Using More Than One Step Solve the perimeter formula $P = 2\ell + 2w$ for w.

$P = 2\ell + 2w$

$P - \square = 2\ell + 2w - \square$ Subtract $\square$ from each side.

$P - 2\ell = 2w$ Simplify.

$\dfrac{\square}{\square}(P - 2\ell) = \dfrac{\square}{\square}(2w)$ Multiply each side by $\dfrac{\square}{\square}$.

$\dfrac{\square}{\square}\square - \square = w$ Use the Distributive Property and simplify.

Quick Check

1. Solve for the indicated variable.

  a. Solve $h = \dfrac{k}{j}$ for k.

  b. Solve $I = prt$ for p.

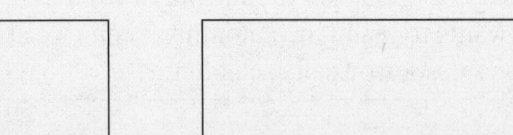

Name_____ Class_____ Date_____

Example

3 **Using a Distance Formula** You plan a 600-mi trip to New York City. You estimate your trip will take about 10 hours. To estimate your average speed, solve the distance formula $d = rt$ for r. Then substitute to find the average speed.

$d = rt$

$\dfrac{d}{\boxed{}} = \dfrac{rt}{\boxed{}}$ Divide each side by $\boxed{}$.

$\dfrac{d}{t} = r$, or $r = \dfrac{d}{t}$ Simplify.

$r = \dfrac{\boxed{}}{\boxed{}}$ Replace d with $\boxed{}$ and t with $\boxed{}$.

$r = \boxed{}$ Simplify.

Quick Check

2. Assume that in Example 3 your average speed is 50 mi/h. Solve the distance formula for the new t.

3. Solve the batting average formula, $a = \dfrac{h}{n}$, for h. Find the number of hits h a batter needs in 40 times at bat n to have an average of 0.275.

Name_____ Class_____ Date_____

Lesson 7-7   Simple and Compound Interest

Lesson Objectives
- Solve simple-interest problems
- Solve compound-interest problems

Take Note

Simple-Interest Formula

$$I = prt,$$

where I is the ☐, p is the ☐,

r is the ☐ per year, and t is the ☐ in years.

Compound-Interest Formula

$$B = p(1 + r)^n,$$

where B is the ☐, p is the ☐,

r is the ☐ for each interest period, and

n is the ☐.

The _____ is the initial amount of an investment or loan.

Interest is _____.

The _____ is the percentage of the balance that an account or investment earns in a fixed period of time.

Simple interest is _____.

_____ is interest paid on the principal and on the interest from previous interest periods.

Balance is _____.

Examples

1 **Finding Simple Interest** Suppose you deposit $1,000 in a savings account that earns 3% per year. Find the simple interest earned in two years. Find the total of principal plus interest.

$I = prt$ Use the simple interest formula.

$I =$ ☐ · ☐ · ☐   Replace p with ☐, r with ☐, and t with ☐.

$I =$ ☐   Simplify.

total = 1,000 + ☐ = ☐   Find the total.

The account will earn ☐ in two years. The total of principal plus interest will be ☐.

Name _____ Class _____ Date _____

❷ Using a Table You deposit $400 in an account that earns 5% interest compounded annually (once per year). The balance after the first four years is $486.20. What is the balance in your account after another 4 years, a total of 8 years? Round to the nearest cent.

Principal at Beginning of Year	Interest	Balance
Year 5: $486.20	486.20 · 0.05 = ☐	486.20 + 24.31 = ☐
Year 6: $ ☐	☐ · 0.05 = ☐	☐ + 25.53 = 536.04
Year 7: $ 536.04	536.04 · 0.05 = ☐	536.04 + 26.80 = ☐
Year 8: $ ☐	☐ · 0.05 = ☐	☐ + 28.14 = 590.98

After four more years, a total of 8 years, the balance is $ ☐.

Quick Check

1. Find the simple interest.
   a. principal = $250, interest rate = 4%
      time = 3 years

   b. principal = $250, interest rate = 3.5%
      time = 6 months

2. Make a table and find the balance. The interest is compounded annually.
   principal = $500
   interest rate = 3%
   time = 2 years

Bal. at Yr. Start	Interest	Bal. at Yr. End

Name_____ Class_____ Date_____

Lesson 8-1   Relations and Functions

Lesson Objectives
- Determine whether a relation is a function
- Graph relations and functions

Vocabulary

A _____ is a set of ordered pairs.

The domain of a relation is _____
_____

The ____ of a _____ is the set of second coordinates.

A function is a relation for which _____
_____

The _____ is a test that determines whether a relation is a function.

Examples

1 **Identifying a Function** Is each relation a function? Explain.

  a. $\{(0,5),(1,5),(2,6),(3,7)\}$

   Domain   Range

   0, 1, 2, 3

   There is [ ] range value for each domain value.

   The relation is a function.

  b. $\{(0,5),(0,6),(1,6),(2,7)\}$

   Domain   Range

   0, 1, 2

   There are [ ] range values for the domain value 0.

   The relation is not a function.

2 **Identifying a Function** Is the time needed to mow a lawn a function of the size of the lawn? Explain. [ ] ; two lawns of the same size ([ ] value) can require different lengths of time ([ ] values) for mowing.

Name _____ Class _____ Date _____

Example

③ Using the Vertical-Line Test

a. Graph the relation shown in the table.

Domain Value	Range Value
−3	5
−5	3
3	5
5	3

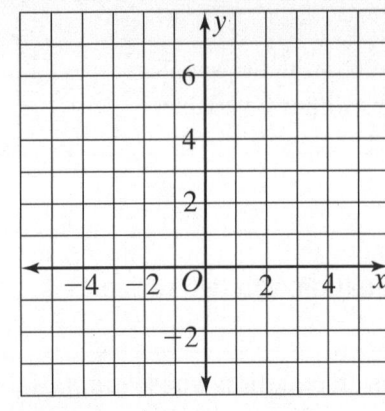

Graph the ordered pairs (−3, 5), (−5, 3), (3, 5) and (5, 3).

b. Use the vertical-line test. Is the relation a function? Explain.

Quick Check

1. Is each relation a function? Explain.

   a. {(−2, 3), (2, 2), (2, −2)}

   b. {(−5, −4), (0, −4), (5, −4)}

2. a. For the United States Postal Service, is package weight a function of the postage paid to mail the package? Explain.

   b. Is the cost of postage a function of package weight? Explain.

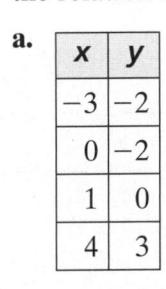

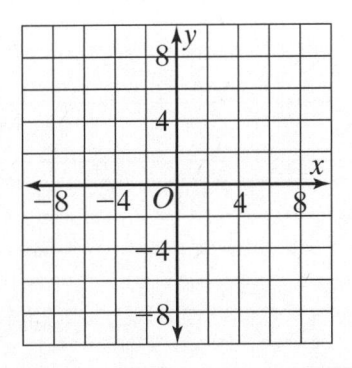

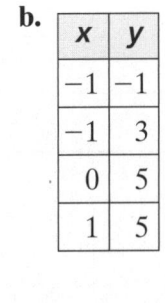

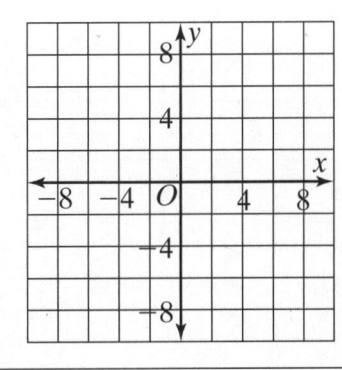

3. **Algebra** Graph the relation shown in each table. Use the vertical-line test. Is the relation a function? Explain.

   a.
x	y
−3	−2
0	−2
1	0
4	3

   b.
x	y
−1	−1
−1	3
0	5
1	5

Name_____ Class_____ Date_____

Lesson 8-2

Equations With Two Variables

Lesson Objectives
- Find solutions of equations with two variables
- Graph linear equations with two variables

Vocabulary

A solution of an equation with two variables is _____
_____

A _____ is an equation whose graph is a line.

Examples

1 **Finding a Solution** Find the solution of $y = 4x - 3$ for $x = 2$.

$y = 4x - 3$

$y = 4(\square) - 3$ Replace x with $\square$.

$y = 8 - 3$ Multiply.

$y = \square$ Subtract.

A solution of the equation is $\square$.

Quick Check

1. Find the solution of each equation for $x = -3$.
   a. $y = 2x + 1$

   b. $y = -4x + 3$

128 *Algebra Readiness* Lesson 8-2   Daily Notetaking Guide

Name _____ Class _____ Date _____

Examples

2 **Using Substitution to Find a Solution** The equation $t = 21 - 0.01n$ models the normal low July temperature in degrees Celsius at Mount Rushmore, South Dakota. In the equation, t is the temperature at n meters above the base of the mountain. Find the normal low July temperature at 500 meters above the base.

$t = 21 - 0.01n$
$t = 21 - 0.01(500)$ **Replace *n* with 500.**
$t = 21 - 5$ **Multiply.**
$t = 16$ **Subtract.**

A solution of the equation is (500, 16). The normal low July temperature at 500 m above the base of the mountain is 16°C.

3 **Graphing a Linear Equation** Graph $y - x = 3$. Is (1, 4) a solution?

Step 1 Make a table of values to show ordered-pair solutions.

x	x + 3	(x, y)
−1	−1 + 3 = ☐	(−1, ☐)
0	0 + 3 = ☐	(0, ☐)
1	1 + 3 = ☐	(1, ☐)

Step 2 Graph the ordered pairs. Draw a line through the points.

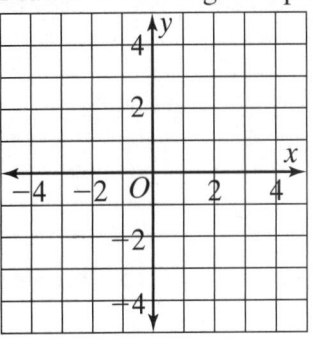

The point (1, 4) appears on the graph, so it is a solution.
Check Substitute (1, 4) in the original equation.
Since $4 - 1 = 3$, (1, 4) is a solution.

Quick Check

2. Find the normal low July temperature at 700 m above the base of Mount Rushmore.

3. Graph each linear equation. Is the given point a solution?
   a. $y = 2x + 1$ (−1, −1) ☐ 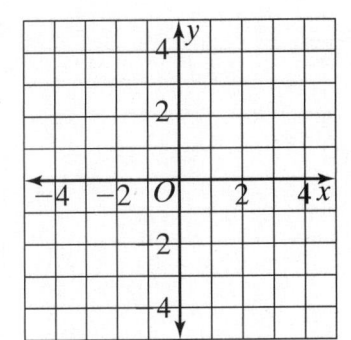
   b. $y = 3x - 2$ (−2, 0) ☐

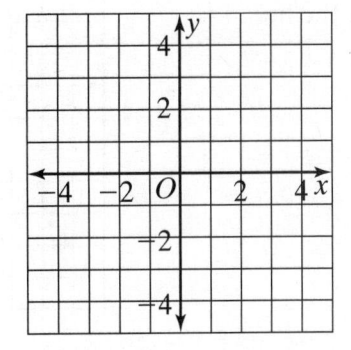

Daily Notetaking Guide   Algebra Readiness Lesson 8-2

Name_____ Class_____ Date_____

Lesson 8-3
Slope and *y*-intercept

Lesson Objectives
- Find the slope of a line
- Use slope-intercept form in graphing a linear equation

Take Note

Slope-intercept Form

The equation ☐ is the slope-intercept form. In this form, *m* is the ☐ of the line, and *b* is the ☐.

$$\text{slope} = \frac{\text{vertical change}}{\text{horizontal change}} = \frac{\boxed{}}{\boxed{}}$$

The *y*-intercept of a line is _____

Example

1 Using Rise and Run to Find Slope Find the slope of the line.

$$\text{slope} = \frac{\text{rise}}{\text{run}} = \frac{\boxed{}}{\boxed{}} = \boxed{}$$

down 6 units
rise = ☐
right 3 units
run = ☐

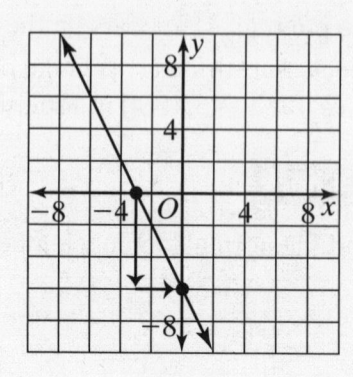

Quick Check

1. Find the slope of the line.

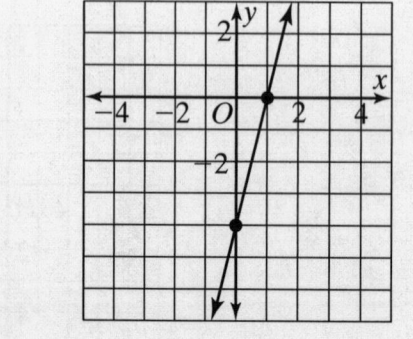

$$\text{slope} = \frac{\text{rise}}{\text{run}} = \frac{\boxed{}}{\boxed{}} = \boxed{}$$

Examples

② Using Coordinates to Find Slope Find the slope of the line through $E(7, 5)$ and $F(-2, 0)$.

$$\text{slope} = \frac{\text{difference in }\boxed{}\text{-coordinates}}{\text{difference in }\boxed{}\text{-coordinates}} = \frac{0 - \boxed{}}{\boxed{} - \boxed{}} = \frac{\boxed{}}{\boxed{}} = \frac{\boxed{}}{\boxed{}}$$

❸ Interpreting Slope in a Real-World Situation A ramp slopes from a warehouse door down to a street. The function $y = -\frac{1}{5}x + 4$ models the ramp, where x is the horizontal distance in feet from the bottom of the door and y is the height in feet above the street. Graph the equation.

Step 1 Since the y-intercept is $\boxed{}$, graph the point $\boxed{}$.

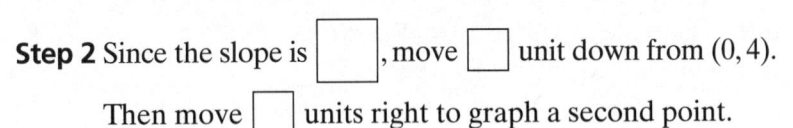

Step 2 Since the slope is $\boxed{}$, move $\boxed{}$ unit down from $(0, 4)$.

Then move $\boxed{}$ units right to graph a second point.

Step 3 Draw a line though the points.

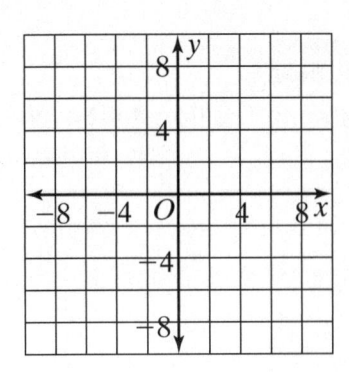

Quick Check

2. Find the slope of the line through $V(8, -1), Q(0, -7)$.

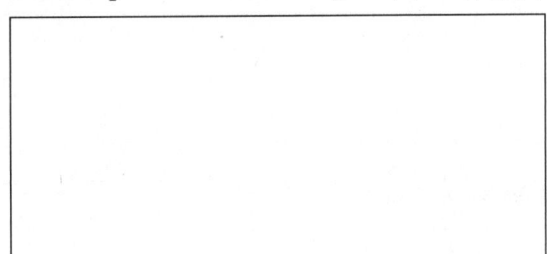

3. Graph each equation.

   a. $y = 2x - 3$

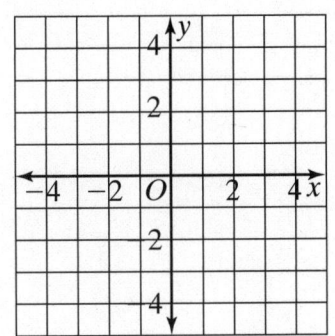

   b. $y = -x + 4$

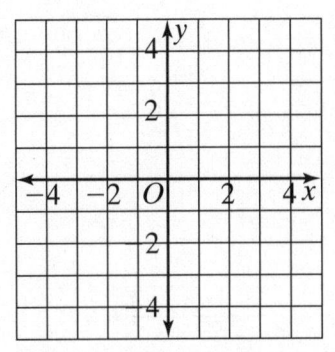

Name_____ Class_____ Date_____

Lesson 8-4   Direct Variation

Lesson Objectives
- Find the constant of variation
- Write a direct variation

Vocabulary

A _____ is a linear function modeled by the equation $y = kx$, where $k = 0$
The constant of variation is _____

Examples

1 Finding the Constant of Variation The table of values models a direct variation. Graph the direct variation. Find the constant of variation.

x	y
0	0
2	1
4	2
6	3

Plot the points on a coordinate plane. Connect the points.

Use a point to find the constant of variation.

$y = kx$ Use the equation for a direct variation.

$5 = k \cdot 2$ Use (2, 5). Substitute.

$\frac{5}{2} = k$ Solve for k.

The constant of variation is $\frac{5}{2}$.

Quick Check

1. The table at the left models a direct variation. Graph the direct variation. Find the constant of variation.

x	y
0	0
3	4
6	8
9	12

Name_____ Class_____ Date _____

Examples

❷ Writing a Direct Variation Your weight w on Earth's surface varies directly with your weight m on the Moon. A person weighing 180 lb on Earth weighs 30 lb on the Moon. About how much does a person weighing 150 lb on Earth weigh on the Moon?

Step 1 Find the constant of variation.

$w = km$ Write the equation for a direct variation.
$180 = k \cdot 30$ Substitute 180 for w and 30 for m.
$\dfrac{180}{30} = \dfrac{30k}{30}$ Divide each side by 30.
$6 = k$ Simplify.

Step 2 Find the weight of a 150-lb person on the Moon.

$w = km$ Write the equation for a direct variation.
$150 = 6m$ Substitute 6 for k and 150 for w.
$25 = m$ Divide each side by 6.

A person weighing 150 lb on Earth weighs about 25 lb on the Moon.

❸ Writing a Direct Variation Using a Point Write an equation for the direct variation that includes $A(-2, 2)$.

Step 1 Find the constant of variation.

$y = kx$ Write the equation for a direct variation.
$2 = k(-2)$ Substitute -2 for x and 2 for y.
$k = -1$ Simplify.

Step 2 Write the equation using the value of k.

$y = kx$ Write the equation for a direct variation.
$y = -x$ Replace k with -1.

Quick Check

2. How much does a person weighing 75 lb on the Moon weigh on Earth?

3. Write an equation for a direct variation that includes $B(3, -5)$.

L1 Daily Notetaking Guide   Algebra Readiness Lesson 8-4   **133**

Name_____ Class_____ Date_____

Lesson 8-5

Reasoning Strategy: Use Multiple Strategies

Lesson Objective
- Solve problems by combining strategies

Example

1 **Apple Display** A grocer stacks apples in the shape of a square pyramid. He wants to make the pyramid have six "layers." How many apples does the grocer need?

Understand the Problem

Read the problem carefully.

1. What do you want to find?

2. What is the relationship between the pyramid layers and the number of apples needed?

Make and Carry Out a Plan

Draw a diagram of each layer of the pyramid of apples.

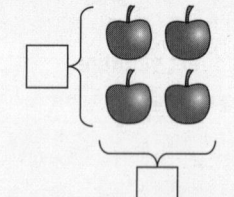

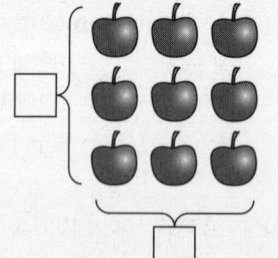

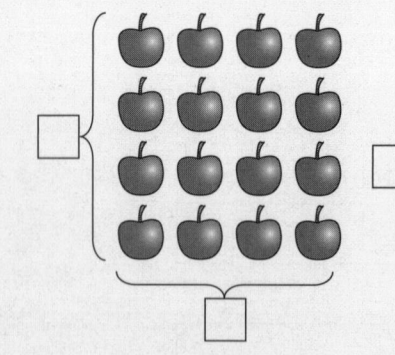

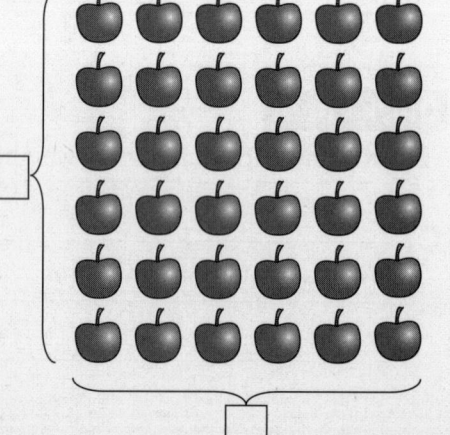

134 Algebra Readiness Lesson 8-5   Daily Notetaking Guide

Make a table.

Layer (from top down)	No. of apples on edge of layer	No. of apples in layer	Total no. of apples
1	1	$1^2 = 1$	1
☐	☐	$2^2 = $ ☐	☐
☐	☐	$☐^2 = $ ☐	☐
☐	☐	$☐^2 = $ ☐	☐
☐	☐	$☐^2 = $ ☐	☐
☐	☐	$☐^2 = $ ☐	☐

The grocer needs ☐ apples.

Check the Answer

The original problem states that the stack of apples is in the shape of a square pyramid. This means that the number of apples in each layer should be a perfect square. In this solution, 4, 9, 16, 25, and 36 are each perfect squares. So the result fits the context of the original problem.

Quick Check

1. Suppose that the pyramid must have 9 layers. Find the number of apples the grocer will need.

Name_____ Class_____ Date_____

Lesson 8-6

Solving Systems of Linear Equations

Lesson Objectives
- Solve systems of linear equations by graphing
- Use systems of linear equations to solve problems

Vocabulary

A system of linear equations is _____

_____

Example

1 Solve a System by Graphing Solve the system $y = x - 7$ and $y = 4x + 2$ by graphing.

Step 1 Graph each line.

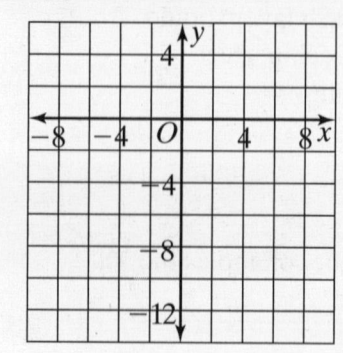

Step 2 Find the point of intersection.

The lines intersect at one point, ☐.

The solution is ☐.

Check See whether $(-3, -10)$ makes both equations true.

$y = x - 7$ Replace x with ☐ $y = 4x + 2$

☐ $\stackrel{?}{=}$ ☐ $- 7$ and y with ☐.   ☐ $\stackrel{?}{=} 4($ ☐ $) + 2$

☐ $=$ ☐ ✔   The solution checks.   ☐ $=$ ☐ ✔

Quick Check

1. Solve each system of equations by graphing. Check the solution.

   $y = x - 6$ and $y = -2x$

   ☐

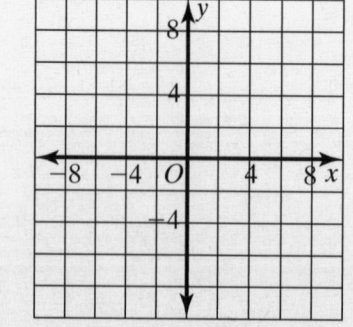

136 Algebra Readiness Lesson 8-6   Daily Notetaking Guide L1

Name_____ Class_____ Date _____

Examples

② Solving Special Systems Solve each system of equations by graphing.

a. $27x + 9y = 36; y = 4 - 3x$

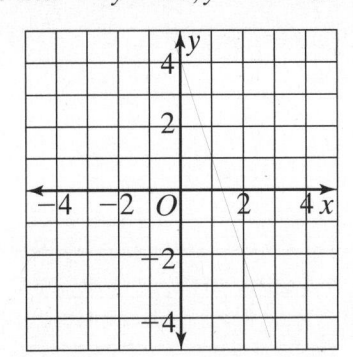

b. $8 = 4x + 2y; 2x + y = 5$

The lines are the same line. There are ☐ many solutions.

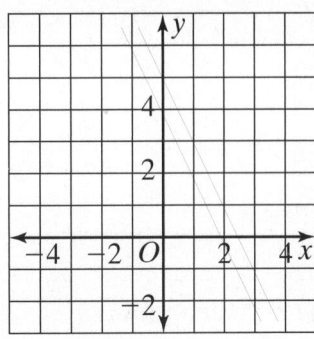

The lines are ☐. They do not intersect. There is ☐ solution.

③ Using a System of Equations Find two numbers with a sum of 10 and a difference of 2.

Step 1 Write equations.

Let x = the greater number.
Let y = the lesser number.

Equation 1 Sum is 10.

☐ + ☐ = ☐

Equation 2 Difference is 2.

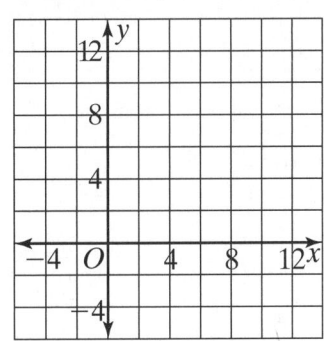

☐ − ☐ = ☐

Step 2 Graph the equations.

The lines intersect at ☐.

The numbers are ☐ and ☐.

Quick Check

2. Solve each system of equations by graphing.
$y = x + 4;$
$y = x$

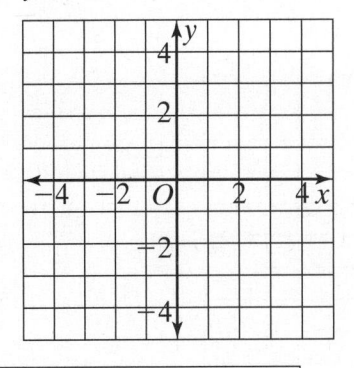

3. Find two numbers with a difference of 2 and a sum of −8.

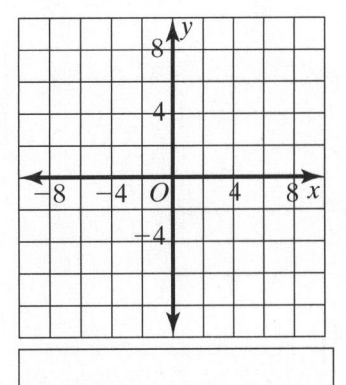

Name_____ Class_____ Date_____

Lesson 8-7   Linear Inequalities

Lesson Objectives
- Graph linear inequalities
- Graph systems of linear inequalities

Vocabulary

A linear inequality is _____

_____

A system of linear inequalities is _____

Example

1 Graphing a Linear Inequality Graph the inequality $y > 2x + 1$ on a coordinate plane.

Step 1 Graph the boundary line.

Points on the boundary line do not make $y > 2x + 1$ true. Use a ☐ line.

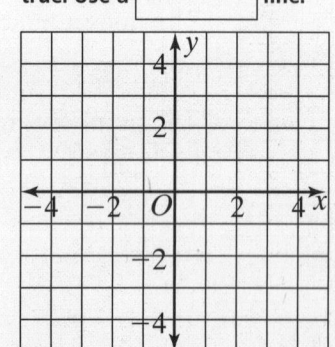

Step 2 Test a point not on the boundary line. Test $(0, 0)$ in the inequality.

$y > 2x + 1$

$☐ \overset{?}{>} 2(☐) + 1$ Substitute.

$0 \overset{?}{>} 0 + 1$

$0 > 1$ ✗   false

Since the inequality is ☐ for $(0, 0)$, shade the region that does not contain $(0, 0)$.

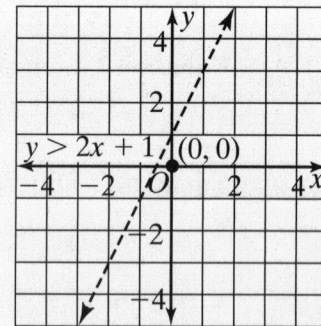

Quick Check

1. Graph each inequality on the coordinate plane.

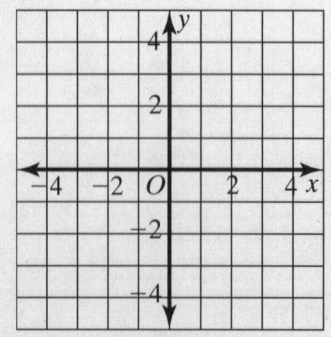

   a. $y \geq 3x - 1$

   b. $y > -x + 3$

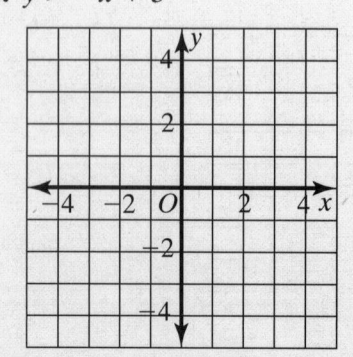

Name _____ Class _____ Date _____

Examples

❷ Using a Linear Inequality Cashews cost $2/lb. Pecans cost $4/lb. You plan to spend no more than $20. Write an inequality to represent the number of pounds of each you can buy.

Words | cost of cashews | plus | cost of pecans | is at most | twenty dollars |

Let $\boxed{y}$ = number of pounds of cashews.

Let $\boxed{x}$ = number of pounds of pecans.

Inequality $\square$ + $\square$ $\square$ $\square$

❸ Solving a System of Linear Inequalities Solve the system $y \geq x + 1$ and $y < 2x + 3$ by graphing.

Step 1 Graph $y \geq x + 1$ and shade in one color.

Step 2 Graph $y < 2x + 3$ and shade in second color.

The solutions are the coordinates of all the points in the region that is shaded in both colors.

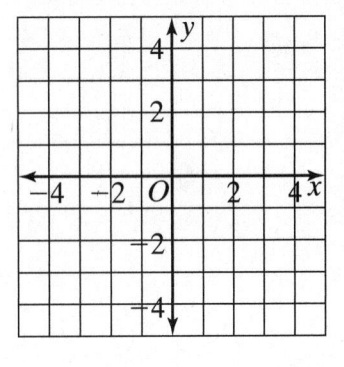

Quick Check

2. Adult tickets to the school play cost $4. Children's tickets cost $2. Your goal is to sell tickets worth at least $30. Let x be the number of children's tickets and y be the number of adult tickets. Graph a linear inequality to show how many of each type of ticket you must sell to earn at least $30.

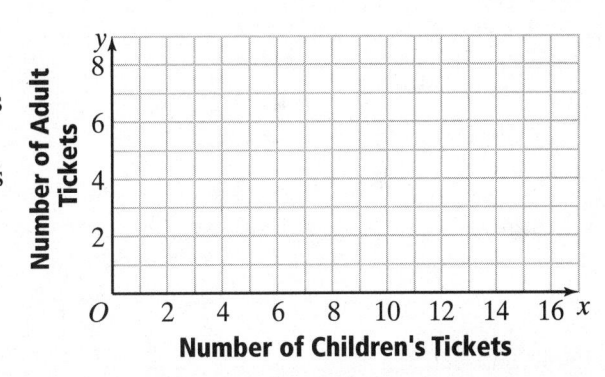

3. Solve each system by graphing.

$y \leq -2x - 5$
$y < \frac{1}{2}x$

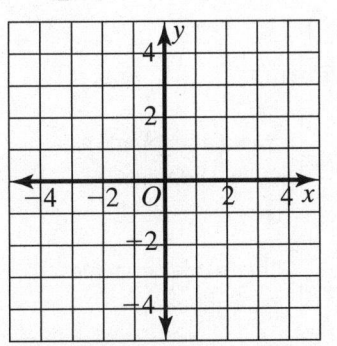

Daily Notetaking Guide — Algebra Readiness Lesson 8-7

Name_____ Class_____ Date_____

Lesson 9-1

Introduction to Geometry: Points, Lines and Planes

Lesson Objectives
- Name basic geometric figures
- Recognize intersecting lines, parallel lines and skew lines

Vocabulary

Basic Geometric Figures

Sample	Symbolic Name	Description
•A	Point A	A _____ is a location in space. It has no size.
A B n (line)	$\overleftrightarrow{AB}$, $\overleftrightarrow{BA}$, or n	A _____ is a series of points that extends in opposite directions without end. A lowercase letter can name a line.
A B M D C	ABCD or M	A _____ is a flat surface with no thickness. It contains many lines and extends without end in the directions of all its lines.
P Q	$\overline{PQ}$, or $\overline{QP}$	A _____ is a part of a line. It has two endpoints. PQ represents the length of $\overline{PQ}$.
C R	$\overrightarrow{CR}$	A _____ is a part of a line. It has exactly one endpoint. Name its endpoint first.

_____ are lines in the same plane that never intersect.

_____ are lines that are not in the same plane, are not parallel, and do not intersect.

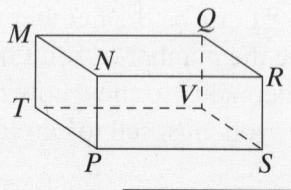

$\overline{MN}$ and $\overline{NP}$ _____.
$\overline{MN}$ and $\overline{QR}$ are _____.
$\overline{MN}$ and $\overline{RS}$ are _____.

Examples

1 Naming Geometric Figures Use the figure to name each of the following.

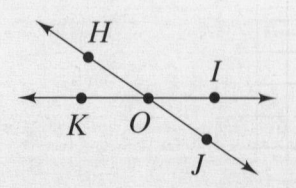

a. four different segments

_____, _____, _____, and _____

Name a segment by its endpoints.

b. four different rays

_____, _____, _____, and _____

The first letter names the endpoint.

140 Algebra Readiness Lesson 9-1 Daily Notetaking Guide

Name_____ Class_____ Date _____

❷ Identifying Segments You are looking at a picture frame. Name each of the following.

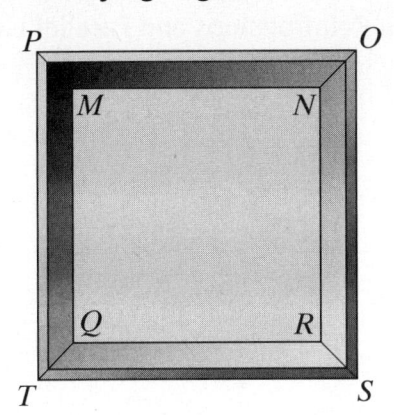

P, O, M, N, Q, R, T, S (picture frame diagram)

a. two segments that intersect $\overline{PT}$
   ☐ , and ☐

b. three segments parallel to $\overline{PT}$
   ☐ , ☐ , and ☐

❸ Drawing Lines Draw two intersecting lines. Then draw a segment that is parallel to one of the intersecting lines.

Use the lines on notebook paper or graph paper. First draw the lines that intersect. Then draw a segment that is parallel to one of the lines.

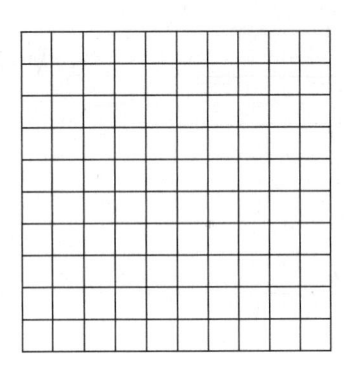

Quick Check

1. Name each figure in the diagram.

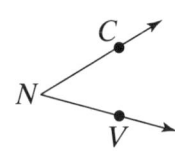

   C, N, V diagram

   a. two segments ☐ and ☐
   b. two rays ☐ and ☐

2. Use the picture in Example 2 to name each of the following:

   a. four segments that intersect $\overline{QR}$
      ☐ , ☐ , ☐ , and ☐

   b. Three segments parallel to $\overline{QR}$
      ☐ , ☐ , and ☐

   c. four segments that are skew to $\overline{QR}$
      ☐ , ☐ , ☐ , and ☐

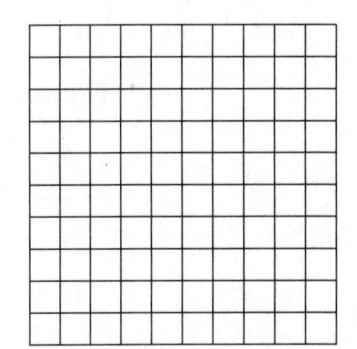

3. Use the grid to draw the figures indicated.
   a. three parallel segments: $\overline{AB}, \overline{CD}, \overline{EF}$
   b. a ray, $\overrightarrow{GH}$, that intersects the parallel segments of part (a)
   c. a line, $\overleftrightarrow{LM}$

L1 Daily Notetaking Guide   Algebra Readiness Lesson 9-1   141

Name_____ Class_____ Date_____

Lesson 9-2 — Angle Relationships and Parallel Lines

Lesson Objectives
- Identify adjacent and vertical angles
- Relate angles formed by parallel lines and a transversal

Vocabulary

Angles 1 and 2 are [_____] angles. They share a [_____] and a side.

Angles 1 and 4 are [_____] angles. They are formed by two [_____] lines.

Line n is a [_____]. It [_____] lines ℓ and m.

Angles 1 and 5 are [_____] angles.

Angles 3 and 6 are [_____] angles.

$\angle ABC$ and $\angle CBD$ are [_____] angles. The sum of their measures is [____].

$\angle ABD$ and $\angle DBE$ are [_____] angles. The sum of their measures is [____].

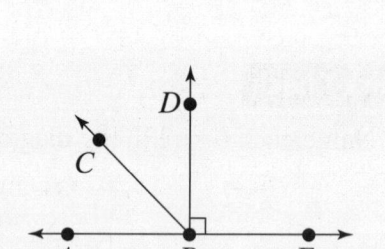

Examples

1 Finding the Measure of an Angle Find the measure of $\angle 3$ if $m\angle 4 = 110°$.

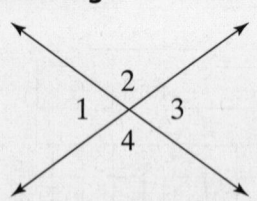

$m\angle 3 + m\angle 4 =$ [____] $\angle 3$ and $\angle 4$ are [_____].

$m\angle 3 +$ [____] $= 180°$ Replace $m\angle 4$ with [____].

$m\angle 3 + 110° -$ [____] $= 180° -$ [____]   Solve for $m\angle 3$.

$m\angle 3 =$ [____]

142 Algebra Readiness Lesson 9-2

② Identifying Congruent Angles In the diagram, $p \parallel q$. Identify each of the following.

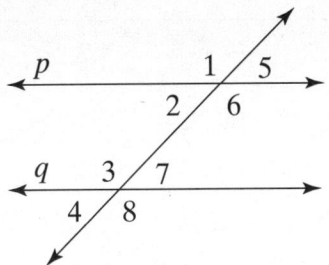

a. congruent corresponding angles

☐ ≅ ☐ , ☐ ≅ ☐ , ☐ ≅ ☐ , ☐ ≅ ☐

b. congruent alternate interior angles

☐ ≅ ☐ , ☐ ≅ ☐

Quick Check

1. If $m\angle 8 = 20°$, find the measures of $\angle 5$, $\angle 6$, and $\angle 7$.

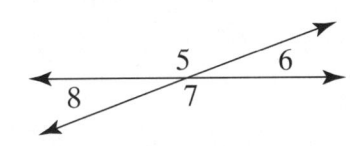

   $m\angle 5 =$ ☐

   $m\angle 6 =$ ☐

   $m\angle 7 =$ ☐

2. In the diagram, $a \parallel b$.

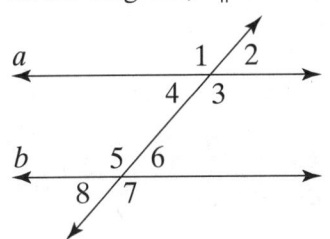

   a. Name four pairs of congruent corresponding angles.

   ☐ ≅ ☐ , ☐ ≅ ☐ , ☐ ≅ ☐ , ☐ ≅ ☐

   b. Name two pairs of congruent alternate interior angles.

   ☐ ≅ ☐ , ☐ ≅ ☐

Name_____ Class_____ Date_____

Lesson 9-3

Classifying Polygons

Lesson Objectives
- Classify triangles
- Classify quadrilaterals

Vocabulary

A _____ is a closed plane figure with at least three sides.

A regular polygon is _____

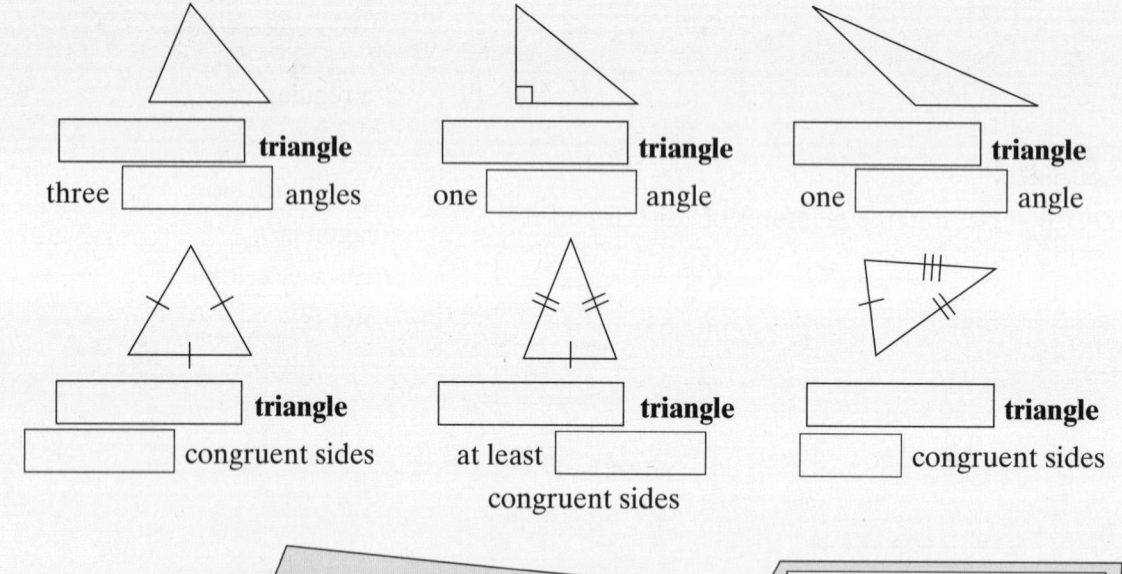

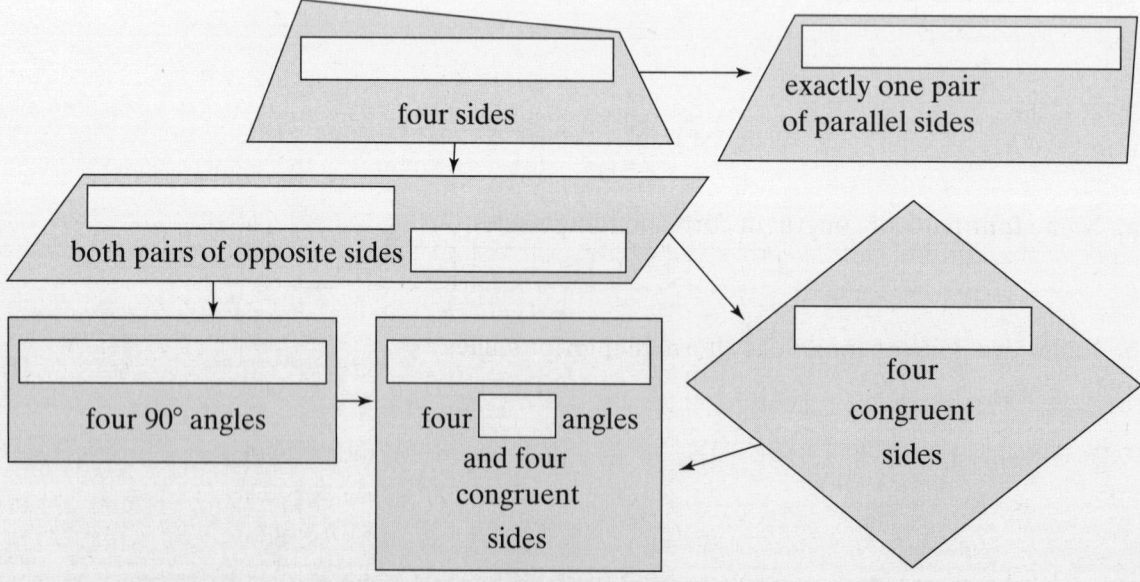

_____

[____] **triangle** three [____] angles

[____] **triangle** one [____] angle

[____] **triangle** one [____] angle

[____] **triangle** [____] congruent sides

[____] **triangle** at least [____] congruent sides

[____] **triangle** [____] congruent sides

[____] four sides

[____] exactly one pair of parallel sides

[____] both pairs of opposite sides [____]

[____] four 90° angles

[____] four [____] angles and four congruent sides

[____] four congruent sides

144 **Algebra Readiness** Lesson 9-3

Name_____ Class_____ Date _____

Examples

① **Classifying a Triangle** Classify the triangle by its sides and angles.

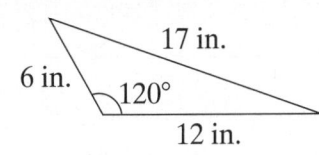

17 in.
6 in. 120°
12 in.

The triangle has [ ] congruent sides and one [ ] angle.

The triangle is a scalene obtuse triangle.

② **Classifying Quadrilaterals** Name the types of quadrilaterals that have at least one pair of parallel sides.

All [ ] and [ ] have at least one pair of parallel sides. Parallelograms include [ ] and [ ].

③ **Finding Perimeter** Write a formula to find the perimeter of a regular dodecagon (12 sides). Evaluate the formula for a side length of 3 ft.

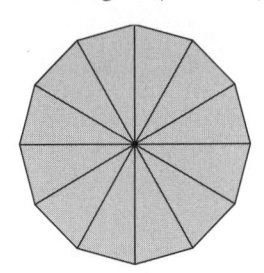

To write a formula, let x = the length of each side.
The perimeter of the regular dodecagon is
$P = x + x + x + x + x + x + x + x + x + x + x + x$.
Therefore a formula for the perimeter is [ ].

$P = 12x$ Write the formula.
$= 12($ [ ] $)$ Substitute [ ] for x.
$=$ [ ]   Simplify.

For a side length of 3 ft, the perimeter is [ ] ft.

Quick Check

1. Judging by appearance, classify each triangle by its sides and angles.

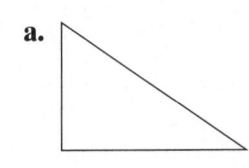

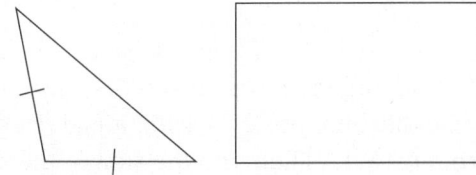

   a.   b.

2. Name the two types of quadrilaterals that have four right angles.

   [ ] and [ ]

3. a. **Algebra** Write a formula to find the perimeter of a regular hexagon. [ ]
   b. Use the formula to find the perimeter if one side is 16 cm. [ ]

Name_____ Class_____ Date_____

Lesson 9-4

Reasoning Strategy: Draw a Diagram

Lesson Objective
- Draw a diagram to solve a problem

Example

1. Drawing a Diagram How many diagonals does a nonagon have?

Understand the Problem
In reading the problem, make sure you understand the meanings of all the terms.

1. What is a nonagon?

2. What is a diagonal?

Make and Carry Out a Plan

One strategy for solving this problem is to draw a diagram and count the diagonals. A nonagon has ☐ sides. You can draw ☐ diagonals from one vertex of a nonagon.

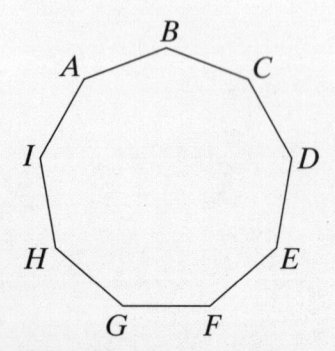

$\overline{AH}, \overline{AG}, \overline{AF}, \overline{AE}, \overline{AD},$ and $\overline{AC}$ are some of the diagonals.

You can organize your results as you count the diagonals. Do not count the same diagonal twice. (The diagonal from A to C is the same as the one from C to A.) Then find the sum of the numbers of diagonals.

Vertex	A	B	C	D	E	F	G	H	I	Total
Number of Diagonals	6									

A nonagon has ☐ diagonals.

---

146 Algebra Readiness Lesson 9-4   Daily Notetaking Guide

Name_____ Class_____ Date _____

Check the Answer

Counting the diagonals after they have all been drawn is not an easy task. To check your results, you may want to try a different approach.

Start with figures with fewer sides and see whether there is a pattern to the total numbers of diagonals as you increase the number of sides.

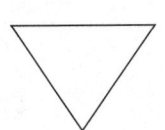

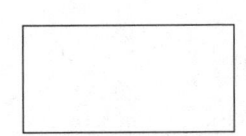

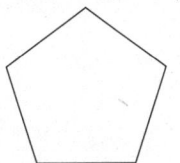

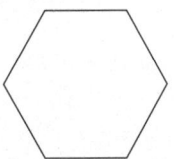

Figure	Number of Sides	Number of Diagonals
Triangle		
Quadrilateral		
Pentagon		
Hexagon		

Notice that the total number of diagonals increases as you increase the number of sides of the polygon. First the number increases by ☐, then by ☐, and then by ☐. Continue the pattern to check your results.

Figure	Number of Sides	Number of Diagonals

Quick Check

1. How many diagonals does a dodecagon have?

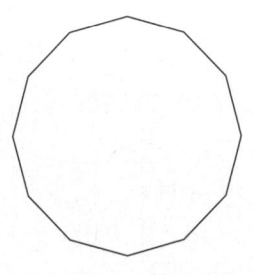

Daily Notetaking Guide   Algebra Readiness Lesson 9-4   147

Lesson 9-5

Congruence

Lesson Objectives
- Identify corresponding parts of congruent triangles
- Determine whether triangles are congruent

Take Note

_____ have figures that have the same size and shape, and their corresponding parts have equal measures.

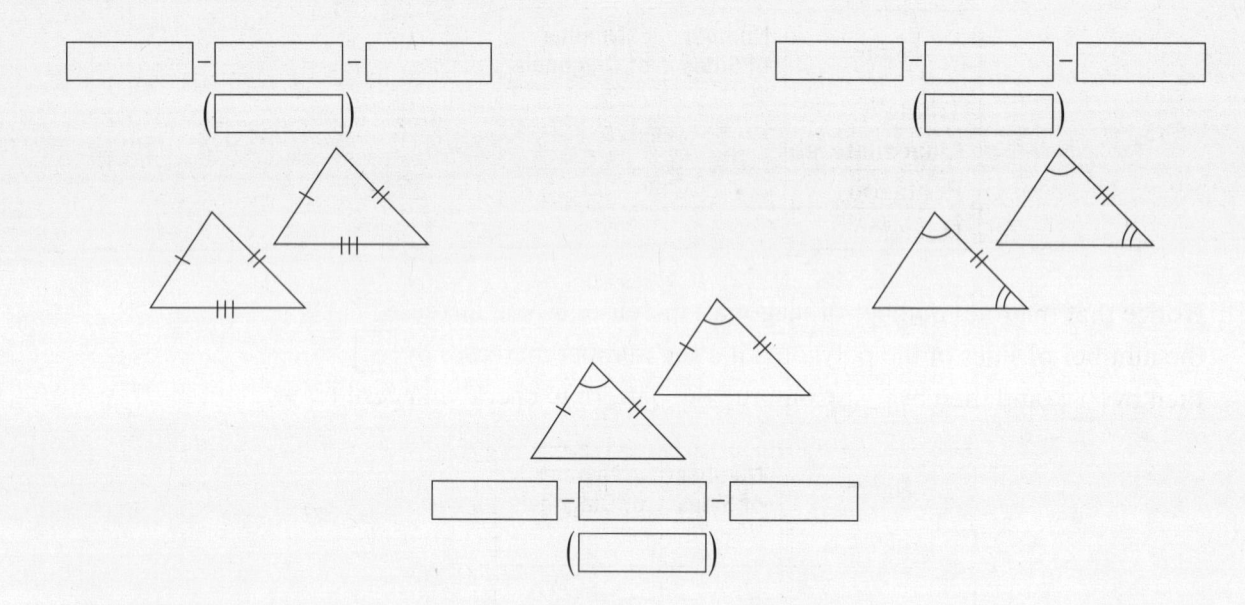

☐ – ☐ – ☐
(☐)

☐ – ☐ – ☐
(☐)

☐ – ☐ – ☐
(☐)

Examples

1 Identifying Congruent Parts In the figure, △TUV ≅ △WUX.

a. Name the corresponding congruent angles.
∠V ≅ ∠☐ , ∠T ≅ ∠☐ , ∠TUV ≅ ∠☐

b. Name the corresponding congruent sides.
$\overline{TV}$ ≅ ☐ , $\overline{TU}$ ≅ ☐ , $\overline{VU}$ ≅ ☐

c. Find the length of $\overline{WX}$.
Since $\overline{WX}$ ≅ ☐ and TV = 300 m, WX = ☐ m.

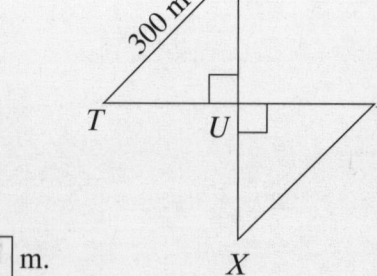

Name_____ Class_____ Date_____

❷ Identifying Congruent Triangles List the congruent corresponding parts of each pair of triangles. Write a congruence statement for the triangles.

a.

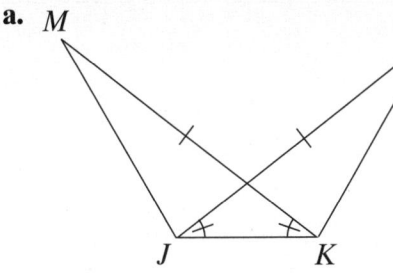

☐ ≅ $\overline{LJ}$ Side

∠☐ ≅ ∠LJK   Angle

☐ ≅ $\overline{JK}$ Side

△☐ ≅ △LJK by ☐.

b.

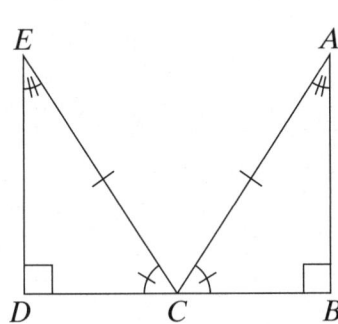

∠ACB ≅ ∠☐   Angle

$\overline{AC}$ ≅ ☐   Side

∠CAB ≅ ∠☐   Angle

△ACB ≅ △☐ by ☐.

Quick Check

1. △ABC ≅ △DEC. List all pairs of congruent corresponding sides and angles. Then find AC.

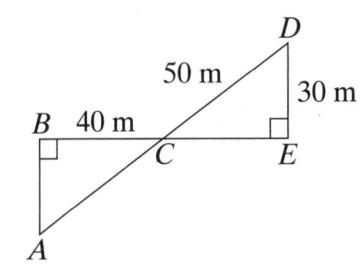

   $\overline{AB}$ ≅ ☐, $\overline{BC}$ ≅ ☐, $\overline{AC}$ ≅ ☐,
   ∠A ≅ ∠☐, ∠B ≅ ∠☐,
   ∠BCA ≅ ∠☐; AC = ☐ m

2. For the two triangles, list the congruent corresponding parts. Write a congruence statement (and reason) for the triangles.

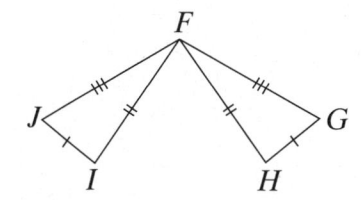

   $\overline{FJ}$ ≅ ☐, $\overline{JI}$ ≅ ☐, $\overline{FI}$ ≅ ☐;
   △JFI ≅ △☐ by ☐

Daily Notetaking Guide   Algebra Readiness Lesson 9-5   **149**

Name_____ Class_____ Date_____

Lesson 9-6   Circles

Lesson Objectives
- Find circumferences
- Find central angles and make circle graphs

Take Note

Circumference of a Circle
The circumference of a circle is π times the diameter.

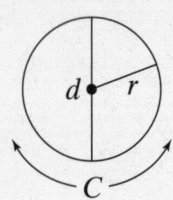

$C = \boxed{} \cdot \boxed{}$

$C = 2\boxed{} \cdot \boxed{}$

A ____ is the set of all points in a plane that are the same distance from a given point, called the center of the circle.

A central angle is _____

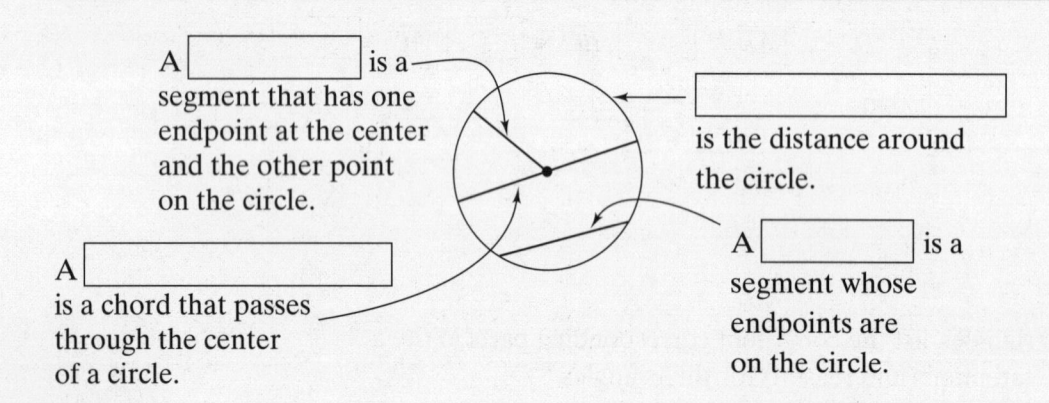

_____

A $\boxed{}$ is a segment that has one endpoint at the center and the other point on the circle.

A $\boxed{}$ is a chord that passes through the center of a circle.

$\boxed{}$ is the distance around the circle.

A $\boxed{}$ is a segment whose endpoints are on the circle.

Examples

1 Finding Circumference Find the circumference of the circle.

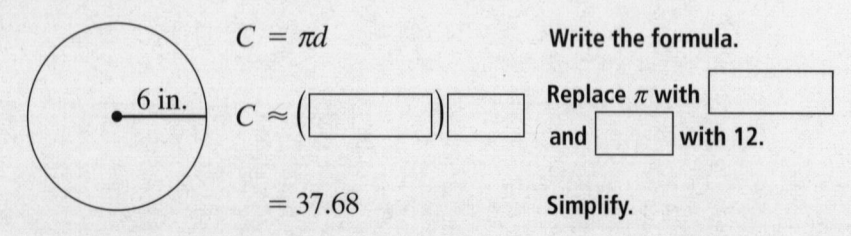

6 in.

$C = \pi d$ Write the formula.

$C \approx (\boxed{})\boxed{}$ Replace π with $\boxed{}$ and $\boxed{}$ with 12.

$= 37.68$ Simplify.

The circumference of the circle is about $\boxed{}$ in.

150 *Algebra Readiness* Lesson 9-6   Daily Notetaking Guide

Name _____ Class _____ Date _____

❷ **Making a Circle Graph** Make a circle graph for Jackie's weekly budget. Use proportions to find the measures of the central angles.

Jackie's Weekly Budget	
Entertainment (e)	20%
Food (f)	20%
Transportation (t)	10%
Savings (s)	50%

$\dfrac{\boxed{}}{100} = \dfrac{e}{360}$ $\dfrac{\boxed{}}{100} = \dfrac{f}{360}$

$e = \boxed{}$ $f = \boxed{}$

$\dfrac{\boxed{}}{100} = \dfrac{t}{360}$ $\dfrac{\boxed{}}{100} = \dfrac{s}{360}$

$t = \boxed{}$ $s = \boxed{}$

Use a compass to draw a circle. Draw the central angles with a protractor. Label each section. Add a title.

Jackie's Weekly Budget

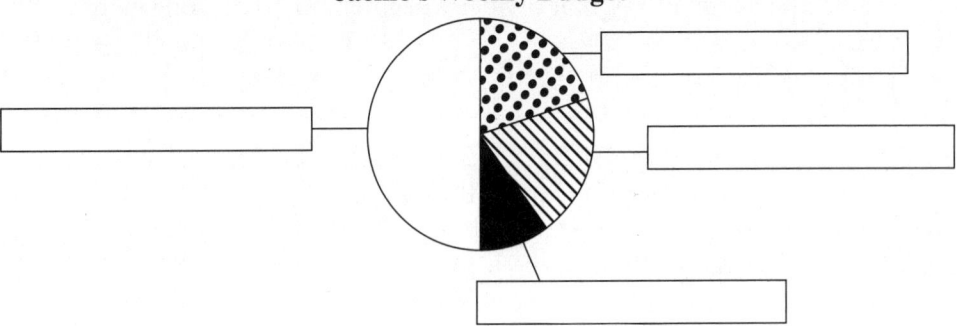

Quick Check

1. Find the circumference of each circle.

   a. diameter = $2\dfrac{4}{5}$ in.

   b. radius = 30 mm

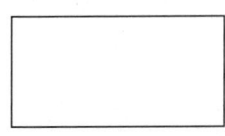

2. Make a circle graph for the data. Round the measure of each central angle to the nearest degree.

   Blood Types of Population

Type A	Type B	Type AB	Type O
40%	12%	5%	43%

   Blood Types of Population

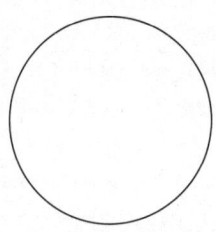

Daily Notetaking Guide   *Algebra Readiness* Lesson 9-6

Name_____ Class_____ Date_____

Lesson 9-7   Constructions

Lesson Objectives
- Construct a segment or an angle congruent to a given segment or angle
- Construct segment bisectors and angle bisectors

Vocabulary

Perpendicular lines, segments, or rays _____

_____

A _____ is a line, segment, or ray that divides a segment into two congruent segments.

A perpendicular bisector is _____

_____

An _____ is a ray that divides an angle into two congruent angles.

Examples

1 Constructing a Congruent Angle Construct an angle congruent to ∠W.

∠ ☐ ≅ ∠NWM

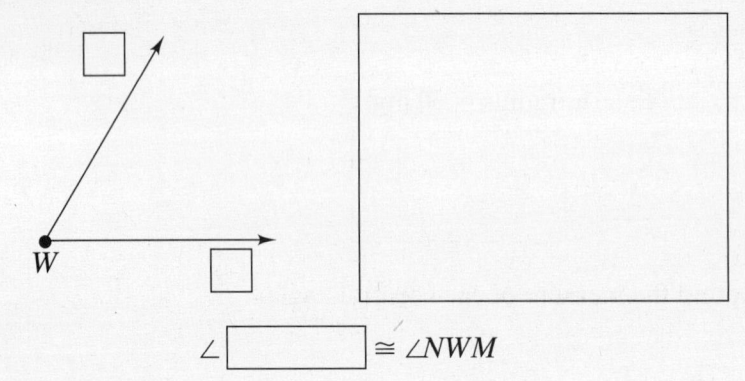

Step 1 Draw a ray with endpoint A.

Step 2 With the compass point at W, draw an arc that intersects the sides of ∠W. Label the intersection points M and N.

Step 3 With the *same* compass setting, put the compass tip on A. Draw an arc that intersects the ray at point B.

Step 4 Open the compass to the length of $\overline{MN}$. Using this setting, put the compass tip at B. Draw an arc to determine the point C. Draw $\overrightarrow{AC}$.

152   Algebra Readiness Lesson 9-7   Daily Notetaking Guide

Name_____ Class_____ Date_____

❷ Constructing a Perpendicular Bisector
Construct the perpendicular bisector of $\overline{WX}$.

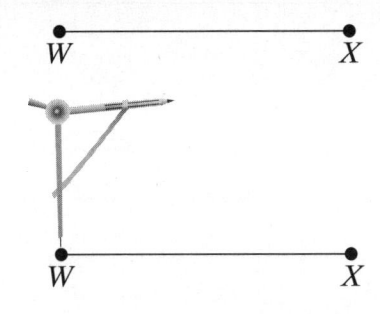

Step 1 Open the compass to more than half the length of $\overline{WX}$. Put the compass tip at W. Draw an arc intersecting $\overline{WX}$. With the same compass setting, repeat from point X.

Step 2 Label the points of intersection S and T. Draw $\overleftrightarrow{ST}$. Label the intersection of $\overleftrightarrow{ST}$ and $\overline{WX}$ point M.

$\overline{ST}$ is [   ] to $\overline{WX}$ and $\overline{ST}$ [   ] $\overline{WX}$.

Quick Check

1. Construct an angle congruent to $\angle A$.

2. Construct the perpendicular bisector of $\overline{CD}$.

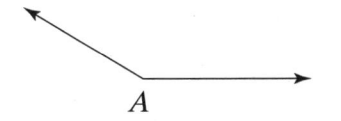

Daily Notetaking Guide — Algebra Readiness Lesson 9-7

Name_____ Class_____ Date_____

Lesson 9-8   Translations

Lesson Objectives
- Graph translations
- Describe translations

Vocabulary

A _____ is a change of position or size of a figure.

A translation is _____

An _____ is the figure you get after a transformation.

Example

1) Translating a Figure Graph the image of △BCD after a translation 3 units to the left and 4 units down.

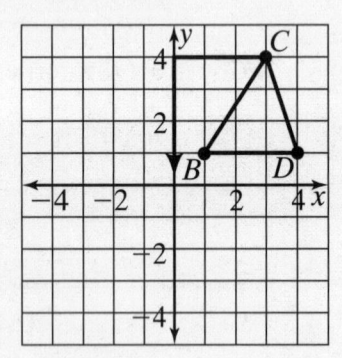

Quick Check

1. On a coordinate plane, draw △BCD from Example 1. Graph the image of △BCD after a translation of △BCD four units to the left.

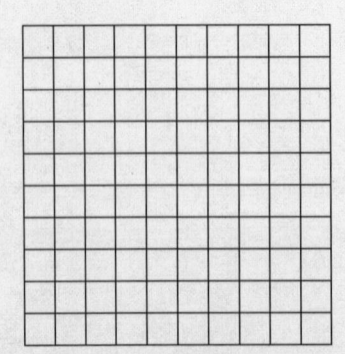

154 Algebra Readiness Lesson 9-8   Daily Notetaking Guide

Name _____ Class _____ Date _____

Examples

② Using Arrow Notation Use arrow notation to describe the translation of X to X'.

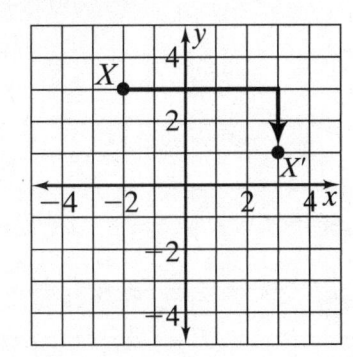

The point moves from $X(-2, 3)$ to $X'(3, 1)$, so the translation is ☐ → ☐.

③ Writing a Rule Write a rule to describe the translation of $\triangle RST$ to $\triangle R'S'T'$.

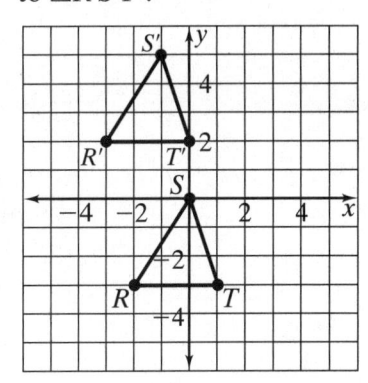

Use $R(-2, -3)$ and its image $R'(-3, 2)$ to find the horizontal and vertical translations.

Horizontal translation: $-3 - (\boxed{}) = \boxed{}$

Vertical translation: $2 - (\boxed{}) = \boxed{}$

The rule is $(x, y) \rightarrow (x - \boxed{}, y + \boxed{})$.

Quick Check

2. Use arrow notation to describe a translation of $B(-1, 5)$ to $B'(3, 1)$.

3. Write a rule to describe the translation of quadrilateral $ABCD$ to quadrilateral $A'B'C'D'$.

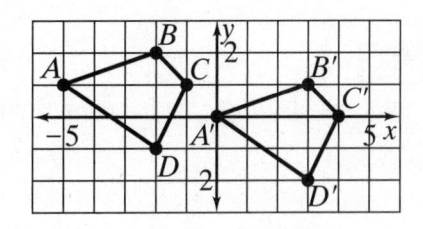

Daily Notetaking Guide   Algebra Readiness Lesson 9-8

Name_____ Class_____ Date_____

Lesson 9-9   Symmetry and Reflections

Lesson Objectives
- Identify a line of symmetry
- Graph a reflection of a geometric figure

Vocabulary

_____ is when one half is a mirror image of the other half.

A line of symmetry is _____

_____

A _____ is a transformation that flips a figure over a line of reflection.

A line of reflection is _____

Example

1. **Finding Lines of Symmetry** Draw the lines of symmetry. Tell how many lines there are.

   a.   b.

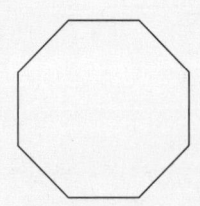

   ☐ lines of symmetry   ☐ lines of symmetry

Quick Check

1. Draw all lines of symmetry for each figure.

   a.   b.

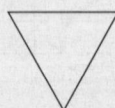

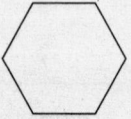

---

156 Algebra Readiness Lesson 9-9   Daily Notetaking Guide

Name _____ Class _____ Date _____

Examples

② Reflecting Over an Axis Graph the image of △EFG after a reflection over the x-axis.

Since F is [ ] units below the x-axis,

F′ is [ ] units above the x-axis.

Reflect the other vertices.
Draw △E′F′G′.

③ Reflecting Over a Line Graph the image of △EFG after a reflection over $y = -1$.

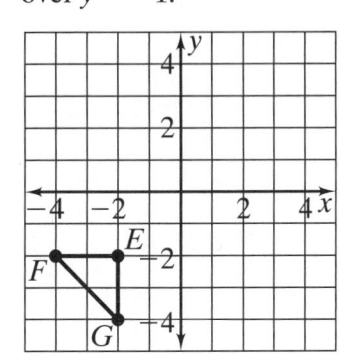

Graph $y = -1$.

Since F is [ ] unit below the line,

F′ is [ ] unit above the line.

Reflect the other vertices.
Draw △E′F′G′.

Quick Check

2. Graph the image of △EFG after a reflection over the y-axis.

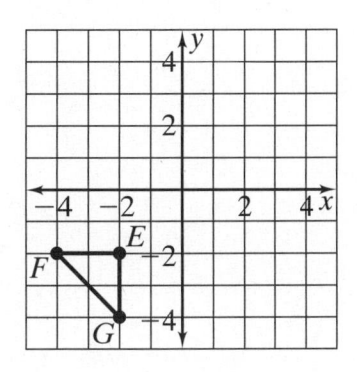

3. Graph △ABC with vertices $A(3, 0)$, $B(2, 3)$, and $C(5, -1)$ and its image after a reflection over the line $x = 2$.

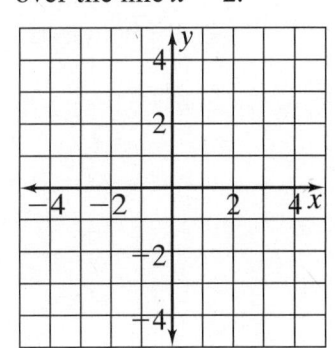

L1 Daily Notetaking Guide   Algebra Readiness Lesson 9-9   **157**

Name_____ Class_____ Date_____

Lesson 9-10　　　　　　　　　　　　　　　　　　　　　　　　　　　Rotations

Lesson Objectives
- Graph rotations
- Identify rotational symmetry

Vocabulary

A _____ is a transformation that turns a figure about a fixed point called the center of rotation.

A center of rotation is _____
_____

An _____ is the angle measure of the rotation.

A figure has rotational symmetry if the _____
_____

Examples

1 Finding a Rotation Image Find the vertices of the image of △RST after a rotation of 90° about the origin.

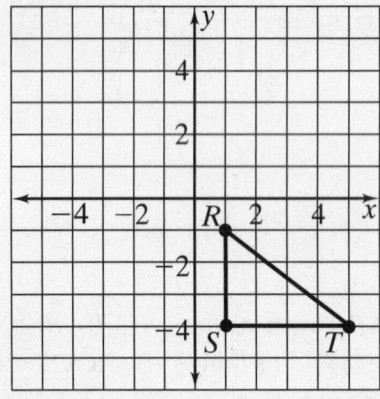

Step 1 Use a blank transparency sheet. Trace △RST, the x-axis, and the y-axis. Then fix the tracing in place at the origin.

Step 2 Rotate the tracing 90° counterclockwise. Make sure the axes line up. Label the vertices R′, S′, and T′. Connect the vertices of the rotated triangle.

The vertices of the image are R′(☐, ☐), S′(☐, ☐), and T′(☐, ☐).

158　Algebra Readiness Lesson 9-10　　　　　　　　　　　　Daily Notetaking Guide

Name _____ Class _____ Date _____

❷ Identifying Rotational Symmetry Judging from appearance, tell whether the star has rotational symmetry. If so, what is the angle of rotation?

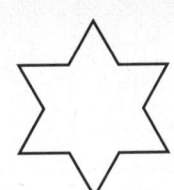

The star can match itself in ☐ positions.

The pattern repeats in ☐ equal intervals.

360° ÷ ☐ = ☐

The figure ☐ rotational symmetry.

The angle of rotation is ☐.

Quick Check

1. Draw the image of △RST in Example 1 after a rotation of 180° about the origin. Name the coordinates of the vertices of the image.

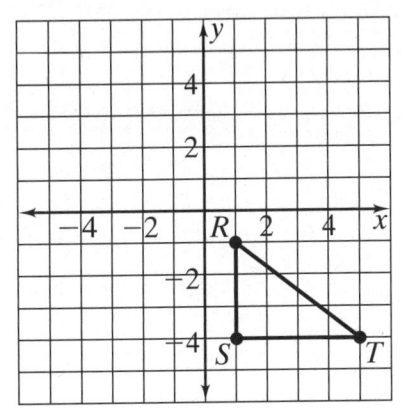

The vertices of the image are $R'(\square, \square)$, $S'(\square, \square)$, and $T'(\square, \square)$.

2. Judging from appearance, tell whether each figure has rotational symmetry. If so, what is the angle of rotation?

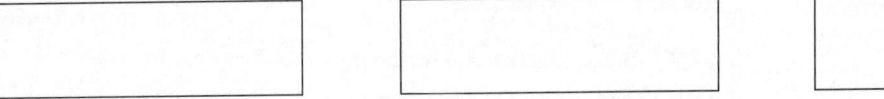

a.

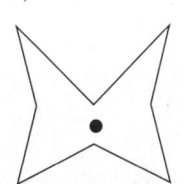

b.

c.

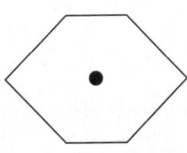

Daily Notetaking Guide — Algebra Readiness Lesson 9-10

Name_____ Class_____ Date_____

Lesson 10-1

Area: Parallelograms

Lesson Objectives
- Find areas of rectangles
- Find areas of parallelograms

Take Note

Area of a Parallelogram
The area of a parallelogram is the product of any base length b and the corresponding height h.

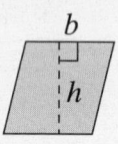

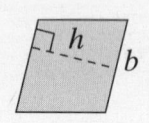

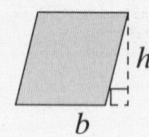

$A = \boxed{} \cdot \boxed{}$

The ____ of a figure is the number of square units it encloses.

An altitude is _____

_____

Examples

1 **Finding Area of a Rectangle** Find the area of the rectangle.

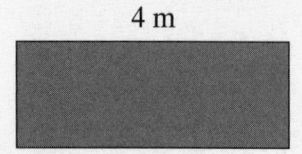

4 m
150 cm

Step 1 Change the units so they are the same.

150 cm = $\boxed{}$ m   Change 150 centimeters to meters.

Step 2 Find the area.

$A = bh$ Use the formula for area of a rectangle.

$= (\boxed{})(\boxed{})$ Replace b and h with the dimensions $\boxed{}$ and $\boxed{}$.

$= \boxed{}$ Simplify.

The area of the rectangle is $\boxed{}$ m^2.

Algebra Readiness Lesson 10-1   Daily Notetaking Guide

Name_____ Class_____ Date _____

❷ Finding Area of a Parallelogram Find the area of each parallelogram.

a.

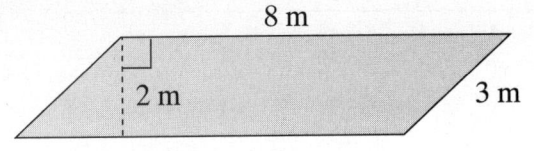

8 m, 2 m, 3 m

$A = bh$ area formula

= (☐)(☐)   Substitute.

= ☐   Simplify.

The area is ☐ m².

b.

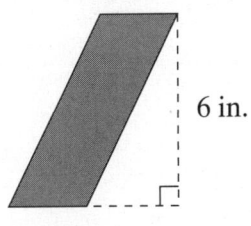

6 in., 2.5 in.

$A = bh$ area formula

= (☐)(☐)   Substitute.

= ☐   Simplify.

The area is ☐ in.².

Quick Check

1. Find the area of each rectangle.

   1 m, 10 cm

   $A = bh$

   = ☐ × ☐

   = ☐

   The area is ☐ cm².

2. Find the area of each parallelogram.

   3 m, 2 m

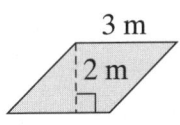

   $A = bh$

   = ☐ × ☐

   = ☐

   The area is ☐ m².

Daily Notetaking Guide   Algebra Readiness Lesson 10-1

Name_____ Class_____ Date_____

Lesson 10-2

Area: Triangles and Trapezoids

Lesson Objectives
- Find areas of triangles
- Find areas of trapezoids

Take Note

Area of a Triangle
The area of a triangle equals half the product of any base length b and the corresponding height h.

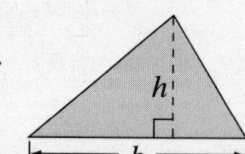

$A = \dfrac{\square}{\square}\square\square$

Area of a Trapezoid
The area of a trapezoid is half the product of the height and the sum of the lengths of the bases.

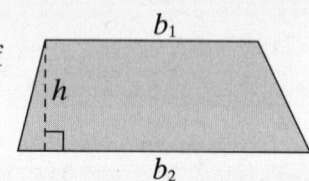

$A = \dfrac{\square}{\square}\square(\square + \square)$

An _____ is the perpendicular segment from a vertex of a triangle to the line containing the opposite side.

Examples

1 Finding Area of a Triangle Find the area of the triangle.

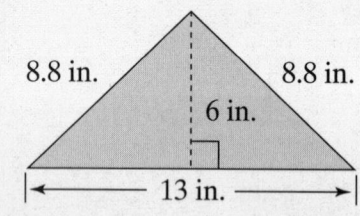

8.8 in.   8.8 in.
6 in.
13 in.

$A = \dfrac{\square}{\square}\square$ Use the formula for area of a triangle.

$= \dfrac{1}{2} \cdot \square \cdot \square$ Replace b with $\square$ and h with $\square$.

$= \square$ Simplify.

The area is $\square$ in.²

162 Algebra Readiness Lesson 10-2

Daily Notetaking Guide

Name_____ Class_____ Date_____

❷ Finding Area of a Trapezoid Suppose that, through the years, a layer of silt and mud settled in the bottom of the Erie Canal. Below is the resulting cross section of the canal. Find the area of the trapezoidal cross section.

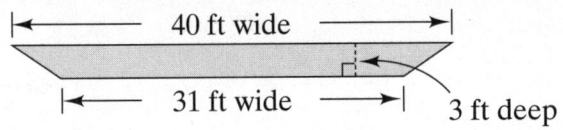

⟵ 40 ft wide ⟶
⟵ 31 ft wide ⟶ 3 ft deep

$A = \dfrac{\Box}{\Box}\Box(\Box + \Box)$ Use the formula for area of a trapezoid.

$A = \dfrac{1}{2} \cdot \Box(\Box + \Box)$ Replace h with $\Box$, b_1 with $\Box$, and b_2 with $\Box$.

$= \dfrac{1}{2} \cdot 3(\Box)$ Add.

$= \dfrac{1}{2} \cdot \Box$ Multiply.

$= \Box$ Simplify.

The area of the cross section is $\Box$ ft².

Quick Check

1. Find the area of each figure.

   a. 5 ft, 4 ft, 1.8 ft, 8.2 ft

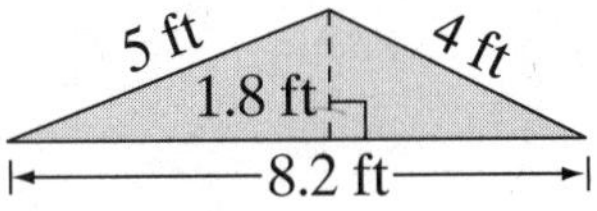

   $A = \dfrac{1}{2}bh$
   $= \dfrac{1}{2}(\Box \times \Box)$
   $= \Box$

   The area is $\Box$ ft².

   b. 2 ft, 4 ft, $4\dfrac{1}{2}$ ft

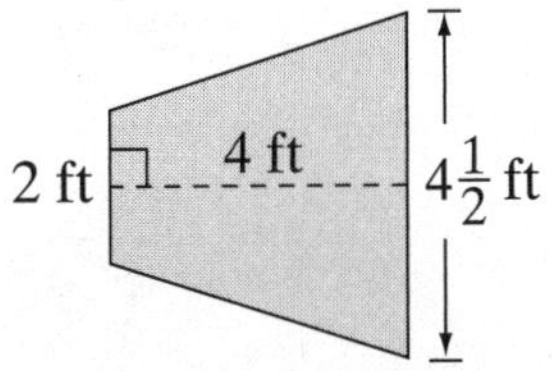

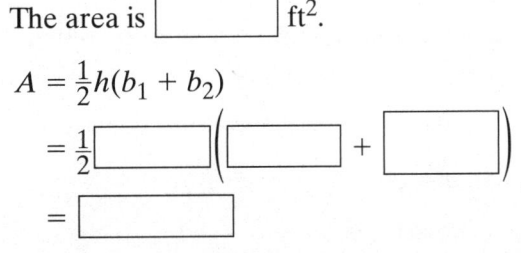

   $A = \dfrac{1}{2}h(b_1 + b_2)$
   $= \dfrac{1}{2}\Box(\Box + \Box)$
   $= \Box$

   The area is $\Box$ ft².

Name_____ Class_____ Date_____

Lesson 10-3 Area: Circles

Lesson Objectives
- Find areas of circles
- Find areas of irregular figures that include parts of circles

Take Note

Area of a Circle

The area of a circle equals the product of π and the square of the radius r.

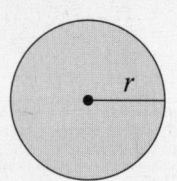

$A = \boxed{}\boxed{}^2$

Examples

1 Finding Area of a Circle Find the exact area of a circle with diameter 20 in.

$A = \boxed{}$ Use the formula for area of a circle.

$= \pi\left(\boxed{}\right)^2$ $r = \frac{1}{2}d$; $r = \boxed{}$

$= \boxed{}$ Simplify.

The area is $\boxed{}$ in.^{2}.

2 Estimating Area of a Circle A TV station's weather radar can detect precipitation in a circular region having a diameter of 100 mi. Find the area of the region.

$A = \boxed{}$ Use the formula for area of a circle.

$= \pi\left(\boxed{}\right)^2$ $r = \frac{1}{2}d$; $r = \boxed{}$

$= 2{,}500\pi$ exact area

$\approx 2{,}500\left(\boxed{}\right)$ Use $\boxed{}$ for π.

$= \boxed{}$ approximate area

The area of the region is about $\boxed{}$ mi^2.

164 Algebra Readiness Lesson 10-3   Daily Notetaking Guide L1

Name _____ Class _____ Date _____

❸ Finding Area of an Irregular Figure A pound of grass seed covers approximately 675 ft². Find the area of the lawn below. Then find the number of bags of grass seed you need to buy to cover the lawn. Grass seed comes in 3-lb bags.

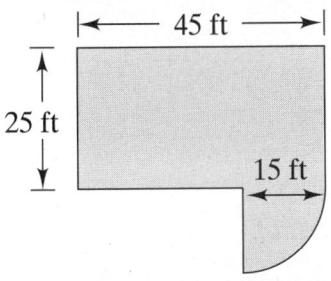

[Figure: L-shaped lawn with rectangle 45 ft × 25 ft and a quarter-circle of radius 15 ft]

Area of region that is one fourth of a circle:

area of a circle = ☐ ☐²

area of a quarter circle = $\frac{\square}{\square}$ ☐ ☐²

$A \approx \frac{1}{4}(\square)(\square)^2$ Replace π with ☐ and r with ☐.

= ☐ ft²

Area of region that is a rectangle:

area of a rectangle = ☐

$A = \square \cdot \square$ Replace b with ☐ and h with ☐.

= ☐ ft²

The area of the lawn is about ☐ ft² + ☐ ft² = ☐ ft².

You need to buy ☐ 3-lb bag(s) of grass seed.

Quick Check

1. Find the exact area of a circle with radius 50 in.

2. Find the approximate area of a circle with radius 6 mi.

3. Find the area of the shaded region to the nearest tenth.

[Figure: rectangle 10 cm × 5 cm with a semicircle of radius 2.5 cm cut out]

Daily Notetaking Guide   Algebra Readiness Lesson 10-3

Name_____ Class_____ Date_____

Lesson 10-4
Space Figures

Lesson Objectives
- Identify common space figures
- Construct nets

Vocabulary

A _____ is a three-dimensional figure.

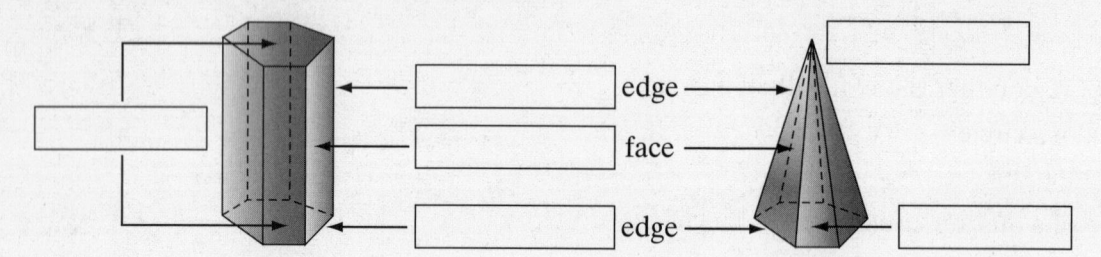

A _____ has two parallel bases that are congruent polygons and lateral faces that are parallelograms.

A pyramid has _____

The lateral faces are [   ].

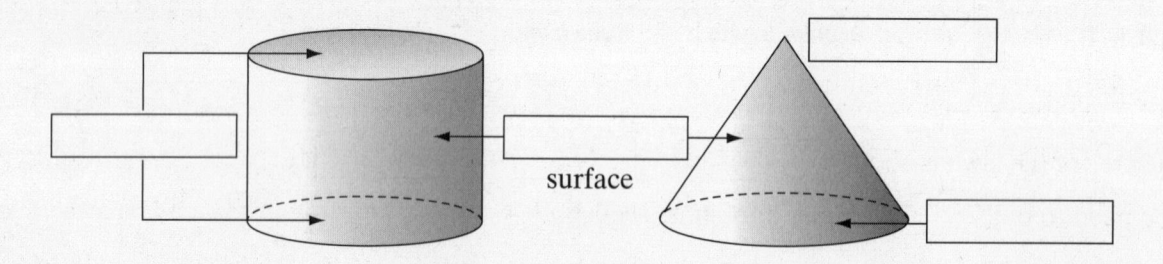

A _____ has two parallel bases that are congruent circles.

A cone has _____

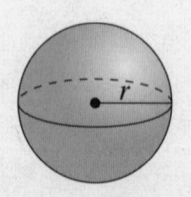

A _____ is the set of all points in space that are a given distance from a given point called the center.

A net is _____

Name_____ Class_____ Date _____

Examples

1 **Naming Space Figures** For each figure, describe the bases and name the figure.

a. 
The bases are [ ]. The figure is a [ ].

b. 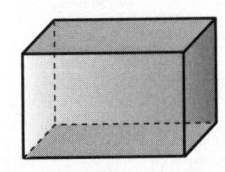
The bases are [ ].
The figure is a [ ].

2 **Naming Space Figures From Nets** Name the space figure you can form from each net.

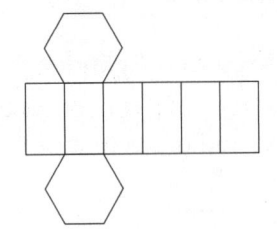

a. With two [ ] bases and [ ] sides, you can form a [ ].

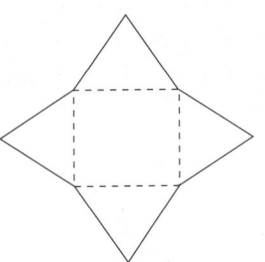

b. With a [ ] base and [ ] sides, you can form a [ ].

Quick Check

1. Name each figure.

   a.

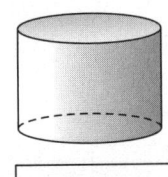

   b.

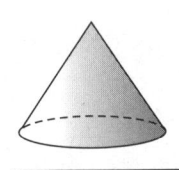

2. Name the space figure you can form from each net.

   a.

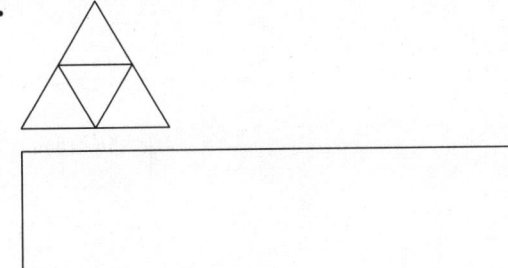

   b.

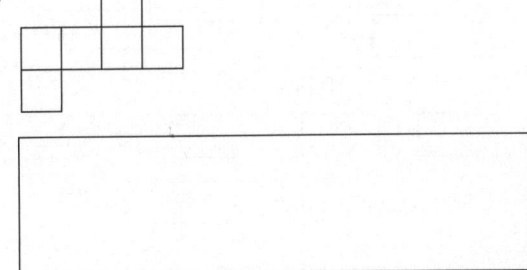

Daily Notetaking Guide   Algebra Readiness Lesson 10-4

Name_____ Class_____ Date_____

Lesson 10-5

Surface Area: Prisms and Cylinders

Lesson Objectives
- Find surface areas of prisms
- Find surface areas of cylinders

Take Note

Surface Area of a Prism

The lateral area of a prism is the product of the perimeter of the base and the height.

L.A. = ☐

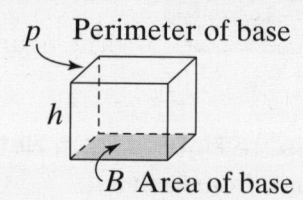

Surface Area of a Cylinder

The lateral area of a cylinder is the product of the circumference of the base and the height of the cylinder.

L.A. = ☐

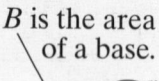

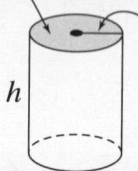

The surface area of a prism or a cylinder is the sum of the lateral area and the areas of the two bases.

S.A. = L.A. + ☐

_____ is the sum of the areas of the base(s) and the lateral faces of a space figure.

Lateral area (L.A.) of a prism is _____

Examples

1 **Finding Surface Area Using a Net** Find the surface area of the rectangular prism using a net.

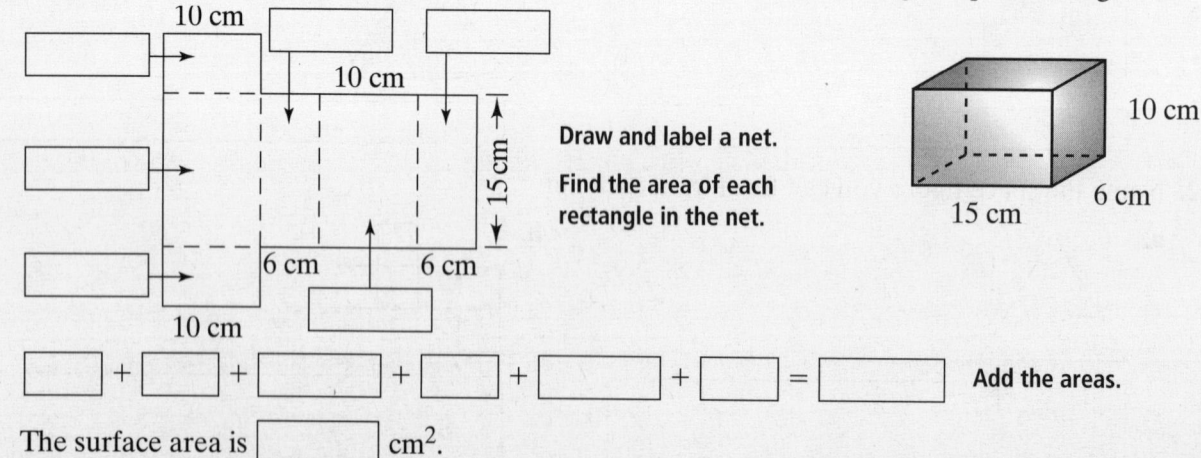

10 cm
10 cm
15 cm
6 cm   6 cm
10 cm

Draw and label a net.

Find the area of each rectangle in the net.

10 cm
15 cm   6 cm

☐ + ☐ + ☐ + ☐ + ☐ + ☐ = ☐   Add the areas.

The surface area is ☐ cm².

168 Algebra Readiness Lesson 10-5   Daily Notetaking Guide L1

Name _____ Class _____ Date _____

❷ **Finding Surface Area Using Formulas** Find the surface area of the cylindrical water tank.

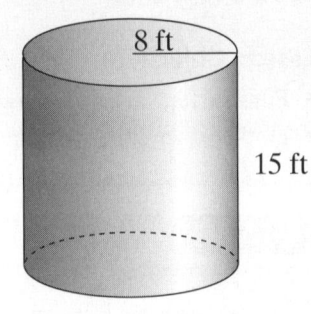

Step 1 Find the lateral area.

L.A. = ☐   Use the formula for lateral area.

≈ 2(3.14)(☐)(☐)

≈ ☐

Step 2 Find the surface area.

S.A. = ☐ + ☐   Use the formula for surface area.

= L.A. + 2(☐)

≈ ☐ + 2(3.14)(☐)^2

= ☐

The surface area of the water tank is about ☐ ft^2.

Quick Check

1. Find the surface area of each prism.

   a. 6 yd, 5 yd, 3 yd, 4 yd

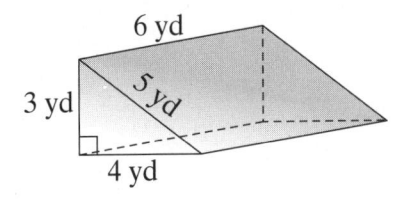

   b. 6 m, 3 m, 4 m

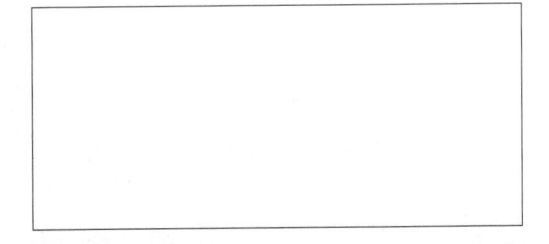

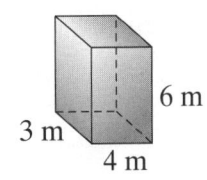

2. Find the surface area of a can with radius 5 cm and height 20 cm.

Daily Notetaking Guide — Algebra Readiness Lesson 10-5

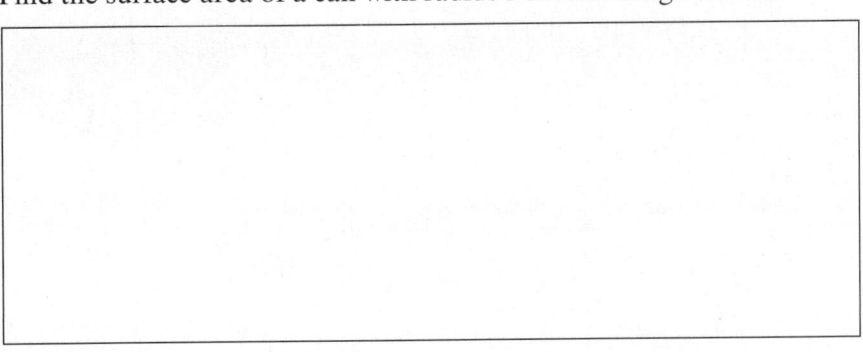

Name_____ Class_____ Date_____

Lesson 10-6

Surface Area: Pyramids, Cones, and Spheres

Lesson Objectives
- Find surface areas of pyramids
- Find surface areas of cones and spheres

Take Note

Surface Area of a Pyramid

The lateral area of a pyramid is one-half the product of the perimeter of the base and the slant height.

L.A. = $\frac{\square}{\square}\square\square$ S.A. = L.A. + $\square$

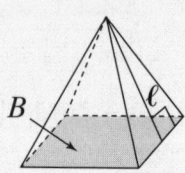

Surface Area of a Cone

The surface area of a cone is the sum of the lateral area and base area.

L.A. = $\square\square\square$ S.A. = L.A. + $\square$

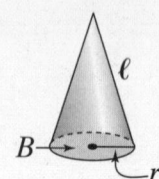

Surface Area of a Sphere

S.A. = $\square\square\square$

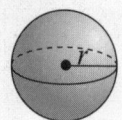

The slant height is _____

Examples

1 Finding Surface Area of a Pyramid Find the surface area of the square pyramid.

Step 1 Find the lateral area.

L.A. = $\frac{\square}{\square}\square$ Use the formula for lateral area.

= $\frac{1}{2} \cdot \square \cdot \square$ $p = 4(\square)$ and $\ell = \square$.

= 80

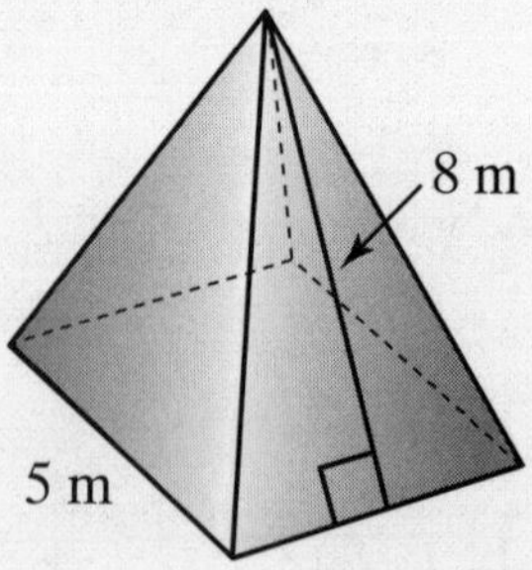

Step 2 Find the surface area.

S.A. = L.A. + B

= 80 + $\square$ Lateral area = $\square$ and $B = \square$.

= 80 + 25 = $\square$

The surface area of the pyramid is $\square$ m².

170 Algebra Readiness Lesson 10-6   Daily Notetaking Guide

Name_____ Class_____ Date _____

② Finding Surface Area of a Cone Find the surface area of the cone.

Step 1 Find the lateral area.

L.A. = $\boxed{}\boxed{}\boxed{}$ Use the formula for lateral area.

≈ (3.14)$\boxed{}$$\boxed{}$ $r =$ $\boxed{}$ and $\ell =$ $\boxed{}$.

≈ $\boxed{}$

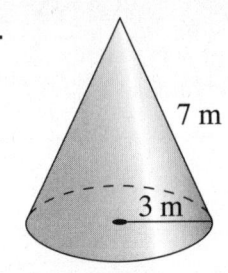

7 m

3 m

Step 2 Find the surface area.

S.A. = L.A. + B   Use the formula for surface area.

≈ $\boxed{}$ + (3.14)$\boxed{}^2$ L.A. ≈ $\boxed{}$ and $B = \pi\left(\boxed{}\right)^2$.

= 65.94 + 28.26

= $\boxed{}$

The surface area of the cone is about $\boxed{}$ m².

③ Finding Surface Area of a Sphere Earth has an approximate radius of 3,963 mi. What is the Earth's approximate surface area to the nearest 1,000 mi²? Assume the Earth is a sphere.

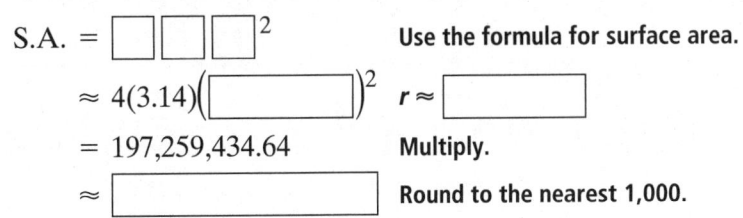

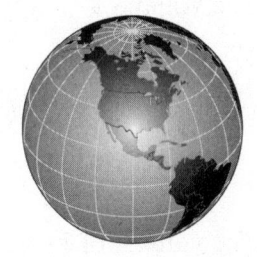

S.A. = $\boxed{}\boxed{}\boxed{}^2$ Use the formula for surface area.

≈ 4(3.14)$\boxed{}^2$ $r ≈$ $\boxed{}$

= 197,259,434.64   Multiply.

≈ $\boxed{}$ Round to the nearest 1,000.

⟵ 7,926 mi ⟶

The surface area of the Earth is about $\boxed{}$ mi².

Quick Check

1. A pyramid has a square base with edge 20 ft. The slant height is 8 ft. Find its surface area.

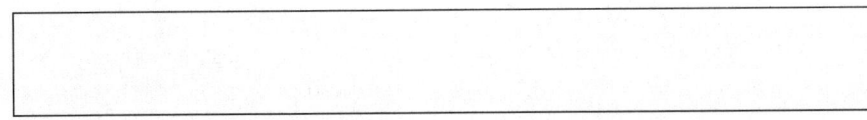

2. A cone has lateral height 39 ft and radius 7 ft. Find its surface area.

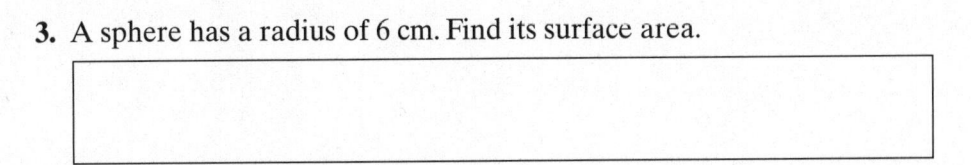

3. A sphere has a radius of 6 cm. Find its surface area.

Daily Notetaking Guide   Algebra Readiness Lesson 10-6   **171**

Name_____ Class_____ Date_____

Lesson 10-7

Volume: Prisms and Cylinders

Lesson Objectives
- Find volumes of prisms
- Find volumes of cylinders

Take Note

Volume of a Prism

The volume V of a prism is the product of the base area B and height h.

$V = \boxed{}\boxed{}$

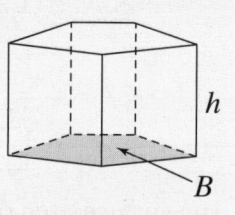

Volume of a Cylinder

The volume V of a cylinder is the product of the base area B and height h.

$V = \boxed{}\boxed{}$

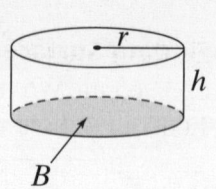

The volume of a three-dimensional figure is _____

_____

A _____ is the space occupied by a cube with sides one unit long.

Examples

1. Finding Volume of a Prism Find the volume of the triangular prism.

$V = \boxed{}$ Use the formula for volume.

$= \boxed{} \cdot 20 \qquad B = \frac{1}{2} \cdot \boxed{} \cdot \boxed{} = \boxed{}$ cm^2

$= \boxed{}$ Simplify.

9 cm
14 cm
20 cm

The volume is $\boxed{}$ cm^3.

172 Algebra Readiness Lesson 10-7

Name_____ Class_____ Date _____

❷ Finding Volume of a Cylinder Find the volume of the juice can to the nearest cubic centimeter.

3.4 cm

16 cm

$V = \boxed{}$ Use the formula for volume.

$V = \boxed{}\, h$ $B = \boxed{}$

$\approx 3.14 \cdot \boxed{}^2 \cdot \boxed{}$ Replace r with $\boxed{}$ and h with $\boxed{}$.

$= \boxed{}$ Simplify.

The volume is about $\boxed{}$ cm^3.

Quick Check

1. Find the volume of the triangular prism.

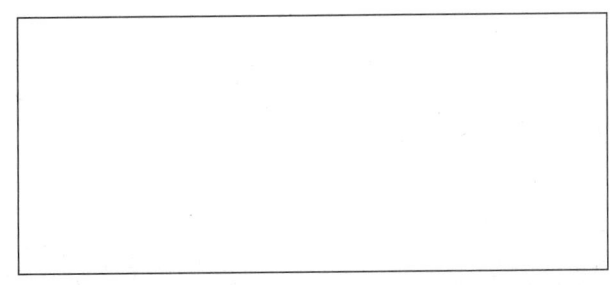

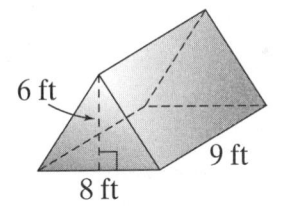

   6 ft
   9 ft
   8 ft

2. Find the volume of the cylinder to the nearest cubic foot.

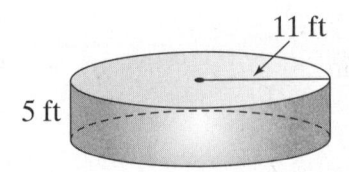

   11 ft
   5 ft

Daily Notetaking Guide   Algebra Readiness Lesson 10-7   173

Name_____ Class_____ Date_____

Lesson 10-8

Reasoning Strategy: Make a Model

Lesson Objective
- Make a model

Example

① Packaging A can company rolls rectangular pieces of metal that measure 8 in. by 10 in. to make the sides of cans. Which height, 8 in. or 10 in., will make a can with the greater volume?

8 in.
10 in.

Understand the Problem

1. What is the goal of the problem?

2. What information do you have to help you build a model?

Make and Carry Out a Plan

You must find the height that gives you the greatest volume. Build two cans using 8 in-by-10 in. pieces of paper. You do not need to make the bases, just the sides.

10 in.

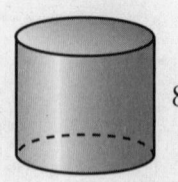

8 in.

174 Algebra Readiness Lesson 10-8   Daily Notetaking Guide

3. Measure your models to find approximate radii.
   a. Radius of 10-in. = high can is approximately [ ] in.
   b. Radius of 8-in. = high can is approximately [ ] in.

   Find the volumes.

   $V = $ [ ] $V = $ [ ]
   $\approx (3.14)([\ ])^2([\ ])$ $\approx (3.14)([\ ])^2([\ ])$
   $= $ [ ] $= $ [ ]

   The volume is [ ] in.³   The volume is [ ] in.³

   The can with the greater volume is the can whose height is [ ].

   Check the Answer

   A table is another way to organize your information and solve the problem.

4. List the height of each can, and then find the radius and the volume of the can.

Height	Radius	Volume
8 in.		
10 in.		

Quick Check

1. Suppose the company uses rectangular pieces of metal that measure 7 in. by 9 in. to form the cans. Build two models to determine which height, 7 in. or 9 in., will make the can with greater volume. Use the table below to organize your information.

Height	Radius	Volume

   The can with the greater volume is the can whose height is [ ].

Daily Notetaking Guide   Algebra Readiness Lesson 10-8

Name_____ Class_____ Date_____

Lesson 10-9
Volume: Pyramids, Cones, and Spheres

Lesson Objectives
- Find volumes of pyramids and cones
- Find volumes of spheres

Take Note

Volume of a Cone and of a Pyramid

The volume V of a cone or a pyramid is $\frac{1}{3}$ the product of the base area B and the height h.

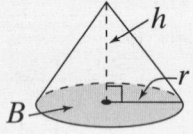

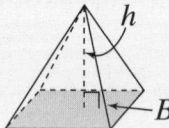

$V = \boxed{}$

Volume of a Sphere

The volume V of a sphere with radius r is $\frac{4}{3}\pi$ times the cube of the radius.

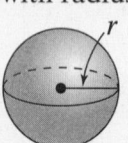

$V = \boxed{}$

Examples

1 **Finding Volume of a Cone** Find the volume of the cone.

$V = \dfrac{\boxed{}}{\boxed{}}$ Use the formula for volume.

$= \dfrac{1}{3} \boxed{} h$ $B = \boxed{}$

$\approx \dfrac{1}{3}(3.14)(\boxed{})^2(\boxed{})$ Replace r with $\boxed{}$, and h with $\boxed{}$. Use 3.14 for π.

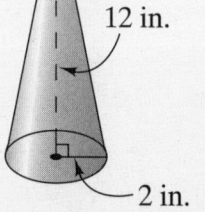

$= \boxed{}$ Simplify.

The volume of the cone is about $\boxed{}$ in.^{3}.

12 in.

2 in.

176 *Algebra Readiness* Lesson 10-9

Name _____ Class _____ Date _____

❷ Finding Volume of a Pyramid Find the volume of the square pyramid.

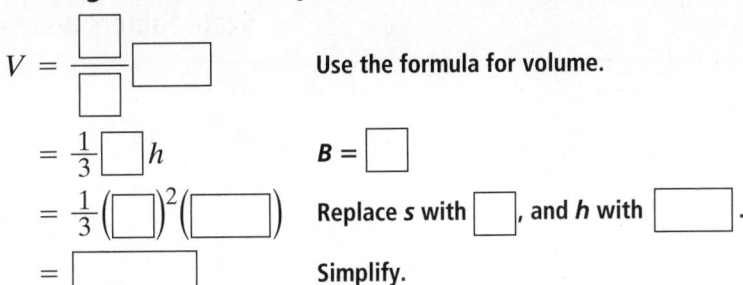

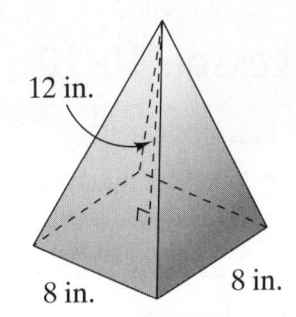

$V = \dfrac{\square}{\square}\square$ Use the formula for volume.

$= \dfrac{1}{3}\square h$ $B = \square$

$= \dfrac{1}{3}(\square)^2(\square)$ Replace s with $\square$, and h with $\square$.

$= \square$ Simplify.

The volume of the pyramid is $\square$ in.^{3}.

12 in.

8 in.   8 in.

❸ Finding Volume of a Sphere Earth has an average radius of 3,963 mi. What is Earth's approximate volume to the nearest 1,000,000 mi^3? Assume that Earth is a sphere.

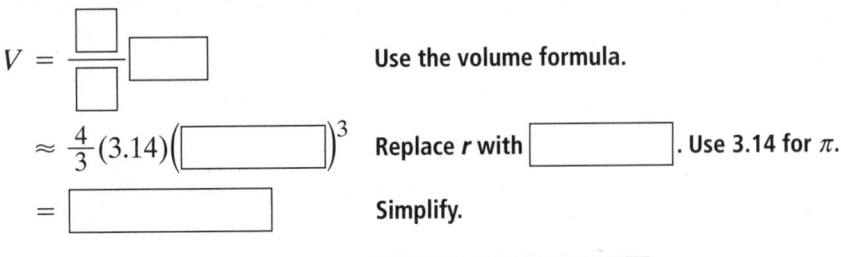

$V = \dfrac{\square}{\square}\square$ Use the volume formula.

$\approx \dfrac{4}{3}(3.14)(\square)^3$ Replace r with $\square$. Use 3.14 for π.

$= \square$ Simplify.

The volume of Earth is about $\square$ mi^3.

Quick Check

1. Find the volume, to the nearest cubic unit, of a cone with height 5 cm and radius of base 2 cm.

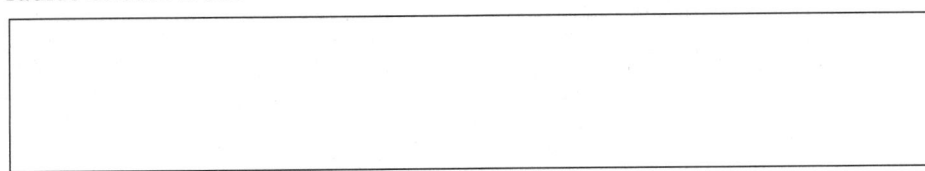

2. Find the volume of a square pyramid that has a side of 5 ft and a height of 20 ft.

3. Find the volume of each sphere to the nearest whole number. Use 3.14 for π.

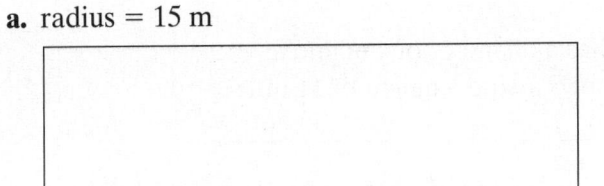

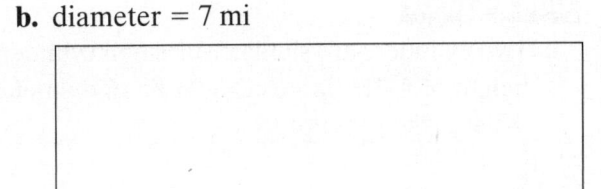

   a. radius = 15 m

   b. diameter = 7 mi

Daily Notetaking Guide   Algebra Readiness Lesson 10-9

Name_____ Class_____ Date_____

Lesson 10-10

Scale Factors and Solids

Lesson Objectives
- Find dimensions of similar solids
- Find surface areas and volumes of similar solids

Take Note

Surface Area and Volume of Similar Solids

If the ratio of the corresponding dimensions of similar solids is $\frac{a}{b}$, then

- the ratio of their surface areas is $\frac{a^2}{b^2}$ and
- the ratio of their volumes is $\frac{a^3}{b^3}$.

Similar solids _____

Scale factor _____

Example

1 **Finding Dimensions of a Similar Solid** At an ice cream shop, the small and large cones are similar. The small cone has a radius of 3 cm and a height of 12 cm. The large cone has a radius of 5 cm. What is the height of the large ice cream cone? Let h = the height of the large cone. Use corresponding parts to write a proportion.

$\dfrac{h}{\square} = \dfrac{\square}{\square}$ ← dimensions of large cone
　　　　　　　　　← dimensions of small cone

$\square \times \dfrac{h}{12} = \dfrac{5}{3} \times 12$ ← Multiply each side by $\square$.

$h = \dfrac{\square}{\square}$ ← Simplify.

$= \square$

The height of the large cone is $\square$.

Quick Check

1. Two cylinders are similar. The small cylinder has a diameter of 4 m and a height of h. The large cylinder has a diameter of 5 m and a height of 11 m. What is the value of h?

_____

178 *Algebra Readiness* Lesson 10-10

Name_____ Class_____ Date _____

Example

❷ **Surface Area and Volume of Similar Solids** A square pyramid has a surface area of 39 cm² and a volume of 12 cm³. The pyramid is similar to a larger pyramid, but its side length is $\frac{2}{3}$ that of the larger pyramid. Find the surface area and volume of the larger pyramid.

The ratio of the side lengths is $\frac{2}{3}$, so the ratio of the surface areas is $\frac{2^2}{3^2}$, or $\frac{\square}{\square}$.

$\dfrac{\text{surface area of the small pyramid}}{\text{surface area of the large pyramid}} = \dfrac{\square}{\square}$ ← Write a proportion.

$\dfrac{\square}{S} = \dfrac{\square}{\square}$ ← Substitute the surface area of the small pyramid.

$39 \cdot \square = S \cdot \square$ ← Multiply.

$S = \square$ ← Simplify.

The surface area of the large pyramid is $\square$.

If the ratio of the side lengths is $\frac{2}{3}$, the ratio of the volumes is $\frac{2^3}{3^3}$, or $\frac{\square}{\square}$.

$\dfrac{\text{volume of the small pyramid}}{\text{volume of the large pyramid}} = \dfrac{\square}{\square}$ ← Write a proportion.

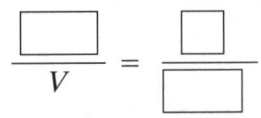

$\dfrac{\square}{V} = \dfrac{\square}{\square}$ ← Substitute the volume of the small pyramid.

$12 \cdot \square = V \cdot \square$ ← Multiply.

$V = \square$ ← Simplify.

The volume of the large pyramid is $\square$.

Quick Check

2. A box has a surface area of about 54 in.² and a volume of about 27 in.³. The edge lengths of the box are about $\frac{1}{3}$ of the edge lengths of a larger box. Find the surface area and volume of the larger box.

Daily Notetaking Guide — Algebra Readiness Lesson 10-10

Name_____ Class_____ Date_____

Lesson 11-1
Square Roots and Irrational Numbers

Lesson Objectives
- Find square roots of numbers
- Classify real numbers

Vocabulary

A _____ is the square of an integer.

Finding a square root is _____
_____

An _____ is a number that cannot be written as the ratio of two integers. The decimal form of an irrational number neither terminates nor repeats.

Examples

1 **Simplifying Square Roots** Simplify each square root.

a. $\sqrt{144}$

$\sqrt{144} = \boxed{}$

b. $-\sqrt{81}$

$-\sqrt{81} = \boxed{}$

2 **Estimating a Square Root** You can use the formula $d = \sqrt{1.5h}$ to estimate the distance d, in miles, to a horizon line when your eyes are h feet above the ground. Estimate the distance to the horizon seen by a lifeguard whose eyes are 20 feet above the ground.

$d = \sqrt{1.5h}$ Use the formula.

$d = \sqrt{1.5(\boxed{})}$ Replace h with $\boxed{}$.

$d = \sqrt{30}$ Multiply.

$\sqrt{25} < \sqrt{30} < \sqrt{36}$ Find the perfect squares close to 30.

$\sqrt{25} = \boxed{}$ Find the square root of the closest perfect square.

The lifeguard can see about $\boxed{}$ miles to the horizon.

Name _____ Class _____ Date _____

Example

3 Identifying Irrational Numbers Identify each number as rational or irrational. Explain.

a. $\sqrt{49}$

b. 0.16

c. $\sqrt{3}$

d. 0.3333…

e. $-\sqrt{15}$

f. 12.69

Quick Check

1. Simplify each square root.

   a. $\sqrt{100}$ ☐   b. $-\sqrt{16}$ ☐

2. Estimate to the nearest integer.

   a. $\sqrt{27}$ b. $-\sqrt{72}$

3. Identify each number as rational or irrational. Explain.

   a. $\sqrt{2}$ b. $-\sqrt{81}$

   c. 0.53   d. $\sqrt{42}$

Daily Notetaking Guide — Algebra Readiness Lesson 11-1

Name_____ Class_____ Date_____

Lesson 11-2
The Pythagorean Theorem

Lesson Objectives
- Use the Pythagorean Theorem
- Identify right triangles

Take Note

Pythagorean Theorem
In any right triangle, the sum of the squares of the lengths of the legs is equal to the square of the length of the hypotenuse.

$$\square^2 + \square^2 = \square^2$$

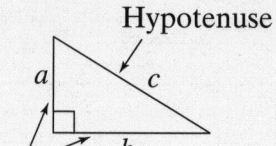

The legs of a right triangle are _____

_____

The _____ is the longest side of a right triangle and is opposite the right angle.

Example

1 Using the Pythagorean Theorem Find c, the length of the hypotenuse.

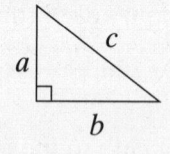

$c^2 = \square^2 + \square^2$ Use the Pythagorean Theorem.

$c^2 = \square^2 + \square^2$ Replace a with $\square$ and b with $\square$.

$c^2 = \square$ Simplify.

$c^2 = \sqrt{1{,}225} = \square$ Find the positive square root of each side.

The length of the hypotenuse is $\square$ cm.

Quick Check

1. The lengths of two sides of a right triangle are given. Find the length of the third side.

   a. legs: 3 ft and 4 ft

   b. leg: 12 m; hypotenuse: 15 m

182 Algebra Readiness Lesson 11-2

Examples

2 **Finding an Approximate Length** In a right triangle, the lengths of the legs are each 10 ft. What is the length of the hypotenuse, to the nearest tenth of a foot?

$c^2 = \boxed{}^2 + \boxed{}^2$ Use the Pythagorean Theorem.

$c^2 = \boxed{}^2 + \boxed{}^2$ Replace a with $\boxed{}$, and b with 10.

$c^2 = \boxed{} + \boxed{}$ Square 10.

$c^2 = \boxed{}$ Add.

$c = \sqrt{\boxed{}}$ Find the positive square root.

$c \approx \boxed{}$ Round to the nearest tenth.

The length of the hypotenuse is about $\boxed{}$ ft.

3 **Finding a Right Triangle** Is a triangle with sides 10 cm, 24 cm, and 26 cm a right triangle?

$a^2 + b^2 = c^2$ Write the equation for the Pythagorean Theorem.

$\boxed{}^2 + \boxed{}^2 \stackrel{?}{=} \boxed{}^2$ Replace a and b with the shorter lengths and c with the longest length.

$\boxed{} + \boxed{} \stackrel{?}{=} \boxed{}$ Simplify.

$\boxed{} = 676$ ✔   Add.

The triangle $\boxed{}$ a right triangle.

Quick Check

2. In a right triangle, the length of the hypotenuse is 15 m and the length of a leg is 8 m. What is the length of the other leg, to the nearest tenth of a meter?

3. Can you form a right triangle with the three lengths given? Explain.

   a. 7 in., 8 in., $\sqrt{113}$ b. 5 mm, 6 mm, 10 mm

Name_____ Class_____ Date_____

Lesson 11-3

Distance and Midpoint Formulas

Lesson Objectives
- Find the distance between two points using the Distance Formula
- Find the midpoint of a segment using the Midpoint Formula

Take Note

Distance Formula

The distance d between any two points (x_1, y_1) and (x_2, y_2) is

$d = \sqrt{(\Box - \Box)^2 + (\Box - \Box)^2}$

Midpoint Formula

The midpoint M of a line segment with endpoints $A(x_1, y_1)$ and $B(x_2, y_2)$ is

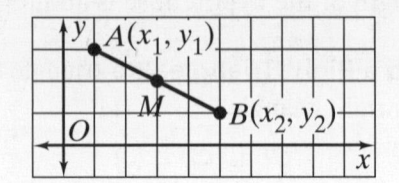

$M\left(\dfrac{\Box + x_2}{2}, \dfrac{\Box + y_2}{2}\right)$

The midpoint of segment $\overline{AB}$ is _____

_____

Example

1 Using the Distance Formula Find the distance between $T(3, -2)$ and $V(8, 3)$.

$d = \sqrt{(x_2 - x_1)^2 + (y_2 - y_1)^2}$ Use the Distance Formula.

$d = \sqrt{(\Box - \Box)^2 + (\Box - (\Box))^2}$ Replace (x_2, y_2) with $(\Box, \Box)$ and (x_1, y_1) with $(\Box, \Box)$.

$d = \sqrt{\Box^2 + \Box^2}$ Simplify.

$d = \sqrt{\Box}$ Find the exact distance.

$d \approx \Box$ Round to the nearest tenth.

The distance between T and V is about $\Box$ units.

Quick Check

1. Find the distance between the two points in each pair. Round to the nearest tenth.

   a. $(3, 8), (2, 4)$ **b.** $(10, -3), (1, 0)$

184 Algebra Readiness Lesson 11-3   Daily Notetaking Guide L1

Name _____ Class _____ Date _____

Example

2 **Finding the Midpoint of a Segment** Find the midpoint of $\overline{TV}$.

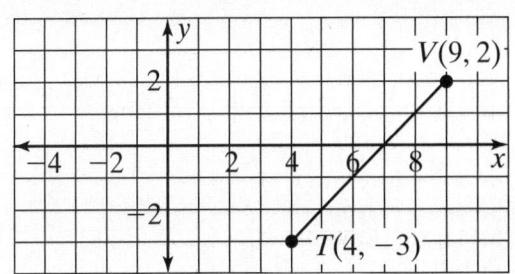

$\left(\dfrac{x_1 + x_2}{2}, \dfrac{y_1 + y_2}{2}\right)$ Use the Midpoint Formula.

$= \left(\dfrac{\square + \square}{2}, \dfrac{\square + \square}{2}\right)$ Replace (x_1, y_1) with $(\square, \square)$ and (x_2, y_2) with $(\square, \square)$.

$= \left(\dfrac{\square}{2}, \dfrac{\square}{2}\right)$ Simplify the numerators.

$= \left(\dfrac{\square}{\square}, \dfrac{\square}{\square}\right)$ Write the fractions in simplest form.

The coordinates of the midpoint of $\overline{TV}$ are $(\square, \square)$.

Quick Check

2. Find the midpoint of each segment.

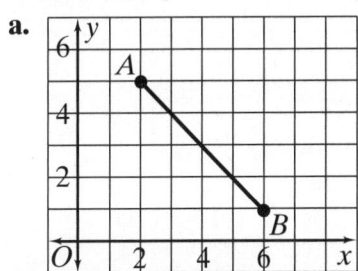

   a.

   b. Find the midpoint of each side of $\triangle DEF$.

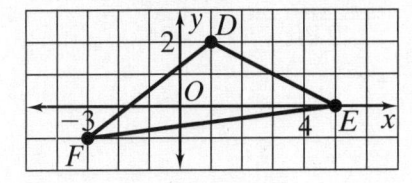

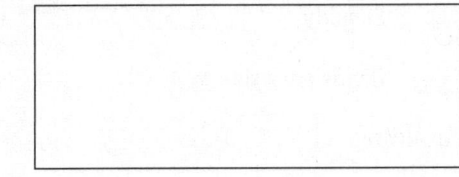

Daily Notetaking Guide   Algebra Readiness Lesson 11-3   185

Name_____ Class_____ Date_____

Lesson 11-4
Write a Proportion

Lesson Objective
- Write a proportion from similar triangles

Example

1 At a given time of day, a building of unknown height casts a shadow that is 24 feet long. At the same time of day, a post that is 8 feet tall casts a shadow that is 4 feet long. What is the height x of the building?

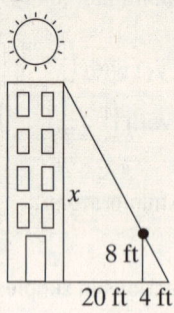

Understand the Problem

1. What information is given?

2. What are you asked to find?

Make and Carry Out a Plan

Since the triangles are similar, and you know three lengths, writing and solving a proportion is a good strategy to use. It is helpful to draw the triangles as separate figures.

Write a proportion using the legs of the similar triangles.

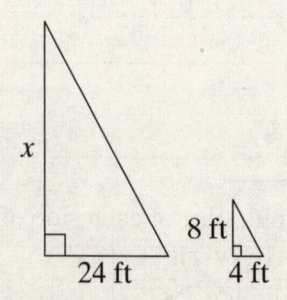

$\dfrac{4}{24} = \dfrac{\boxed{}}{\boxed{}}$ Write a proportion.

$\boxed{}x = \boxed{}(\boxed{})$ Write cross products.

$4x = \boxed{}$ Simplify.

$x = \boxed{}$ Divide each side by 4.

The height of the building is $\boxed{}$ ft.

186 *Algebra Readiness* Lesson 11-4

Name _____ Class _____ Date _____

Example
Check the Answer

Solving problems that involve indirect measurement often makes use of figures that overlap.

Quick Check

1. Use the diagram of the building in Example 1 to answer the following questions.
   a. Which segments overlap?

   b. A common error students make is to use part of a side in a proportion. For example, some students might think $\frac{4}{20}$ is equal to $\frac{8}{x}$. How does drawing the triangles as separate figures help you avoid this error?

Daily Notetaking Guide — Algebra Readiness Lesson 11-4 — 187

Name_____ Class_____ Date_____

Lesson 11-5

Graphing Nonlinear Functions

Lesson Objectives
- Graph quadratic functions
- Graph absolute value functions

Vocabulary

A _____ is a function based on squaring the input variable.

A cubic function is _____
_____

Examples

1 Graphing a Quadratic Function For the function $y = -x^2$, make a table with integer values of x from -2 to 2. Then graph the function.

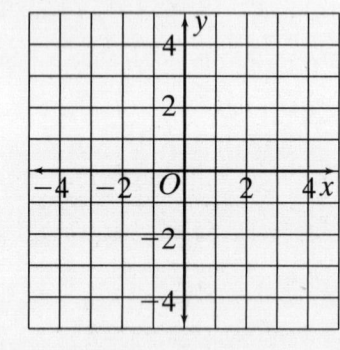

x	$-x^2 = y$	(x, y)
-2	$-(-2)^2 = \square$	$(-2, \square)$
-1	$-(-1)^2 = -1$	$(-1, -1)$
0	$-(\square)^2 = 0$	$(\square, 0)$
1	$-(1)^2 = \square$	$(1, \square)$
2	$-(2)^2 = -4$	$(2, -4)$

2 Graphing a Cubic Function Graph the function $y = x^3$.

x	$x^3 = y$	(x, y)
-2	$(-2)^3 = \square$	$(-2, \square)$
-1	$(-1)^3 = -1$	$(-1, -1)$
0	$(0)^3 = 0$	$(0, 0)$
1	$(1)^3 = 1$	$(1, 1)$
2	$(2)^3 = \square$	$(2, \square)$

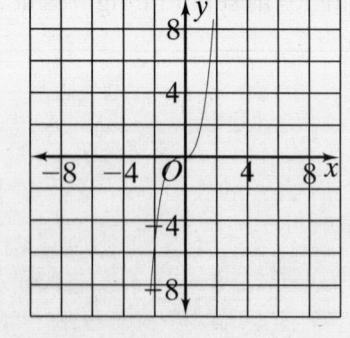

Algebra Readiness Lesson 11-5

Name _____ Class _____ Date _____

Quick Check

1. For each function, make a table with integer values of x from -2 to 2. Then graph each function.

    a. $y = -2x^2$

x	$-2x^2 = y$	(x, y)
-2		
-1		
0		
1		
2		

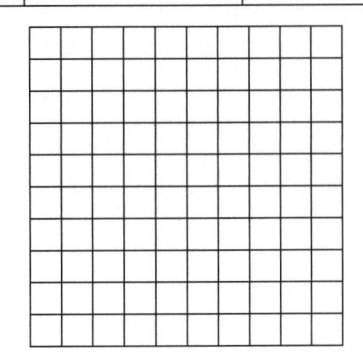

    b. $y = 3x^3$

x	$y = 3x^3$	(x, y)
-2		
-1		
0		
1		
2		

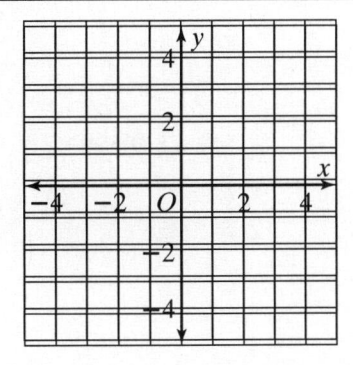

Name_____ Class_____ Date_____

Lesson 12-1

Mean, Median, and Mode

Lesson Objectives
- Find mean, median, and mode of a set of data
- Choose the best measure of central tendency

Vocabulary

Three measures of central tendency are ☐, ☐, and ☐.

A mean is _____

_____

A median is _____

_____

If there is an even number of data values, the median is _____

_____

A mode is _____

An outlier is _____

_____

Examples

1 Finding the Mean, Median, and Mode Six elementary students are participating in a one-week Readathon to raise money for a good cause. Use the graph to find the (a) mean, (b) median, and the (c) mode of the data if you leave out the number of pages Latana has read.

a. Mean = $\dfrac{\text{sum of data values}}{\text{number of data values}}$

= $\dfrac{\boxed{} + \boxed{} + \boxed{} + \boxed{} + \boxed{}}{5}$

= $\dfrac{\boxed{}}{5}$

= $\boxed{}$

The mean is ☐.

b. Median: 40 45 48 50 50   Write the data in order.

The median is the ☐ number, or ☐.

c. Mode: Find the data value that occurs most often.

40 45 48 |50 50|

The mode is ☐.

Readathon (Pages Read): Nick 40, Bettina 45, Kyle 48, Larry 50, Marita 50, Latana 59

190 Algebra Readiness Lesson 12-1

❷ Identifying Outliers Use the data 7%, 4%, 10%, 33%, 11%, 12%.

a. Which data value is an outlier? The data value [ ] is an outlier.

It is an outlier because it is much [ ] than the other data values.

b. How does the outlier affect the mean?

$\frac{77}{6} \approx$ [ ]   Find the mean with the outlier.

$\frac{44}{5} \approx$ [ ]   Find the mean without the outlier.

[ ] − [ ] = [ ]

The outlier raises the mean by about [ ] points.

❸ Identifying the Best Measure Which measure of central tendency best describes each situation? Explain.

a. the monthly amount of rain for a year

[ ]; since the average monthly amount of rain for a year is not likely to have an outlier, [ ] is the appropriate measure. When the data have no outliers, use the [ ].

b. the most popular color of shirt

[ ]; since the data are not numerical, the [ ] is the appropriate measure. When determining the most frequently chosen item, or when the data are not numerical, use the [ ].

c. time student leaves home to get to school

[ ]; since a few students may leave much earlier or much later than most of the students, the [ ] is the appropriate measure. When an outlier may significantly influence the mean, use the [ ].

Quick Check

1. Find the mean, median, and mode of each group of data.

    a. 2.3   4.3   3.2   2.9   2.7   2.3

    mean = [ ], median = [ ], mode = [ ]

    b. $20 $26 $27 $28 $21 $42 $18 $20

    mean = [ ], median = [ ], mode = [ ]

2. Find an outlier in each group of data below and tell how it affects the mean.

    a. 9   10   12   13   8   9   31   9   b. 1   17.5   18   19.5   16   17.5

Name_____ Class_____ Date_____

Lesson 12-2

Frequency Tables, Line Plots, and Histograms

Lesson Objectives
- Display data in frequency tables and line plots
- Display data in histograms

Vocabulary

A frequency table is a data display that _____

_____

A line plot is a data display that _____

_____

The range of the data is _____

_____

Example

1 Using a Line Plot A survey asked 22 students how many hours of TV they watched daily. The results are below. Display the data in a frequency table. Then make a line plot.

| 1 | 3 | 4 | 3 | 1 | 1 | 2 | 3 | 4 | 1 | 3 |
| 2 | 2 | 1 | 4 | 2 | 1 | 2 | 3 | 2 | 4 | 3 |

List the numbers of hours in order.   Use a tally mark for each result.   Count the tally marks and record the frequency.

Number	Tally	Frequency
1	⊮⊮ I	6

For a line plot, follow the steps ①, ②, and ③.

③ Write a title that describes the data.

② Mark an **X** for each response.

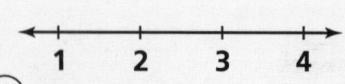

① Draw a number line with the choices below it.

   1 2 3 4

Quick Check

1. Display the data below in a frequency table. Then make a line plot.

10 12 13 15 10 11 14 13 10 11 11 12 10 10 15

Number	Tally	Frequency

Name _____ Class _____ Date _____

Example

② Displaying Data in a Histogram Twenty-one judges were asked how many cases they were trying on Monday. The frequency table below shows their responses. Display the data in a histogram. Then find the range.

"How many cases are you trying?"

Number	Frequency
0	3
1	5
2	4
3	5
4	4

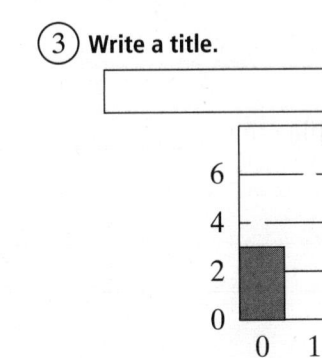

For a histogram, follow the steps ①, ②, and ③.

③ Write a title.

② Draw bars equal in height to the frequency.

① Label each axis.

The greatest value in the data set is ☐ and the least value is ☐.
The range is ☐ − ☐ or ☐.

Quick Check

2. **a.** Display the data below in a histogram. Then find the range.
   Miles from home to the mall:
   2, 4, 3, 7, 3, 1, 4, 2, 2, 6, 3, 5, 1, 8, 3

   b. What is the range of the data below?
   Prices of a gallon of regular gas at different gas stations:
   $1.48, $1.32, $1.30, $1.35, $1.41, $1.29, $1.32, $1.43, $1.36

Name_____ Class_____ Date_____

Lesson 12-3   Box-and-Whisker Plots

Lesson Objectives
- Make box-and-whisker plots
- Analyze data in box-and-whisker plots

Vocabulary

A box-and-whisker plot is a data display that _____
_____

Quartiles _____

The median is _____

Example

1 **Making a Box-and-Whisker Plot** The data below represent the wingspans in centimeters of captured birds. Make a box-and-whisker plot.

    61 35 61 22 33 29 40 62 21 49 72 75 28 21 54

Step 1 Arrange the data in order from least to greatest. Find the median.

☐ ☐ ☐ ☐ ☐ ☐ ☐ ☐ ☐ ☐ ☐ ☐ ☐ ☐ ☐

Step 2 Find the lower quartile and upper quartile, which are the medians of the lower and upper halves.

    lower quartile ☐   upper quartile ☐

Step 3 Draw a number line. Mark the least and greatest values, the median, and the quartiles. Draw a box from the first to the third quartile. Mark the median with a vertical segment. Draw whiskers from the box to the least and greatest values.

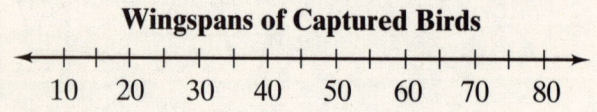

    Wingspans of Captured Birds

    10 20 30 40 50 60 70 80

Quick Check

1. Draw a box-and-whisker plot for the distances of migration of birds (thousands of miles): 5, 2.5, 6, 8, 9, 2, 1, 4, 6.2, 18, 7.

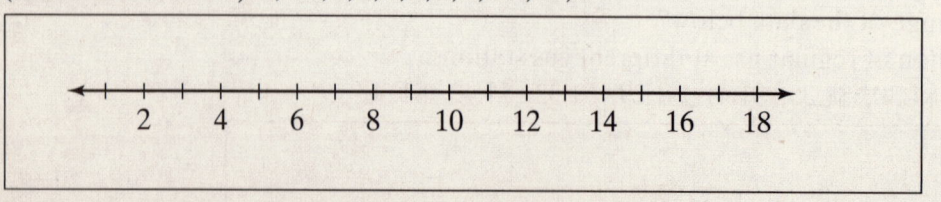

    2 4 6 8 10 12 14 16 18

Name_____ Class_____ Date _____

Example

❷ **Using a Box-and-Whisker Plot to Draw Conclusions** The plots below compare the percents of students who were eligible to those who participated in extracurricular activities in one school from 1992 to 2002. What conclusions can you draw?

Percents of Students Who Were Eligible and Participated in Activities from 1992 to 2002

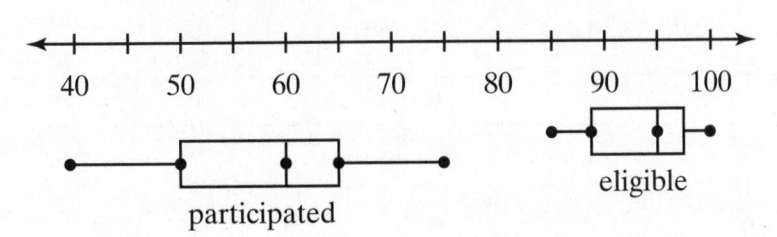

About [ ] of the students were eligible to participate in extracurricular activities. Around [ ] of the students did participate. A little less than [ ] of the eligible students participated in extracurricular activities.

Quick Check

2. Use the box-and-whisker plots below. What conclusions can you draw about the heights of Olympic basketball players?

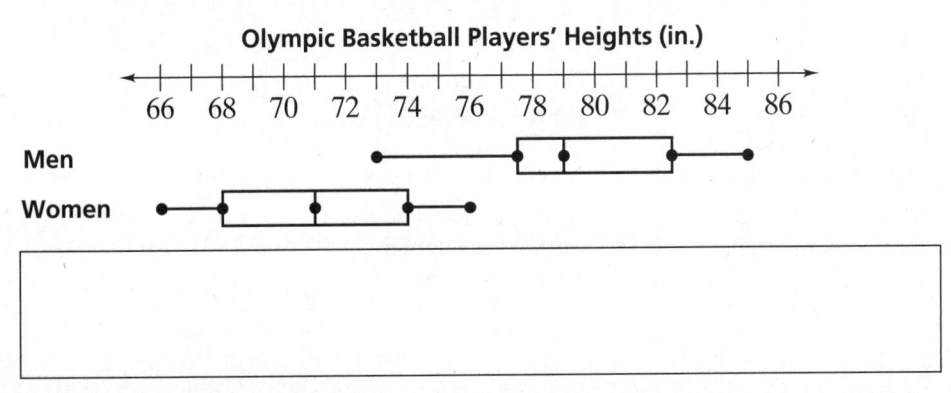

3. Compare annual video sales and CD sales by making two box-and-whisker plots below one number line.
   videos (millions of units): 28, 24, 15, 21, 22, 16, 22, 30, 24, 17
   CDs (millions of units) 16, 17, 22, 16, 18, 24, 15 16, 25, 18

Daily Notetaking Guide — Algebra Readiness Lesson 12-3

Name_____ Class_____ Date_____

Lesson 12-4

Stem-and-Leaf Plots

Lesson Objective	
To represent and interpret data using stem-and-leaf plots	

Vocabulary

A stem-and-leaf plot is _____

_____

Example

1 Making Stem-and-Leaf Plots Make a stem-and-leaf plot for the data.

51, 56, 67, 44, 50, 63, 65, 58, 49, 51, 66, 59, 63, 47

Step 1 Choose the stems. The least value is [ ]; the greatest value is [ ]. Leaves are single digits, so use the first digits as the [ ]. The stems in this case are [ ], [ ], and [ ].

Step 2 Draw the stem-and-leaf plot. Include a key.

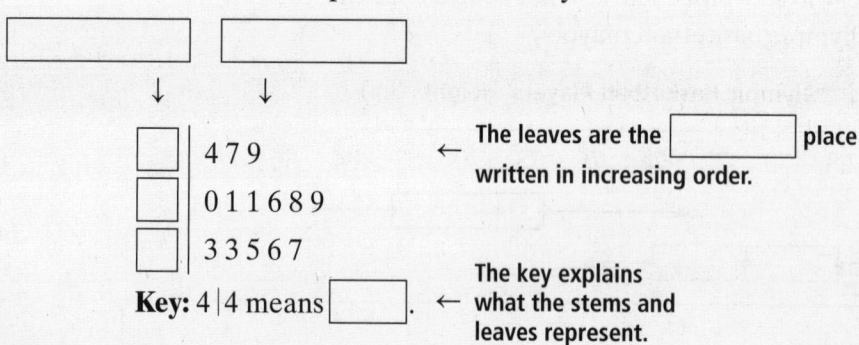

[ ]   [ ]
 ↓   ↓

[ ] | 4 7 9
[ ] | 0 1 1 6 8 9
[ ] | 3 3 5 6 7

← The leaves are the [ ] place written in increasing order.

Key: 4 | 4 means [ ].   ← The key explains what the stems and leaves represent.

Quick Check

1. Below are the monthly high temperatures for Death Valley, California. Make a stem-and-leaf plot for the data.

   87 91 101 111 120 125 134 126 120 113 97 86

Algebra Readiness Lesson 12-4   Daily Notetaking Guide

Name _____ Class _____ Date _____

Example

2 Using Back-to-Back Stem-and-Leaf Plots Compare the number of basketball and baseball cards using the mode of each data set.

Basketball and Baseball Cards

```
Basketball     Baseball
     9 9 8 | 1 |
   4 2 1 0 | 2 | 8 9
           | 3 | 1 2 2 3 4
```

Key: means ☐ ← 4|2|9 → means ☐

The mode for basketball cards is ☐ cards, while the mode for baseball cards is ☐ cards. This measure of central tendency gives the impression that the number of baseball cards is ☐ than the number of basketball cards.

Quick Check

2. Compare the city mileage to the highway mileage using the mean and median.

New Car Mileage (mi/gal)

```
  City        Highway
 9 8 8 | 1 |
 7 4 2 | 2 | 4 5 7 8
     0 | 3 | 3 3
       | 4 | 0
```

Key: means 27 ← 7|2|8 → means 28

Daily Notetaking Guide   Algebra Readiness Lesson 12-4   **197**

Name_____ Class_____ Date_____

Lesson 12-5

Scatter Plots

Lesson Objectives
- Interpret and draw scatter plots
- Use scatter plots to find trends

Vocabulary

A scatter plot is _____

_____

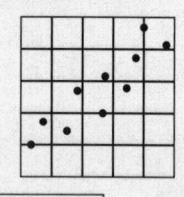

[ ] **correlation**
As one set of values increases, the other set tends to increase.

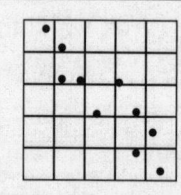

[ ] **correlation**
As one set of values increases, the other set tends to decrease.

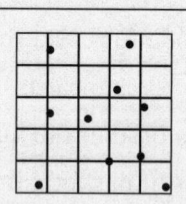

[ ] **correlation**
The values show no relationship.

Example

1 The scatter plot shows education and income data.

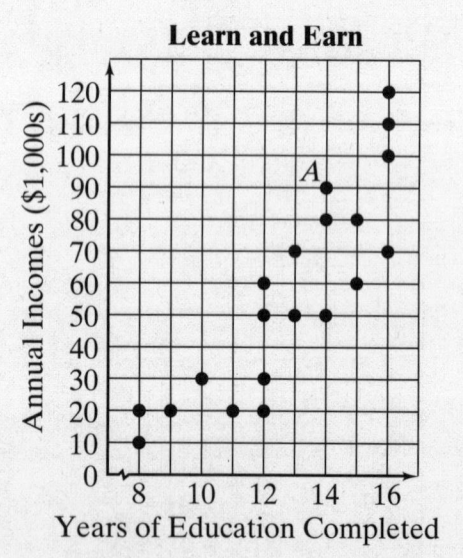

a. Describe the person represented by the point with coordinates (10, 30).

This person has [ ] years of education and earns [ ] each year.

b. How many people have exactly 14 years of education? What are their incomes?

The points (14, [ ]), (14, [ ]), and (14, [ ]) have education coordinate 14. The three people they represent earn [ ], [ ], and [ ], respectively.

Learn and Earn

(Annual Incomes ($1,000s) vs. Years of Education Completed)

c. Is there a *positive correlation*, a *negative correlation*, or *no correlation* between education and income? Explain.

As the years of education [ ], annual income [ ].
There is a [ ] correlation.

198 Algebra Readiness Lesson 12-5

Name _____ Class _____ Date _____

Example

2 Use the table to make a scatter plot of the elevation and precipitation data.

Elevation and Precipitation

City	Elevation Above Sea Level (ft)	Mean Annual Precipitation (in.)
Atlanta, GA	1,050	51
Boston, MA	20	42
Chicago, IL	596	36
Honolulu, HI	18	22
Miami, FL	11	56
Phoenix, AZ	1,072	8
Portland, ME	75	44
San Diego, CA	40	10
Wichita, KS	1,305	29

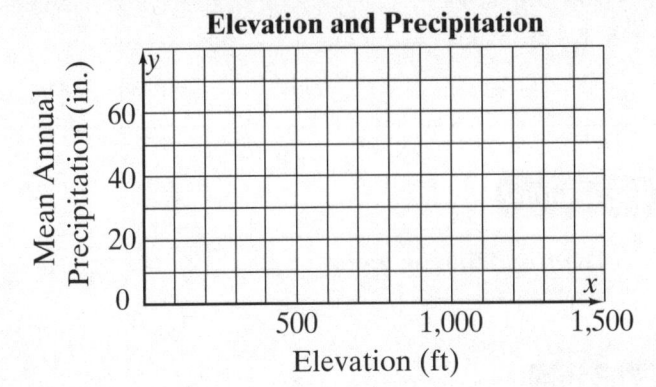

Quick Check

1. **a.** Use the information in Example 1 to describe the person represented by point A.

   b. How many people have exactly 12 years of education?

2. Use the table at the right. Make a scatter plot of the latitude and precipitation data.

Climate Data

City	Location (degrees north latitude)	Mean Annual Precipitation (inches)
Atlanta, GA	34	51
Boston, MA	42	42
Chicago, IL	42	36
Duluth, MN	47	30
Honolulu, HI	21	22
Houston, TX	30	46
Juneau, AK	58	54
Miami, FL	26	56
Phoenix, AZ	33	8
Portland, ME	44	44
San Diego, CA	33	10
Wichita, KS	38	29

SOURCES: *The World Almanac* and *The Statistical Abstract of the United States*. Go to www.PHSchool.com for a data update.
Web Code: adg-2041

Daily Notetaking Guide — Algebra Readiness Lesson 12-5

Name_____ Class_____ Date_____

Lesson 12-6

Solve by Graphing

Lesson Objective
- Solve problems by graphing

Vocabulary

The trend line on a scatter plot _____

Example

1. Use the data in the table below. Suppose this year there are 12 wolves on the island. Predict how many moose are on the island.

Isle Royale Populations

Year	Wolf	Moose	Year	Wolf	Moose	Year	Wolf	Moose
1982	14	700	1988	12	1,653	1994	15	1,800
1983	23	900	1989	11	1,397	1995	16	2,400
1984	24	811	1990	15	1,216	1996	22	1,200
1985	22	1,062	1991	12	1,313	1997	24	500
1986	20	1,025	1992	12	1,600	1998	14	700
1987	16	1,380	1993	13	1,880	1999	25	750

SOURCE: Isle Royale National Park Service

Understand the Problem

1. What are the two variables?
2. What are you trying to predict?

Make and Carry Out a Plan You can graph the data in a scatter plot. If the points show a correlation, you can draw a trend line. You can use the line to predict other data values.

Step 1 Make a scatter plot by graphing the (wolf, moose) ordered pairs. Use the x-axis for _____ and the y-axis for _____.

Step 2 Sketch a trend line. The line should be as close as possible to each data point. There should be about as many points above the trend line as below it.

200 Algebra Readiness Lesson 12-6 Daily Notetaking Guide

Name _____ Class _____ Date _____

Example

Isle Royale Populations

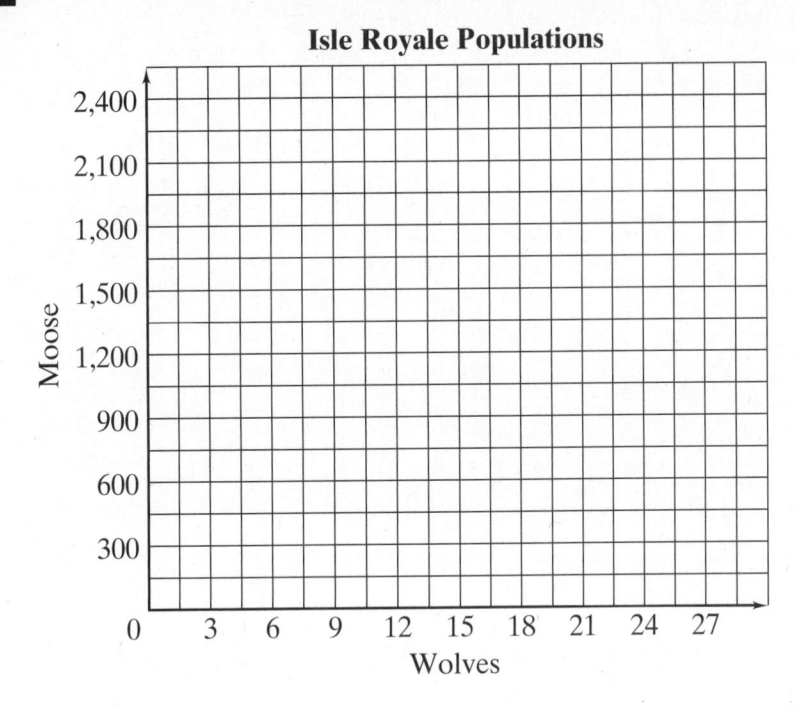

[Graph with Moose on y-axis (0 to 2,400 by 300) and Wolves on x-axis (0 to 27 by 3)]

Step 3 To predict the number of moose when there are 12 wolves, find 12 along the ☐ axis. Look up to find the point on the trend line that corresponds to 12 wolves. Then look across to the value on the ☐ axis, which is about ☐. There are about ☐ moose on the island.

Check the Answer You can write an equation for a trend line. You can use the equation to make predictions.

Quick Check

1. **a.** What is the y-intercept of the trend line above?

   ☐

   b. Locate one other point on the trend line. Then find the slope of the trend line.

   ☐

   c. Write an equation for the trend line in slope-intercept form.

   ☐

   d. Use the equation you wrote in part (c). Find the solution of the equation when $x = 12$.

   ☐

Daily Notetaking Guide — Algebra Readiness Lesson 12-6

A Note to the Student:

This section of your workbook contains a series of pages that support your mathematics understandings for each chapter and lesson presented in your student edition.

- Practice pages provide additional practice for every lesson.

- Guided Problem Solving pages lead you through a step-by-step solution to an application problem in each lesson.

- Vocabulary pages contain a variety of activities to increase your reading and math understanding, ranging from graphic organizers to vocabulary review puzzles.

Practice • Guided Problem Solving • Vocabulary

Name _____ Class _____ Date _____

Practice 1-1

Variables and Expressions

Write an expression for each quantity.

1. the value in cents of 5 quarters _____

2. the value in cents of q quarters _____

3. the number of months in 7 years _____

4. the number of months in y years _____

Write an algebraic expression for each word phrase.

5. 9 less than k _____

6. m divided by 6 _____

7. 4 more than twice x _____

8. the sum of eighteen and b _____

Tell whether each expression is a numerical expression or an algebraic expression. For an algebraic expression, name the variable.

9. $4d$ _____

10. $\dfrac{4(9)}{6}$ _____

11. $5k - 9$ _____

12. $19 + 3(12)$ _____

Write an expression for each quantity.

13. the number of hours in 5 days

_____

14. the number of weeks in d days

_____

L1 Practice

Algebra-Readiness Lesson 1-1 205

Name _____ Class _____ Date _____

1-1 • Guided Problem Solving

GPS Exercise 29

Mia has $20 less than Brandi. Brandi has d dollars. Write an algebraic expression for the amount of money Mia has.

Understand the Problem

1. Who has more money, Brandi or Mia? _____

2. What operation do you think of when you hear the phrase *less than*? _____

3. Describe how much money Mia has, compared to how much Brandi has. _____

4. What does the variable d represent? _____

5. The problem asks you to write an expression for what? _____

Make and Carry Out a Plan

6. You are given two pieces of information in the problem: the amount of money that Brandi has and the fact that Mia has $20 less than Brandi.
To write an expression for the amount Mia has, start by writing the amount that Brandi has. _____

7. To complete the expression, show the subtraction of $20 from the amount that Brandi has. _____

Check the Answer

8. You know that Brandi has $20 more than Mia. To check that your expression for this amount is correct, add $20 to it to see whether you get Brandi's amount.

_____

Solve Another Problem

9. Deena has 5 more marbles than Jonna. Jonna has m marbles. Write an expression to represent the number of marbles Deena has. _____

Name _____ Class _____ Date _____

Practice 1-2

The Order of Operations

Simplify each expression.

1. $3 + 15 - 5 \cdot 2$ _____

2. $5 \cdot 6 + 2 \cdot 4$ _____

3. $68 - 12 \div 2 \div 3$ _____

4. $6(2 + 7)$ _____

5. $25 - (6 \cdot 4)$ _____

6. $3[9 - (6 - 3)] - 10$ _____

7. $60 \div (3 + 12)$ _____

8. $18 \div (5 - 2)$ _____

9. $\frac{16 + 24}{30 - 22}$ _____

10. $(8 \div 8 + 2 + 11) \div 2$ _____

Insert grouping symbols to make each number sentence true.

11. $3 + 5 \cdot 8 = 64$

12. $(4 \cdot 6) - 2 + 7 = 23$

Compare. Use >, <, or = to complete each statement.

13. $(24 - 8) \div 4$ ☐ $24 - 8 \div 4$

14. $3 \cdot (4 - 2) \cdot 5$ ☐ $3 \cdot 4 - 2 \cdot 5$

15. $11 \cdot 4 - 2$ ☐ $11 \cdot (4 - 2)$

16. $(7 \cdot 3) - (4 \cdot 2)$ ☐ $7 \cdot 3 - 4 \cdot 2$

L1 Practice

Algebra-Readiness Lesson 1-2 **207**

Name _____ Class _____ Date _____

1-2 • Guided Problem Solving

GPS Exercise 39

A part-time employee worked 4 hours on Monday and 7 hours each day for the next 3 days. Write and simplify an expression that shows the total number of hours worked.

Understand the Problem

1. How many hours did the employee work on Monday? _____

2. How many hours did the employee work each day on Tuesday, Wednesday, and Thursday? _____

3. For how many days did the employee work 7 hours? _____

Make and Carry Out a Plan

4. What operation should you use to find the total number of hours worked in the 3 days that the employee worked 7 hours each day? _____

5. Write an expression to find the total number of hours worked during those 3 days. _____

6. What operation should you use to combine the hours the employee worked on Monday with the hours worked in the next 3 days? _____

7. Write an expression for the total number of hours worked on Monday and the number of hours worked in the next 3 days. _____

8. Simplify the expression you wrote for Step 7 to find the total number of hours worked. Remember to use the correct order of operations. _____

Check the Answer

9. You can check your work by writing an expression that adds the number of hours worked on each day. This expression should simplify to the number of hours you found in Step 8 above.

   _____

Solve Another Problem

10. Carter bought 4 books for $8 each and another book for $5. Write and simplify an expression to find the total cost of the books he bought.

    _____

208 Algebra-Readiness Lesson 1-2 — Guided Problem Solving

Practice 1-3

Writing and Evaluating Expressions

Evaluate each expression.

1. xy, for $x = 3$ and $y = 5$ _____
2. $24 - p \cdot 5$, for $p = 4$ _____
3. $9 - k$, for $k = 2$ _____
4. $6x$, for $x = 3$ _____
5. $2 + n$, for $n = 3$ _____
6. $63 \div p$, for $p = 7$ _____
7. $10 - r + 5$, for $r = 9$ _____
8. $10 - x$, for $x = 3$ _____
9. $4m + 3$, for $m = 5$ _____
10. $35 - 3x$, for $x = 10$ _____
11. $3ab - c$, for $a = 4$, $b = 2$, and $c = 5$ _____
12. $\frac{ab}{2} + 4c$, for $a = 6$, $b = 5$, and $c = 3$ _____
13. $x(y + 5) - z$, for $x = 3$, $y = 2$, and $z = 7$ _____
14. A tree grows 5 in. each year.

    a. Write an expression for the tree's height after x years. _____

    b. Evaluate the expression to find the height of the tree after 36 years. _____

Name _____ Class _____ Date _____

1-3 • Guided Problem Solving

GPS Exercise 38

A fitness club requires a $100 initiation fee and dues of $25 each month. Write an expression for the cost of membership for n months. Then find the cost of membership for one year.

Understand the Problem

1. What is the initiation fee for the club? _____

2. What are the monthly dues for the club? _____

3. What does the variable n represent? _____

4. You are asked to write an expression. What does this expression represent? _____

5. What are you asked to find? _____

Make and Carry Out a Plan

6. What operation must you use to find the amount of dues for n months? _____

7. Write an expression to represent the cost of dues for n months. _____

8. The total cost of membership for n months includes the initiation fee and the cost of monthly dues for n months. What operation must you use to find the total cost of membership? _____

9. Write an expression for the total cost of membership for n months, including the initiation fee. _____

10. Substitute $n = 12$, the number of months in a year, into the expression in Step 9. _____

11. Simplify the expression to find the cost of membership for one year. _____

Check the Answer

12. Look at the expression you found in Step 9. Which operation do you perform first? _____

Solve Another Problem

13. Carly belongs to a book-of-the-month club. She paid $10 to sign up and then pays $5 for a new book each month. Write an expression for the cost of belonging to the club for n months. Then find the cost of belonging to the club for 8 months. _____

210 Algebra-Readiness Lesson 1-3   Guided Problem Solving

Name _____ Class _____ Date _____

Practice 1-4

Integers and Absolute Value

Graph each set of numbers on a number line. Then order the numbers from least to greatest.

1. $-4, -8, 5$

2. $3, -3, -2$

Write an expression to represent each quantity.

3. c degrees below zero _____

4. h ft above sea level _____

Simplify each expression.

5. $|-9|$ _____

6. $-|-25|$ _____

7. the opposite of $|-8|$ _____

8. $|847|$ _____

Write the integer represented by each point on the number line.

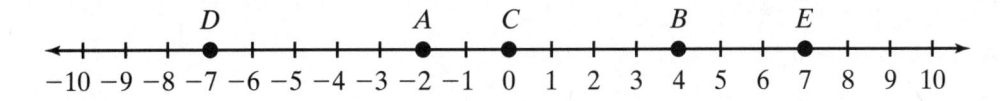

9. A _____

10. B _____

11. C _____

12. D _____

Compare. Use >, <, or = to complete each statement.

13. $|-2|$ ☐ $|2|$

14. $|-1|$ ☐ -6

15. $|4|$ ☐ $|-5|$

16. 0 ☐ $|-7|$

L1 Practice

Algebra-Readiness Lesson 1-4

Name _____ Class _____ Date _____

1-4 • Guided Problem Solving

GPS Exercise 7

Graph the set of numbers on a number line. Then order the numbers from least to greatest.

$-2, 8, -9$

Understand the Problem

1. What are you asked to do? _____

2. What are the three numbers? _____

Make and Carry Out a Plan

3. Draw a number line from -10 to 10 in the space below.

4. Negative numbers are to the left of zero and positive numbers are to the right of zero. Plot $-2, 8,$ and -9 on the number line.

5. Numbers on a number line increase in value from left to right. Which number is farthest to the left on the number line? _____

6. Order the numbers from least to greatest. _____

Check the Answer

7. To check your answer, find the absolute value of each negative number.

   _____

   The negative number with the greatest absolute value comes first when ordering numbers from least to greatest.

Solve Another Problem

Graph the set of numbers on a number line. Then order the numbers from least to greatest.

8. $4, -3, -8$ _____

212 Algebra-Readiness Lesson 1-4   Guided Problem Solving

Practice 1-5

Adding Integers

Write a numerical expression. Find the sum.

1. climb up 26 steps, then climb down 9 steps

   _____

2. earn $100, spend $62, earn $35, spend $72

   _____

Find each sum.

3. $-8 + (-3)$

4. $12 + (-7) + 3 + (-8)$

5. $9 + (-11)$

6. $6 + (-5) + (-4)$

7. The price of a share of stock started the day at $37. During the day it went down $3, up $1, down $7, and up $4. What was the price of a share at the end of the day?

Without adding, tell whether each sum is positive, negative, or zero.

8. $192 + (-129)$

9. $-417 + (-296)$

10. $-175 + 87$

Evaluate each expression for $n = -12$.

11. $n + 8$

12. $n + (-5)$

13. $12 + n$

Compare. Write >, <, or = to complete each statement.

14. $-7 + 5$ ☐ $3 + (-6)$

15. $4 + (-9)$ ☐ $6 + (-7) + (-4)$

Name _____ Class _____ Date _____

1-5 • Guided Problem Solving

GPS Exercise 49

Maria had $123. She spent $35, loaned $20 to a friend, and received her $90 paycheck. How much does she have now?

Understand the Problem

1. How much money did Maria start with? _____

2. What amount did she spend? _____

3. How much money did she loan to a friend? _____

4. What was the amount of Maria's paycheck? _____

Make and Carry Out a Plan

5. Look at the amounts below. Tell whether each amount should be added to or subtracted from Maria's $123.

   a. $35 _____

   b. $20 _____

   c. $90 _____

6. Write an expression to show the original amount of $123 and the amounts that should be added or subtracted. _____

7. Simplify the expression to find the amount of money Maria has now. _____

Check the Answer

8. To check your work, start with the amount you found in Step 7 and work backward. Subtract 90, add 20, and add 35. Is your result the same as the amount Maria started with?

   _____
   _____

Solve Another Problem

9. Alec had $55. He earned $25 mowing lawns in his neighborhood. He spent $10 on a new baseball card for his collection. Then he spent $6 on lunch with a friend. How much money does Alec have now? _____

214 Algebra-Readiness Lesson 1-5   Guided Problem Solving

Name _____ Class _____ Date _____

Practice 1-6

Subtracting Integers

Use models to help you find each difference.

1. $8 - 12$
2. $13 - 6$
3. $9 - (-12)$

4. $-98 - 103$
5. $-25 - 25$
6. $-16 - (-16)$

Find each difference.

7. $6 - 9$
8. $14 - 8$
9. $-15 - 3$

Round each number. Then estimate the sum or difference.

10. $-57 + (-98)$
11. $448 - 52$
12. $-191 + (-511)$

13. $-361 - (-58)$
14. $888 + 1{,}177$
15. $-484 - 1{,}695$

Write a numerical expression. Simplify.

16. A balloon goes up 2,300 ft, then goes down 600 ft.

17. The Glasers had $317 in their checking account. They wrote checks for $74, $132, and $48. What is their checking account balance?

Name _____ Class _____ Date _____

1-6 • Guided Problem Solving

GPS Exercise 26

Suppose you have a score of 35 in a game. You get a 50-point penalty. What is your new score?

Understand the Problem

1. What is your original score? _____

2. How many points is your penalty? _____

3. What are you asked to find? _____

Make and Carry Out a Plan

4. Is your original score positive or negative? _____

5. Should you add or subtract your penalty from your original score?
   _____

6. Write an expression to show how to combine a 50-point penalty with the original 35-point score.
   _____

7. Simplify the expression from Step 6 to find your new score.
   _____

Check the Answer

8. Write the expression from Step 6 as a sum.
   _____

9. Find the sum. _____

Solve Another Problem

10. Trevor has a score of 55 in a game. He gets a 75-point penalty. What is his new score? _____

Name _____ Class _____ Date _____

Practice 1-7

Inductive Reasoning

Write a rule for each pattern. Find the next three numbers in each pattern.

1. 3, 6, 9, 12, 15, _____, _____, _____

    Rule: _____

2. 1, 2, 4, 8, 16, _____, _____, _____

    Rule: _____

3. 6, 7, 14, 15, 30, 31, _____, _____, _____

    Rule: _____

4. 34, 27, 20, 13, 6, _____, _____, _____

    Rule: _____

Is each conjecture correct or incorrect? If it is incorrect, give a counterexample.

5. All roses are red.
   _____

6. The difference of two numbers is always less than at least one of the numbers.
   _____

Describe the next figure in each pattern. Then draw the figure.

7.

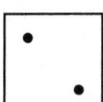

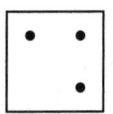

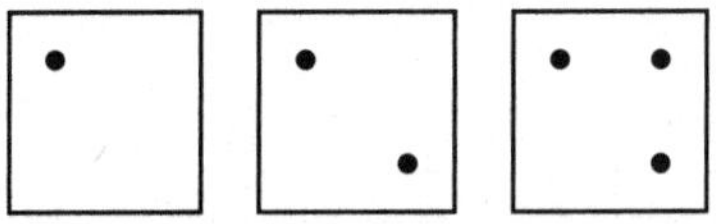

8.

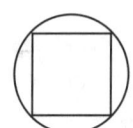

9.

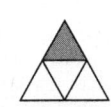

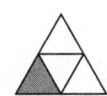

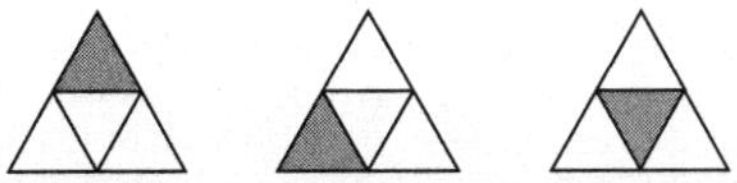

10.

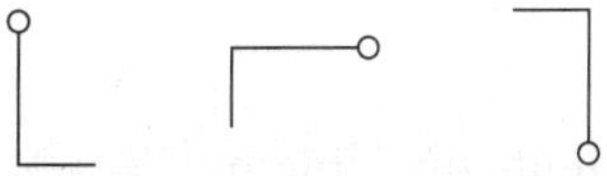

Practice

Algebra-Readiness Lesson 1-7   217

Name _____ Class _____ Date _____

1-7 • Guided Problem Solving

GPS Exercise 21

Reasoning Is the conjecture correct? If incorrect, give a counterexample.
A whole number is divisible by 3 if the sum of its digits is divisible by 3.

Understand the Problem

1. Write the conjecture in your own words. _____
   _____

Make and Carry Out a Plan

2. An example of a whole number whose digits have a sum that is divisible by 3 is 27. List three other such whole numbers. _____

3. Show that each whole number you found in Step 2 is divisible by 3.
   _____

4. The sum of the digits of 102 is divisible by 3.
   Also, 102 is divisible by 3. What are two other three-digit numbers for which the sum of the digits is divisible by 3? _____

5. Is each number you named in Step 4 also divisible by 3? _____

6. Based on your trials, does the conjecture seem correct or incorrect? Explain. _____
   _____

Check the Answer

7. Test the conjecture using the number 5,112.
   Is the sum of the digits divisible by 3? Is 5,112 divisible by 3? _____

Solve Another Problem

8. Is the conjecture correct or incorrect? If it is incorrect, give a counterexample.
   A whole number is divisible by 2 if the sum of its digits is divisible by 2.
   _____
   _____

218 Algebra-Readiness Lesson 1-7   Guided Problem Solving

Practice 1-8

Reasoning Strategy: Look for a Pattern

Look for a Pattern to help you solve each problem.

1. Each row in a window display of storage boxes contains two more boxes than the row above. The first (top) row has one box.

   a. Complete the table.

Row Number	1	2	3	4	5	6
Boxes in the Row						
Total Boxes in the Display						

   b. Describe the pattern in the numbers you wrote.

   _____

   _____

   c. Find the number of rows in a display containing the given number of boxes.

   81 _____   144 _____   400 _____

2. A computer multiplied 100 nines. You can use patterns to find the ones digit of the product.

   $9 \times 9 \times 9 \times 9 \times \cdots \times 9$ (100 times)

   a. Find the ones digit for the product of:

   1 nine ____   2 nines ____   3 nines ____   4 nines ____

   b. Describe the pattern. _____

   _____

   _____

   _____

   c. What is the ones digit of the computer's product? _____

Name _____ Class _____ Date _____

1-8 • Guided Problem Solving

GPS Exercise 2

Look for a Pattern to help you solve each problem.

Students are to march in a parade. There will be one first grader, two second graders, three third graders, and so on, through the twelfth grade. How many students will march in the parade?

Understand the Problem

1. How many first graders will march in the parade? _____

2. How many second graders will march in the parade? Third graders? _____

3. What are you asked to find? _____

Make and Carry Out a Plan

4. Make a table to organize the information. Complete the table with the information you know about the number of first, second, and third graders.

Grade	1	2	3	4	5	6	7	8	9	10	11	12
Number of Students in the Parade												

5. Look for a pattern in the number of students. What pattern do you see? _____

6. Use the pattern to complete the table above.

7. Add the number of students from each grade who will march in the parade. How many students will march in the parade? _____

Check the Answer

8. To check your answer, draw a diagram on a separate piece of paper. Use a dot to represent each student. In the first row of your diagram, draw the number of first graders, in the second row the number of second graders, and so on. The number of dots should be equal to the number of students from Question 7. _____

Solve Another Problem

9. At Highland Elementary School, one first grader, three second graders, five third graders and so on through the sixth grade are crossing guards. How many students are crossing guards? _____

Algebra-Readiness Lesson 1-8   Guided Problem Solving

Name _____ Class _____ Date _____

Practice 1-9   Multiplying and Dividing Integers

Use repeated addition, patterns, or rules to simplify each product or quotient.

1. $8 \cdot 7(-6)$ 2. $-17 \cdot 3$ 3. $-24 \div 4$

4. $117 \div (-1)$ 5. $-30 \div (-6)$ 6. $5(-1)(-9)$

7. $-3 \cdot 7(-2)$ 8. $\dfrac{-15(-3)}{-9}$

Compare. Use >, <, or = to complete each statement.

9. $-7(5) \square -6 \cdot (-6)$ 10. $-20 \cdot (-5) \square 10 \cdot |-10|$

11. $3(-6) \square -3(6)$ 12. $-54 \div 9 \square 21 \div (-3)$

For each group, find the average.

13. temperatures: $6°, -15°, -24°, 3°, -25°$ _____

14. bank balances: $52, -$7, $20, -$63, -$82 _____

15. stock price changes: $6, -$6, -$9, $1, $3 _____

16. golf scores: $-2, 0, 3, -2, -3, 1, -4$ _____

Write a multiplication or division sentence to answer the question.

17. The temperature rose 4° each hour for 3 hours. What was the total change in temperature?

_____

Name _____ Class _____ Date _____

1-9 • Guided Problem Solving

GPS Exercise 8

The temperature dropped 5 degrees each hour for 7 h. Use an integer to represent the total change in temperature.

Understand the Problem

1. How many degrees did the temperature drop each hour? _____

2. For how many hours did the temperature drop? _____

3. What are you asked to do? _____

Make and Carry Out a Plan

4. Use repeated subtraction to solve the problem. How many times will you subtract 5 degrees? _____

5. Use a number line to show your repeated subtraction. Continue on the number line below until you have subtracted −5 the correct number of times.

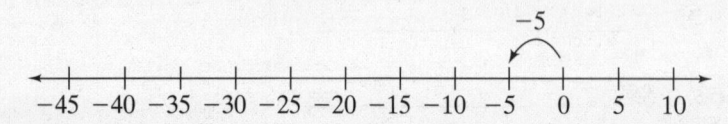

```
              −5
          ⌒
←+––+––+––+––+––+––+––+––+––+––+→
−45 −40 −35 −30 −25 −20 −15 −10 −5  0   5  10
```

6. What integer represents the total change in temperature? _____

Check the Answer

7. To check your answer, multiply the number of degrees the temperature dropped each hour by the number of hours. _____
Your answer should be the same as your answer to Question 6.

Solve Another Problem

8. A scuba diver descends 10 ft every 10 seconds. Use an integer to represent the position of the diver after 1 min (60 seconds). _____

222 Algebra-Readiness Lesson 1-9   Guided Problem Solving

Practice 1-10

The Coordinate Plane

Graph each point.

1. $A(-2, 2)$
2. $B(0, 3)$
3. $C(-3, 0)$
4. $D(2, 3)$
5. $E(-1, -2)$
6. $F(4, -2)$
7. Connect the points B, D, F, and E in that order. Connect the last point to the first. Name the figure.

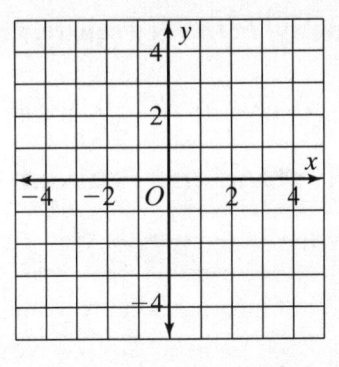

_____

Write the coordinates of each point.

8. A _____
9. B _____
10. C _____
11. D _____

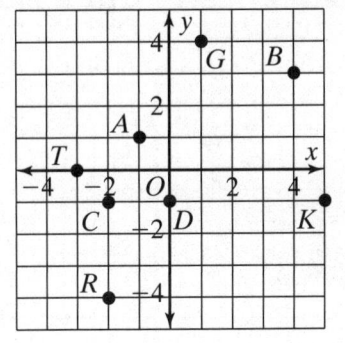

In which quadrant or on what axis does each point lie?

12. A _____
13. B _____
14. C _____
15. D _____

Name the point with the given coordinates.

16. $(1, 4)$ _____
17. $(-3, 0)$ _____

Complete using *positive*, *negative*, or *zero*.

18. In Quadrant II, x is _____ and y is _____.

19. On the x-axis y is _____.

Practice — Algebra-Readiness Lesson 1-10

Name _____ Class _____ Date _____

1-10 • Guided Problem Solving

GPS Exercise 45

Geometry *PQRS* is a square. Find the coordinates of *S*.

$P(-5, 0), Q(0, 5), R(5, 0), S(\blacksquare, \blacksquare)$

Understand the Problem

1. What shape is *PQRS*? _____

2. What information are you given about points *P*, *Q*, and *R*? _____

3. What are you asked to find? _____

Make and Carry Out a Plan

4. Graph *P*, *Q*, and *R* on the graph below.

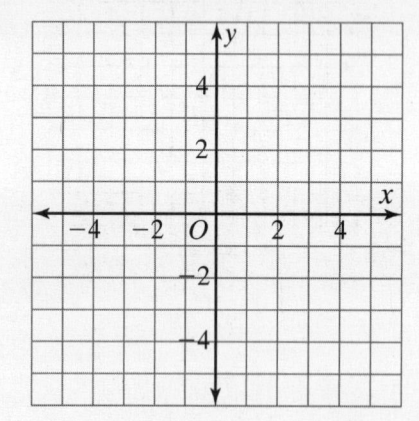

5. Draw lines to connect *P* to *Q* and *Q* to *R*. These are two sides of the square.

6. What is true about the four sides of a square? _____

7. Draw the two missing sides of the square.

8. *S* is the point where the two new sides meet. What are the coordinates of *S*? _____

Check the Answer

9. To check your answer, use a ruler to measure each side. _____
   Since *PQRS* is a square, all four sides should have the same length.

Solve Another Problem

10. *JKLM* is a rectangle. Find the coordinates of *M*.
    $J(-4, 2), K(-4, -2), L(4, -2), M(\blacksquare, \blacksquare)$ _____

224 Algebra-Readiness Lesson 1-10   Guided Problem Solving

Name _____ Class _____ Date _____

1A: Graphic Organizer

For use before Lesson 1-1

Study Skill Take a few minutes to explore the general contents of this text. Begin by looking at the cover. What does the cover art say about mathematics? What do the pages before the first page of Chapter 1 tell you? What special pages are in the back of the book to help you?

Write your answers. Use the Table of Contents page for this chapter at the front of the book.

1. What is the title of this chapter? _____

2. Name four topics that you will study in this chapter.

   _____   _____

   _____   _____

3. What is the topic of the Reasoning Strategy lesson? _____

4. Complete the graphic organizer below as you work through the chapter.
   1. Write the title of the chapter in the center oval.
   2. When you begin a lesson, write the name of the lesson in a rectangle.
   3. When you complete that lesson, write a skill or key concept from that lesson in the outer oval linked to that rectangle.
   Continue with steps 2 and 3 clockwise around the graphic organizer.

Vocabulary and Study Skills

Algebra-Readiness Chapter 1   225

Name _____ Class _____ Date _____

1B: Reading Comprehension

For use after Lesson 1-4

Study Skill When you read a paragraph in mathematics, read it twice. Read it the first time to get an overview of the content. Read it a second time to find the essential details and information. Write down key words that tell you the topic for each paragraph.

Read the passage below and answer the questions that follow.

> Algebra is a part of mathematics that uses variables as well as the operations that combine variables. Some operations in algebra are the ones you learned in arithmetic $(+, -, \times, \div)$. In algebra, however, you might add two variables such as a and b. Then you could substitute different values for these variables. So, for example, $a + b$ can represent $3 + 4$ or $13.5 + 24.7$ or any other numbers you choose.
>
> Two different people have commonly been called "the father of algebra." One is Diophantus, a Greek mathematician who lived in the third century. He was the first to use symbols to represent frequently used words. The other is the Arab mathematician Al-Khowarizmi. In the ninth century, he published a clear and complete explanation of how to solve an equation. Our word "algebra" comes from the word *al-jabr*, which appears in the title of his work.

1. What is the subject of the first paragraph? What is the subject of the second paragraph?
   _____

2. How are numbers used in the passage? _____
   _____

3. What are the names of the mathematicians mentioned in the passage?
   _____

4. What title do they share? _____

5. How much time passed between the lives of these two mathematicians? _____

6. According to this passage, what is the same in arithmetic and algebra? _____
   _____

7. Which operations are named in this passage? _____

8. What was the origin of the word *algebra*? _____

9. **High-Use Academic Words** In the first paragraph of the passage, what does it mean to *substitute*?

   a. to use in place of another   **b.** to prove

226 *Algebra-Readiness* Chapter 1   Vocabulary and Study Skills

Name _____ Class _____ Date _____

1C: Reading/Writing Math Symbols For use after Lesson 1-9

Study Skill Plan your time, whether you are studying or taking a test. Look at the entire amount of time you have and divide it into portions that you allocate to each task. Keep track of whether you are on schedule.

Write an explanation in words for the meaning of each mathematical expression or statement.

1. $2 \div p$ _____

2. $|x|$ _____

3. -10 _____

4. $y < -2$ _____

5. $7a$ _____

Write each expression or statement with math symbols.

6. the sum of a and b _____

7. 3 divided by 15 _____

8. 2 times the sum of x and y _____

9. The opposite of m is less than 2. _____

10. 6 less than p _____

11. the quotient of 12 and t _____

12. the absolute value of 3 _____

Vocabulary and Study Skills   Algebra-Readiness Chapter 1

Name _____ Class _____ Date _____

1D: Visual Vocabulary Practice   For use after Lesson 1-10

Study Skill The Glossary contains the key vocabulary for this course.

Concept List

opposites	ordered pair	origin
quadrants	variable	algebraic expression
x-axis	y-axis	y-coordinate

Write the concept that best describes each exercise. Choose from the concept list above.

1. The letter "c" in $24c + 8$

2. $10d - 3 + a$

3. -9 and 9

4. [grid with quadrants I, II, III, IV labeled, y-axis highlighted]

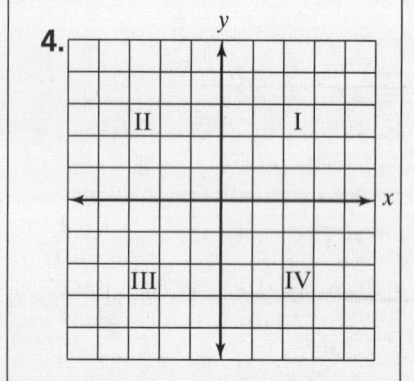

5. [grid with quadrants I, II, III, IV labeled, arrow on y-axis]

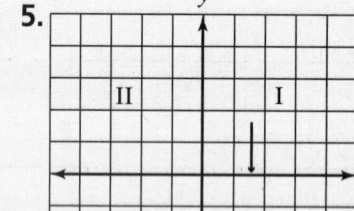

6. [grid with quadrants I, II, III, IV labeled, arrow on x-axis]

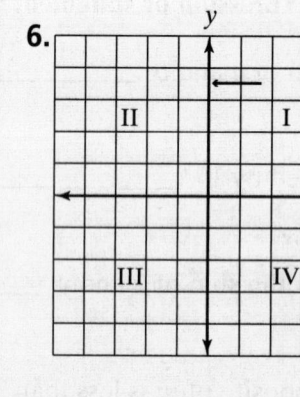

7. $(2, -3)$

8. [grid with quadrants I, II, III, IV labeled, point near origin]

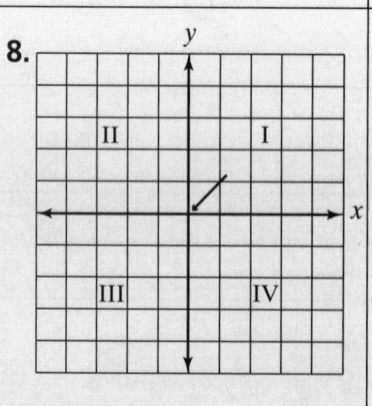

9. The number 8 in $(5, 8)$

228 Algebra-Readiness Chapter 1   Vocabulary and Study Skills

Name _____ Class _____ Date _____

1E: Vocabulary Check

For use after Lesson 1-7

Study Skill Strengthen your vocabulary. Use these pages and add cues and summaries by applying the Cornell Notetaking style.

Write the definition for each word at the right. To check your work, fold the paper back along the dotted line to see the correct answers.

_____ Integers

_____

_____

_____ Absolute value

_____

_____

_____ Inductive reasoning

_____

_____

_____ Conjecture

_____

_____

_____ Counterexample

_____

_____

Vocabulary and Study Skills   Algebra-Readiness Chapter 1

1E: Vocabulary Check (continued)

For use after Lesson 1-7

Write the vocabulary word for each definition. To check your work, fold the paper forward along the dotted line to see the correct answers.

The whole numbers and their opposites.

_____

The distance of a number from zero on a number line.

_____

Making conclusions based on patterns you observe.

_____

A conclusion reached through inductive reasoning.

_____

An example that proves a statement false.

_____

Name _____ Class _____ Date _____

1F: Vocabulary Review Puzzle

For use with Chapter Review

Study Skill The language of mathematics has precise definitions for each vocabulary word or phrase. To help you learn these definitions, keep a list of the new words in each chapter, along with their definitions and an example.

Write the vocabulary word for each description. Complete the word search puzzle by finding and circling each vocabulary word. For help, use the glossary in your textbook. Remember that a word may go right to left, left to right, or it may go up as well as down.

1. a conclusion reached by observing patterns _____

2. the plane formed by the intersection of two number lines _____

3. a whole number or its opposite _____

4. reasoning that makes conclusions based on patterns _____

5. the horizontal or vertical number line on the coordinate plane _____

6. a letter that stands for a number _____

7. one of the four parts of the coordinate plane _____

8. point of intersection for the axes _____

9. kind of value that gives the distance of a number from zero _____

10. replacing each variable with a number in an expression and simplifying the result _____

```
I N T E G E R O T E U D Q
E T E E E A G V A T C L O
E N I E T R N D E A E I I
R A R U A B D J L U A E A
U R T U N O N B B L I E N
T D E A I V E T A A C T N
C A I N D U C T I V E U U
E U U T R B N O R E B L E
J Q A A O R I E A L S O I
N E D O O T T A V U X S I
O G A O C O R I G I N B N
C A X I S U T T I V E A N
```

Vocabulary and Study Skills

Algebra-Readiness Chapter 1

231

Practice 2-1

Properties of Numbers

Use mental math to simplify each expression.

1. $4 \cdot 13 \cdot 25$
2. $700 + 127 + 300$
3. $68 + 85 + 32$

4. $2 \cdot 3 \cdot 4 \cdot 5$
5. $-14 + 71 + 29 + (-86)$
6. $20 \cdot 7 \cdot 5$

7. $39 + 27 + 11$
8. $19 + 0 + (-9)$
9. $-6 \cdot 1 \cdot 30$

Write the letter of the property shown.

10. $14(mn) = (14m)n$ _____

11. $k \cdot 1 = k$ _____

12. $(x + y) + z = x + (y + z)$ _____

13. $p = 0 + p$ _____

14. $(x + p) + (r + t) = (r + t) + (x + p)$ _____

15. $x + yz = x + zy$ _____

a. Commutative Property of Addition
b. Associative Property of Addition
c. Commutative Property of Multiplication
d. Associative Property of Multiplication
e. Additive Identity
f. Multiplicative Identity

Evaluate each expression.

16. $q + r + s$, for $q = 46, r = 19, s = 54$ _____

17. $a(b)(-c)$, for $a = 7, b = -2, c = 15$ _____

Name _____ Class _____ Date _____

2-1 • Guided Problem Solving

GPS Exercise 26

Mental Math Loryn is flying roundtrip from Dallas, Texas, to Minneapolis, Minnesota. The fare for her ticket is $308. Each airport charges a $16 airport fee. There is also a tax of $12 on the fare. What is the total cost of Loryn's ticket?

Understand the Problem

1. What is the fare for Loryn's flight? _____

2. What is the tax on the fare? _____

3. What are the airport fees for each airport? _____

4. How many airports will charge airport fees? _____

5. What are you asked to find? _____

Make and Carry Out a Plan

6. Write an expression to find the total cost of airport fees for Loryn's flight. _____

7. Write an expression to add the cost of the fare, the total cost of airport fees, and the tax on the fare. _____

8. Which operation should you perform first to simplify the expression? _____

9. Write the simplified expression. _____

10. Use the Commutative Property of Addition to rewrite the expression so it is easier to simplify using mental math. _____

11. Use the Associative Property of Addition to group the two terms in the expression that are easiest to add. _____

12. What is the total cost of Loryn's ticket? _____

Check the Answer

13. How do the Commutative and Associative Properties help you use mental math to solve the problem? _____

Solve Another Problem

14. Terry purchased a new seat for his bicycle for $24. He also bought a new helmet for $35 and two new reflectors for $3 each. How much did Terry spend? _____

234 Algebra-Readiness Lesson 2-1   Guided Problem Solving

Practice 2-2

The Distributive Property

Write an expression using parentheses for each model. Then multiply.

1. _____ 2. _____

Multiply each expression.

3. $6(h - 4)$ _____ 4. $(p + 3)5$ _____

5. $-3(x + 8)$ _____ 6. $(4 - y)(-9)$ _____

Use the Distributive Property to simplify.

7. $98 \cdot 7$ _____

8. $9 \cdot 28$ _____

9. $78 \cdot 8$ _____

10. $8 \cdot 5 - 12 \cdot 5$ _____

11. $7 \cdot 10 + 7(-3)$ _____

12. $-4(3) + (-4)(6)$ _____

13. $6(8) + 6(-2)$ _____

Solve using mental math.

14. A shipping container holds 144 boxes. How many boxes can be shipped in 4 containers? _____

Name _____ Class _____ Date _____

2-2 • Guided Problem Solving

GPS Exercise 13

Solve using mental math.

A theater sold out its evening performances four nights in a row. The theater has 294 seats. How many people attended the theater in the four nights?

Understand the Problem

1. How many seats does the theater have? _____

2. How many nights in a row did the theater sell all of its seats? _____

3. What are you asked to find? _____

Make and Carry Out a Plan

4. Write an expression to find the number of people that attended the theater in the four nights. _____

5. In what other way can you write 294 so it will be easier to simplify the expression using mental math? _____

6. Rewrite the expression from Step 4 using your new way to write 294. _____

7. Use the Distributive Property to simplify the expression. _____

8. How many people attended the theater in the four nights? _____

Check the Answer

9. How can the Distributive Property help you find the answer mentally? _____

Solve Another Problem

10. Forty-eight people visited the information booth at a town fair on each day of the fair. If the fair was open for three days, how many people visited the information booth in all? _____

Algebra-Readiness Lesson 2-2   Guided Problem Solving

Name _____ Class _____ Date _____

Practice 2-3

Simplifying Algebraic Expressions

Simplify each expression.

1. $16 + 7y - 8$

2. $18m - 7 + 12m$

3. $5(3t) - 7(2t)$

4. $2x - 9y + 7x + 20y$

5. $-7a + 3(a - c) + 5c$

6. $6(g - h) - 6(g - h)$

Name the coefficients, the like terms, and the constants.

	Coefficients	Like Terms	Constants
7. $3x + 7$	_____	_____	_____
8. $4m + (-3n) + n$	_____	_____	_____
9. $6kp + 9k + kp - 14$	_____	_____	_____
10. $c + 2c + c - 5c + 1$	_____	_____	_____

Use a model to simplify each expression.

11. $1y + 4 + 3y - 5 + 2y$ _____

12. $4x - 6 - 2x + 3x + 1$ _____

L1 Practice

Algebra-Readiness Lesson 2-3 237

Name _____ Class _____ Date _____

2-3 • Guided Problem Solving

GPS Exercise 33

Juan bought supplies for his new gecko. He bought four plants for p dollars each. He also bought a 10-gallon tank for $10 and a water dish for $3. Write an expression Juan could use to find the total cost of the supplies.

Understand the Problem

1. What does the variable p represent? _____

2. How much did Juan spend on the 10-gallon tank? _____

3. How much did Juan spend on the water dish? _____

4. For what situation are you asked to write an expression? _____
   _____

Make and Carry Out a Plan

5. Write an expression to represent the amount Juan paid for the four plants. _____

6. Write an expression to represent the amount Juan paid in all for the plants, the 10-gallon tank, and the water dish. _____

7. Simplify the expression by combining like terms and any constants. _____

Check the Answer

8. How do you know the expression is simplified? _____
   _____

Solve Another Problem

9. Josie bought new school supplies. She bought three notebooks for n dollars each. She also bought a new calculator for $12 and a new pen for $2. Write an expression Josie could use to find the total cost of the school supplies. _____

238 Algebra-Readiness Lesson 2-3   Guided Problem Solving

Name _____ Class _____ Date _____

Practice 2-4

Variables and Equations

Is the given number a solution of the equation?

1. $9k = 10 - k$; -1 _____
2. $-7r - 15 = -2r$; -3 _____
3. $3g \div (-6) = 5 - g$; -10 _____
4. $-3p = 4p + 35$; -5 _____
5. $8 - e = 2e - 16$; 8 _____
6. $6a + 3 = 3(3a - 2)$; 4 _____

State whether each equation is *true*, *false*, or an *open sentence*.

7. $14 = x - 9$

8. $8 + 7 = 10$

9. $4 - 15 = 22 - 33$

10. $-7(5 - 9) = 19 - 3(-3)$

Write an equation for each sentence. State whether the equation is *true*, *false*, or an *open sentence*.

11. One fifth of a number n is equal to -7.

12. Fifty-four divided by six equals negative nine.

13. Seven less than the product of a number z and 3 is equal to 4.

Write an equation. Is the given value a solution?

14. A truck driver drove 468 miles on Tuesday. That was 132 miles farther than she drove on Monday. Let d represent the distance she drove on Monday. Did she drive 600 miles on Monday?

Name _____ Class _____ Date _____

2-4 • Guided Problem Solving

GPS Exercise 20

Write an equation. Is the given value a solution?

A veterinarian weighs 140 lb. When she steps on a scale while holding a dog, the scale shows 192 lb. Let d represent the weight of the dog. Does the dog weigh 52 lb?

Understand the Problem

1. How much does the veterinarian weigh? _____

2. What does the variable d represent? _____

3. How much do the dog and veterinarian weigh together? _____

4. What are you asked to do? _____

Make and Carry Out a Plan

5. Write a variable expression to represent the total weight of the veterinarian and dog. _____

6. Write an equation in which the variable expression is equal to the scale weight of the veterinarian and dog. _____

7. Is the equation you wrote true, false, or an open sentence? _____

8. Substitute 52 for d in the equation. _____

9. Is the equation true or false? _____

10. Does the dog weigh 52 lb? _____

Check the Answer

11. Subtract 52 lb from 192 lb. _____
    If the dog weighs 52 lb, the difference will be equal to the weight of the veterinarian.

Solve Another Problem

12. Drew has 32 trading cards. Together, Beth and Drew have 56 trading cards. Let b represent the number of trading cards Beth has. Write an equation to find out whether Beth has 25 trading cards.

    _____

Name _____ Class _____ Date _____

Practice 2-5

Solving Equations by Adding or Subtracting

Use mental math to solve each equation.

1. $-52 = -52 + k$ _____
2. $837 = p + 37$ _____
3. $x - 155 = 15$ _____
4. $180 = 80 + n$ _____
5. $2{,}000 + y = 9{,}500$ _____
6. $81 = x - 19$ _____
7. $111 + f = 100$ _____
8. $w - 6 = -16$ _____

Solve each equation.

9. $m - 17 = -8$ _____
10. $19 = c - (-12)$ _____
11. $x + 14 = 21$ _____
12. $31 = p + 17$ _____
13. $-88 + z = 0$ _____
14. $-33 + (-7) = 29 + m$ _____

15. The combined enrollment in the three grades at Jefferson Middle School is 977. There are 356 students in the seventh grade and 365 in the eighth grade. Write and solve an equation to find how many students are in the ninth grade.

    Equation _____

    Solution _____

L1 Practice

Algebra-Readiness Lesson 2-5 241

Name _____ Class _____ Date _____

2-5 • Guided Problem Solving

GPS Exercise 29

Multiple Choice In one year, 487 million people across the world spoke English. This was 512 million people fewer than the number who spoke Mandarin Chinese. Which equation could you use to find the number of millions of people n who spoke Mandarin Chinese?

A $487 = n - 512$ **C** $487 = 512 - n$

B $487 = n \times 512$ **D** $487 = 512 \div n$

Understand the Problem

1. How many people in the world spoke English in that year? _____

2. What information are you given about the number of people who spoke Mandarin Chinese in that year? _____

_____

3. What are you asked to do? _____

_____

Make and Carry Out a Plan

4. Each of the equation choices uses the variable n to represent an unknown quantity. What is the unknown quantity in the problem statement?

_____

5. What mathematical operation is implied by the phrase "512 fewer than n"? Explain.

_____

6. Which equation represents 487 is 512 fewer than n? _____

Check the Answer

7. According to the problem statement, fewer people spoke English than Mandarin Chinese. Check the reasonableness of your answer by determining whether the equation you chose makes n bigger or smaller than 487.

_____

Solve Another Problem

8. There are 32 students taking physical science. This is 119 fewer than the number of students taking Earth science. Write an equation to find the number of students s taking Earth science.

_____

242   *Algebra-Readiness Lesson 2-5*   Guided Problem Solving

Practice 2-6
Solving Equations by Multiplying or Dividing

Solve each equation.

1. $\frac{k}{-5} = -5$ _____
2. $-3 = \frac{n}{7}$ _____
3. $-6 = \frac{m}{-2}$ _____
4. $\frac{y}{-4} = -12$ _____
5. $\frac{s}{30} = 6$ _____
6. $\frac{1}{9}z = 0$ _____
7. $-\frac{m}{55} = 1$ _____
8. $-3x = 18$ _____
9. $8p = -8$ _____
10. $-2x = 34$ _____
11. $\frac{x}{-9} = -11$ _____
12. $-17v = -17$ _____
13. $\frac{y}{-21} = -21$ _____
14. $\frac{m}{-3} = 21$ _____

Write an equation for the sentence. Solve the equation.

15. Carl drove 561 miles. His car averages 33 miles per gallon of gas. Write and solve an equation to find how much gas Carl's car used. Let g represent the amount of gas Carl's car used.

   Equation: _____ Solution: _____

For what values of y is each equation true?

16. $-5|y| = -25$ _____
17. $\frac{|y|}{2} = 28$ _____

Practice — Algebra-Readiness Lesson 2-6 243

Name _____ Class _____ Date _____

2-6 • Guided Problem Solving

GPS Exercise 43

One of the world's tallest office buildings is in Malaysia. The building has 88 stories. The height of the 88 stories is 1,232 ft. What is the height of one story?

- **A** 9 ft high
- **B** 11 ft high
- **C** 14 ft high
- **D** 88 ft high

Understand the Problem

1. How many stories does the building have? _____

2. How tall is the building? _____

3. What are you asked to find? _____

Make and Carry Out a Plan

4. Choose a variable to represent the height of one story. _____

5. Use the sentence "The 1,232-ft height of the building is equal to 88 stories times the height of one story," and your variable for the height of one story, to write an equation. _____

6. What should you do to get the variable alone on one side of the equation? _____

7. Solve the equation for the variable. _____

8. What is the height of one story? _____

Check the Answer

9. Multiply the height of one story by the number of stories. _____ The result should be equal to the height of the building.

Solve Another Problem

10. You have 34 sections of fencing, all of equal length. You put them together to build a fence 136 ft long. Write an equation and solve to find the length of one section. _____

Algebra-Readiness Lesson 2-6

Name _____ Class _____ Date _____

Practice 2-7

Reasoning Strategy: Try, Test, Revise

Use the Try, Test, Revise strategy to solve each problem.

1. The length of a rectangle is 9 in. greater than the width. The area is 36 in.^{2} Area equals length times width. Find the dimensions. _____

Width						
Length						
Area						

2. Shari Williams, a basketball player, scored 30 points on 2-point and 3-point goals. She hit 5 more 2-pointers than 3-pointers. How many of each did she score? _____

3-Pointers						
2-Pointers						
Points						

3. The sums and products of pairs of integers are given. Find each pair of integers.

   a. sum = −12, product = 36 _____

   b. sum = −12, product = 35 _____

   c. sum = −12, product = 11 _____

   d. sum = −12, product = 0 _____

Solve using any strategy.

4. Jess had 3 more nickels than dimes for the total of $1.50. How many of each coin did he have?

   _____

5. A brush cost $2 more than a comb. The brush and the comb together cost $3.78. Find the cost of each.

   _____

L1 Practice

Algebra-Readiness Lesson 2-7 245

Name _____ Class _____ Date _____

2-7 • Guided Problem Solving

GPS Exercise 8

In a group of quarters and nickels, there are four more nickels than quarters. How many nickels and quarters are there if the coins are worth $2.30?

Understand the Problem

1. What two types of coins are in the group? _____

2. How many more nickels are there than quarters? _____

3. How much are the coins worth altogether? _____

4. What are you asked to find? _____

Make and Carry Out a Plan

5. To find their worth, by what number must you multiply the number of nickels? The number of quarters? _____

6. Copy the table at right. Record your conjectures about the number of quarters and nickels, adding rows as necessary.

Quarters	Nickels	Total Worth
1	5	1(0.25) + 5(0.05) = 0.50

7. a. Test the first conjecture. Are the numbers of quarters and nickels too high or too low? _____

   b. How should you revise your conjecture? _____

8. Continue until you find the correct numbers of nickels and quarters. How many nickels and quarters have a total worth of $2.30? _____

Check the Answer

9. How did you know whether to increase or decrease the numbers of nickels and quarters in each conjecture? _____

Solve Another Problem

10. Kai has nickels and dimes in his pocket. The coins are worth $1.85. He has five fewer nickels than dimes. How many dimes and nickels does he have? _____

Algebra-Readiness Lesson 2-7   Guided Problem Solving

Practice 2-8

Inequalities and Their Graphs

Write an inequality for each sentence.

1. The total t is less than sixteen. _____

2. The price p is less than or equal to $25. _____

3. A number n is negative. _____

Write an inequality for each graph.

4. (number line with closed dot at -7, shaded left) _____

5. (number line with open dot at -10, shaded right) _____

6. (number line with open dot at 2, shaded left) _____

7. (number line with closed dot at -3, shaded right) _____

Graph the solutions of each inequality on a number line.

8. $x < -2$

9. $y \geq -1$

10. $k > 1$

11. $p \leq 4$

Write an inequality for each situation. Use the variable given.

12. The speed limit is 60 miles per hour. Let s be the speed of a car driving within the limit.
_____

13. You have $4.50 to spend on lunch. Let c be the cost of your lunch.
_____

Practice · Algebra-Readiness Lesson 2-8

Name _____ Class _____ Date _____

2-8 • Guided Problem Solving

GPS Exercise 32

Write an inequality to describe this situation. A student pays for three movie tickets with a twenty-dollar bill and gets change back. Let t be the cost of a movie ticket.

Understand the Problem

1. How many movie tickets did the student buy? _____

2. How did the student pay for the movie tickets? _____

3. What does the variable t represent? _____

Make and Carry Out a Plan

4. Write an expression to represent the cost of three movie tickets. _____

5. What information tells you that the three movie tickets cost less than twenty dollars? _____
_____

6. Write the inequality using the expression from Step 4. _____

Check the Answer

7. How would the problem read differently if the three tickets cost more than twenty dollars? _____
_____

Solve Another Problem

8. Write an inequality for this situation. Katrina bought four greeting cards. She gave the clerk a five-dollar bill plus some change to pay for the cards. Let g be the cost of a greeting card. _____

248 Algebra-Readiness Lesson 2-8   Guided Problem Solving

Name _____ Class _____ Date _____

Practice 2-9
Solving One-Step Inequalities by Adding or Subtracting

Write an inequality for each sentence. Then solve the inequality.

1. Six less than n is less than -4.
   _____

2. The sum of a number k and five is greater than or equal to two.
   _____

3. Nine more than a number b is greater than negative three.
   _____

4. You must be at least 48 inches tall to ride an amusement park ride, and your little sister is 39 inches tall. How many inches i must she grow before she may ride the ride?
   _____

Solve each inequality. Graph the solutions.

5. $7 + x \geq 9$ _____
   (number line: $-16, -12, -8, -4, 0, 4$)

6. $-5 \leq x - 6$ _____
   (number line: $-5, -4, -3, -2, -1, 0, 1, 2, 3, 4, 5$)

7. $13 + x \geq 13$ _____
   (number line: $-5, -4, -3, -2, -1, 0, 1, 2, 3, 4, 5$)

8. $x - 8 > -5$ _____
   (number line: $-5, -4, -3, -2, -1, 0, 1, 2, 3, 4, 5$)

9. $4 + x < -2$ _____
   (number line: $-8, -7, -6, -5, -4, -3, -2, -1, 0, 1, 2$)

10. $x - 9 > -11$ _____
    (number line: $-5, -4, -3, -2, -1, 0, 1, 2, 3, 4, 5$)

11. $x - 6 \leq -1$ _____
    (number line: $-5, -4, -3, -2, -1, 0, 1, 2, 3, 4, 5$)

12. $-4 + x < -4$ _____
    (number line: $-5, -4, -3, -2, -1, 0, 1, 2, 3, 4, 5$)

L1 Practice

Algebra-Readiness Lesson 2-9   249

Name _____ Class _____ Date _____

2-9 • Guided Problem Solving

GPS Exercise 14

You are saving to buy a bicycle that will cost at least $120. Your parents give you $45 toward the bicycle. How much money will you have to save?

Understand the Problem

1. How much money will the bicycle cost? _____

2. How much money did your parents give you? _____

3. What are you asked to find? _____

Make and Carry Out a Plan

4. Write an inequality to represent the situation "The amount of money my parents gave me, plus m, the amount of money I will have to save, is at least $120." _____

5. What number must you subtract from each side of the inequality to solve for m? _____

6. Solve the inequality for m. _____

7. How much money will you have to save to buy the bicycle? _____

Check the Answer

8. Subtract from $120 the amount of money stated in your answer to Step 7. _____
The result should be equal to the amount of money your parents gave you.

Solve Another Problem

9. Shana is saving money to buy a CD player that will cost at least $65. She has $27. How much money will she have to save? _____

250   Algebra-Readiness Lesson 2-9   Guided Problem Solving

Practice 2-10

Solving One-Step Inequalities by Multiplying or Dividing

Write an inequality for each sentence. Then solve the inequality.

1. The product of k and -5 is no more than 30.

2. Half of p is at least -7.

3. The product of k and 9 is no more than 18.

4. One-third of p is at least -17.

Solve each inequality.

5. $-5x < 10$ _____

6. $\frac{x}{4} > 1$ _____

7. $-8 < -8x$ _____

8. $\frac{1}{3}x > -2$ _____

9. $\frac{x}{5} < -4$ _____

10. $-x \leq 2$ _____

Justify each step.

11. $-5n \geq 45$

$\frac{-5n}{-5} \leq \frac{45}{-5}$ _____

$n \leq -9$ _____

Practice — Algebra-Readiness Lesson 2-10

Name _____ Class _____ Date _____

2-10 • Guided Problem Solving

GPS Exercise 32

Marnie pays $.06 per kilowatt-hour for electricity. She has budgeted $72 for her electricity. What is the greatest number of kilowatt-hours Marnie can use and stay within her budget?

Understand the Problem

1. How much does Marnie pay per kilowatt-hour of electricity? _____

2. How much has Marnie budgeted for her electricity? _____

3. What are you asked to do? _____
   _____

Make and Carry Out a Plan

4. Let k represent the number of kilowatt-hours. Use the sentence "$.06 per kilowatt-hour multiplied by the number of kilowatt-hours is less than or equal to $72" to write an inequality. _____

5. What number should you divide each side of the inequality by to get the variable k alone on one side? _____

6. Solve the inequality for k. _____

7. What is the greatest number of kilowatt-hours of electricity Marnie can use and stay in budget? _____

Check the Answer

8. To check your answer, multiply your answer by the price per kilowatt-hour Marnie pays for electricity. _____
   The product should be less than or equal to $72.

Solve Another Problem

9. Derek enjoys going to movies. He budgets $30 a month for movies. Admission for one movie costs $7.25. How many movies can he see in one month and stay within budget? _____

252 Algebra-Readiness Lesson 2-10   Guided Problem Solving

Name _____ Class _____ Date _____

2A: Graphic Organizer
For use before Lesson 2-1

Study Skill As you begin each new chapter, ask yourself: *What is the main idea of this chapter?* and *How is the material divided?*

Write your answers. Use the Table of Contents page for this chapter at the front of the book.

1. What is the title of this chapter? _____

2. Name four topics that you will study in this chapter.

   _____   _____

   _____   _____

3. What is the topic of the Reasoning Strategy lesson? _____

4. Complete the graphic organizer as you work through the chapter.
   1. Write the title of the chapter in the center oval.
   2. When you begin a lesson, write the name of the lesson in a rectangle.
   3. When you complete that lesson, write a skill or key concept from that lesson in the outer oval linked to that rectangle.

   Continue with steps 2 and 3 clockwise around the graphic organizer.

Vocabulary and Study Skills   Algebra-Readiness Chapter 2   **253**

Name _____ Class _____ Date _____

2B: Reading Comprehension

For use after Lesson 2-8

Study Skill When you take notes, either as you read or as you listen to a class discussion or the teacher, you can write more quickly if you use shortcuts. Make a list of the abbreviations and symbols that you use in your notes so that you can remember the meanings of these shortcuts when you review your notes later.

Read the instructions in the box and then answer the questions about steps I–V. You do not have to do the activity in the box.

> I. Write an inequality that shows that Carlos has more than 15 books.
> II. List these numbers on your paper: 20, 18, 15, 12, 6, 5.
> III. Look at the numbers in the list.
>   a. Draw a red circle around every number in the list that is a solution.
>   b. Make a blue line through every number in the list that is not a solution.
> IV. a. How many red circles did you draw?
>   b. How many blue lines did you make?
>   c. Are there any numbers that have two color marks?
>   d. Are there any numbers that have no color marks?
> V. Graph the solutions of your inequality.

1. Read quickly through ALL the steps in the instructions. What supplies will you need to complete this task?

   _____

2. What will be the result of the action you take in step I?

   _____

3. What will be the result of the action you take in step II?

   _____

4. Notice that step III has two parts.
   List the verbs that tell you what actions to take.

   _____

5. What will be the *form* of your answers to parts (a) and (b) of step IV?

   _____

6. What will be the *form* of your answers to parts (c) and (d) of step IV?

   _____

7. **High-Use Academic Words** In step V, what does *graph* mean for you to do?

   a. make a picture   **b.** make a table

Algebra-Readiness Chapter 2   Vocabulary and Study Skills

Name_____ Class_____ Date_____

2C: Reading/Writing Math Symbols   For use after Lesson 2-3

Study Skill Taking notes in class, or while you study, helps you remember the content. Your notes also help you to review what you have learned. Write your notes clearly so that you will be able to read them accurately later, when you may have forgotten some of the words.

Write the symbol(s), letter(s), or number(s) described in each of the following. The first one is done for you.

1. the constant term in $5x + 6$

   _____6_____

2. the number of like terms in $3a + 4b - 7a + 9d$

   _____

3. the identity element for multiplication

   _____

4. the number to be distributed in $7(2m + 3p)$

   _____

5. the variable to be distributed in $a(b + c)$

   _____

6. the identity element for addition

   _____

7. the number of terms in $3x + 2y$

   _____

8. the coefficient of b in $12a + 13b + 14$

   _____

9. the like terms in $2x - 2y + 3x$

   _____

10. the coefficient of p in $-5p - 2q$

    _____

2D: Visual Vocabulary Practice

For use after Lesson 2-5

Study Skill Mathematics builds on itself so build a strong foundation.

Concept List

coefficient	constant	equation
expression	graph	inverse operations
open sentence	solution of equation	terms

Write the concept that best describes each exercise. Choose from the concept list shown above.

1. $4x$ and 9 in $4x + 9$	2. (number line with point at -2, marks at $-4, -2, 0, 2, 4, 6$)	3. 9 in $2n - 6m + 9$
4. The 3 and 6 in $3a + 6b - 10$	5. The number 3 if $y + 19 = 22$	6. $4c - 6 = c$
7. $5(4 - 2) = 10$	8. addition and subtraction	9. $-8x + 6xy + 7y$

256 *Algebra-Readiness* Chapter 2   Vocabulary and Study Skills

Name _____ Class _____ Date _____

2E: Vocabulary Check

For use after Lesson 2-9

Study Skill Strengthen your vocabulary. Use these pages and add cues and summaries by applying the Cornell Notetaking style.

Write the definition for each word at the right. To check your work, fold the paper back along the dotted line to see the correct answers.

_____ Constant
_____
_____

_____ Like terms
_____
_____

_____ Open Sentence
_____
_____

_____ Equation
_____
_____

_____ Inequality
_____
_____

Vocabulary and Study Skills   *Algebra-Readiness* Chapter 2   **257**

Name _____ Class _____ Date _____

2E: Vocabulary Check (continued)   For use after Lesson 2-9

Write the vocabulary word for each definition. To check your work, fold the paper forward along the dotted line to see the correct answers.

A term that has no variable.   _____

Terms with the same variable(s) raised to the same power(s).   _____

An equation with one or more variables.   _____

A mathematical sentence with an equal sign, =.   _____

A sentence that uses one or more of the symbols <, >, ≥, ≤, or ≠.   _____

258 *Algebra-Readiness* Chapter 2   Vocabulary and Study Skills

Name _____ Class _____ Date _____

2F: Vocabulary Review

For use with Chapter Review

Study Skill To succeed in mathematics, you need to understand the language and the words. Learn the new math terms one at a time by drawing a diagram or by writing a sentence to make the meaning clear.

Match each word or phrase in the left column with the best example in the right column. Some words or phrases may have more than one example, but only one example is the best match.

Word or Phrase

1. Addition Property of Equality
2. Additive Identity
3. Associative Property
4. Commutative Property
5. Multiplicative Identity

Example or Definition

A. $w + 0 = w$

B. $n \cdot 1 = n$

C. $(pq)r = p(qr)$

D. If $a = c$, then $a + b = c + b$.

E. $x \cdot y = y \cdot x$

Word or Phrase

6. constant
7. open sentence
8. equation
9. solution
10. term

Example or Definition

A. $6 + 22 = 28$

B. $13y$

C. $17 + b = 47$

D. 75

E. When $x + 37 = 62$, $x = 25$.

Vocabulary and Study Skills — Algebra-Readiness Chapter 2

Name _____ Class _____ Date _____

Practice 3-1   Rounding and Estimating

Estimate using front-end estimation.

1. 6.3 + 8.55 _____

2. 4.60 + 5.53 _____

3. $6.14 + $9.38 _____

4. 9.71 + 3.94 _____

Estimate using clustering.

5. $7.04 + $5.95 + $6.08 + $5.06 + $6.12 _____

6. 9.3 + 8.7 + 8.91 + 9.052 _____

Estimate by rounding each number to the same place.

7. 14.66 + 25.19 _____

8. 8.7 + 3.21 + 3.899 _____

9. $86.91 − $67.20 _____

10. 800 − 301.47 _____

Round to the underlined place.

11. 6.739 _____

12. 52.192 _____

13. 0.61 _____

14. 348.508 _____

Estimate. State your method (rounding, front-end, or clustering).

15. 91.7 + 88.6 + 89.1 + 92.5 + 90.6 _____

16. 3.9 + 8.1 + 2.06 _____

Name _____ Class _____ Date _____

3-1 • Guided Problem Solving

GPS Exercise 27

Mobile, Alabama, has an average annual rainfall of 63.96 in. The average annual rainfall in San Francisco, California, is 19.70 in. About how much more rain falls each year in Mobile than in San Francisco?

Understand the Problem

1. What is the average annual rainfall in Mobile, Alabama? _____

2. What is the average annual rainfall in San Francisco, California? _____

3. What are you asked to find? _____
   _____

Make and Carry Out a Plan

4. Round the average annual rainfall in Mobile to the nearest inch. _____

5. Round the average annual rainfall in San Francisco to the nearest inch. _____

6. Write an expression, using your estimates, to find about how much more rain falls annually in Mobile than in San Francisco. _____

7. Simplify the expression. _____

8. About how many more inches of rain fall each year in Mobile than in San Francisco? _____

Check the Answer

9. Round the average annual rainfalls in Mobile and San Francisco to the tens place. Then subtract to find about how many more inches of rain fall in Mobile than in San Francisco each year. _____
   The result should be close to your answer to Question 8.

Solve Another Problem

10. A snowstorm dropped 13.88 inches of snow on Minneapolis, Minnesota. Only 8.12 inches of snow fell in Chicago, Illinois from the same storm. About how much more snow fell in Minneapolis than in Chicago? _____

Algebra-Readiness Lesson 3-1

Practice 3-2

Estimating Decimal Products and Quotients

Determine whether each product or quotient is reasonable. If it is not reasonable, find a reasonable result.

1. $(55.14)(4.98) = 275$ _____

2. $15.14 \div 2.96 = 54.5$ _____

3. $2.65(-0.84) = -0.2226$ _____

4. $381.274 \div 5.07 = 75.2$ _____

5. $59.45 \div 7.25 = 8.2$ _____

6. $-40.1(-1.99) = 7.2954$ _____

7. $1.939(6.1) = 115.857$ _____

8. $3.276 \div 0.63 = 5.2$ _____

Estimate each product or quotient.

9. $8.73 \cdot 6.01$ _____

10. $11.042(4.56)$ _____

11. $29.5 \div 5.1$ _____

12. $\$41.59 \div \$6.88$ _____

13. $148.8 \div 9.8$ _____

14. $\$74.77 \div \$24.89$ _____

Solve the following problems by estimating a quotient or a product.

15. Apples cost $.89 per lb. Estimate the cost of three 5-lb bags. _____

16. You worked 16 hours last week and received $92.70 in your paycheck. Estimate your hourly pay.

_____

Name _____ Class _____ Date _____

3-2 • Guided Problem Solving

GPS Exercise 34

Shari is planning a 450-mi car trip. Her car can travel about 39 mi on a gallon of gasoline. Gasoline costs $1.89/gal. About how much will the gas cost for her trip?

Understand the Problem

1. How many miles is the car trip Shari is planning? _____

2. About how many miles can Shari's car travel on a gallon of gasoline? _____

3. How much does gasoline cost per gallon? _____

4. What are you asked to find? _____

Make and Carry Out a Plan

5. Write an expression using the total number of miles in the trip and the number of miles Shari can drive on one gallon of gasoline to find how many gallons of gasoline Shari will need to complete her trip. _____

6. Since the question says "about," round the divisor to the nearest ten. _____

7. Round the dividend to a multiple of the rounded divisor. Keep the rounded dividend close to 450. _____

8. Rewrite your expression from Step 5 using your rounded values from Steps 6 and 7. Simplify. _____

9. Round $1.89 to the nearest dollar. _____

10. Write an expression to find the approximate cost of the gasoline for Shari's trip. _____

11. About how much will the gas cost for Shari's trip? _____

Check the Answer

12. Use a calculator to simplify your expression from Step 5 and multiply by 1.89 to find the exact answer to the problem. _____
    The result should be close to your answer to Question 11.

Solve Another Problem

13. Julia is planning to drive to see her sister, who lives 285 mi away. Her car can travel about 32 mi on a gallon of gasoline. Gasoline costs $1.85 a gallon. About how much will gasoline cost for her trip? _____

Algebra-Readiness Lesson 3-2

Practice 3-3

Using Formulas

Use the formula $P = 2l + 2w$. Find the perimeter of each rectangle.

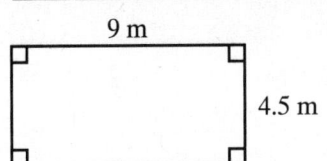

1. _____

   9 m, 4.5 m

2. _____

   5 ft, 1.5 ft

Use the formula $A = lw$. Find the area of each rectangle above.

3. _____   4. _____

5. Use the formula $d = rt$ to find how far each animal in the table can travel in 5 seconds.

Animal	Speed (ft/s)	Distance in 5 s (ft)
Pronghorn antelope	89.5	
Gray fox	61.6	
Wild turkey	22.0	
Chicken	13.2	

6. While vacationing on the Mediterranean Sea, Angie recorded the temperature several times during a 24-hour period. Use the formula $F = 1.8C + 32$ to change the temperatures Angie recorded from Celsius to Fahrenheit.

Time	Temperature (°C)	Temperature (°F)
4:00 A.M.	19	
8:00 A.M.	22	
12:00 P.M.	30	
4:00 P.M.	28	
8:00 P.M.	24	
12:00 A.M.	20	

L1 Practice   Algebra-Readiness Lesson 3-3

Name _____ Class _____ Date _____

3-3 • Guided Problem Solving

GPS Exercise 25

Geometry Use the formula $P = 2\ell + 2w$. Find the perimeter of the rectangle. Then use the formula $A = \ell w$ to find the area.

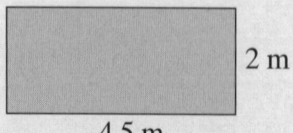

3.7 m
7.3 m

Understand the Problem

1. What is the width of the rectangle? _____

2. What is the length of the rectangle? _____

3. What are you asked to find? _____

Make and Carry Out a Plan

4. Replace ℓ with 7.3 and w with 3.7 in the formula $P = 2\ell + 2w$. _____

5. Simplify by multiplying. _____

6. Add. What is the perimeter of the rectangle? _____

7. Replace ℓ with 7.3 and w with 3.7 in the formula $A = \ell w$. _____

8. Multiply. What is the area of the rectangle? _____

Check the Answer

9. To check your answer to Question 6, add the measurements of the 4 sides together. _____
   Your answer should be the same as your answer to Question 6.

10. To check your answer to Question 7, divide your answer by the length of the rectangle. _____
    Your answer should be the width of the rectangle.

Solve Another Problem

11. Use the formula $P = 2\ell + 2w$. Find the perimeter of the rectangle. Then use the formula $A = \ell w$ to find the area. _____

2 m
4.5 m

266 Algebra-Readiness Lesson 3-3   Guided Problem Solving

Name _____ Class _____ Date _____

Practice 3-4   Solving Equations by Adding or Subtracting Decimals

Solve each equation.

1. $3.81 = n - 3.62$

2. $x - 19.7 = -17.48$

3. $y - 48.763 = 0$

4. $-25 = p + 10.7$

5. $x + (-0.0025) = 0.0024$

6. $-0.08 = f + 0.07$

7. $0 = a + 27.98$

8. $5.4 = t + (-6.1)$

9. $z - 1.6 = -1.6$

10. $4.87 = n + 0.87$

Use mental math to solve each equation.

11. $k + 23.7 = 23.7$

12. $5.63 = n + 1.63$

13. $x - 3.2 = 4.1$

14. $p - 0.7 = 9.3$

Name _____ Class _____ Date _____

3-4 • Guided Problem Solving

GPS Exercise 20

Michael Johnson's world record in the 200-m sprint is 19.32 s. His 400-m world record is 23.86 s slower than his 200-m record. Write and solve an equation to find Johnson's 400-m record.

Understand the Problem

1. What is Michael Johnson's world record in the 200-m sprint? _____

2. How much slower is his 400-m world record than his 200-m world record? _____

3. What are you asked to do? _____
   _____

Make and Carry Out a Plan

4. Let r represent Michael Johnson's 400-m world record. Use the sentence "Michael Johnson's 400-m record minus 23.86 s is equal to his 200-m world record" to write an equation to represent the situation. _____

5. For your equation from Question 4, what number must you add to both sides to get r alone on one side? _____

6. Solve the equation for r. _____

7. What is Michael Johnson's 400-m world record? _____

Check the Answer

8. To check your answer, subtract 23.86 from your answer to Question 7. _____
   The result should be Michael Johnson's 200-m world record.

Solve Another Problem

9. Karin's best time in the 50-yd freestyle is 25.68 s. Her best time in the 100-yd freestyle is 32.85 s slower. Write and solve an equation to find Karin's best time in the 100-yd freestyle. _____

268 *Algebra-Readiness* Lesson 3-4 Guided Problem Solving

Name _____ Class _____ Date _____

Practice 3-5
Solving Equations by Multiplying or Dividing Decimals

Use mental math to solve each equation.

1. $0.7h = 4.2$ _____
2. $\dfrac{x}{2.5} = -3$ _____
3. $38.7 = -100k$ _____
4. $-45.6e = -4.56$ _____

Solve each equation.

5. $\dfrac{p}{2.9} = 0.55$ _____
6. $9.1 = \dfrac{x}{-0.7}$ _____
7. $-6.4 = \dfrac{y}{8.5}$ _____
8. $\dfrac{k}{-1.2} = -0.07$ _____
9. $-9k = 2.34$ _____
10. $-12.42 = 0.03p$ _____
11. $-7.2y = 61.2$ _____
12. $-0.1035 = 0.23n$ _____

Write an equation for each sentence. Solve for the variable.

13. The opposite of seventy-five hundredths times some number n equals twenty-four thousandths. Find the value of n.

_____

14. A number n divided by -3.88 equals negative two thousand. Find the value of n.

_____

Algebra-Readiness Lesson 3-5

Name_____ Class_____ Date_____

3-5 • Guided Problem Solving

GPS Exercise 37

Number Sense The weight of a record-setting onion was 12.25 lb. An average-sized onion weighs 0.5 lb. About how many average-sized onions have a total weight equal to the record-setting onion?

Understand the Problem

1. How much did the record-setting onion weigh? _____

2. How much does an average-sized onion weigh? _____

3. What are you asked to find? _____
   _____

Make and Carry Out a Plan

4. Let *n* represent the number of average-sized onions. Use the sentence "The number of average-sized onions times the weight of an average-sized onion equals the weight of the record-setting onion" to write a multiplication equation to represent the situation. _____

5. For your equation from Question 4, by what number must you divide each side to get *n* alone on one side? _____

6. Solve the equation for *n*. _____

7. About how many average-sized onions have a total weight equal to the record-setting onion? Round your answer to the nearest integer. _____

Check the Answer

8. Find the total weight of the number of onions you found in Question 7. _____
   It should be equal to the weight of the record-setting onion.

Solve Another Problem

9. Doug has a marble collection. Altogether, his marbles weigh 232.8 g. Each marble weighs about 9 g. About how many marbles does Doug have? _____

270 Algebra-Readiness Lesson 3-5   Guided Problem Solving

Practice 3-6

Using the Metric System

Write the metric unit that makes each statement true.

1. 7.84 cm = 78.4 _____
2. 423 m = 0.423 _____
3. 2.8 m = 280 _____
4. 6.5 km = 650,000 _____

Complete each statement.

5. 3.4 cm = _____ mm
6. 197.5 cm = _____ m
7. 7 L = _____ mL
8. 5,247 mg = _____ g
9. 87 g = _____ kg
10. 9,246 mL = _____ L

Choose a reasonable estimate. Explain your choice.

11. the amount of water a cup would hold: 250 mL   250 L
_____

12. the mass of a bag of apples: 2 g   2 kg
_____

Choose an appropriate metric unit of measure. Explain your choice.

13. distance between two cities
_____

14. the mass of a pencil
_____

15. the capacity of an automobile's gas tank
_____

16. A fish pond holds 2,500 liters of water. How many kiloliters is this?
_____

Practice

Algebra-Readiness Lesson 3-6   271

Name _____ Class _____ Date _____

3-6 • Guided Problem Solving

GPS Exercise 45

A hippopotamus is so large that it has a stomach 304.8 cm long, yet it is agile enough to outrun a human. How long is the stomach of a hippopotamus in meters?

Understand the Problem

1. How long is the stomach of a hippopotamus in centimeters? _____

2. What are you asked to find? _____
_____

Make and Carry Out a Plan

3. How many centimeters are in a meter? _____

4. Use the sentence "Length in centimeters divided by number of centimeters per meter equals length in meters" to write an equation to find the length of the hippopotamus's stomach in meters. _____

5. Calculate to find the length in meters of the stomach of a hippopotamus. _____

Check the Answer

6. Convert the length of a hippopotamus's stomach in meters (from Question 5) back to centimeters. _____

Solve Another Problem

7. Grace is 143.7 cm tall. What is her height in meters? _____

Name _____ Class _____ Date _____

Practice 3-7

Reasoning Strategy: Act It Out

Solve by acting out each problem.

1. A house-number manufacturer sold numbers to retail stores for $.09 per digit. A hardware store bought enough digits for two of every house number from 1 to 999. How many digits did the store purchase for house numbers:

    a. 1–9 _____   b. 10–99 _____   c. 100–999 _____

    d. Find the total cost of the house numbers. _____

2. A tic-tac-toe diagram uses 2 vertical lines and 2 horizontal lines to create 9 spaces. How many spaces can you create using:

    a. 1 vertical line and 1 horizontal line _____

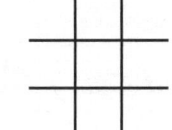

    b. 2 vertical lines and 1 horizontal line _____

    c. 3 vertical lines and 3 horizontal lines _____

    d. 4 vertical lines and 5 horizontal lines _____

3. Each side of each triangle in the figure has length 1 cm. The perimeter (the distance around) the first triangle is 3 cm. Find the perimeter of the figure formed by connecting:

    a. 2 triangles _____   b. 3 triangles _____

    c. 4 triangles _____

Solve using any strategy.

4. At the inauguration, the President was honored with a 21-gun salute. The report from each gunshot lasted 1 s. Four seconds elapsed between shots. How long did the salute last?

    _____

L1 Practice

Algebra-Readiness Lesson 3-7   **273**

Name _____ Class _____ Date _____

3-7 • Guided Problem Solving

GPS Exercise 4

The school store buys pencils for $.20 each. It sells the pencils for $.25 each. How much profit does the store make if it sells five dozen pencils?

Understand the Problem

1. How much does the school store pay for pencils? _____

2. For how much does the school store sell the pencils? _____

3. What are you asked to find? _____
_____

Make and Carry Out a Plan

4. Write an expression to find the amount of profit the store makes on one pencil. Simplify. _____

5. How many pencils are in one dozen? _____

6. How many pencils are in five dozen? _____

7. Write an expression to find the amount of profit the store makes on five dozen pencils. _____

8. How much profit does the store make if it sells five dozen pencils? _____

Check the Answer

9. Solve the problem another way to check your answer. First, find the amount of money the store pays for five dozen pencils. _____

10. Next, find the amount of money for which the store sells five dozen pencils. _____

11. Finally, subtract the amount you found in Question 9 from the amount in Question 10 to find the store's profit on the five dozen pencils. _____
Compare with your answer to Question 8.

Solve Another Problem

12. A store sells watchbands for $4.25 each. It buys the watchbands for $2.10 each. If the store sells 20 watchbands, how much profit does the store make? _____

274 Algebra-Readiness Lesson 3-7   Guided Problem Solving

Name _____ Class _____ Date _____

3A: Graphic Organizer

For use before Lesson 3-1

Study Skill Keep notes as you work through each chapter to help you organize your thinking and to make it easier to review the material when you complete the chapter.

Write your answers. Use the Table of Contents page for this chapter at the front of the book.

1. What is the title of this chapter? _____

2. Name four topics that you will study in this chapter.

   _____ _____

   _____ _____

3. What is the topic of the Reasoning Strategy lesson? _____

4. Complete the graphic organizer as you work through the chapter.
   1. Write the title of the chapter in the center oval.
   2. When you begin a lesson, write the name of the lesson in a rectangle.
   3. When you complete that lesson, write a skill or key concept from that lesson in the outer oval linked to that rectangle.
   Continue with steps 2 and 3 clockwise around the graphic organizer.

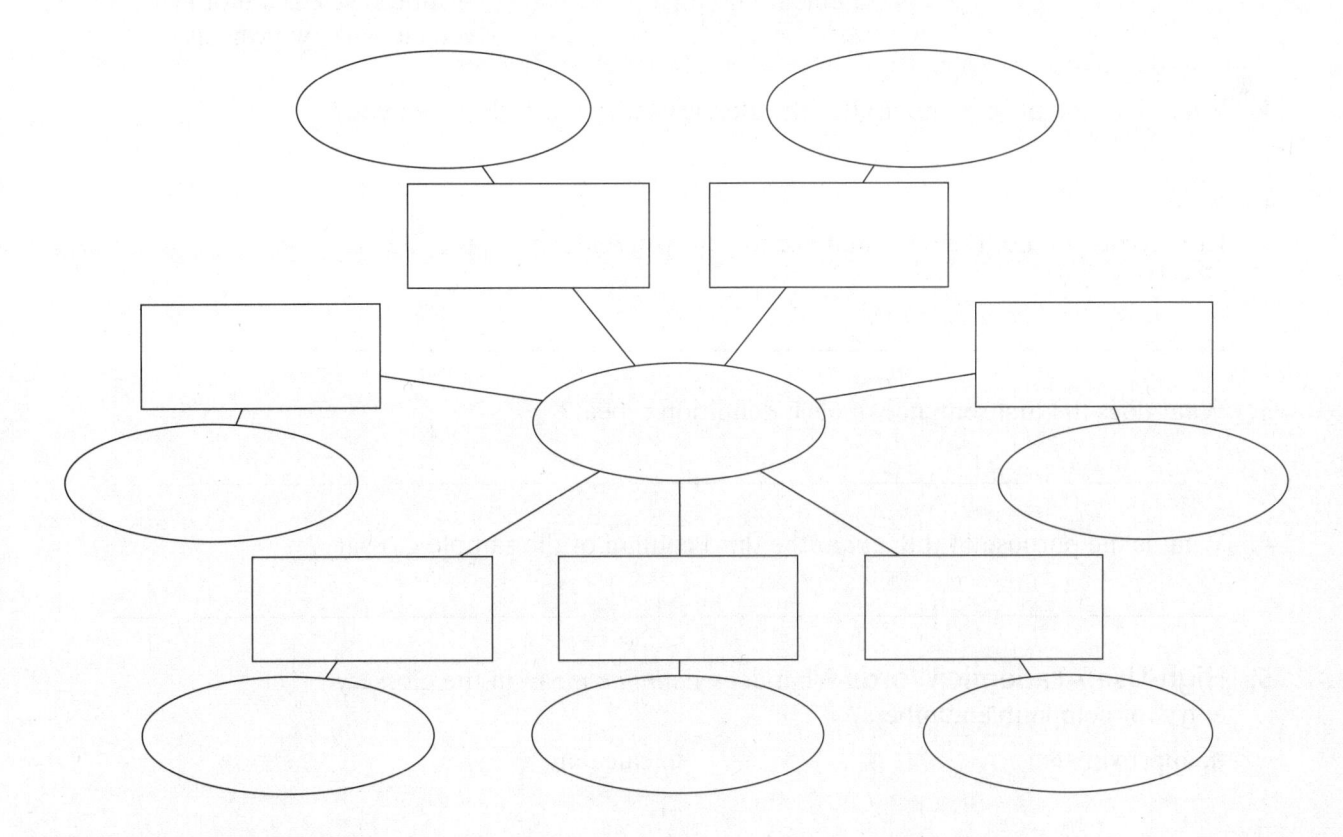

Vocabulary and Study Skills   *Algebra-Readiness* Chapter 3   **275**

Name _____ Class _____ Date _____

3B: Reading Comprehension

For use after Lesson 3-2

Study Skill If you cannot identify the meaning of unfamiliar words from the context of the sentence, list the word and its page number on a piece of paper. After you finish reading, use a dictionary to look up and record the meanings of the unfamiliar words on your list. Then look back at the pages where you found the unfamiliar words and read the passages again.

Read the entries from this sample glossary. Then answer the questions about how to read glossary entries.

Compatible numbers (p. 133)	Compatible numbers are numbers that are close in value to the numbers you want to add, subtract, multiply, or divide, and for which the computation is easy to perform mentally.	Estimate $151 \div 14.6$. $151 \approx 150$ $14.6 \approx 15$ $150 \div 15 = 10$ $151 \div 14.6 \approx 10$
Composite number (p. 182)	A composite number is an integer greater than 1 with more than two positive factors.	24 is a composite number that has 1, 2, 3, 4, 6, 8, 12, and 24 as factors.
Counterexample (p. 37)	A counterexample is an example that proves a statement false.	Statement: Motor vehicles have four wheels. Counterexample: A motorcycle is a motor vehicle with two wheels.

1. What does the page number after the glossary entry most likely tell you?
   _____

2. How could you use the page number to help you understand the glossary entry?
   _____

3. What does the first sentence of each definition repeat?
   _____

4. What is the purpose of the text in the third column of the sample glossary?
   _____

5. **High-Use Academic Words** What does *Estimate* mean in the glossary entry for compatible numbers?

   a. approximate   b. calculate

276 *Algebra-Readiness* Chapter 3   Vocabulary and Study Skills

Name_____ Class_____ Date_____

3C: Reading/Writing Math Symbols   For use after Lesson 3-6

Study Skill You may want to save time as you take notes in any subject by using abbreviations and symbols. Here are some common symbols:
@ (at); # (number); w/ (with); w/o (without); & (and).

On the blank, rewrite the expression or statement using symbols in place of words.

1. p divided by 0.7

2. b is less than or equal to -23.

3. 7 meters

4. $t + 5$ is less than 28.

5. 3 more than h

6. 56.9 centimeters

7. 7 is greater than or equal to g.

8. two thirds plus three fourths

9. eleven less than four and five tenths

10. negative seven twelfths

11. fifteen times a number

Vocabulary and Study Skills   Algebra-Readiness Chapter 3

Name _____ Class _____ Date _____

3D: Visual Vocabulary Practice
High-Use Academic Words

For use after Lesson 3-3

Study Skill If a word is not in the Glossary, use a dictionary to find its meaning.

Concept List

compare	convert	define
describe	estimate	evaluate
explain	identify	model

Write the concept that best describes each exercise. Choose from the concept list above.

1. Let n = number of CDs.	2. $3a + 4$ for $a = -5$ $3 \cdot a + 4 = 3 \cdot (-5) + 4$ $ = -15 + 4$ $ = -11$	3. $4.72 \cdot 1.8 \approx 10$
4. $8 \div 4 = 2$ — dividend, quotient, divisor	5. $2 + (-5)$ -3 $2 + (-5) = -3$	6. Three items are priced at $4.59, $2.75, and $3.40.
7. $-6 < 5$	8. To plot (x, y), start at the origin. Move horizontally x units. Then move vertically y units.	9. The length of the table is 72 inches, or 6 feet.

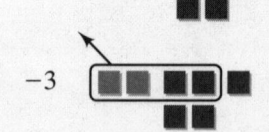

278 Algebra-Readiness Chapter 3 — Vocabulary and Study Skills

Name _____ Class _____ Date _____

3E: Vocabulary Check

For use after Lesson 3-7

Study Skill Strengthen your vocabulary. Use these pages and add cues and summaries by applying the Cornell Notetaking style.

Write the definition for each word at the right. To check your work, fold the paper back along the dotted line to see the correct answers.

_____

_____

_____ Compatible numbers

_____

_____

_____

_____ Formula

_____

_____

_____

_____ Perimeter

_____

_____

_____

_____ Term

_____

_____

_____

_____ Significant digits

_____

_____

Vocabulary and Study Skills   Algebra-Readiness Chapter 3

Name _____ Class _____ Date _____

3E: Vocabulary Check (continued)   For use after Lesson 3-7

Write the vocabulary word for each definition. To check your work, fold the paper forward along the dotted line to see the correct answers.

Numbers that are easy to divide mentally.   _____

An equation that shows a relationship between quantities that are represented by variables.   _____

The distance around a figure.   _____

A number, a variable, or the product of a number and variable(s).   _____

The digits that represent the actual measurement.   _____

280   *Algebra-Readiness* Chapter 3   Vocabulary and Study Skills

3F: Vocabulary Review Puzzle

Study Skill When you are learning a new skill or new vocabulary words, stay alert so that you will store what you read or hear in your memory. If your mind wanders, take written notes to help you stay focused.

Use words from the list to complete the crossword puzzle. For help, use the Glossary in your textbook.

formula	conjecture
metric	variable
perimeter	coefficient
compatible	equation

ACROSS

4. numbers that are easy to divide mentally
5. conclusion you reach by inductive reasoning
6. distance around a figure
7. system of measurement units based on 10

DOWN

1. equation that relates quantities represented by variables
2. mathematical sentence with an equal sign
3. letter that stands for a number
4. number that multiplies a variable

Practice 4-1

Divisibility and Factors

List the positive factors of each integer.

1. 6 _____

2. 15 _____

3. 41 _____

4. 27 _____

5. 100 _____

6. 39 _____

State whether each number is divisible by 2, 3, 5, 9, 10, or none.

7. 85 _____

8. 1,011 _____

9. 2,070 _____

10. 3,707 _____

Write the missing digit to make each number divisible by 9.

11. 7☐1

12. 2,2☐2

13. 88,☐12

14. There are two different digits which, when inserted in the blank space in the number 7,16☐, make the number divisible by 5. Write them.

15. There are five different digits which, when inserted in the blank space in the number 99,99☐, make the number divisible by 2. Write them.

Name_____ Class_____ Date_____

4-1 • Guided Problem Solving

GPS Exercise 45

Reasoning John made oatmeal cookies for a class bake sale. The cookies need to be distributed equally on 2 or more plates. If each plate gets at least 7 cookies, what are the possible combinations for the totals below?

a. 42 cookies   **b.** 56 cookies   **c.** 60 cookies   **d.** 144 cookies

Understand the Problem

1. At least how many plates must John use to distribute the cookies? _____

2. At least how many cookies must be on each plate? _____

Make and Carry Out a Plan

3. List the different ways that 42 can be written as the product of two factors. _____

4. What are the possible combinations of plates and cookies for 42 cookies? (Remember, the number of plates must be 2 or greater and the number of cookies must be 7 or greater.) _____
_____

5. What are the possible combinations for 56 cookies? _____
_____

6. What are the possible combinations for 60 cookies? _____
_____

7. What are the possible combinations for 144 cookies? _____
_____

Check the Answer

8. Why do the combinations of plates and cookies need to be factors of the number of cookies? _____
_____

Solve Another Problem

9. Jenna is looking at ways to seat the guests at her wedding. There will be at least 8 tables and each table must have at least 4 guests. What are the possible combinations for 64 guests? _____

Algebra-Readiness Lesson 4-1   Guided Problem Solving

Name _____ Class _____ Date _____

Practice 4-2   Exponents

Evaluate each expression.

1. m^4, for $m = 5$ _____   2. $(5a)^3$, for $a = -1$ _____

3. $-(2p)^2$, for $p = 7$ _____   4. $-n^6$, for $n = 2$ _____

5. $(6 + h^2)^2$, for $h = 3$ _____   6. $x^2 + 3x - 7$, for $x = -4$ _____

Write using exponents.

7. $3 \cdot 3 \cdot 3 \cdot 3$ _____

8. $k \cdot k \cdot k \cdot k \cdot k$ _____

9. $g \cdot g \cdot g \cdot g \cdot h$ _____

10. $7 \cdot a \cdot a \cdot b \cdot b \cdot b$ _____

Simplify.

11. $(-2)^3$ and -2^3 _____   12. 0^{12} _____

13. 2^8 and 4^4 _____   14. $-5^2 + 4 \cdot 2^3$ _____

15. $3(8 - 6)^2$ _____   16. $-6^2 + 2 \cdot 3^2$ _____

Name _____ Class _____ Date _____

4-2 • Guided Problem Solving

GPS Exercise 28

Error Analysis A student gives ab^3 as an answer when asked to write the expression $ab \cdot ab \cdot ab$ using exponents. What is the student's error?

Understand the Problem

1. What expression was the student asked to write using exponents? _____

2. What was the answer the student gave? _____

3. What are you asked to do? _____

Make and Carry Out a Plan

4. Rewrite $ab \cdot ab \cdot ab$ so that the like terms are grouped together. _____

5. Rewrite your expression from Step 4 using exponents. _____

6. How is what you wrote in Step 5 different from the answer the student gave, ab^3? _____
_____

7. What is the student's error? _____
_____

Check the Answer

8. Evaluate $ab \cdot ab \cdot ab$ for $a = 1$ and $b = 2$. _____

9. Evaluate your answer to Step 5 for $a = 1$ and $b = 2$. If you wrote $ab \cdot ab \cdot ab$ using exponents correctly, your answers for Steps 8 and 9 will be the same. _____

Solve Another Problem

10. When asked to write the expression $(-4)(-4)(-4)(-4)$ using exponents, Jeremiah wrote -4^4. What error did he make? _____
_____

286 Algebra-Readiness Lesson 4-2   Guided Problem Solving

Name _____ Class _____ Date _____

Practice 4-3 Prime Factorization and Greatest Common Divisor

Find each GCD.

1. 4, 8 _____
2. 36, 54 _____
3. 5, 7 _____
4. 14, 21 _____
5. $30m, 36n$ _____
6. $75x^3y^2, 100xy$ _____
7. 15, 24, 30 _____
8. 32, 48, 80 _____

Is each number prime, composite, or neither? For each composite number, write the prime factorization.

9. 75 _____
10. 152 _____
11. 160 _____
12. 108 _____
13. 19 _____
14. 143 _____
15. 83 _____
16. 137 _____

Name _____ Class _____ Date _____

4-3 • Guided Problem Solving

GPS Exercise 28

A math teacher and a science teacher combine their first-period classes for a group activity. The math class has 24 students and the science class has 16 students. The teachers need to divide the students into groups of the same size. Each group must have the same number of math students. Find the greatest number of groups possible.

Understand the Problem

1. How many students are in the math class? _____

2. How many students are in the science class? _____

3. What must be true about the groups into which the students are divided? _____
_____

4. What are you asked to find? _____

Make and Carry Out a Plan

5. The 24 math students are divided equally. List the factors of 24. _____

6. For the groups to have the same size, the science students must also be divided equally. List the factors of 16. _____

7. What factors do 24 and 16 have in common? _____

8. What is the greatest common factor of 24 and 16? _____

9. What is the greatest number possible of groups that are the same size with the same number of math students? _____

Check the Answer

10. Explain why the greatest common factor of 24 and 16 is the greatest number of possible groups. _____
_____

Solve Another Problem

11. Derek and Trevor are planning a treasure hunt for a group of friends. There are 12 adults and 18 children. They need to divide their friends into groups of the same size. Each group must have the same number of adults. Find the greatest number of groups possible. _____

288 Algebra-Readiness Lesson 4-3   Guided Problem Solving

Name _____ Class _____ Date _____

Practice 4-4   Simplifying Fractions

Write each fraction in simplest form.

1. $\dfrac{8}{12}$ _____

2. $\dfrac{5}{10}$ _____

3. $\dfrac{26}{39}$ _____

4. $\dfrac{7b}{9b}$ _____

5. $\dfrac{16y^3}{20y^4}$ _____

6. $\dfrac{8x}{10y}$ _____

7. $\dfrac{abc}{10abc}$ _____

8. $\dfrac{30hxy}{54kxy}$ _____

9. Joel completed 21 passes in 35 attempts. What fraction of his passes did Joel complete? Write in simplest form.

_____

Find two fractions equivalent to each fraction.

10. $\dfrac{1}{4}$ _____

11. $\dfrac{2}{3}$ _____

12. $\dfrac{3}{5}$ _____

13. $\dfrac{3}{18}$ _____

14. $\dfrac{8k}{16k}$ _____

15. $\dfrac{3m}{8n}$ _____

Name _____ Class _____ Date _____

4-4 • Guided Problem Solving

GPS Exercise 17

Doctors suggest that most people need about 8 hours of sleep each night to stay healthy. What fraction of the day is this? Write your answer in simplest form.

Understand the Problem

1. How many hours of sleep do doctors suggest people need each night to stay healthy? _____

2. What are you asked to find? _____

3. How should you write your answer? _____

Make and Carry Out a Plan

4. What will be the numerator of the fraction? _____

5. What will be the denominator of the fraction? _____

6. Write the fraction that represents 8 hours of a day. _____

7. What is the greatest common factor of the numerator and denominator? _____

8. Divide the numerator and the denominator by the greatest common factor and simplify. _____

9. What fraction of the day do doctors recommend people sleep? _____

Check the Answer

10. How many hours are in the fraction of the day you found in Step 9? _____

Solve Another Problem

11. Marnie practices piano 2 hours every day in the summer. What fraction of the day is this? Write your answer in simplest form. _____

Algebra-Readiness Lesson 4-4 — Guided Problem Solving

Practice 4-5

Solve a Simpler Problem

Solve each problem by solving a simpler problem.

1. A baseball team has 4 pitchers and 3 catchers. How many different pitcher-catcher combinations are possible? One way to solve this problem is to make a list like the one started below. Finish the list.

   P1-C1   P2-C1
   P1-C2   P2-C2

   _____   _____

   _____   _____

   _____   _____

   _____   _____

2. The baseball team has 2 first basemen, 3 second basemen, and 2 third basemen. How many combinations of the three positions are possible?

3. A quarter is tossed 3 times. In how many different orders can heads and tails be tossed?

4. Curtains are manufactured in 3 different styles and 5 different colors.
   a. How many different style-color combinations are possible?

   b. The curtains are produced in 2 different fabrics. How many different style-color-fabric combinations are possible?

Practice   Algebra-Readiness Lesson 4-5   **291**

Name _____ Class _____ Date _____

4-5 • Guided Problem Solving

GPS Exercise 3

You have pepperoni, mushrooms, onions, and green peppers. How many different pizzas can you make by using one, two, three, or four of the toppings?

Understand the Problem

1. What toppings do you have? _____

2. What are you asked to find? _____

Make and Carry Out a Plan

3. How many different pizzas can you make with only one topping each? _____

4. Complete the organized list of different pizzas with two toppings.

   pepperoni ⟨ mushrooms, onions, green peppers   mushrooms ⟨ ?, ?   onions — ?

5. How many different pizzas can you make with two toppings? _____

6. How many different pizzas can you make with three toppings? (Hint: Think about a pizza with all four toppings. How many different ways could you remove one topping?) _____

7. How many different pizzas can you make with four toppings? _____

8. Find the sum of your answers to Steps 3, 5, 6, and 7. How many different pizzas can you make? _____

Check the Answer

9. Use a diagram to find the number of two-topping pizzas you can make. Draw line segments connecting the toppings to show all possible pizzas.

   pepperoni   **mushrooms**

   onions   **green peppers**

Solve Another Problem

10. Caleb has salami, cheese, and turkey to put on a sandwich for lunch. How many different sandwiches could he make by using one, two, or three of the sandwich fixings? _____

292 *Algebra-Readiness* Lesson 4-5   Guided Problem Solving

Practice 4-6

Rational Numbers

Use the number line below to order the set of rational numbers from least to greatest.

1. $\frac{3}{4}, -\frac{1}{4}, -0.5, 0.3$

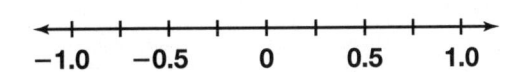

$$\begin{array}{c} \longleftarrow | \quad | \quad | \quad | \quad | \quad | \quad | \quad | \quad | \longrightarrow \\ -1.0 \quad -0.5 \quad\; 0 \quad\; 0.5 \quad\; 1.0 \end{array}$$

Evaluate. Write in simplest form.

2. $\frac{x}{y}$, for $x = 12, y = 21$ _____

3. $\frac{n}{n+p}$, for $n = 9, p = 6$ _____

4. $\frac{m}{-n}$, for $m = 6, n = 7$ _____

5. $\frac{x-y}{-21}$, for $x = -2, y = 5$ _____

Write three fractions equivalent to each fraction.

6. $\frac{5}{7}$ _____

7. $\frac{-4}{-6}$ _____

8. $\frac{24}{30}$ _____

9. $\frac{6}{16}$ _____

10. Which of the following rational numbers are equal to $-\frac{17}{10}$?

    $-17, -1.7, -\frac{34}{20}, 0.17$ _____

11. Which of the following rational numbers are equal to $\frac{3}{5}$?

    $\frac{12}{20}, \frac{-3}{-5}, 0.3, \frac{6}{10}$ _____

12. Which of the following rational numbers are equal to $\frac{12}{15}$?

    $\frac{4}{5}, \frac{40}{50}, -\frac{8}{10}, \frac{8}{10}$ _____

Practice

Algebra-Readiness Lesson 4-6

Name _____ Class _____ Date _____

4-6 • Guided Problem Solving

GPS Exercise 35

The formula $s = \dfrac{1{,}600}{d^2}$ gives the strength s of a radio signal at a distance d miles from the transmitter. What is the strength at 5 mi? Write your answer in simplest form.

Understand the Problem

1. What does the variable s represent? _____

2. What does the variable d represent? _____

3. What does the formula give? _____
   _____

4. What are you asked to find? _____

Make and Carry Out a Plan

5. Substitute 5 for d in the formula. _____

6. Simplify the denominator of the fraction. _____

7. Write the fraction in simplest form. _____

8. What is the strength of the radio signal 5 mi from the transmitter? _____

Check the Answer

9. In simplifying the answer, why did you simplify the denominator first? _____

10. Substitute your answer for s in the formula and solve for d. What is the distance? _____

Solve Another Problem

11. The acceleration in meters per second per second (m/s^2) of a racing car at 100 meters after it starts moving is given by $a = \dfrac{200}{t^2}$, where a is acceleration and t is time in seconds. What is the acceleration of the car if it takes 4 seconds to travel 100 meters? _____

294 Algebra-Readiness Lesson 4-6   Guided Problem Solving

Practice 4-7

Exponents and Multiplication

Complete each equation.

1. $9^3 \cdot 9^{\underline{}} = 9^7$

2. $6^5 \cdot 6^{\underline{}} = 6^{14}$

3. $n^{\underline{}} \cdot n^5 = n^{15}$

4. $(a^{\underline{}})^8 = a^{24}$

Simplify each expression.

5. $(z^3)^5$ _____

6. $-(m^4)^3$ _____

7. $(-3^2)^3$ _____

8. $(x^3)(x^4)$ _____

9. $y^4 \cdot y^5$ _____

10. $(-y^5)(y^2)$ _____

Find the area of each rectangle.

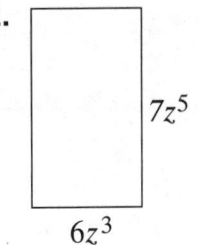

11. [rectangle with sides $3p^4$ and p^2]

_____

12. [rectangle with sides $6z^3$ and $7z^5$]

_____

Compare. Use >, <, or = to complete each statement.

13. $(4^3)^2 \ \square \ (4^2)^3$

14. $3^4 \ \square \ 9^2$

15. $(9^7)^9 \ \square \ (9^8)^8$

16. $5^2 \cdot 5^6 \ \square \ 5^7$

Practice

Algebra-Readiness Lesson 4-7 **295**

Name _____ Class _____ Date _____

4-7 • Guided Problem Solving

GPS Exercise 33

Writing in Math Explain why $x^8 \cdot x^2$ has the same value as $x^5 \cdot x^5$.

Understand the Problem

1. What are the two expressions? _____

2. What are you asked to do? _____

Make and Carry Out a Plan

3. Simplify the expression $x^8 \cdot x^2$ by adding the exponents of powers with the same base. _____

4. Simplify the expression $x^5 \cdot x^5$ by adding the exponents of powers with the same base. _____

5. Explain why $x^8 \cdot x^2$ and $x^5 \cdot x^5$ are equivalent. _____
_____

Check the Answer

6. Write another product that is equivalent to $x^8 \cdot x^2$ and $x^5 \cdot x^5$. _____

Solve Another Problem

7. Explain why $(x^2)^4$ is equivalent to $(x^4)^2$. _____
_____

Algebra-Readiness Lesson 4-7

Name _____ Class _____ Date _____

Practice 4-8

Exponents and Division

Complete each equation.

1. $\dfrac{8^n}{8^7} = 8^2$, $n =$ _____

2. $\dfrac{12x^5}{4x} = 3x^n$, $n =$ _____

3. $\dfrac{1}{h^5} = h^n$, $n =$ _____

4. $\dfrac{p^n}{p^8} = p^{-6}$, $n =$ _____

Simplify each expression.

5. $\dfrac{x^7}{x^7}$ _____

6. $\dfrac{2f^{10}}{f^5}$ _____

7. $\dfrac{3y^4}{6y^{-4}}$ _____

8. n^{-5} _____

9. $\dfrac{3xy^4}{9xy}$ _____

10. $(-15)^0$ _____

Write each expression without a fraction bar.

11. $\dfrac{a^7}{a^{10}}$ _____

12. $\dfrac{4x^2y}{2x^3}$ _____

13. $\dfrac{x^3y^4}{x^9y^2}$ _____

14. $\dfrac{12mn}{12m^3n^5}$ _____

Practice

Algebra-Readiness Lesson 4-8

Name _____ Class _____ Date _____

4-8 • Guided Problem Solving

GPS Exercise 26

The *magnitude* of an earthquake is a measure of the amount of energy released. An earthquake of magnitude 6 releases about 30 times as much energy as an earthquake of magnitude 5. The magnitude of the 1989 earthquake in Loma Prieta, California, was about 7. The magnitude of the 1933 earthquake in Sanriku, Japan, was about 9. Simplify $\frac{30^9}{30^7}$ to find how many times as much energy was released in the Sanriku earthquake.

Understand the Problem

1. What is the magnitude of an earthquake? _____

2. What was the magnitude of the Loma Prieta earthquake? _____

3. What was the magnitude of the Sanriku earthquake? _____

4. What are you asked to do? _____

Make and Carry Out a Plan

5. Start simplifying $\frac{30^9}{30^7}$ by subtracting exponents. _____

6. Simplify your result from Step 5. _____

7. How many times as much energy was released in the Sanriku earthquake as in the Loma Prieta earthquake? _____

Check the Answer

8. What rule did you follow to simplify the expression? _____

9. Explain how using this rule makes simplifying the expression easier. _____

Solve Another Problem

10. A video game is set up so that each level is 10 times more difficult than the previous level. Simplify $\frac{10^6}{10^3}$ to find how many times more difficult Level 6 is than Level 3. _____

298 Algebra-Readiness Lesson 4-8   Guided Problem Solving

Name _____ Class _____ Date _____

Practice 4-9

Scientific Notation

Write each number in standard notation.

1. 3.77×10^4 _____
2. 8.5×10^3 _____
3. 9.002×10^{-5} _____
4. 1.91×10^{-3} _____

Write each number in scientific notation.

5. Pluto is about 3,653,000,000 mi from the sun. _____

6. There are 63,360 in. in a mile. _____

7. At its closest, Mercury is about 46,000,000 km from the sun. _____

8. 77,250,000 _____
9. 526,000 _____
10. 0.00000073 _____
11. 0.000903 _____

Multiply. Express each result in scientific notation.

12. $(2 \times 10^5)(3 \times 10^2)$
13. $(1.5 \times 10^5)(4 \times 10^9)$

14. $(6 \times 10^{-4})(1.2 \times 10^{-3})$
15. $(5 \times 10^3)(1.7 \times 10^{-5})$

Order from least to greatest.

16. $72 \times 10^5, 6.9 \times 10^6, 23 \times 10^5$

17. $19 \times 10^{-3}, 2.5 \times 10^{-4}, 1.89 \times 10^{-4}$

Practice

Algebra-Readiness Lesson 4-9

Name _____ Class _____ Date _____

4-9 • Guided Problem Solving

GPS Exercise 30

An ant weighs about 2×10^{-5} lb. There are about 10^{15} ants on Earth. How many pounds of ants are on Earth?

Understand the Problem

1. About how much does an ant weigh? _____

2. About how many ants are on Earth? _____

3. What are you asked to find? _____

Make and Carry Out a Plan

4. Write an expression to multiply the number of ants on Earth by the weight of each ant. (Write 10^{15} as 1×10^{15}.) _____

5. Rewrite the expression using the Commutative Property of Multiplication. _____

6. Simplify by multiplying 2 and 1. _____

7. Simplify by adding the exponents. _____

8. How many pounds of ants are on Earth? _____

Check the Answer

9. To check your answer, divide it by the number of ants on Earth. Remember to subtract the exponents when you divide. _____
Your answer should be equal to the approximate weight of one ant.

Solve Another Problem

10. Marcella has a large jar of beads she uses for making bracelets and necklaces. She has about 10^3 beads in her jar right now. All of her beads are the same size, and each one weighs about 4×10^{-4} lb. About how much do all of the beads in her jar weigh? _____

Algebra-Readiness Lesson 4-9

Name_____ Class_____ Date_____

4A: Graphic Organizer

For use before Lesson 4-1

Study Skill You can get a general idea about what you will learn in a chapter when you preview the chapter. Look at the titles of the lessons in this chapter. From reading these titles, what do you predict you might learn in each lesson? Write notes about your predictions and then, as you finish a lesson, compare your notes with what you actually learned. Then change and add to your notes.

Write your answers. Use the Table of Contents page for this chapter at the front of the book.

1. What is the title of this chapter? _____

2. Name four topics that you will study in this chapter:

   _____   _____

   _____   _____

3. What is the topic of the Reasoning Strategy lesson? _____

4. Complete the graphic organizer as you work through the chapter.
   1. Write the title of the chapter in the center oval.
   2. When you begin a lesson, write the name of the lesson in a rectangle.
   3. When you complete that lesson, write a skill or key concept from that lesson in the outer oval linked to that rectangle.

   Continue with steps 2 and 3 clockwise around the graphic organizer.

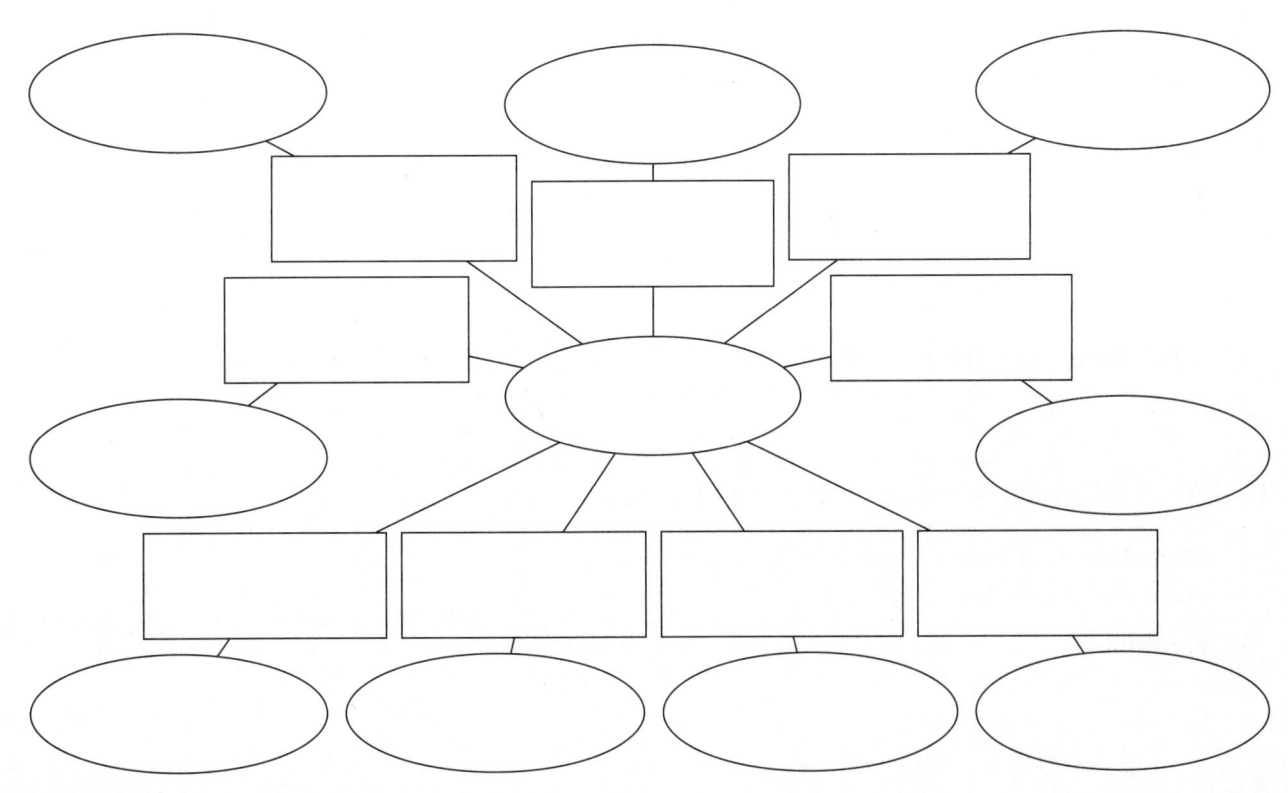

Vocabulary and Study Skills

Algebra-Readiness Chapter 4

301

Name _____ Class _____ Date _____

4B: Reading Comprehension   For use after Lesson 4-8

Study Skill When you have several assignments to do, try starting with the one that you find the most challenging, so that you are doing it while you are at your best. Save the one that is most familiar and easiest for last, when you may be tired.

When you read exponents, the positions of the exponent and parentheses tell you what the base is for that exponent.

Use these expressions to answer the questions about reading exponents.

$a + b^2$ $(a+b)^3$ $-a^4$

$(-a)^6$ a^{-1} $a - b^5$

1. Identify the base for the exponent 2. _____

2. Identify the base for the exponent 3. _____

3. Identify the base for the exponent 4. _____

4. Identify the base for the exponent 6. _____

5. Identify the base for the exponent −1. _____

6. Identify the base for the exponent 5. _____

Write your answers.

7. How can you simplify an expression in which a base has exponent −1?
   _____

8. In the expression ab^0, what is the base for the exponent 0? _____

9. What is the value of the expression ab^0? _____

10. In the expression $(ab)^0$, what is the base for the exponent 0? _____

11. What is the value of the expression $(ab)^0$? _____

12. **High-Use Academic Words** In Questions 1–6, what does *identify* mean for you to do?

    a. evaluate   b. name

302 *Algebra-Readiness* Chapter 4   Vocabulary and Study Skills

Name _____ Class _____ Date _____

4C: Reading/Writing Math Symbols
For use after Lesson 4-2

Study Skill After you take notes in class or while studying, take the time to go back and highlight what you have written. Mark key words or phrases in color to indicate the separate topics in your notes. In this way, you can quickly find the information you need as you review for a test.

Write a brief answer to each of these questions.

1. What effect does 2 have when you evaluate $2x$ for a given value of x?

   _____

   _____

2. What effect does 2 have when you evaluate x^2 for a given value of x?

   _____

   _____

3. What effect does 7 have when you evaluate $7(x + y)$ for given values of x and y?

   _____

   _____

4. What effect does 3 have when you evaluate $\frac{p}{3}$ for a given value of p?

   _____

   _____

5. What effect does 2 have when you evaluate ab^2 for given values of a and b?

   _____

   _____

6. What effect does 3 have when you evaluate x^3 for a given value of x?

   _____

   _____

Vocabulary and Study Skills   Algebra-Readiness Chapter 4

4D: Visual Vocabulary Practice

For use after Lesson 4-9

Study Skill When a math exercise is difficult, try to determine what makes it difficult. Is it a word that you don't understand? Are the numbers difficult to use?

Concept List

base	equivalent fractions	exponent
greatest common divisor	prime numbers	rational number
scientific notation	simplest form	standard notation

Write the concept that best describes each exercise. Choose from the concept list above.

1. 2 in 9^2	2. 7 in 7^3	3. relationship of 5 to the numbers 25 and 30
4. 3, 7, and 13	5. $\frac{2}{3}$ for the fraction $\frac{10}{15}$	6. $\frac{8}{16}$ and $\frac{2}{4}$
7. $\frac{a}{b}$ where a and b are integers and b is not 0	8. 42,000,000	9. 2.5×10^5

304 *Algebra-Readiness* Chapter 4   Vocabulary and Study Skills

4E: Vocabulary Check

For use after Lesson 4-3

Study Skill Strengthen your vocabulary. Use these pages and add cues and summaries by applying the Cornell Notetaking style.

Write the definition for each word at the right. To check your work, fold the paper back along the dotted line to see the correct answers.

_____ Divisible

_____

_____ Factor

_____

_____ Composite number

_____

_____ Prime factorization

_____

_____ Greatest common divisor

_____

4E: Vocabulary Check (continued)

For use after Lesson 4-3

Write the vocabulary word for each definition. To check your work, fold the paper back along the dotted line to see the correct answers.

When one integer can be divided by another integer with a remainder of zero. _____

An integer that can divide another nonzero integer with a remainder of zero. _____

An integer greater than 1 with more than two positive factors. _____

The expression of a number as the product of its prime factors. _____

The greatest factor two or more numbers have in common. _____

Name _____ Class _____ Date _____

4F: Vocabulary Review

For use with Chapter Review

Study Skill Many words in English have more than one meaning. You can often figure out which meaning to use by looking at the sentence that contains the word. To help you decide what a word means, consider the surroundings, or context, in which you see the word.

Match each word or phrase in the left column with the best example in the right column. Some words or phrases may have more than one example, but only one example is the best match.

Word or Phrase

1. exponent _____
2. base _____
3. factors _____
4. scientific notation _____
5. standard notation _____
6. prime factorization _____
7. equivalent fractions _____

Example

A. the 5 in 5^2

B. 4.06×10^3

C. $\frac{3}{4} = \frac{6}{8}$

D. both the 3 and the 5 in $3 \cdot 5$

E. 4,060

F. the 2 in 5^2

G. $60 = 2 \cdot 2 \cdot 3 \cdot 5$

Word or Phrase

8. formula _____
9. dividend _____
10. like terms _____
11. coefficient _____
12. term _____
13. prime number _____
14. rational number _____

Example

A. the 4 in $4x$

B. the $5x$ in $5x - 2$

C. 10 in $10 \div 5 = 2$

D. $3x$ and $7x$

E. 11

F. $P = 2\ell + 2w$

G. $\frac{2}{3}$

Vocabulary and Study Skills

Algebra-Readiness Chapter 4

307

Practice 5-1

Comparing and Ordering Rational Numbers

Compare. Use >, <, or = to complete each statement.

1. $\frac{2}{3}$ ☐ $\frac{7}{9}$
2. $\frac{3}{5}$ ☐ $\frac{7}{10}$
3. $-\frac{3}{4}$ ☐ $-\frac{13}{16}$
4. $\frac{9}{21}$ ☐ $\frac{6}{14}$
5. $\frac{4}{7}$ ☐ $2\frac{4}{7}$
6. $\frac{-9}{-11}$ ☐ $\frac{9}{11}$

Find the LCM.

7. 7, 21 _____
8. 24, 32 _____
9. 15, 50 _____
10. $9a^3b$, $18abc$ _____

Solve the following problems by finding the LCM and comparing fractions.

11. A stock sold for $3\frac{5}{8}$ one day and $3\frac{1}{2}$ the next. Did the value of the stock go up or down? Explain.

_____

12. Marissa needs $2\frac{2}{3}$ yards of ribbon for a wall-hanging she wants to make. She has $2\frac{3}{4}$ yards. Does she have enough ribbon? Explain.

_____

Order from least to greatest.

13. $\frac{2}{3}, \frac{3}{4}, \frac{1}{2}$
14. $\frac{2}{5}, \frac{1}{3}, \frac{3}{7}, \frac{4}{9}$
15. $\frac{8}{11}, \frac{9}{10}, \frac{7}{8}, \frac{3}{4}$

Name _____ Class _____ Date _____

5-1 • Guided Problem Solving

GPS Exercise 43

The manager of Frank's Snack Shop buys hot dogs in packages of 36. He buys hot dog buns in packages of 20. He cannot buy part of a package. What is the least number of packages of each product he can buy to have an equal number of hot dogs and buns?

Understand the Problem

1. How many hot dogs are there in one package? _____

2. How many hot dog buns are there in one package? _____

3. What are you asked to find? _____

Make and Carry Out a Plan

4. List the first 10 multiples of 36. _____

5. List the first 10 multiples of 20. _____

6. Circle the common multiples of 36 and 20. _____

7. What is the least common multiple of 36 and 20? _____
   This is the smallest number of hot dogs with buns that can be made from packages of 36 hot dog buns and packages of 20 hot dogs.

8. To find the number of packages of hot dogs the manager should buy, divide the least common multiple by 36. _____

9. To find the number of packages of buns the manager should buy, divide the lowest common multiple by 20. _____

Check the Answer

10. To check your answer, find the least common multiple of 36 and 20 using prime factorization. _____
    It should be the same as your answer to question 7.

Solve Another Problem

11. An office manager buys company letterhead in boxes of 40 sheets and envelopes in boxes of 32. He cannot buy part of a box. What is the least number of boxes of each he can buy to have an equal number of sheets of letterhead and envelopes? _____

310 Algebra-Readiness Lesson 5-1   Guided Problem Solving

Practice 5-2

Fractions and Decimals

Write each decimal as a fraction or a mixed number in simplest form.

1. 2.34 _____
2. 0.75 _____
3. 0.16 _____
4. 8.8 _____

Write each fraction or mixed number as a decimal.

5. $3\frac{1}{8}$ _____
6. $\frac{7}{8}$ _____
7. $-\frac{9}{16}$ _____
8. $6\frac{9}{32}$ _____
9. $4\frac{31}{50}$ _____
10. $\frac{15}{11}$ _____

Order from least to greatest.

11. $0.4, \frac{3}{5}, \frac{1}{2}, \frac{3}{10}$ _____

12. $-\frac{3}{8}, -\frac{3}{4}, -0.38, -0.6$ _____

13. $\frac{1}{4}, -\frac{1}{5}, 0.2, \frac{2}{5}$ _____

Write each decimal as a fraction or a mixed number in simplest form.

14. $10.0\overline{7}$ _____
15. 0.375 _____
16. $-4.\overline{27}$ _____

Compare. Use <, >, or = to complete each statement.

17. $\frac{5}{6}$ ☐ 0.8
18. $\frac{7}{11}$ ☐ 0.65
19. $4.\overline{2}$ ☐ $4\frac{2}{9}$

Name _____ Class _____ Date _____

5-2 • Guided Problem Solving

GPS Exercise 32

Number Sense A carpenter has a bolt with diameter $\frac{5}{32}$ in. Will the bolt fit in a hole made by a drill bit with diameter 0.2 in.? Explain.

Understand the Problem

1. What is the diameter of the carpenter's bolt? _____

2. What is the diameter of the drill bit? _____

3. What is the diameter of a hole made by the drill bit? _____

4. What are you asked to do? _____

Make and Carry Out a Plan

5. The diameter of the bolt is given as a fraction. Change it to a decimal. _____

6. Compare the decimal diameter of the bolt to the diameter of the hole made by the drill bit. Which is greater? _____

7. Will the bolt fit into the hole? Justify your reasoning. _____

Check the Answer

8. Check your answer by writing 0.2 in., the diameter of the drill bit, as a fraction and comparing it to $\frac{5}{32}$, the diameter of the bolt. _____

Solve Another Problem

9. A wooden peg has a diameter of 0.5 in. Will the peg fit into a hole that has a diameter of $\frac{7}{16}$ in.? Justify your reasoning. _____

Algebra-Readiness Lesson 5-2

Name _____ Class _____ Date _____

Practice 5-3

Adding and Subtracting Fractions

Find each sum or difference. Simplify if possible.

1. $\frac{2}{3} + \frac{1}{6}$ _____
2. $\frac{5}{8} - \frac{1}{4}$ _____
3. $\frac{1}{4} - \frac{1}{3}$ _____
4. $\frac{x}{3} + \frac{x}{5}$ _____
5. $3\frac{1}{5} + 2\frac{2}{5}$ _____
6. $1\frac{5}{8} - 1\frac{1}{8}$ _____
7. $\frac{3}{5y} + \frac{1}{5y}$ _____
8. $2\frac{7}{10} - 3\frac{7}{20}$ _____

Find each sum using mental math.

9. $3\frac{3}{8} + 2\frac{1}{8} + 1\frac{3}{8}$ _____
10. $6\frac{7}{12} + 4\frac{5}{12}$ _____
11. $8\frac{3}{16} + 2\frac{5}{16} + 4\frac{7}{16}$ _____
12. $7\frac{9}{10} + 3\frac{3}{10}$ _____

Estimate each sum or difference.

13. $13\frac{4}{5} - 2\frac{9}{10}$ _____
14. $18\frac{3}{8} + 11\frac{6}{7}$ _____
15. $23\frac{6}{13} + 32\frac{7}{8}$ _____
16. $26\frac{9}{10} + 72\frac{5}{6}$ _____

Use prime factors to find the LCD. Then simplify each expression.

17. $\frac{7}{30} - \frac{29}{75}$ _____
18. $\frac{3}{14} + \frac{17}{63}$ _____
19. $\frac{5}{42} + \frac{5}{12}$ _____
20. $2\frac{5}{6} - 2\frac{5}{22}$ _____

Name _____ Class _____ Date _____

5-3 • Guided Problem Solving

GPS Exercise 40

There were three snowstorms last winter. The storms dropped $3\frac{1}{2}$ in., $6\frac{1}{16}$ in., and $10\frac{3}{4}$ in. of snow. What was the combined snowfall of the three storms?

Understand the Problem

1. How much snow did each of the three storms drop? _____

2. What are you asked to find? _____

Make and Carry Out a Plan

3. Write an expression to find the combined snowfall of the three storms. _____

4. Rewrite $3\frac{1}{2}$, $6\frac{1}{16}$, and $10\frac{3}{4}$ as improper fractions. _____

5. Rewrite the expression using a common denominator. _____

6. Simplify the expression. _____

7. Rewrite the improper fraction as a mixed number. _____

8. What was the combined snowfall of the three storms? _____

Check the Answer

9. What steps do you follow to write a mixed number as an improper fraction? _____
_____

10. What steps do you follow to write an improper fraction as a mixed number? _____
_____

Solve Another Problem

11. Alexis has three pieces of ribbon. Their lengths are $4\frac{1}{3}$ in., $8\frac{5}{6}$ in., and $12\frac{1}{2}$ in. How many inches of ribbon does she have in all? _____

Algebra-Readiness Lesson 5-3   Guided Problem Solving

Name _____ Class _____ Date _____

Practice 5-4
Multiplying and Dividing Fractions

Find each quotient. Simplify if possible.

1. $\frac{1}{2} \div \frac{5}{8}$ _____
2. $-\frac{5}{24} \div \frac{7}{12}$ _____
3. $8 \div \frac{4}{5}$ _____
4. $6\frac{1}{4} \div 2\frac{1}{2}$ _____
5. $\frac{6}{35t} \div \frac{3}{7t}$ _____
6. $1\frac{3}{7} \div \left(-2\frac{1}{7}\right)$ _____

Find each product. Simplify if possible.

7. $\frac{2}{5} \cdot \frac{3}{7}$ _____
8. $\frac{5}{9} \cdot \frac{3}{5}$ _____
9. $4\frac{7}{8} \cdot 6$ _____
10. $\frac{5x}{7} \cdot \frac{3}{10}$ _____
11. $\frac{9a}{10} \cdot \frac{5}{12a}$ _____
12. $\frac{9t}{16} \cdot \frac{12}{17}$ _____

Solve the following problems by finding a product or a quotient.

13. You are making cookies for a bake sale. The recipe calls for $2\frac{3}{4}$ cups of flour. How much flour will you need if you triple the recipe?

_____

14. It took you 1 hour to read $1\frac{3}{8}$ chapters of a novel. At this rate, how many chapters can you read in three hours?

_____

Practice

Algebra-Readiness Lesson 5-4

Name _____ Class _____ Date _____

5-4 • Guided Problem Solving

GPS Exercise 59

You are hiking along a trail that is $13\frac{1}{2}$ mi long. You plan to rest every $2\frac{1}{4}$ mi. How many rest stops will you make?

Understand the Problem

1. How long is the trail you are hiking? _____

2. How often do you plan to rest? _____

3. What are you asked to find? _____

Make and Carry Out a Plan

4. Write an expression to divide the length of the trail into $2\frac{1}{4}$-mi sections. _____

5. Change the fractions in the expression to improper fractions. _____

6. What is the reciprocal of the divisor? _____

7. Rewrite the division as multiplication by the reciprocal. _____

8. Divide the common factors and simplify. _____

9. How many $2\frac{1}{4}$-mi sections are there in the $13\frac{1}{2}$-mi trail? _____

10. How many rest stops will you make? Note that the last $2\frac{1}{4}$-mi section will not have a rest stop because you will be finished. _____

Check the Answer

11. If you divide the $13\frac{1}{2}$-mi trail by your answer to Step 9, what result would show that your work is correct? _____

Solve Another Problem

12. You have a piece of fabric that is $8\frac{1}{4}$ yd long. You want to cut the fabric into pieces that are $\frac{3}{8}$ yd long. How many pieces of fabric will you have? _____

316 *Algebra-Readiness Lesson 5-4*   Guided Problem Solving

Name _____ Class _____ Date _____

Practice 5-5
Using Customary Units of Measurement

Use estimation, mental math, or paper and pencil to complete each statement.

1. 2 gal 2 qt = _____ qt
2. 3 yd = _____ ft
3. 30 in. = _____ ft
4. 20 fl oz = _____ c
5. 20 oz = _____ lb
6. $2\frac{1}{2}$ pt = _____ c

Is each measurement reasonable? If not, give a reasonable measurement.

7. A glass of milk holds about 8 pt.
_____

8. A newborn baby weighs about $7\frac{1}{2}$ oz.
_____

9. A phonebook is $\frac{3}{4}$ ft wide.
_____

Choose an appropriate unit of measure. Explain your choice.

10. weight of a whale
_____

11. sugar in a cookie recipe
_____

12. length of a mouse
_____

Is each item likely to be measured by *length*, *weight*, or *capacity*?

13. amount of soup in a can
_____

14. heaviness of a can
_____

15. diameter of a can
_____

Algebra-Readiness Lesson 5-5

Name _____ Class _____ Date _____

5-5 • Guided Problem Solving

GPS Exercise 27

You are hiking a 2-mi-long trail. You pass by a sign showing that you have hiked 1,000 ft. How many feet are left?

Understand the Problem

1. How long is the trail you are hiking? _____

2. How far have you hiked? _____

3. What are you asked to find? _____

Make and Carry Out a Plan

4. How many feet are in a mile? _____

5. What is the conversion factor for converting miles to feet? _____

6. Multiply 2 mi by the conversion factor to find the number of feet in 2 mi. _____

7. Write an expression to find the number of feet you still have to hike on the 2-mi trail. _____

8. How many feet are left to hike? _____

Check the Answer

9. To check your work, add 1,000 to your answer. Then convert the sum to miles. _____

Solve Another Problem

10. You are in-line skating around a 3-mi loop. You just passed a marker showing you have skated 5,000 ft. How many feet are left? _____

318 Algebra-Readiness Lesson 5-5   Guided Problem Solving

Name _____ Class _____ Date _____

Practice 5-6   Work Backward

Work backward to solve each problem.

1. Manuel's term paper is due on March 31. He began doing research on March 1. He intends to continue doing research for 3 times as long as he has done already. Then he will spend a week writing the paper and the remaining 3 days typing. What day is it? (Assume he will finish typing on March 30.)

2. A disc jockey must allow time for 24 minutes of commercials every hour, along with 4 minutes for news, 3 minutes for weather, and 2 minutes for public-service announcements. If each record lasts an average of 3 minutes, how many records per hour can the DJ play?

3. On Monday the low temperature at the South Pole dropped 9°F from Sunday's low. On Tuesday it fell another 7°, then rose 13° on Wednesday, and 17° more on Thursday. Friday it dropped 8° to −50°F. What was Sunday's low temperature?

4. Each problem lists the operations performed on n to produce the given result. Find n.
   a. Multiply by 3, add 4, divide by 5, subtract 6; result, −1.
   _____

   b. Add 2, divide by 3, subtract 4, multiply by 5; result, 35.
   _____

Name _____ Class _____ Date _____

5-6 • Guided Problem Solving

GPS Exercise 7

You spent half of your money at the amusement park and had $15 left. How much money did you have originally?

Understand the Problem

1. What fraction of your money did you spend at the amusement park? _____

2. How many dollars did you have left after you had spent money at the amusement park? _____

3. What are you asked to find? _____

Make and Carry Out a Plan

4. If you spent half of your money at the amusement park, what fraction of the original amount of money do you have left? _____

5. Use the variable m to represent your original amount of money. Write a variable expression for the amount of money you have left. _____

6. Set the expression you wrote in Step 5 equal to $15, the dollar amount of money you have left. Solve for m to find the original amount of money you had. _____

Check the Answer

7. How did you decide what fraction of money you had left? _____
_____

8. Divide your answer in half. Then subtract the quotient from the original amount. The result should be the amount of money you have left. _____

Solve Another Problem

9. Two-thirds of the students in Tristan's class chose to participate in choir. If 8 students from Tristan's class do not participate in choir, how many students are in Tristan's class? _____

320 Algebra-Readiness Lesson 5-6   Guided Problem Solving

Practice 5-7

Solving Equations by Adding or Subtracting Fractions

Solve and check each equation.

1. $m - \left(-\frac{7}{10}\right) = -1\frac{1}{5}$ _____

2. $k - \frac{3}{4} = \frac{2}{5}$ _____

3. $x + \frac{5}{8} = \frac{7}{8}$ _____

4. $k + \frac{4}{5} = 1\frac{3}{5}$ _____

5. $d + 1 = \frac{4}{9}$ _____

6. $e - \frac{11}{16} = -\frac{7}{8}$ _____

7. $a - 9\frac{1}{6} = -3\frac{19}{24}$ _____

8. $f + \left|-3\frac{11}{12}\right| = 18$ _____

9. $z + \left(-3\frac{2}{5}\right) = -4\frac{1}{10}$ _____

10. $x - \frac{7}{15} = \frac{7}{60}$ _____

Solve each equation using mental math.

11. $x + \frac{3}{7} = \frac{5}{7}$ _____

12. $k - \frac{8}{9} = -\frac{1}{9}$ _____

13. $a + \frac{1}{9} = \frac{3}{9}$ _____

14. $g - \frac{4}{5} = -\frac{2}{5}$ _____

Write an equation to solve each problem.

15. Pete's papaya tree grew $3\frac{7}{12}$ ft during the year. If its height at the end of the year was $21\frac{1}{6}$ ft, what was its height at the beginning of the year?

    _____

16. Lee is $1\frac{3}{4}$ ft taller than Jay. If Lee is $6\frac{1}{4}$ ft tall, how tall is Jay?

    _____

Name _____ Class _____ Date _____

5-7 • Guided Problem Solving

GPS Exercise 25

A restaurant chef needs $8\frac{1}{2}$ lb of salmon. To get a good price, he buys more than he needs. He ends up with $4\frac{7}{8}$ lb too much. How much salmon did he buy?

Understand the Problem

1. How much salmon does the chef need? _____

2. How much extra salmon did the chef buy? _____

3. What are you asked to find? _____

Make and Carry Out a Plan

4. Use the sentence "The amount of salmon the chef bought minus the amount of salmon he needs equals the amount of extra salmon he has" to write an equation to represent the situation. Let s represent the amount of salmon he bought. _____

5. Write the mixed numbers in the equation as improper fractions. _____

6. What fraction must you add to each side to solve for s? _____

7. Rewrite the equation using a common denominator. _____

8. Simplify to solve the equation for s. _____

9. Change the result to a mixed number. _____

10. How much salmon did the chef buy? _____

Check the Answer

11. Add the amount of extra salmon the chef had to the amount he needed. _____
    The result should be the amount of salmon he bought.

Solve Another Problem

12. Each month, Sally buys a $37\frac{1}{2}$ lb bag of food for her dog. This month, she bought $5\frac{1}{4}$ lb more than she needed because the larger bag was on sale. How many pounds of dog food are in the larger bag? _____

322 *Algebra-Readiness* Lesson 5-7   Guided Problem Solving

Name _____ Class _____ Date _____

Practice 5-8

Solving Equations by Multiplying Fractions

Solve each equation.

1. $\frac{3}{4}x = \frac{9}{16}$ _____

2. $-\frac{1}{3}p = \frac{1}{4}$ _____

3. $\frac{-3}{8}k = \frac{1}{2}$ _____

4. $\frac{1}{8}h = \frac{1}{10}$ _____

5. $-\frac{1}{3}p = \frac{1}{18}$ _____

6. $\frac{11}{-12}w = -1$ _____

7. $-3\frac{4}{7}x = 0$ _____

8. $\frac{4}{7}y = 4$ _____

9. $\frac{10}{11}n = \frac{2}{11}$ _____

10. $\frac{7}{8}c = \frac{7}{6}$ _____

Solve each equation using mental math.

11. $7d = 42$ _____

12. $\frac{1}{4}y = 5$ _____

13. $-3h = \frac{3}{8}$ _____

14. $\frac{1}{5}k = -\frac{1}{3}$ _____

Write an equation to solve each problem.

15. It takes Nancy $1\frac{2}{3}$ min to read 1 page in her social studies book. It took her $22\frac{1}{2}$ min to complete her reading assignment. How long was the assignment? Let m represent the number of pages she read.

_____

16. It takes Gary three hours to drive to Boston. If the trip is 156 miles, what is Gary's average number of miles per hour? Let x represent the miles per hour.

_____

Algebra-Readiness Lesson 5-8

Name _____ Class _____ Date _____

5-8 • Guided Problem Solving

GPS Exercise 50

Biology In ideal conditions, the kudzu plant can grow at least $1\frac{3}{20}$ ft per week. At this rate, how many weeks would it take a kudzu plant to grow 23 ft?

Understand the Problem

1. How many feet can a kudzu plant grow each week in ideal conditions? _____

2. What are you asked to find? _____
   _____

Make and Carry Out a Plan

3. Use the sentence "Feet per week times number of weeks is 23 feet" to write an equation to represent the situation. Let w represent number of weeks. _____

4. Write $1\frac{3}{20}$ as an improper fraction in the equation. _____

5. By what number must you multiply each side of the equation to get w alone on one side? _____

6. Divide common factors and simplify the equation. _____

7. How many weeks would it take a kudzu plant to grow 23 feet? _____

Check the Answer

8. Divide 23 feet by the number of weeks you found. _____
   The result should be the number of feet per week a kudzu plant grows.

Solve Another Problem

9. A Jersey cow produces an average of $3\frac{1}{2}$ gallons of milk per day. How many days will it take a Jersey cow to produce 21 gallons of milk? _____

Algebra-Readiness Lesson 5-8

Name _____ Class _____ Date _____

Practice 5-9   Powers of Products and Quotients

Simplify each expression.

1. $\left(\frac{5}{6}\right)^2$ _____
2. $\left(-\frac{4}{9}\right)^2$ _____
3. $\left(\frac{x^2}{5}\right)^3$ _____
4. $(2x)^3$ _____
5. $(-3y^2)^2$ _____
6. $(5ab^2)^3$ _____
7. $-(a^2b^2)^3$ _____
8. $(2a^3b^2)^4$ _____
9. $\left(\frac{2x}{y}\right)^2$ _____
10. $\left(\frac{3y^2}{x}\right)^3$ _____

Evaluate for $a = 2$, $b = -1$, and $c = \frac{1}{3}$.

11. $(a^2)^3$ _____
12. $2b^3$ _____
13. $(a^2b)^2$ _____
14. $(ac)^2$ _____

Complete each equation.

15. $(3b\text{———})^2 = 9b^{10}$
16. $(m^2n)^{\text{———}} = m^8n^4$
17. $(xy\text{———})^2 = x^2y^6$
18. $\left(\frac{3s^2}{r}\right)^{\text{———}} = \frac{9s^4}{r^2}$

19. Write an expression for the area of a square with a side of length $4a^2$. Simplify your expression.

_____

Practice   Algebra-Readiness Lesson 5-9   **325**

Name _____ Class _____ Date _____

5-9 • Guided Problem Solving

GPS Exercise 46

A square table has sides that measure $3x^2$ ft. Write an expression for the area of the tabletop. Simplify your expression.

Understand the Problem

1. What is the length of a side of the table? _____

2. What are you asked to do? _____

Make and Carry Out a Plan

3. Let s represent the length of the side of the table. Write an expression for the area of the tabletop. _____

4. Replace s with $3x^2$ in the expression. _____

5. Use the rule for raising a product to a power to evaluate the expression you wrote for Step 4. _____

6. Simplify the expression. _____

7. What is the area of the tabletop? _____

Check the Answer

8. What rule did you use to simplify $(x^2)^2$? _____

Solve Another Problem

9. The length of the side of a square is $4x^3$. Write an expression for the area of the square. Simplify the expression. _____

326 Algebra-Readiness Lesson 5-9 — Guided Problem Solving

Name _____ Class _____ Date _____

5A: Graphic Organizer

For use before Lesson 5-1

Study Skill Get a general overview of the main features by skimming or surveying this chapter. Read the title, headings, and the first and last paragraphs of each lesson. This helps you outline in your mind a general framework for what you are going to study in this chapter.

Write your answers. Use the Table of Contents page for this chapter at the front of the book.

1. What is the title of this chapter? _____

2. Name four topics that you will study in this chapter:

   _____ _____

   _____ _____

3. What is the topic of the Reasoning Strategy lesson? _____

4. Complete the graphic organizer as you work through the chapter.
   1. Write the title of the chapter in the center oval.
   2. When you begin a lesson, write the lesson name in a rectangle.
   3. When you complete that lesson, write a skill or key concept from that lesson in the outer oval linked to that rectangle.
   Continue with steps 2 and 3 clockwise around the graphic organizer.

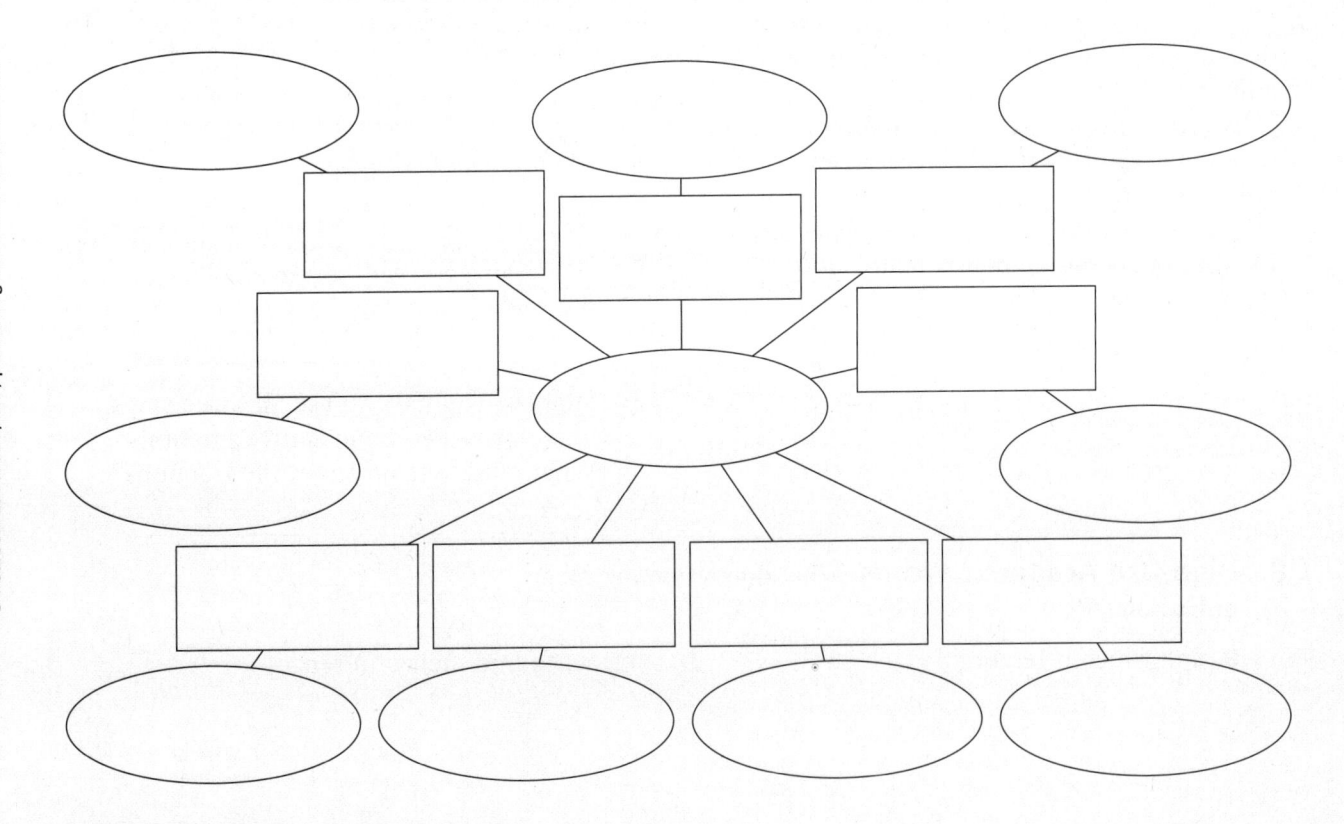

Vocabulary and Study Skills

Algebra-Readiness Chapter 5

327

Name _____ Class _____ Date _____

5B: Reading Comprehension

For use after Lesson 5-3

Study Skill Instead of relying on your memory, keep a special notebook where you write down your daily assignments and directions. Make notes of hints and suggestions that may be given when an assignment is explained. Check off the work as you complete it.

Read the review at the left, and then answer the questions at the right.

Summary of multiples:

An integer is a multiple of
- 2 if it ends in 0, 2, 4, 6, or 8
- 5 if it ends in 0 or 5
- 10 if it ends in 0
- 3 if the sum of its digits is divisible by 3
- 9 if the sum of its digits is divisible by 9

Summary for finding the LCM:

To find the Least Common Multiple for two integers,
- write the prime factorization for each,
- circle the greatest power of each factor,
- multiply the circled powers.

Summary for comparing nonnegative fractions:

- If two fractions have the same denominator, then the greater fraction has the greater numerator.
- If two fractions have the same numerator, then the greater fraction has the lesser denominator.
- Otherwise, rewrite both fractions using the LCM as the common denominator, and then compare.

To remember the information in this review, first look at the way the review is organized.

1. How many main parts are there in this review?
   _____

2. How many tests for finding multiples are listed?
   _____

3. Is it possible for an integer to pass more than one of the "multiples" tests?
   _____

4. According to the summary of multiples, what must be true of an integer that is a multiple of 2 and 9?
   _____

5. What does LCM mean?
   _____

6. How many steps are given to find the LCM?
   _____

7. Suppose you have to use all three steps to compare two nonnegative fractions. What must be true about the fractions?
   _____

8. **High-Use Academic Words** What does *compare* mean in Exercise 7?

   a. find which is larger   b. subtract to find their difference

328 *Algebra-Readiness* Chapter 5   Vocabulary and Study Skills

Name _____ Class _____ Date _____

5C: Reading/Writing Math Symbols
For use after Lesson 5-8

Study Skill When you write symbols, make them clear and complete so that you will be able to read them correctly at a later time. If you create your own symbols and abbreviations, be sure to write a key to remind you of their meanings.

On the blank on the right, write one symbol or abbreviation to complete each statement.

1. $2\frac{1}{3} = 2 \underline{} \frac{1}{3}$ _____

2. $ab = a \underline{} b$ _____

3. $\frac{5}{7} = 5 \underline{} 7$ _____

4. The opposite of 7 is $\underline{}$ 7.   _____

5. 56 feet is 56 $\underline{}$.   _____

6. 3 cups of flour is 3 $\underline{}$ of flour.   _____

7. The value of 5 dimes = 5 $\underline{}$ $.10.   _____

8. 8 pounds is 8 $\underline{}$.   _____

9. $3 \div \frac{2}{3} = 3 \underline{} \frac{3}{2}$ _____

10. $\frac{3}{4}$ of $p = \frac{3}{4} \underline{} p$ _____

11. 15 centimeters is 15 $\underline{}$.   _____

12. 12 is greater than x is 12 $\underline{}$ x.   _____

13. y minus the opposite of 7 is $y \underline{} 7$.   _____

14. 4 increased by b is 4 $\underline{} b$.   _____

Vocabulary and Study Skills   Algebra-Readiness Chapter 5

Name _____ Class _____ Date _____

5D: Visual Vocabulary Practice

For use after Lesson 5-6

Study Skill When you come across something you don't understand, view it as an opportunity to increase your brain power.

Concept List

conversion factor	equivalent fractions	greatest common divisor
least common denominator	least common multiple	prime factorization
reciprocals	repeating decimal	terminating decimal

Write the concept that best describes each exercise. Choose from the concept list shown above.

1. Relationship of 15 to the numbers 3 and 5	2. Relationship of 20 to the denominators of the fractions $\frac{1}{2}, \frac{3}{4},$ and $\frac{3}{5}$	3. 0.75
4. 0.333...	5. $\frac{3}{4}$ and $\frac{4}{3}$	6. $\frac{12 \text{ in.}}{1 \text{ ft}}$ and $\frac{4 \text{ qt}}{1 \text{ gal}}$
7. Relationship of 3 to the numbers 3, 6, and 9	8. $30 = 2 \cdot 3 \cdot 5$	9. $\frac{6}{10}$ and $\frac{12}{20}$

330 Algebra-Readiness Chapter 5   Vocabulary and Study Skills

Name _____ Class _____ Date _____

5E: Vocabulary Check

For use after Lesson 5-5

Study Skill Strengthen your vocabulary. Use these pages and add cues and summaries by applying the Cornell Notetaking style.

Write the definition for each word. To check your work, fold the paper back along the dotted line to see the correct answers.

_____ Multiple

_____

_____

_____ Least common multiple

_____

_____ Least common denominator

_____

_____ Terminating decimal

_____

_____ Repeating decimal

_____

Vocabulary and Study Skills

Algebra-Readiness Chapter 5

5E: Vocabulary Check (continued)

For use after Lesson 5-5

Write the vocabulary word for each definition. To check your work, fold the paper forward along the dotted line to see the correct answers.

The product of a number and any nonzero whole number.

_____

The least number that is a multiple of two or more numbers.

_____

The least common multiple of the denominators of two or more fractions.

_____

A decimal with a finite number of digits.

_____

A decimal in which the same block of digits repeats without end.

_____

Name _____ Class _____ Date _____

5F: Vocabulary Review Puzzle
For use with Chapter Review

Study Skill After you complete a vocabulary puzzle, word search, or game, review the list of words and say the meaning of each vocabulary term to yourself. Pay special attention to how the word is spelled.

Unscramble the UPPERCASE letters to form a math word or phrase that completes each sentence.

1. When you divide the numerator of a fraction by the denominator, and the quotient is a GATTEMINNIR decimal, then the division ends with a remainder of zero. _____

2. When two fractions describe the same part of a whole, the two fractions are VAQUITLEEN. _____

3. The PRICOLACER of 2 is one-half. _____

4. A fraction is in TESLIMPS form when the only common factor of the numerator and denominator is one. _____

5. A GREATPINE decimal is one that has the same block of digits repeating without end. _____

6. When you look at units to decide which conversion factors to use, you are doing LANDMINESOI analysis. _____

7. The SETTGEAR common divisor of 24 and 36 is 12. _____

8. Twenty-eight is a PLLTMIUE of both 4 and 7. _____

9. The least NOMMOC multiple of 4 and 25 is 100. _____

10. SECCNTIIFI notation is a shorthand way of writing numbers using powers of 10. _____

Vocabulary and Study Skills   Algebra-Readiness Chapter 5

Name _____ Class _____ Date _____

Practice 6-1

Ratios and Unit Rates

Find each unit rate.

1. 78 mi on 3 gal _____

2. $60.00 in 8 h _____

3. 416 mi in 8 h _____

Write each ratio as a fraction in simplest form.

4. 7th-grade boys to 8th-grade boys _____

5. 7th-grade girls to 7th-grade boys _____

6. 7th graders to 8th graders _____

	Boys	Girls
7th Grade	26	34
8th Grade	30	22

Write three different ratios for each model.

7.

8.

9.

_____   _____   _____

Complete each statement.

10. 180 m/day = ☐ m/min

11. 2.5 gal/min = ☐ qt/h

12. 45 yd/min = ☐ in./s

13. 0.3 km/s = ☐ m/min

14. 15 kg/min = ☐ g/s

15. 5 oz/min = ☐ qt/day

L1 Practice

Algebra-Readiness Lesson 6-1

335

Name _____ Class _____ Date _____

6-1 • Guided Problem Solving

GPS Exercise 19

What is the rate in meters per second of a jetliner that is traveling at a rate of 846 km/h?

Understand the Problem

1. How fast is the jetliner traveling? _____

2. What are you asked to find? _____

Make and Carry Out a Plan

3. How many meters are in 1 kilometer? _____

4. What conversion factor will you use to change the number of kilometers to meters? _____

5. How many seconds are in one hour? _____

6. What conversion factor will you use to change the number of hours to seconds? _____

7. Multiply $\frac{846 \text{ km}}{1 \text{ h}}$ by the two conversion factors. _____

8. What is the rate of the jetliner in meters per second? _____

Check the Answer

9. To check to make sure you have converted correctly, convert the meters per second rate back to kilometers per second. _____

Solve Another Problem

10. What is the rate in feet per minute of a car that is traveling 68 mi/h on an interstate freeway? _____

336 Algebra-Readiness Lesson 6-1   Guided Problem Solving

Name _____ Class _____ Date _____

Practice 6-2

Proportions

Write a proportion for each phrase. Then solve. When necessary, round to the nearest hundredth.

1. 420 ft² painted in 36 min; f ft² painted in 30 min

   _____

2. 75 points scored in 6 games; p points scored in 4 games

   _____

3. 6 apples for $1.00; 15 apples for d dollars

   _____

Tell whether the two ratios form a proportion.

4. $\frac{3}{4}$ and $\frac{9}{12}$ _____   5. $\frac{25}{40}$ and $\frac{5}{8}$ _____

6. $\frac{4}{5}$ and $\frac{5}{6}$ _____   7. $\frac{13}{15}$ and $\frac{4}{5}$ _____

Solve each proportion. Where necessary, round to the nearest tenth.

8. $\frac{3}{5} = \frac{15}{x}$ _____   9. $\frac{15}{30} = \frac{n}{34}$ _____

10. $\frac{h}{36} = \frac{21}{27}$ _____   11. $\frac{11}{6} = \frac{f}{60}$ _____

12. $\frac{36}{j} = \frac{7}{20}$ _____   13. $\frac{r}{23} = \frac{17}{34}$ _____

14. You estimate that you can do 12 math problems in 45 min. How long should it take you to do 20 math problems?

    _____

L1 Practice

Algebra-Readiness Lesson 6-2

Name _____ Class _____ Date _____

6-2 • Guided Problem Solving

GPS Exercise 54

A microchip inspector found three defective chips in a batch containing 750 chips. At that rate, how many defective chips would there be in 10,000 chips?

Understand the Problem

1. How many defective chips did the inspector find? _____

2. How many chips did the inspector inspect? _____

3. What are you asked to find? _____

Make and Carry Out a Plan

4. Write the ratio of the number of defective chips the inspector found to the total number of chips inspected. _____

5. Let c represent the number of defective chips in 10,000. Write the ratio of the number of defective chips to the total number of chips, 10,000. _____

6. Use the two ratios to write a proportion. _____

7. Write the cross-product equation. _____

8. By what number must you divide each side of the equation to solve for c? _____

9. About how many defective chips would there be in 10,000 chips? _____

Check the Answer

10. To check your answer, use the Multiplication Property of Equality to solve the proportion from Step 6. What is the value of c? _____

Solve Another Problem

11. In Mr. Schulte's eighth-grade class, 17 of the 20 students participate in after-school activities. At that rate, how many of 300 eighth-grade students have after-school activities? _____

Algebra-Readiness Lesson 6-2   Guided Problem Solving

Name ____________________ Class ____________________ Date ____________________

Practice 6-3

Similar Figures and Scale Drawings

The scale of a map is $\frac{1}{2}$ in. : 8 mi. Find the actual distance for each map distance.

1. 2 in. ____________________

2. 5 in. ____________________

3. $3\frac{1}{2}$ in. ____________________

4. 10 in. ____________________

Each pair of figures is similar. Find the missing length. Round to the nearest tenth where necessary.

5.

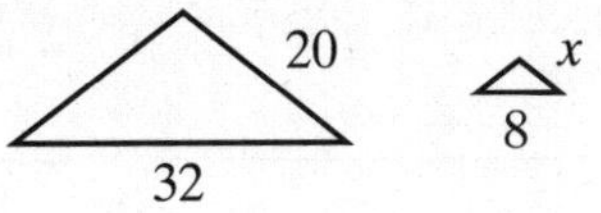

$x =$ ____________________

6.

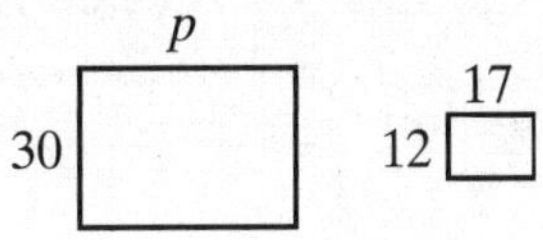

$p =$ ____________________

7.

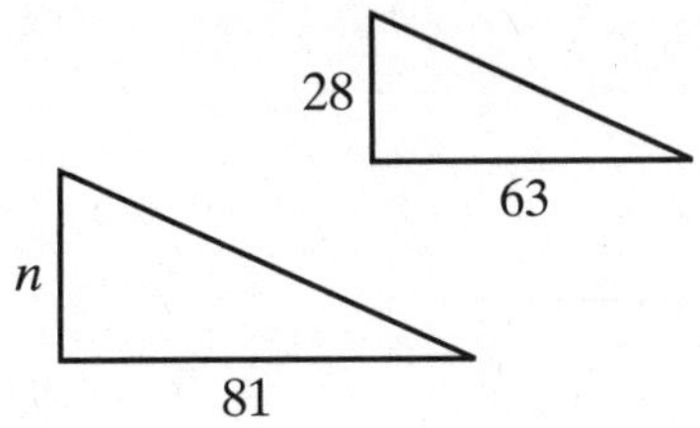

$n =$ ____________________

8.

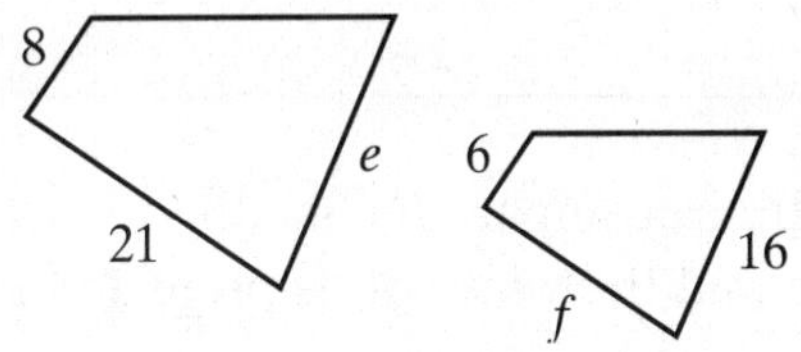

$e \approx$ ____________________ $f \approx$ ____________________

A scale drawing has a scale of $\frac{1}{4}$ in. : 6 ft. Find the length on the drawing for each actual length.

9. 18 ft ____________________

10. 66 ft ____________________

11. 204 ft ____________________

Name _____ Class _____ Date _____

6-3 • Guided Problem Solving

GPS Exercise 12

An image on a slide is similar to its projected image. A slide is 35 mm wide and 21 mm high. Its projected image is 85 cm wide. To the nearest centimeter, how high is the image?

Understand the Problem

1. How wide is the slide? _____

2. How high is the slide? _____

3. What is the width of the slide's projected image? _____

4. What are you asked to find? _____

Make and Carry Out a Plan

5. What is true about the lengths of corresponding sides of similar figures?. _____
   _____

6. Write a ratio to compare the width of the slide and the width of its projected image. _____

7. Let h represent the height of the projected image. Write a ratio to compare the height of the slide to the height of its projected image. _____

8. Use the two ratios to write a proportion. _____

9. Write the cross-product equation. _____

10. By what number must you divide each side to solve for h? _____

11. How high is the projected image? _____

Check the Answer

12. To check your answer, use the Multiplication Property of Equality to solve the proportion in Step 8. What is the value of h? _____

Solve Another Problem

13. Marianna scans a picture into her computer so she can make an enlargement that is similar to the original. The original picture is 4 in. wide and 6 in. long. She wants the enlargement to be 12 in. long. How wide must it be? _____

340 Algebra-Readiness Lesson 6-3

Name _____ Class _____ Date _____

Practice 6-4

Fractions, Decimals, and Percents

Write each decimal or fraction as a percent. Round to the nearest tenth of a percent where necessary.

1. 0.16 _____
2. 0.72 _____
3. $\frac{24}{25}$ _____
4. $\frac{31}{40}$ _____
5. 3.04 _____
6. $\frac{403}{1,000}$ _____

Write each percent as a decimal.

7. 8% _____
8. 0.07% _____
9. $7\frac{1}{2}$% _____
10. $15\frac{1}{4}$% _____

Write each percent as a fraction or mixed number in simplest form.

11. 60% _____
12. 5% _____
13. 32% _____
14. 140% _____

Compare. Use >, <, or = to complete each statement.

15. 0.7 ☐ 7%
16. 80% ☐ $\frac{4}{5}$

17. In the United States in 1990, about one person in twenty was 75 years old or older. Write this fraction as a percent.

_____

Name _____ Class _____ Date _____

6-4 • Guided Problem Solving

GPS Exercise 71

Jeanette answered 32 questions correctly on a 45-question test. The passing grade was 70%. Did Jeanette pass? Justify your answer.

Understand the Problem

1. How many questions did Jeanette answer correctly? _____

2. How many questions were on the test? _____

3. What was a passing grade for the test? _____

4. What are you asked to do? _____

Make and Carry Out a Plan

5. What fraction of the questions on the test did Jeanette answer correctly? _____

6. Write the fraction as a decimal. Divide the numerator by the denominator and round to two decimal places. _____

7. Write the decimal as a percent. (Move the decimal point two places to the right.) _____

8. Is your answer greater than, equal to, or less than 70%? _____

9. Did Jeanette pass? Explain your answer. _____
   _____

Check the Answer

10. To check your answer, find Jeanette's incorrect answer rate. An incorrect answer rate greater than 30% is a failing grade. How does her incorrect answer rate support your answer to Step 9? _____
    _____

Solve Another Problem

11. Ms. Martinez's class is voting on whether to take its science quiz a day early. Of 26 students, 19 vote yes. A yes vote of 70% or better is needed to change the quiz day. Will the class take the quiz early? Explain. _____
    _____

342 Algebra-Readiness Lesson 6-4   Guided Problem Solving

Name _____ Class _____ Date _____

Practice 6-5

Proportions and Percents

Write and solve a proportion. Where necessary, round to the nearest tenth or tenth of a percent.

1. 120% of y is 42. What is y? _____

2. 300% of m is 600. What is m? _____

3. What percent of 40 is 12? _____

4. What percent of 48 is 18? _____

5. What percent is 54 of 60? _____

6. What percent is 39 of 50? _____

7. Find 80% of 25. _____

8. Find 150% of 74. _____

9. Find 44% of 375. _____

10. Find 65% of 180. _____

11. Thirty-five of 40 students surveyed said that they favored recycling. What percent of those surveyed favored recycling?

    _____

Name _____ Class _____ Date _____

6-5 • Guided Problem Solving

GPS Exercise 36

You invested some money and made a profit of $55. Your profit was 11% of your investment. How much did you invest?

Understand the Problem

1. What was the profit on the money you invested? _____

2. What percent of the investment was the profit? _____

3. What are you asked to find? _____

Make and Carry Out a Plan

4. Write 11% as a fraction. _____

5. Let n represent the amount of money invested. Write the amount of profit as a fraction of the amount of money invested. _____

6. Use the two fractions to write a proportion. _____

7. Write the cross-product equation. _____

8. By what number must you divide each side to solve for n? _____

9. Simplify to find how much money you invested. _____

Check the Answer

10. To check your answer, multiply it by 11%. _____
    The result should be the amount of profit you made.

Solve Another Problem

11. Simon puts 15% of his monthly allowance into his savings account. If he saves $9 each month, what is his monthly allowance? _____

344 Algebra-Readiness Lesson 6-5   Guided Problem Solving

Name _____ Class _____ Date _____

Practice 6-6
Percents and Equations

Write and solve an equation. Where necessary, round to the nearest tenth or tenth of a percent.

1. What percent of 25 is 17? _____

2. What percent is 10 of 8? _____

3. What percent is 63 of 84? _____

4. What percent is 3 of 600? _____

5. Find 45% of 60. _____

6. Find 325% of 52. _____

7. Find 1% of 3,620. _____

8. 300% of k is 42. What is k? _____

9. $33\frac{1}{3}$% of p is 19. What is p? _____

10. 70% of c is 49. What is c? _____

11. Nine hundred thirty-six students, 65% of the entire student body, attended the football game. Find the size of the student body.

_____

Name _____ Class _____ Date _____

6-6 • Guided Problem Solving

GPS Exercise 28

A salesperson receives 5.4% commission. On one sale, she received $6.48. What was the amount of the sale?

Understand the Problem

1. What percent commission does the salesperson receive? _____

2. What cash commission did she receive on one sale? _____

3. What are you asked to find? _____

Make and Carry Out a Plan

4. Use the sentence "$6.48 is 5.4% of the amount of the sale" to write an equation. Let *s* represent the amount of the sale, and write 5.4% as a decimal. _____

5. By what number must you divide each side of the equation to solve for *s*? _____

6. Solve the equation to find the amount of the sale. _____

Check the Answer

7. To check your answer, multiply it by 5.4%. _____
   The product should be equal to the amount of commission the salesperson received.

Solve Another Problem

8. Tasha works in a bicycle shop. She receives 3.5% commission on each bicycle she sells. She received a $28 commission on one bicycle. What was the selling price of the bicycle? _____

346 *Algebra-Readiness* Lesson 6-6   Guided Problem Solving

Name _____ Class _____ Date _____

Practice 6-7

Percent of Change

Find each percent of change. Where necessary, round to the nearest tenth of a percent. Tell whether the change is an increase or a decrease.

1. 24 to 21 _____
2. 64 to 80 _____
3. 100 to 113 _____
4. 50 to 41 _____
5. 80 to 24 _____
6. 20 to 24 _____
7. 44 to 22 _____
8. 16 to 12 _____
9. 10 to 100 _____
10. 20 to 40 _____
11. 10 to 50 _____
12. 12 to 16 _____
13. 80 to 100 _____
14. 88 to 26 _____

15. Mark weighed 110 pounds last year. He weighs 119 pounds this year. What is the percent of increase in his weight, to the nearest tenth of a percent?

   _____

16. Susan had $140 in her savings account last month. She added $20 this month and earned $.50 interest. What is the percent of increase in the amount in her savings account to the nearest tenth of a percent?

   _____

L1 Practice

Algebra-Readiness Lesson 6-7

Name _____ Class _____ Date _____

6-7 • Guided Problem Solving

GPS Exercise 36

The average cost of a gallon of gasoline was $1.29 in 1997 and $2.96 in 2006. Find the percent of increase.

Understand the Problem

1. What was the average cost of a gallon of gasoline in 1997? _____

2. What was the average cost of a gallon of gasoline in 2006? _____

3. What are you asked to find? _____

Make and Carry Out a Plan

4. Write an expression to find the amount of increase in the average price of a gallon of gasoline from 1997 to 2006. _____

5. What is the amount of increase? _____

6. Write the formula for percent of change. _____

7. Replace the amount of change with the amount of increase you found in Step 5. Replace the original amount with the gallon cost for 1997. _____

8. Write the fraction as a decimal. Divide the numerator by the denominator and round to three decimal places. _____

9. Write the decimal as a percent. Multiply by 100 and write a percent sign. _____

10. What is the percent of increase? (Round to the nearest tenth.) _____

Check the Answer

11. To check your answer, multiply it by $1.29. _____
    The product should be the same as the difference between $1.29 and $2.96.

Solve Another Problem

12. A store usually sells a particular game for $21.95. The game is now on sale for $18.05. Find the percent of decrease to the nearest percent. _____

348 Algebra-Readiness Lesson 6-7   Guided Problem Solving

Name _____ Class _____ Date _____

Practice 6-8

Markup and Discount

Find each sale price. Round to the nearest cent where necessary.

	Regular Price	Percent of Discount	Sale Price
1.	$4.00	25%	
2.	$1.40	10%	
3.	$87	50%	
4.	$675	20%	

Find each selling price. Round to the nearest cent where necessary.

	Cost	Percent Markup	Selling Price
5.	$1.00	75%	
6.	$25	50%	
7.	$100	25%	
8.	$10.65	20%	

9. A company buys a sweater for $14 and marks it up 90%. It later discounts the sweater 25%.

   a. Find the selling price of the sweater after markup.

   b. How much was the discount?

   c. Find the sale price after the discount.

   d. The company's profit on the sweater can be found by subtracting the final selling price minus the cost. What was the company's profit on the sweater?

   e. The profit was what percent of the cost?

L1 Practice

Algebra-Readiness Lesson 6-8   **349**

Name _____ Class _____ Date _____

6-8 • Guided Problem Solving

GPS Exercise 18

Store A is selling a video for 20% off the store's regular price of $25.95. Store B is selling the same video for 30% off the store's regular price of $29.50. Which store's sale price is lower? How much lower is it?

Understand the Problem

1. What is the regular price of the video at Store A? _____

2. What is the percent of discount on the video at Store A? _____

3. What is the regular price of the video at Store B? _____

4. What is the percent of discount on the video at Store B? _____

5. What are you asked to find? _____

Make and Carry Out a Plan

6. Write 20% as a decimal. _____

7. Multiply the original price of the video at Store A by the decimal from Step 6 to find the discount. _____

8. Subtract the discount from the original price to find the sale price of the video at Store A. _____

9. Repeat Steps 6–8 to find the sale price of the video at Store B. _____

10. Which store has the lower sale price? Subtract the lower sale price from the higher sale price to find out how much lower it is. _____

Check the Answer

11. To check your answer, find the sale price of each video directly.

   For Store A, find 80% of $25.95. _____

   For Store B, find 70% of $29.50. _____

   Which store has the lower sale price? _____

Solve Another Problem

12. Sherry bought a CD that was on sale for 25% off the regular price of $15.99. Tate bought a CD that was on sale for 30% off the regular price of $16.99. Who paid less for the CD? How much less? _____

Algebra-Readiness Lesson 6-8   Guided Problem Solving

Practice 6-9

Applications of Rational Numbers

Solve the following problems by applying your knowledge of rational numbers.

1. There were 120 students asked to identify their favorite subject. 20% of the students chose English, 0.4 chose Physical Education, 3/10 chose Art, and the remaining 12 students chose Social Studies. Which subject did most of the students select? How many selected it?

2. Rez can run 18 miles in 4 hours. Jamie can run 2/3 as many miles in 2 hours. Who runs faster?

3. Estimate a 15% tip on a $34.80 dinner bill.

4. You want to buy a jacket that costs $57.95. Your parents agree to pay 27% of the cost. Estimate the amount your parents will contribute.

Use >, <, or = to complete each statement.

5. 32% of 176 ☐ $\frac{7}{16}$ of 195

6. $\frac{3}{7}$ of 426 ☐ 0.3 of 152

Name_____ Class_____ Date_____

6-9 • Guided Problem Solving

GPS Exercise 17

The chart represents the number of musicians in each section of a 96-member orchestra. Estimate the number of musicians in the woodwind section.

Orchestra Sections

(Pie chart: Percussion & Brass $\frac{3}{16}$; Woodwind x; Strings 65%)

Understand the Problem

1. What do you know about the percussion & brass and the strings sections of a 96-member orchestra? _____

2. What are you asked to find? _____

Make and Carry Out a Plan

3. How can you find out what fraction of the orchestra makes up the percussion & brass section and the strings section? _____

4. Write 65% as a fraction. _____

5. Add the fraction expressing the number of musicians in percussion & brass section and the fraction expressing the number of musicians in the strings section. _____

6. What fraction of the orchestra musicians is in the woodwind section of the orchestra? _____

7. To find the number of musicians in the woodwind section of the orchestra, multiply the fraction of the orchestra musicians in the woodwind section by 96. _____

8. Estimate the number of musicians in the woodwind section of the orchestra. _____

Check the Answer

9. To check your result, find the number of musicians in each section of the orchestra. The numbers from each section should add up to 96. _____

Solve Another Problem

10. Estimate the number of musicians in the woodwind section of the orchestra if the orchestra has 116 musicians. Assume that the fraction of woodwind players is the same as in the 96-member orchestra. _____

352 Algebra-Readiness Lesson 6-9   Guided Problem Solving

Practice 6-10

Reasoning Strategy: Make a Table

Make a table to solve each problem.

1. A car was worth $12,500 in 2005. Its value depreciates, or decreases, 15% per year. Find its value in 2009.

Year	2005	2006	2007	2008	2009
Car's Value	$12,500				

2. Marcus spent $105 on 6 items at a sale. Videotapes were on sale for $15 each and music CDs were on sale for $20 each. How many of each item did Marcus buy?

Number of Videotapes	1	2	3	4	5
Number of CDs	5	4	3	2	1
Total Cost					

3. How many ways can you have 25 cents in change?

4. How many different sandwiches can you make from 3 types of bread, 2 types of cheese, and 2 types of meat? Assume that only one type of each item is used per sandwich.

5. A bus leaves a station at 8:00 A.M. and averages 30 mi/h. Another bus leaves the same station following the same route two hours after the first and averages 50 mi/h. When will the second bus catch up with the first bus?

Name _____ Class _____ Date _____

6-10 • Guided Problem Solving

GPS Exercise 9

A family went to the movies. Tickets cost $4 for each child and $6 for each adult. The total admission charge for the family was $26. List all the possible numbers of adults and children in the family.

Understand the Problem

1. What was the price of a movie ticket for a child? _____

2. What was the price of a movie ticket for an adult? _____

3. What was the total admission charge for the family? _____

4. What are you asked to find? _____

Make and Carry Out a Plan

5. On a separate piece of paper, make a table to list all of the possible combinations. Begin with one adult and one child. Continue increasing the number of children with one adult until the total admission charge reaches $26 or more. Then increase the number of adults by one and repeat the process. Continue the table until the total admission price for the adults is greater than $26.

Number of Adults $6 Each	Number of Children $4 Each	Total Admission Charge
1	1	$10
1	2	$14

6. Which combinations of adults and children have a total admission charge of $26? _____

Check the Answer

7. To check your answer, multiply $6 by the number of adults and $4 by the number of children in each of the combinations from Step 6 and add the products. What result will tell you that your answers to Step 6 are correct? _____

Solve Another Problem

8. Dane bought new hand towels and bath towels. Hand towels cost $4 each and bath towels cost $6 each. He spent a total of $22. List all the possible numbers of hand towels and bath towels he bought. _____

354 Algebra-Readiness Lesson 6-10   Guided Problem Solving

Name _____ Class _____ Date _____

6A: Graphic Organizer
For use before Lesson 6-1

Study Skill Look at the pages before the first page of the first lesson in this chapter. What do they tell you about the chapter? Reading takes concentration and effort, so as you read these introductory pages, pay attention to what you are reading so that you could, for example, explain the contents to a friend. Take notes on any questions that you have about the chapter, and look back at these questions later to see if you have found the answers.

Write your answers. Use the Table of Contents page for this chapter at the front of the book.

1. What is the title of this chapter? _____

2. Name four topics that you will study in this chapter:

   _____   _____
   _____   _____

3. What is the topic of the Reasoning Strategy lesson? _____

4. Complete the graphic organizer as you work through the chapter.
   1. Write the title of the chapter in the center oval.
   2. When you begin a lesson, write the name of the lesson in a rectangle.
   3. When you complete a lesson, write a skill or key concept from that lesson in the outer oval linked to that rectangle.
   Continue with steps 2 and 3 clockwise around the graphic organizer.

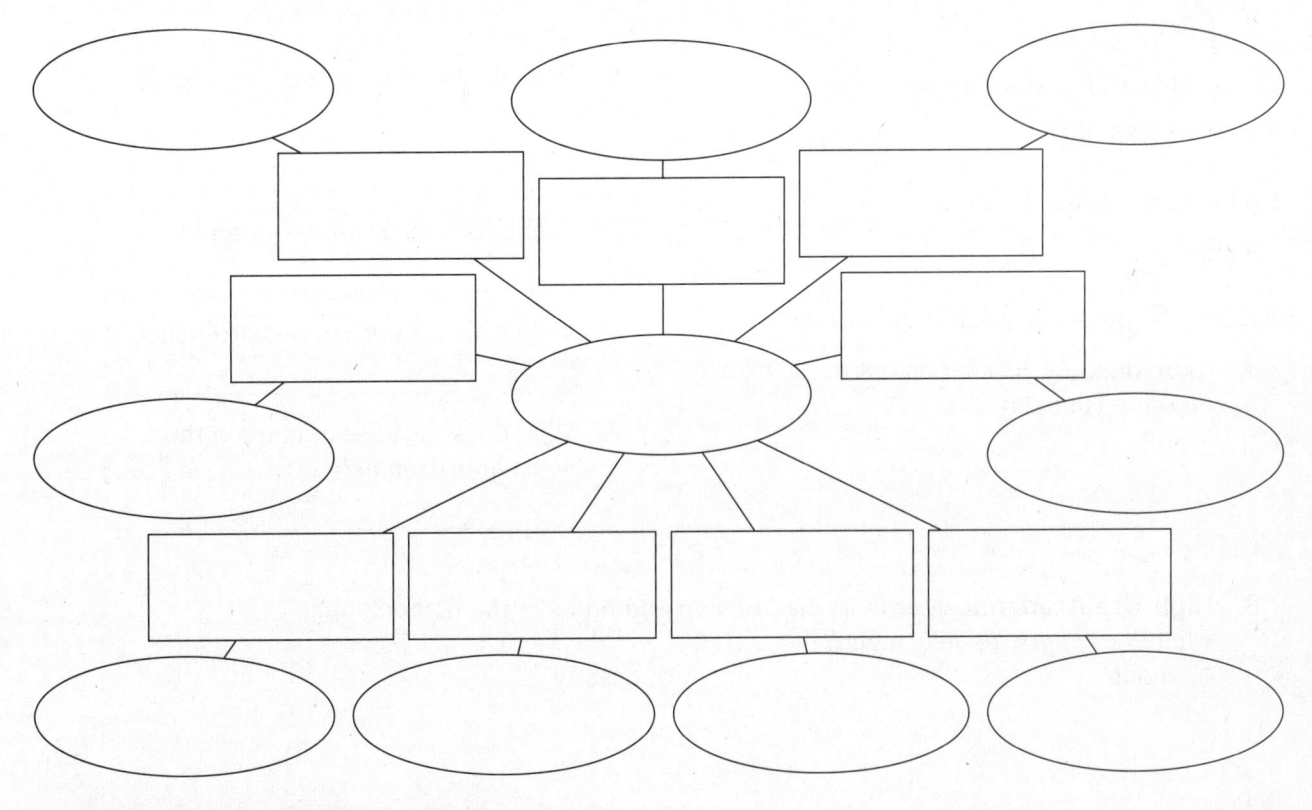

Vocabulary and Study Skills   *Algebra-Readiness* Chapter 6   **355**

Name _____ Class _____ Date _____

6B: Reading Comprehension

For use after Lesson 6-8

Study Skill As you read or study, take notes that summarize the key points and information. Use these notes to help you review for a test.

Read the steps and notes in the example at the left, and answer the questions at the right.

EXAMPLE Solving With a Proportion

Seven of the twenty-three students in the class voted to have the test on Thursday. What percent of the class voted for Thursday?

Write a proportion.

- $\frac{7}{23} = \frac{c}{100}$

Write the cross products.

- $7 \cdot 100 = 23c$

Simplify.

- $700 = 23c$

Divide each side by 23.

- $\frac{700}{23} = c$

Use a calculator to simplify $700 \div 23$.

- $30.434783 \approx c$

Round to the nearest tenth.

- $30.4 \approx c$

Answer the question asked in the problem.

- Approximately 30.4% percent of the class voted for Thursday.

1. Read the title of the example. What process are you going to use to solve the problem?
   _____

2. What is a proportion?
   _____

3. What does writing the cross products mean?
   _____
   _____

4. Why do you divide both sides by 23?
   _____
   _____

5. What does the symbol $\approx$ stand for?
   _____

6. Why is the $\approx$ used in this problem?
   _____

7. Why does the answer contain the word *approximately*?
   _____
   _____

8. **High-Use Academic Words** In the last step and notes in the first column, what does *approximately* mean?
   a. about   **b.** exactly

356 *Algebra-Readiness* Chapter 6   Vocabulary and Study Skills

Name _____ Class _____ Date _____

6C: Reading/Writing Math Symbols For use after Lesson 6-3

Study Skill Whenever you work on an assignment or a test, read the instructions or direction line two times to make sure you understand what to do. Before you begin to work, think about what the final result will look like and the form it will take.

In mathematics, the order of the numerals and symbols has meaning and is important. Under each pair of math expressions, explain how changing the order changes the meaning.

1. $3 - 2$ $2 - 3$
_____

2. $(2, -3)$ $(-3, 2)$
_____

3. 2^3 3^2
_____

4. 3 miles per hour   3 hours per mile
_____

5. $2 \div 3$ $3 \div 2$
_____

6. $2 < 3$ $3 < 2$
_____

7. 3 snacks for 6 people   6 snacks for 3 people
_____

8. $1 : 2$ $2 : 1$
_____

9. $\angle PQR$ $\angle PRQ$
_____

Vocabulary and Study Skills   Algebra-Readiness Chapter 6   **357**

Name _____ Class _____ Date _____

6D: Visual Vocabulary Practice
For use after Lesson 6-5

Study Skill When you come across something you don't understand, view it as an opportunity to increase your brain power.

Concept List

cross products	ratio	indirect measurement
proportion	markup	scale
similar figures	percent of change	unit rate

Write the concept that best describes each exercise. Choose from the concept list above.

1. $\frac{18}{16}$ and 4.5 : 4	2. A 6-ft-tall person standing near a building has a shadow that is 60 ft long. This can be used to determine the height of the building.	3. $\frac{\text{amount of change}}{\text{original amount}}$
4. A store buys a DVD for $12 and sells it for $15. This is $3.	5. $\frac{30}{75} = \frac{x}{5}$	6. For the equation $\frac{15}{16} = \frac{3z}{4}$, these are represented by 15×4 and $3z \times 16$.
7. The equation $\frac{1}{2}$ in. = 50 mi represents this on a map.	8. $\frac{\$4.25}{5 \text{ lb}} = \$.85/\text{lb}$	9. [rectangle 25.5 × 12; rectangle 8.5 × 4]

358 *Algebra-Readiness* Chapter 6   **Vocabulary and Study Skills**

6E: Vocabulary Check

For use after Lesson 6-9

Study Skill Strengthen your vocabulary. Use these pages and add cues and summaries by applying the Cornell Notetaking style.

Write the definition for each word. To check your work, fold the paper back along the dotted line to see the correct answers.

_____ Rate

_____ Unit rate

_____ Commission

_____ Markup

_____ Discount

6E: Vocabulary Check (continued)

For use after Lesson 6-9

Write the vocabulary word for each definition. To check your work, fold the paper forward along the dotted line to see the correct answers.

A ratio that compares quantities measured in different units.

_____

A rate that has a denominator of 1.

_____

Pay that is equal to a percent of sales.

_____

The amount of increase in price.

_____

The amount by which a price is decreased.

_____

360 Algebra-Readiness Chapter 6   Vocabulary and Study Skills

Name _____ Class _____ Date _____

6F: Vocabulary Review Puzzle

For use with Chapter Review

Study Skill You may have noticed that math tests often contain word problems for you to solve. In order to read and understand the problems, so that you can solve them, you must know the meanings of the words used to state the problems. The next time you study for a math test, be sure to begin by studying the vocabulary involved.

Write the words that are described below. Complete the word search puzzle by finding the words. For help, use the Chapter Review in your textbook. Remember that a word may go right to left, left to right, or it may go up as well as down.

1. an equality of two ratios _____
2. the amount of price decrease _____
3. ratio comparing a number to 100 _____
4. ratio comparing quantities in different units _____
5. amount you are paid based on amount you sell _____
6. comparison of two quantities by division _____
7. amount of increase over cost _____

```
E D I S C O U N T M O P E
M M O E N R T R A M D T R
S S R O A N E P M T D N I
E C A D R A T E O O S E O
C I T T P E R C E N T M U
E C I P N O I A E U N E M
P P O S O E A T T N T L N
E P R O P O R T I O N P E
C M S T R N M C P A E M C
O T O U T C O M E R V O O
C O M M I S S I O N E C E
C N O V M A R K U P N C O
R N T T U E U U C P P K T
```

Vocabulary and Study Skills

Algebra-Readiness Chapter 6

361

Name _____ Class _____ Date _____

Practice 7-1

Solving Two-Step Equations

Solve each equation.

1. $4x - 17 = 31$ _____
2. $15 = 2m + 3$ _____
3. $\frac{k}{3} + 3 = 8$ _____
4. $7 = 3 + \frac{h}{6}$ _____
5. $14 = 5k - 31$ _____
6. $\frac{t}{9} - 7 = -5$ _____

Solve each equation using mental math.

7. $3p + 5 = 14$ _____
8. $\frac{k}{2} - 5 = 1$ _____
9. $\frac{m}{7} - 3 = 0$ _____
10. $10v - 6 = 24$ _____
11. $8 + \frac{x}{2} = -7$ _____
12. $7 = 6r - 17$ _____

Write an equation to describe the situation. Solve.

13. A waitress earned $73 for 6 hours of work. The total included $46 in tips. What was her hourly wage?

    _____

    _____

14. You used $6\frac{3}{4}$ c of sugar while baking muffins and nutbread for a class party. You used a total of $1\frac{1}{2}$ c of sugar for the muffins. Your nutbread recipe calls for $1\frac{3}{4}$ c of sugar per loaf. How many loaves of nutbread did you make?

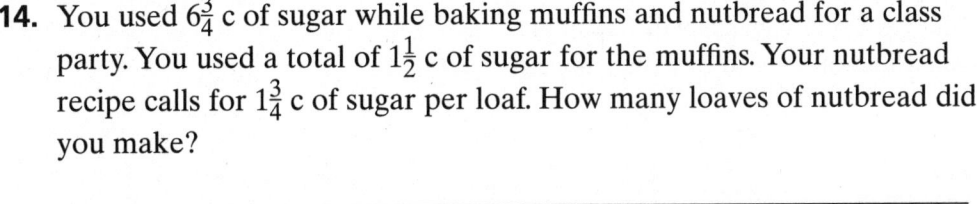

    _____

    _____

Name _____ Class _____ Date _____

7-1 • Guided Problem Solving

GPS Exercise 27

Carmela wants to buy a digital camera for $249. She has $24 and is saving $15 each week. Solve the equation $15w + 24 = 249$ to find how many weeks w it will take Carmela to save enough to buy the digital camera.

Understand the Problem

1. What does the variable w represent? _____

2. What are you asked to find? _____

Make and Carry Out a Plan

3. To solve the equation $15w + 24 = 249$, you must undo the addition operation first. What value should you subtract from each side of the equation? _____

4. Subtract the answer from Step 3 from each side of the equation. What expression are you left with? _____

5. By what value must you divide each side of the equation to find the value of w? _____

6. Divide each side of the equation by your answer to Step 5 and simplify. How many weeks will Carmela have to save to have enough money to buy the camera? _____

Check the Answer

7. Replace w in the original equation with your result from Step 6. Do you get a true statement? _____

Solve Another Problem

8. Kirk has $240 in his savings account. He deposits $20 in his account every week, working toward the goal of saving $500. Solve the equation $20w + 240 = 500$ to find how many weeks he will need to save to reach his goal. _____

364 *Algebra-Readiness Lesson 7-1*   Guided Problem Solving

Name _____ Class _____ Date _____

Practice 7-2

Solving Multi-Step Equations

Solve and check each equation.

1. $\frac{p}{3} - 7 = -2$

2. $2(n - 7) + 3 = 9$

3. $0 = 5(k + 9)$

4. $4h + 7h - 6 = 16$

5. $3(2n - 7) = 9$

6. $-27 = 8x - 5x$

7. $-37 = 3x + 11 - 7x$

8. $\frac{1}{6}(y + 42) - 15 = -3$

Write and solve an equation for each situation.

9. Find two consecutive integers whose sum is 33.

10. Find three consecutive integers whose sum is −15.

11. Jack's overtime wage is $3 per hour more than his regular hourly wage. He worked for 5 hours at his regular wage and 4 hours at the overtime wage. He earned $66. Find his regular wage.

Algebra-Readiness Lesson 7-2

Name _____ Class _____ Date _____

7-2 • Guided Problem Solving

GPS Exercise 9

Bill and Jasmine together have 94 glass marbles. Bill has 4 more than twice as many marbles as Jasmine. If Jasmine has m marbles, then Bill has $2m + 4$ marbles. Solve the equation $m + 2m + 4 = 94$. Find how many glass marbles each has.

Understand the Problem

1. What does the variable m represent? _____

2. What are you asked to find? _____

Make and Carry Out a Plan

3. To solve the equation $m + 2m + 4 = 94$, you must combine like terms first. What are the like terms in the equation? _____

4. Combine the like terms. What expression are you left with? _____

5. Undo the addition operation by subtracting from each side of the equation. What expression are you left with? _____

6. Divide each side of the equation by the same number and simplify. Solve the equation for m. _____

7. How many marbles does Jasmine have? _____

8. How many marbles does Bill have? _____

Check the Answer

9. Check to see whether your answer is reasonable. Add the number of marbles Bill has and the number of marbles Jasmine has. Is your answer reasonable? _____

Solve Another Problem

10. Tanya and her brother, Jake, collect rare stamps. Together, they have 43 stamps. Tanya calculated she has 1 fewer than 3 times as many stamps as Jake. If Jake has m stamps, then Tanya has $(3m - 1)$ stamps. Solve the equation $m + (3m + 1) = 43$. How many rare stamps does Tanya have? How many does Jake have? _____

366 Algebra-Readiness Lesson 7-2   Guided Problem Solving

Name _____ Class _____ Date _____

Practice 7-3   Two-Step Equations With Fractions and Decimals

Solve and check each equation.

1. $0.7n - 1.5 + 7.3n = 14.5$

2. $18p - 45 = 0$

3. $16.3k + 19.2 + 7.5k = -64.1$

4. $h + 3h + 4h = 100$

5. $40 - 5n = -2$

6. $\frac{2}{3}y - 6 = 2$

7. $1.2m + 7.5m + 2.1 = 63$

8. $\frac{7}{8}h - \frac{5}{8} = 2$

9. $9w - 16.3 = 5.3$

10. $22.7 - 4.6 = -8.58$

11. $-15.3 = -7.5k + 55.2$

12. $26e + 891 = -71$

Write an equation to describe each situation. Solve.

13. Jolene bought 3 blouses at one price and 2 blouses priced $3 below the others. The total cost was $91.50. Find the prices of the blouses.

By what number would you multiply each equation to clear denominators or decimals? Do not solve.

14. $\frac{1}{3}z + \frac{1}{6} = 5\frac{1}{6}$

15. $3.7 + 2.75k = 27.35$

Practice   Algebra-Readiness Lesson 7-3

Name _____ Class _____ Date _____

7-3 • Guided Problem Solving

GPS Exercise 39

A pair of athletic shoes is on sale for $\frac{1}{4}$ off the original cost. The sale price is $49.95. Solve the equation $c - \frac{1}{4}c = 49.95$ to find the original cost c of the shoes.

Understand the Problem

1. What does the variable c represent? _____

2. What does $\frac{1}{4}c$ represent? _____

Make and Carry Out a Plan

3. First, combine like terms and write the new expression. _____

4. How can you use a reciprocal to solve the equation? _____
   _____

5. What is the reciprocal of $\frac{3}{4}$? _____

6. Multiply each side of the equation by your answer to step 5 to solve the equation for c. _____

7. What was the original cost of the shoes? _____

Check the Answer

8. Why is the equation $c - \frac{1}{4}c = 49.95$ used to find the original cost of the shoes? _____
   _____

Solve Another Problem

9. A framed picture is on sale for $\frac{1}{5}$ off the original cost. The sale price of the picture is $63.60. Use the equation $c - \frac{1}{5}c = 63.60$ to find the original cost c of the picture. _____

Algebra-Readiness Lesson 7-3

Name _____ Class _____ Date _____

Practice 7-4

Reasoning Strategy: Write an Equation

Write an equation. Then solve.

1. Bill purchased 4 pens for $3.32, including $.16 sales tax. Find the cost of 1 pen.

2. Adrianna weighed 3.2 kg at birth. She gained 0.17 kg per week. How old was she when she weighed 5.75 kg?

3. The product of 6 and 3 more than k is 48.

4. A bottle and a cap together cost $1.10. The bottle costs $1 more than the cap. How much does each cost?

5. The perimeter of a rectangular garden is 40 ft. The width is 2 ft more than one half the length. Find the length and width.

L1 Practice

Algebra-Readiness Lesson 7-4 369

Name _____ Class _____ Date _____

7-4 • Guided Problem Solving

GPS Exercise 5

Lamar's summer job is mowing lawns for a landscaper. His pay is $7.50/h. Lamar also makes $11.25/h for any time over 40 h that he works in one week. He worked 40 h last week plus n overtime hours and made $339.38. How many overtime hours did he work?

Understand the Problem

1. What is Lamar's hourly pay? _____

2. What is Lamar's hourly pay for working overtime hours? _____

3. What does the variable n represent? _____

4. How much money did Lamar make last week? _____

5. What are you asked to find? _____

Make and Carry Out a Plan

6. Use the sentence "$7.50/h multiplied by 40 hours plus $11.25/h multiplied by n hours equals $339.38" to write an equation to represent the situation. _____

7. Simplify by multiplying. _____

8. What number must you subtract from each side of the equation? _____

9. By which number must you then divide each side of the equation? _____

10. Solve for n. _____

11. How many overtime hours did Lamar work last week? _____

Check the Answer

12. To check your answer, multiply your answer by 11.25 and multiply 7.5 by 40. Add the products. _____ The sum should be the amount of money Lamar made last week.

Solve Another Problem

13. Jonna works in the summer as a lifeguard. She earned $435 last week for working 40 hours plus 5 overtime hours. If she earns $15/h for overtime, what is her normal hourly pay? _____

370 Algebra-Readiness Lesson 7-4   Guided Problem Solving

Name _____ Class _____ Date _____

Practice 7-5
Solving Two-Step Inequalities

Solve each inequality. Graph the solutions on a number line.

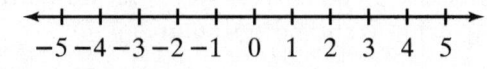

1. $2x + 2 \leq 8$ _____

2. $7x + 2x \geq 21 - 3$ _____

3. $9 - x > 10$ _____

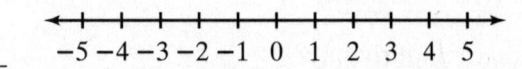

4. $-6x < 12$ _____

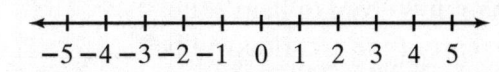

5. $\frac{x}{-4} > 0$ _____

Solve each inequality.

6. $2x - 5 > 1$ _____

7. $9x - 7 \leq 38$ _____

8. $3 < \frac{1}{2}x + 1$ _____

9. $-12 < -12x$ _____

10. $50 < 8 - 6x$ _____

11. $\frac{1}{5}x + 6 > -3$ _____

Write an inequality for each situation. Then solve.

12. Abigail drove h hours at a rate of 55 mi/h. She did not reach her goal of driving 385 miles for the day. How long did she drive?

_____

_____

Practice — Algebra-Readiness Lesson 7-5

Name _____ Class _____ Date _____

7-5 • Guided Problem Solving

GPS Exercise 29

You want to spend at most $10 for a taxi ride. Before you go anywhere, the taxi driver sets the meter at the initial charge of $2. The meter then adds $1.25 for every mile driven. If you plan on a $1 tip, what is the farthest you can go?

Understand the Problem

1. What are you asked to find? _____

2. What information is given to help you
   find what the cost of the taxi ride will be? _____
   _____

Make and Carry Out a Plan

3. Write an expression for the cost of the taxi
   ride using the variable *m* for the number of miles. _____

4. Use the expression to write an inequality showing
   that the cost of the taxi ride is less than or equal to $10. _____

5. Solve the inequality for *m*. _____

6. How many miles can you go for at most $10? _____

Check the Answer

7. Why is the expression for the cost of
   the taxi ride set less than or equal to 10? _____
   _____

8. To test your answer, find the cost of a taxi ride
   that is 5.7 miles. What does the result tell you? _____
   _____

Solve Another Problem

9. You have $15 to spend on a pizza. A 16-inch pizza
   costs $7 plus $2 per topping. What is the greatest
   number of toppings you can afford to get on a 16-inch pizza? _____

372 Algebra-Readiness Lesson 7-5   Guided Problem Solving

Practice 7-6

Transforming Formulas

Solve for the indicated variable.
Shopping City has a 6% sales tax.

1. Solve the formula $c = 1.06p$ for p, where c is the cost of an item at Shopping City, including tax, and p is the selling price.

   _____

2. Maria spent $37.10 on a pair of shoes at Shopping City. What was the selling price of the shoes?

   _____

3. Manuel spent $10.59 on a golf balls at Shopping City. What was the selling price of the golf balls?

   _____

Transform the formulas.

4. The area of a triangle A can be found with the formula $A = \frac{1}{2}bh$ where b is the length of the base of the triangle and h is the height of the triangle. Solve the formula for h.

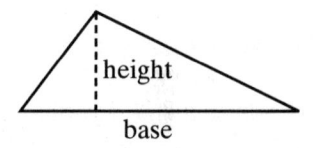

   _____

5. Solve the formula $A = \frac{1}{2}bh$ for b.

   _____

Find the missing part of each triangle.

6. $A = 27$ cm^2

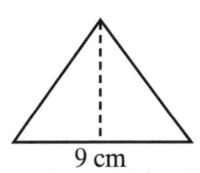

   9 cm

   $h = $ _____

Solve for the indicated variable.

7. $V = \frac{1}{3}lwh$, for w

   _____

Practice

Algebra-Readiness Lesson 7-6   **373**

Name _____ Class _____ Date _____

7-6 • Guided Problem Solving

GPS Exercise 14

a. Bricklayers use the formula $N = 7LH$ to estimate the number N of bricks needed in a wall. L is the length of the wall and H is the height. Solve the formula for H.

b. If 1,134 bricks are used to build a wall that is 18 ft long, how high is the wall?

Understand the Problem

1. What does each variable stand for? _____

2. What are you asked to do in part (a)? _____

3. What are you asked to find in part (b)? _____

Make and Carry Out a Plan

4. To solve for H, by what quantity must you divide each side of $N = 7LH$? _____

5. What is the formula for H? _____

6. Replace N with 1,134 and L with 18. Simplify to find H. _____

7. What is the height of the wall? _____

Check the Answer

8. Why did part (a) ask you to solve the formula for H? _____
_____

9. Use the formula $N = 7LH$ to test your answer. Replace N with 1,134, L with 18, and H with 9, and then simplify. Is the resulting statement true? _____
_____

Solve Another Problem

10. The number of feet of fencing needed to enclose a square-shaped backyard is found by the formula $4s = P$, where s is the length of a side and P is the perimeter. Solve the formula for s. What is the length of a side of the backyard if its area is 272 square feet? _____

374 *Algebra-Readiness Lesson 7-6*   Guided Problem Solving

Practice 7-7

Simple and Compound Interest

Find each balance.

	Principal	Interest Rate	Compounded	Time (years)	Balance
1.	$400	7%	annually	3	
2.	$1,200	4%	semi-annually	2	

Find the simple interest.

3. $900 deposited at an interest rate of 3% for 5 years

4. $674 deposited at an interest rate of 5% for 18 months

Complete each table. Compound the interest annually.

5. $5,000 at 6% for 4 years

Principal at Beginning of Year	Interest	Balance
Year 1: $5,000		
Year 2:		
Year 3:		

6. $7,200 at 3% for 4 years

Principal at Beginning of Year	Interest	Balance
Year 1: $7,200		
Year 2:		
Year 3:		

Name _____ Class _____ Date _____

7-7 • Guided Problem Solving

GPS Exercise 12

You deposit $600 in a savings account for 3 years.
The account pays 8% annual interest compounded quarterly.
a. What is the quarterly interest rate?
b. What is the number of payment periods?
c. Find the final balance in the account.

Understand the Problem

1. How much is deposited in the savings account? _____

2. How long is the money in the savings account? _____

3. What interest does the account pay? _____

4. What are you asked to find in part (a)? _____

5. What are you asked to find in part (b)? _____

6. What are you asked to find in part (c)? _____

Make and Carry Out a Plan

7. Divide the annual interest rate by the number of
   interest periods in one year to find the quarterly interest rate. _____

8. Multiply the number of payment periods in one
   year by 3 to find the total number of payment periods. _____

9. Use the compound interest formula $B = p(1 + r)^n$.
   Replace p with 600, r with the quarterly interest
   rate, and n with the total number of payment periods. _____

10. Solve the equation for B. Round your answer to the nearest hundredth. _____

11. What is the balance in the account after 3 years? _____

Check the Answer

12. To check your answer, replace B with your answer
    in the compound interest formula and solve for p. _____
    Remember, p should be equal to the original amount deposited in the account.

Solve Another Problem

13. You deposit $500 in a savings account for 5 years. The account pays 6% annual interest
    compounded semiannually.
    a. What is the semiannual interest rate? _____
    b. What is the number of payment periods? _____
    c. Find the balance in the account. _____

Algebra-Readiness Lesson 7-7   Guided Problem Solving

Name _____ Class _____ Date _____

7A: Graphic Organizer
For use before Lesson 7-1

Study Skill Compare the title of this chapter to the titles of the chapters before this one. Ask yourself how the contents of this chapter might connect to the contents of previous chapters. What did you learn before that you may need as you learn the topics in this chapter?

Write your answers. Use the Table of Contents page for this chapter at the front of the book.

1. What is the title of this chapter? _____

2. Name four topics that you will study in this chapter:

   _____   _____

   _____   _____

3. What is the topic of the Reasoning Strategy lesson? _____

4. Complete the graphic organizer as you work through the chapter.
   1. Write the title of the chapter in the center oval.
   2. When you begin a lesson, write the name of the lesson in a rectangle.
   3. When you complete that lesson, write a skill or key concept from that lesson in the outer oval linked to that rectangle.
   Continue with steps 2 and 3 clockwise around the graphic organizer.

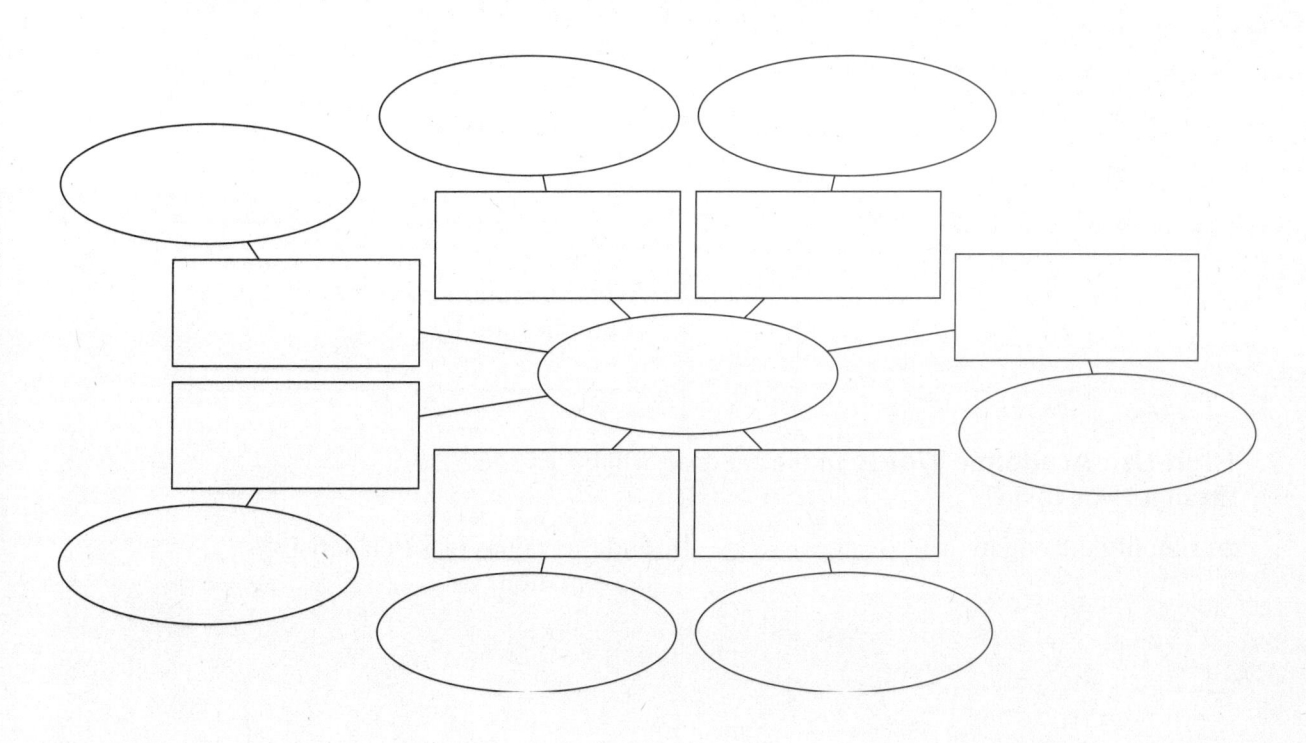

Vocabulary and Study Skills

Algebra-Readiness Chapter 7

377

Name _____ Class _____ Date _____

7B: Reading Comprehension
For use after Lesson 7-4

Study Skill Sometimes you can better remember what you read by forming a "picture" in your mind of what the words say. Make mental pictures of the content, like a "mind movie," to help you recall the material later.

Read the directions for the exercise below.

Solve $-2(3x - 1) + x = 27$ and check.

Read the steps in the solution below, and answer the questions at the right.

$$-2(3x - 1) + x = 27$$
$$-6x + 2 + x = 27$$
$$-6x + x + 2 = 27$$
$$-5x + 2 = 27$$
$$-5x + 2 - 2 = 27 - 2$$
$$-5x + 0 = 25$$
$$-5x = 25$$
$$x = \frac{25}{-5}$$
$$x = -5$$

Check:

$$-2(3x - 1) + x = 27$$
$$-2[3(-5) - 1] + (-5) \stackrel{?}{=} 27$$
$$-2[-16] + (-5) \stackrel{?}{=} 27$$
$$32 - 5 \stackrel{?}{=} 27$$
$$27 = 27 \checkmark$$

1. What is the variable in the equation?
   _____

2. When you have solved the equation, what should your result look like?
   _____

3. What are you to do after you solve the equation?
   _____

4. Refer to the solution steps. What property do you use in the first step?
   _____

5. What property simplifies $-5x + 0$ to $-5x$?
   _____

6. What operation do you use to undo multiplication by -5?
   _____

7. **High-Use Academic Words** In the exercise, what does *solve* mean for you to do?

   a. simplify the equation

   b. find the values of x that satisfy the equation

7C: Reading/Writing Math Symbols

For use after Lesson 7-6

Study Skill As you study, have a dictionary close by so that you can look up the meaning of any words or symbols that you find confusing. When you look something up, be sure to add it to your personal written vocabulary list.

Write the meaning of each symbol on the line provided.

1. ≈ _____

2. % _____

3. △ used in an expression such as △ABC _____

4. P used in an expression such as P(odd number) or P(heads) _____

5. ≠ _____

6. ≟ _____

7. ~ _____

8. : used in an expression such as 1 ft : 10 yd _____

9. < _____

10. ∘⟶ used as a graph on a number line _____

11. ≥ _____

12. | | used in an expression such as | z | _____

13. / used in a spreadsheet or calculator _____

14. · used in an expression such as a · b _____

15. ‾ used in an expression such as $0.\overline{3}$ _____

Name _____ Class _____ Date _____

7D: Visual Vocabulary Practice
For use after Lesson 7-6

Study Skill One way to check if you understand something is to try to explain it to someone else.

Concept List

area formula	Distributive Property	consecutive integers
inequality	least common multiple	perimeter formula
distance formula	two-step inequality	variable

Write the concept that best describes each exercise. Choose from the concept list above.

1. 181, 182, 183	2. $3(b + 4) = 3b + 12$	3. $A = lw$
4. $P = 2l + 2w$	5. $3x + 4 \geq -2$	6. $d = rt$
7. a in $3a - 4 = 5$	8. 20 for the numbers 5 and 4	9. $5c \geq 2b + 9$

380 Algebra-Readiness Chapter 7 Vocabulary and Study Skills

7E: Vocabulary Check

For use after Lesson 7-7

Study Skill Strengthen your vocabulary. Use these pages and add cues and summaries by applying the Cornell Notetaking style.

Write the definition for each word at the right. To check your work, fold the paper back along the dotted line to see the correct answers.

Principal

Interest

Interest Rate

Simple Interest

Compound Interest

7E: Vocabulary Check (continued)

For use after Lesson 7-7

Write the vocabulary word for each definition. To check your work, fold the paper forward along the dotted line to see the correct answers.

The initial amount of an investment or loan. _____

An amount paid for the use of money. _____

The percentage of the balance that an account or investment earns in a fixed period of time. _____

Interest paid only on the principal. _____

Interest paid on both the principal and the interest earned in previous interest periods. _____

Name_____ Class_____ Date_____

7F: Vocabulary Review

For use with Chapter Review

Study Skill Often when you learn about a new topic in mathematics, you also learn several new words. To understand the new vocabulary, take the time to review some of the vocabulary terms from previous topics, and see how they relate to the new words. In general, you will keep adding to your active math vocabulary and reusing the terms you learned before.

Many mathematical ideas are opposites, inverses, or contrasts. For each pair, write a brief explanation of how to tell the difference between the two mathematical ideas in the pair. For help, use the Glossary in your textbook.

1. simple interest/compound interest

   _____
   _____
   _____

2. principal /interest

   _____
   _____
   _____

3. consecutive even integers/consecutive odd integers

   _____
   _____
   _____

4. equation/expression

   _____
   _____
   _____

5. interest/interest rate

   _____
   _____
   _____

Vocabulary and Study Skills

Algebra-Readiness Chapter 7

Name _____ Class _____ Date _____

Practice 8-1

Relations and Functions

Graph each relation. Is the relation a function? Explain.

1.

x	y
−1	4
2	3
4	−1
−1	−2

_____
_____
_____

2.

x	y
2	−4
−4	0
−2	3
3	−1

_____
_____
_____

Graph each relation shown. Use the vertical-line test.
Is the relation a function? Explain.

3. $\{(7, -2), (8, -2), (-5, 7), (-9, 1)\}$

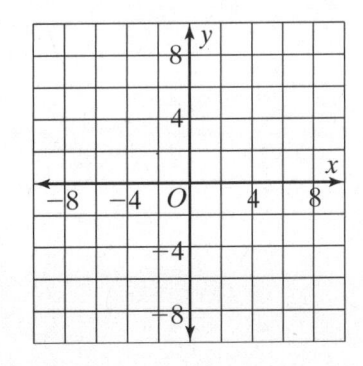

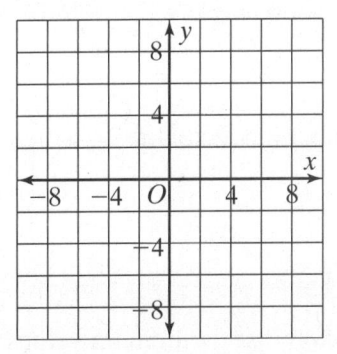

4. $\{(-8, 0), (10, 6), (10, -2), (-5, 7)\}$

Function? _____   Function? _____

_____   _____

5. Is the time is takes you to run a 100-meter race a function of the speed you run? Explain.

_____

Practice Algebra-Readiness Lesson 8-1

Name _____ Class _____ Date _____

8-1 • Guided Problem Solving

GPS Exercise 17

Graph the relation shown at right. Is the relation a function? Explain.

x	y
–5	6
–2	3
3	2
4	6

Understand the Problem

1. List the ordered pairs in the relation. _____

2. What are you asked to do? _____

Make and Carry Out a Plan

3. Graph the ordered pairs in the relation in the coordinate plane.

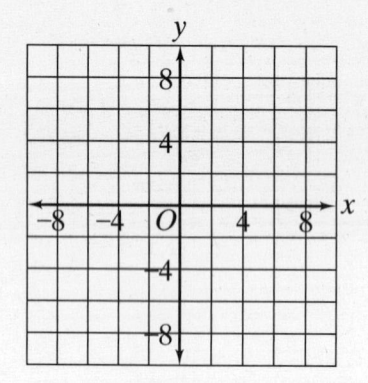

4. What test can you use to decide whether the relation is a function? _____

5. Hold a pencil parallel to the y-axis and move it across the graph from left to right. Does the line of the pencil ever pass through more than one point of the graph? What does this tell you? _____
_____

6. Is the relation a function? Explain. _____
_____

Check the Answer

7. To check your answer, list the domain values and the range values in order. Draw arrows from the domain values to their range values. Is each member of the domain paired with exactly one member of the range? _____

   What does this tell you? _____

Solve Another Problem

8. Graph the relation
{(1, –4), (2, 5), (4, –1), (5, 3)}.
Is the relation a function? Explain. _____

386 Algebra-Readiness Lesson 8-1   Guided Problem Solving

Practice 8-2

Equations With Two Variables

Solve each equation for y.

1. $3y = 15x - 12$

    $y = $ _____

2. $5x + 10 = 10y$

    $y = $ _____

3. $3y - 21 = 12x$

    $y = $ _____

4. $5y + 3 = 2y - 3x + 5$

    $y = $ _____

Graph each linear equation.

5. $y = -0.5x + 4$

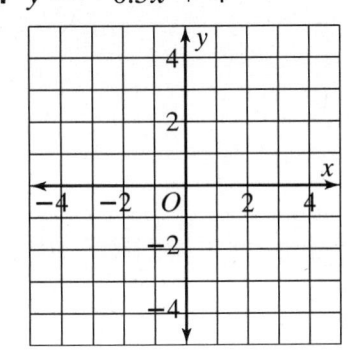

6. $y = 4$

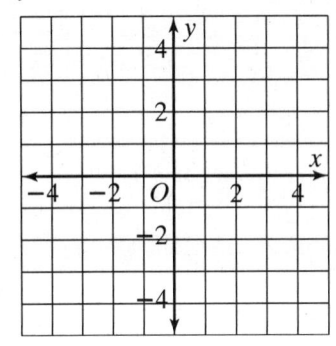

7. $2x - 3y = 6$

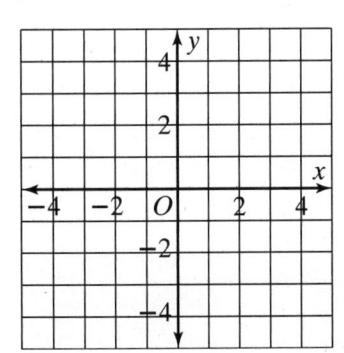

    $y = $ _____

8. $-10x = 5y$

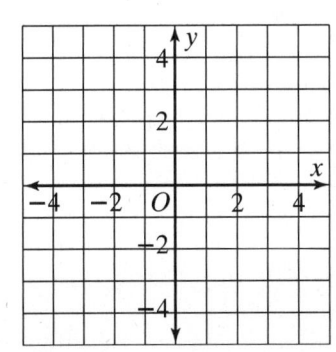

    $y = $ _____

Find the solution of $y = 3x - 4$ for the given value of x.

9. 3 _____

10. −2 _____

11. 0 _____

12. 5 _____

Name _____ Class _____ Date _____

8-2 • Guided Problem Solving

GPS Exercise 28

José is driving on a highway. The equation $d = 55t$ relates the number of miles d and the amount of time in hours t. About how many hours does José spend driving 100 mi?

Understand the Problem

1. What does the variable d represent? _____

2. What does the variable t represent? _____

3. What equation relates d and t? _____

4. What are you asked to find? _____
   _____

Make and Carry Out a Plan

5. Replace d in the equation with 100. _____

6. By what number must you divide each side of the equation to solve for t? _____

7. Solve the equation for t. _____

8. About how many hours does José spend driving 100 mi? _____

Check the Answer

9. To check your answer, replace t in the equation with your answer and solve the equation for d. _____
   The result should be about the number of miles José will drive.

Solve Another Problem

10. The equation $c = \$6.50t$ relates the number of tickets t purchased for a baseball game and the total cost c of the tickets. What is the total cost of 15 tickets? _____

Algebra-Readiness Lesson 8-2

Guided Problem Solving

Practice 8-3

Slope and y-intercept

Find the slope of the line through each pair of points.

1. $A(1, 1), B(6, 3)$

2. $J(-4, 6), K(-4, 2)$

3. $P(3, -7), Q(-1, -7)$

4. $M(7, 2), N(-1, 3)$

Complete the table.

Equation	Equation in Slope-Intercept Form	Slope	y-intercept
5. $5x - y = 6$			
6. $7x + 2y = 10$			

Find the slope of each line.

7. _____

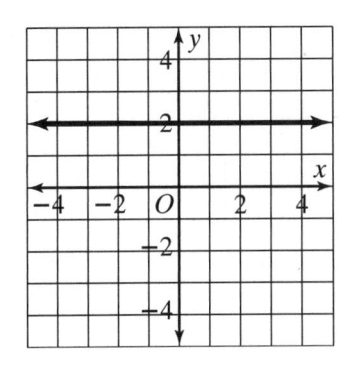

8. _____

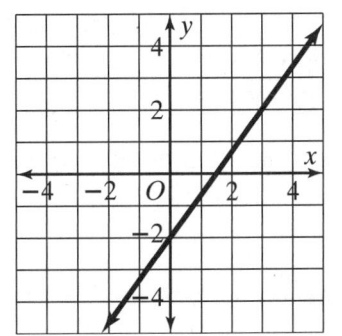

Graph each equation.

9. $y = -2x + 3$

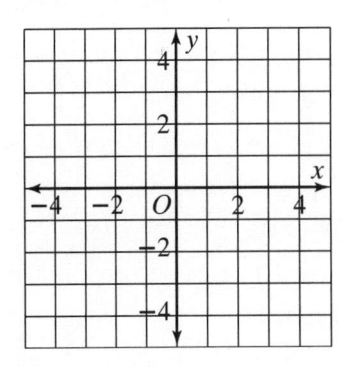

10. $y = \frac{1}{3}x - 1$

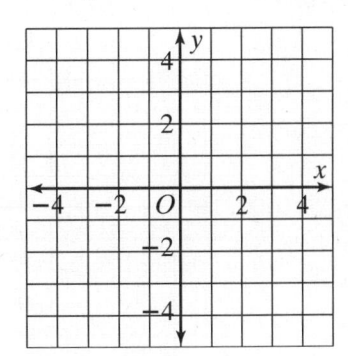

Practice Algebra-Readiness Lesson 8-3

Name _____ Class _____ Date _____

8-3 • Guided Problem Solving

GPS Exercise 23

Find the slope of the line.

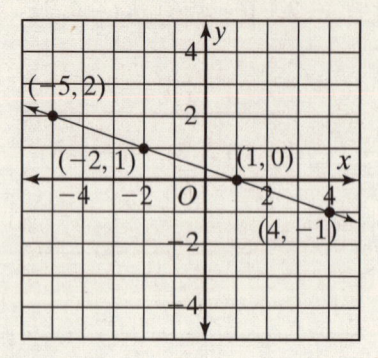

Understand the Problem

1. What are you asked to find? _____

2. What four points are given on the line? _____

Make and Carry Out a Plan

3. What is the formula for finding slope of a line using the coordinates of two points on the line? _____

4. Choose two points on the line. Write a ratio to show the difference in the *y*-coordinates over the difference in the *x*-coordinates. _____

5. Subtract the *y*-coordinates and the *x*-coordinates. _____

6. Simplify. What is the slope of the line? _____

Check the Answer

7. To check your answer, find the slope of the line by using the other two points labeled on the line. _____

Solve Another Problem

8. Find the slope of the line.

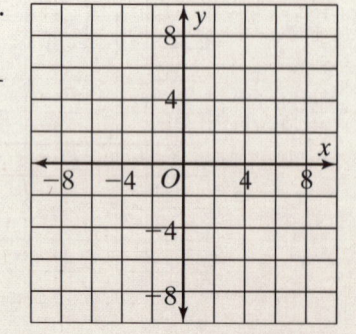

_____

390 Algebra-Readiness Lesson 8-3   Guided Problem Solving

Practice 8-4

Direct Variation

Graph the direct variation. Find the constant of variation.

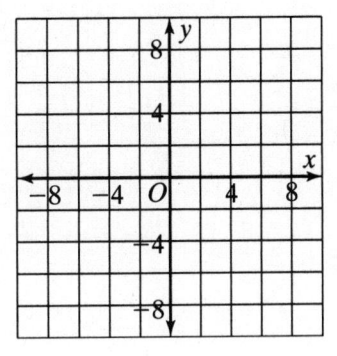

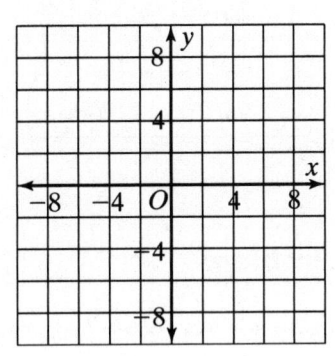

1.
x	y
−1	−4
0	0
1	4
2	8

2.
x	y
0	0
2	−3
4	−6
6	−9

3. The amount of money you earn varies directly with the number of hours you work. You work for 8 h and earn $98. How many hours do you need to work to earn $441?

Write an equation for a direct variation that includes each point.

4. $H(-6, -1)$

5. $G(-3, 8)$

6. $F(5, 2)$

Practice

Algebra-Readiness Lesson 8-4 391

Name _____ Class _____ Date _____

8-4 • Guided Problem Solving

GPS Exercise 14

The equation $V = kT$ models the volume and the temperature of air in a balloon. Use the data in the table to find the temperature when the volume is 12.6.

Air in a Balloon

Volume V (liters)	Temperature T (kelvins)
125	▆
300	400

Understand the Problem

1. What does the variable V represent? _____

2. What does the variable T represent? _____

3. What does the variable k represent? _____

4. What are you asked to find? _____

Make and Carry Out a Plan

5. Use the information in the table to find k. Divide the given volume 300 by the given temperature 400. _____

6. Replace k in the equation with the result. Replace V in the equation with 12.6. _____

7. By what number must you multiply each side of the equation to solve for T? _____

8. Solve the equation for T. _____

Check the Answer

9. To check your answer, replace T in the equation with your answer and solve the equation for V. The result should be about 12.6. _____

Solve Another Problem

10. A worker earns $306.25 for 35 hours of work. About how much will the worker earn for working 72 hours? _____

Algebra-Readiness Lesson 8-4   Guided Problem Solving

Practice 8-5

Reasoning Strategy: Use Multiple Strategies

Combine multiple strategies to solve each problem.

1. A rectangle has length $(x - 3)^2$ and width 4. The perimeter of the rectangle is 40. Find the length.

2. A rectangular prism has length $x + 2$, width $x + 1$, height 4, and volume 24. Find the length and the width.

3. A piece of cardboard measures 12 ft by 12 ft. Corners are to be cut from it as shown by the broken lines, and the sides folded up to make a box with an open top. What size corners should be cut from the cardboard to make a box with the greatest possible volume?

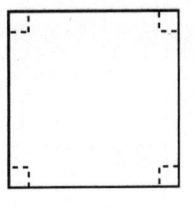

4. What size corners should be cut from a piece of cardboard that measures 30 in. by 30 in. to make an open-top box with the greatest possible volume?

5. The perimeter of a right triangle is 24 in. Find the dimensions of the triangle if the sides are all whole-number lengths.

Name _____ Class _____ Date _____

8-5 • Guided Problem Solving

GPS Exercise 8

Geometry A lot measures 50 ft by 100 ft. The house on the lot measures 25 ft by 50 ft. What is the area of the lawn?

Understand the Problem

1. What are the measurements of the lot? _____

2. What are the measurements of the house? _____

3. What are you asked to find? _____

4. Draw and label a diagram of the house on the lot in the space below.

Make and Carry Out a Plan

5. Use the formula for area of a rectangle to find the area of the lot. _____

6. Find the area of the house. _____

7. Use the area of the lot and the area of the house to write an expression for the area of the lawn. _____

8. Simplify to find the area of the lawn. _____

Check the Answer

9. To check your answer, rewrite the expression, $50 \cdot 100 - 50 \cdot 25$ using the Distributive Property and simplify. _____
The result should be the same as the area of the lawn you found in Question 8.

10. Does it make a difference where you place the house? Explain. _____

Solve Another Problem

11. A deli plate has a radius of 50 cm. The undecorated part has a radius of 17 cm. What is the area of the plate?

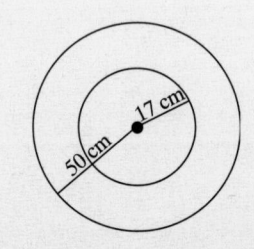

394 Algebra-Readiness Lesson 8-5   Guided Problem Solving

Practice 8-6

Linear Inequalities

Is each ordered pair a solution of the given system? Write *yes* or *no*.

1. $y = 6x + 12$
   $2x - y = 4$

   $(-4, -12)$ _____

2. $x + 2y = 2$
   $2x + 5y = 2$

   $(6, -2)$ _____

Solve each system of equations by graphing. Check your solution.

3. $x + y = 3$
   $x - y = -1$
   Solution:

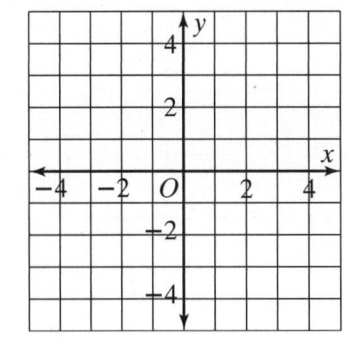

   _____

4. $y + 2 = 0$
   $2x + y = 0$
   Solution:

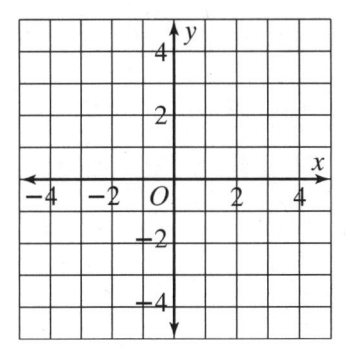

   _____

Write a system of linear equations. Solve by graphing.

5. The sum of two numbers is 3. Their difference is 1. Find the numbers.

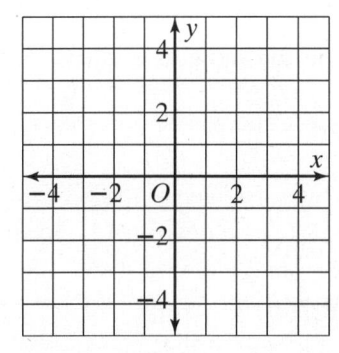

   _____

   _____

   _____

Practice   Algebra-Readiness Lesson 8-6

Name _____ Class _____ Date _____

8-6 • Guided Problem Solving

GPS Exercise 22

There are 11 animals in a barnyard. Some are chickens and some are cows. There are 38 legs in all. Let x be the number of chickens and y be the number of cows. How many of each animal are in the barnyard?

Understand the Problem

1. How many animals are in the barnyard? _____

2. How many legs are in the barnyard? _____

3. What does the variable x represent? _____

4. What does the variable y represent? _____

5. What are you asked to do? _____

Make and Carry Out a Plan

6. How many legs does a chicken have? A cow? _____

7. Write an expression to represent the number of chicken legs in the barnyard. _____

8. Write an expression to represent the number of cow legs in the barnyard. _____

9. Use the two expressions to write an equation for the total number of legs in the barnyard. _____

10. Use x and y to write an equation for the number of animals in the barnyard. _____

11. Use graph paper. Graph the two equations.

12. At what point do the two lines intersect? _____

13. How many chickens and cows are in the barnyard? _____

Check the Answer

14. To check your answer, replace x and y in the two equations with the values you found for Question 12. Do the values make both equations true? _____

Solve Another Problem

15. There are seven vehicles parked in a garage. Some are bicycles and some are cars. There are 18 wheels in all. Let x be the number of bicycles and y be the number of cars. How many bicycles are in the garage? How many cars are in the garage? _____

Algebra-Readiness Lesson 8-6   Guided Problem Solving

Practice 8-7

Linear Inequalities

Graph each inequality.

1. $y < x$

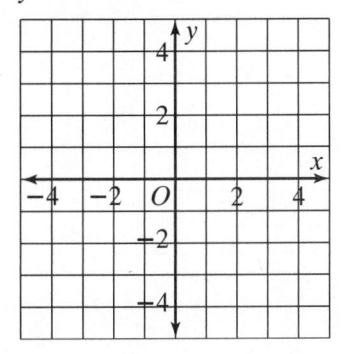

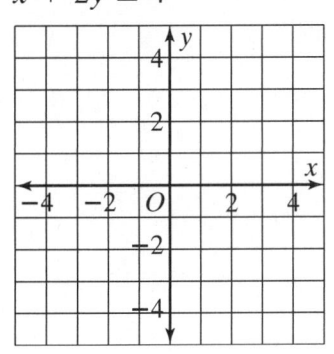

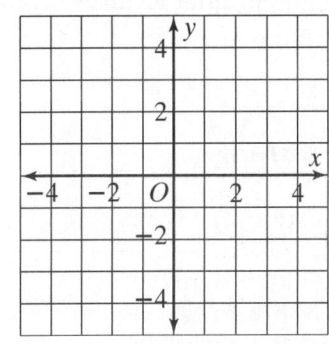

2. $x + y \leq 2$

3. $x + 2y \geq 4$

4. $x > -2$

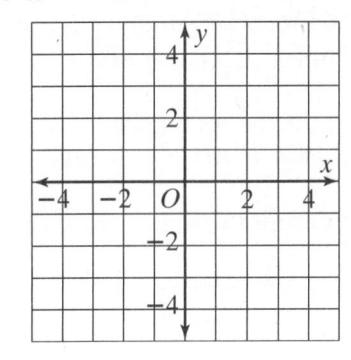

Solve each system of inequalities by graphing.

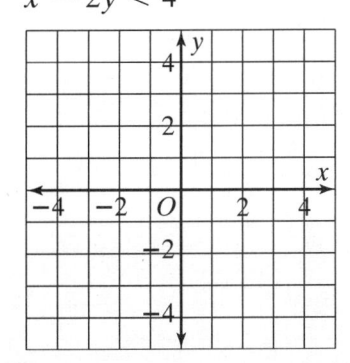

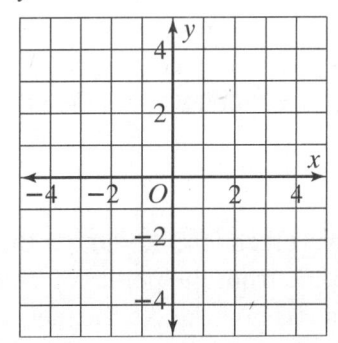

5. $y \geq -x - 2$
   $x - 2y < 4$

6. $x + y < 3$
   $y \geq 3x - 2$

7. Is the origin included in the solution to the system in Exercise 5? _____

8. Is (1, 0) a solution to the system in Exercise 6? _____

Name _____ Class _____ Date _____

8-7 • Guided Problem Solving

GPS Exercise 15

A number is greater than or equal to three times another number. What are the numbers?

Understand the Problem

1. What information are you given about the two numbers? _____

2. What are you asked to do? _____

Make and Carry Out a Plan

3. Let y represent a number and x represent another number. Use the sentence "A number is greater than or equal to three times another number" to write an inequality. _____

4. Write an equation for the inequality. This is the equation of the boundary line. _____

5. Use graph paper. Graph the equation of the boundary line.

6. Choose a point on the boundary line. Does the point make the inequality you wrote in Step 3 true or false? _____
If the point makes the equation true, make the boundary line solid. If the point does not make the inequality true, make the boundary line dashed.

7. Choose a point not on the boundary line to test in the inequality. Does the point make the inequality you wrote in Step 3 true or false? _____
If the point makes the inequality true, shade the region containing the point. If the point does not make the inequality true, shade the region that does not contain the point.

Check the Answer

8. To check your answer, choose a point on the other side of the line from the point you chose in Question 7. Does this point make the inequality true or false? _____

   How does this support how you shaded your graph? _____

Solve Another Problem

9. A number is greater than three more than two times another number. Show all the solutions by writing and graphing a linear inequality. Use graph paper.

Name _____ Class _____ Date _____

8A: Graphic Organizer

For use before Lesson 8-1

Study Skill Look at the title of this chapter. Do you already know the meaning of the words *linear functions* in the title? Look at the titles of the lessons in this chapter. Do they give you any clues about the meaning of *linear functions*? Write notes to record your thoughts about the meaning of the words in these titles. As you finish a lesson, review your notes and update them to contain what you have learned about linear functions.

Write your answers. Use the Table of Contents page for this chapter at the front of the book.

1. What is the title of this chapter? _____

2. Name four topics that you will study in this chapter:

   _____   _____

   _____   _____

3. What is the topic of the Reasoning Strategy lesson? _____

4. Complete the graphic organizer as you work through the chapter.
   1. Write the title of the chapter in the center oval.
   2. When you begin a lesson, write the name of the lesson in a rectangle.
   3. When you complete that lesson, write a skill or key concept from that lesson in the outer oval linked to that rectangle.
   Continue with steps 2 and 3 clockwise around the graphic organizer.

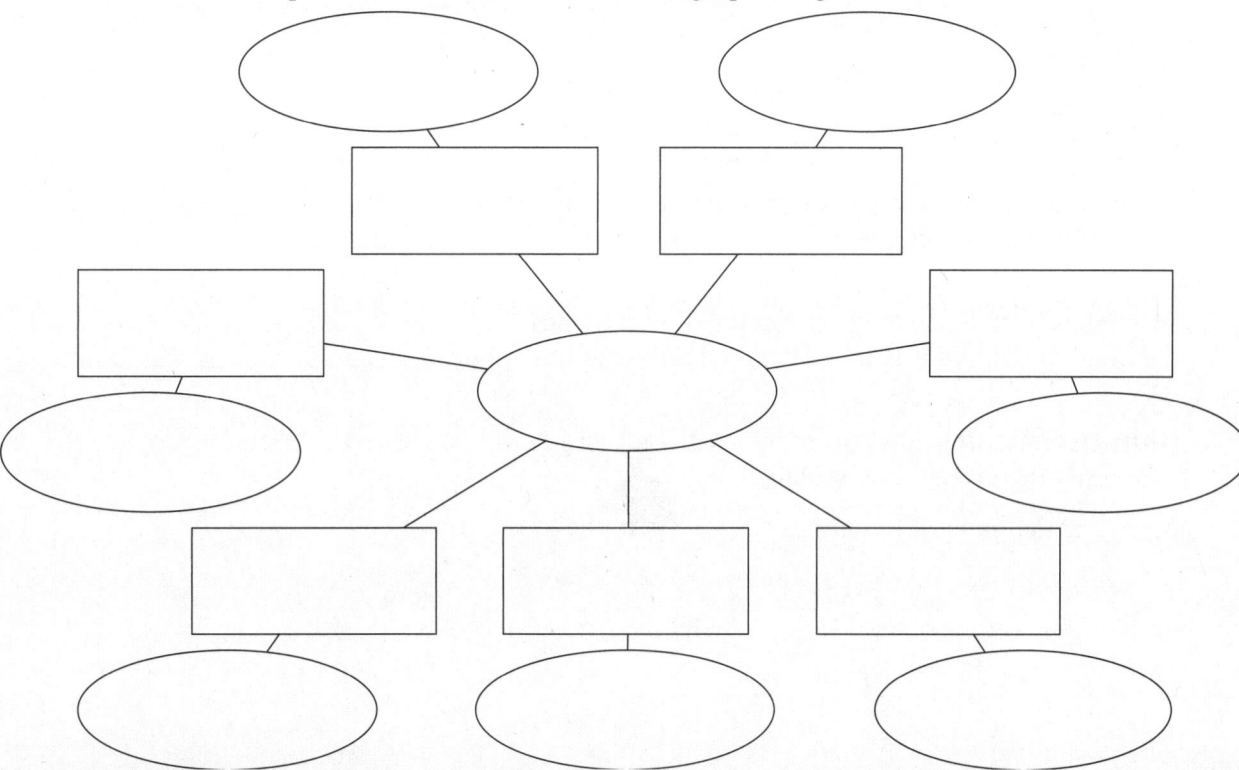

Vocabulary and Study Skills

Algebra-Readiness Chapter 8

399

Name _____ Class _____ Date _____

8B: Reading Comprehension
For use after Lesson 8-6

Study Skill The notes you take in class should contain all of the important information. In general, anything your teacher writes on the board or overhead projector should go into your notes. Other signals that information is important are repetition and emphasis. If your teacher presents a math idea more than once, then it belongs in your written notes.

Answer the questions below about how to read this graph.

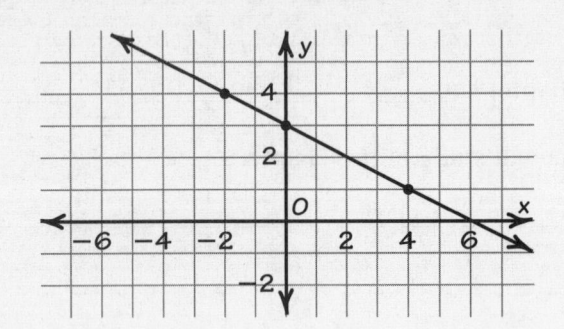

1. What is the label on the horizontal axis? _____

2. What is the label on the vertical axis? _____

3. What marks on the horizontal and vertical axes show that these lines extend without ending? _____

4. Write the coordinates of the ordered pair that names the point where the graphed line crosses the *y*-axis. _____

5. Write the coordinates of the ordered pair that names the point where the graphed line crosses the *x*-axis. _____

6. Write the coordinates of the ordered pair that names the point in Quadrant II that is marked on the graphed line. _____

7. **High-Use Academic Words** In questions 1 and 2, you are asked to identify the *label*. What is a label?

    a. writing that names something   b. the key feature

400 *Algebra-Readiness* Chapter 8   Vocabulary and Study Skills

Name _____ Class _____ Date _____

8C: Reading/Writing Math Symbols   For use after Lesson 8-4

Study Skill As you listen and take notes in class, bear in mind that you will probably want to use your notes to do your homework and study for tests. Take time to make your notes clear, using full sentences or phrases instead of isolated words. Write an example whenever you can.

Answer the following questions about math symbols in the space provided.

1. Complete the sentence that describes this expression: $\{(2, 3), (2, 4), (4, 3)\}$.

   These symbols show a relation consisting of _____

   _____

2. Describe this expression: $\{(0, 1), (1, 2), (2, 2), (3, 4)\}$.

   _____

   _____

3. On a coordinate system, both the *x*-axis and the *y*-axis have arrowheads at the ends. The graph of a line also has arrowheads drawn at both ends. Write a sentence that explains what these arrowhead symbols mean.

   _____

   _____

4. For the expression $y = kx$, what does the variable *k* represent?

   _____

   _____

5. In the slope-intercept form of a linear equation, $y = mx + b$, describe the meaning of *m*.

   _____

   _____

6. In the slope-intercept form of a linear equation, $y = mx + b$, what does *b* represent?

   _____

   _____

Vocabulary and Study Skills   Algebra-Readiness Chapter 8   **401**

8D: Visual Vocabulary Practice

For use after Lesson 8-7

Study Skill When learning about a new concept, try to draw a picture to illustrate it.

Concept List

constant of variation	linear equation	linear inequality
relation	direct variation	vertical-line test
slope	slope-intercept form	system of linear equations

Write the concept that best describes each exercise. Choose from the concept list shown above.

1. $y = 2x + 1$

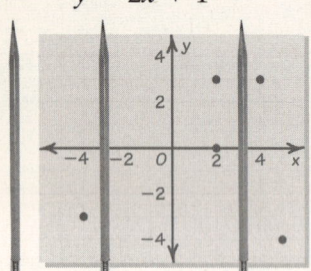

2. $\dfrac{\text{rise}}{\text{run}}$

3. $y = mx + b$

4. $(0, 1), (1, 2), (2, 3)$

5. k in $y = kx$

6. $y = kx$

7.

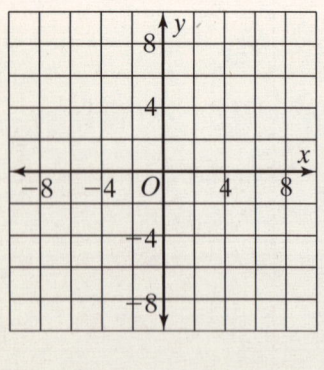

8. $y = x,\ y = 2x + 3$

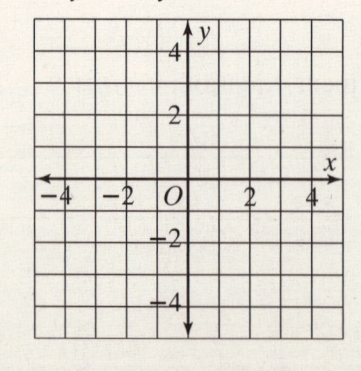

9.

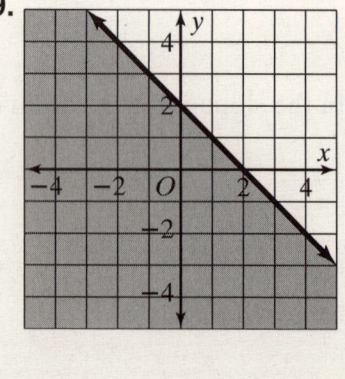

Algebra-Readiness Chapter 8 — Vocabulary and Study Skills

8E: Vocabulary Check

For use after Lesson 8-5

Study Skill Strengthen your vocabulary. Use these pages and add cues and summaries by applying the Cornell Notetaking style.

Write the definition for each word at the right. To check your work, fold the paper back along the dotted line to see the correct answers.

_____

Domain

_____

Range

_____

Function

_____

Slope

_____

Vertical-line Test

8E: Vocabulary Check (continued)

For use after Lesson 8-5

Write the vocabulary word for each definition. To check your work, fold the paper forward along the dotted line to see the correct answers.

The set of first coordinates of the ordered pairs of the relation.

_____

The set of second coordinates of the ordered pairs of a relation.

_____

A relationship in which each member of the domain is paired with exactly one member of the range.

_____

A ratio that describes the tilt of a line.

_____

A test that allows you to describe graphically whether a relation is a function.

_____

Name _____ Class _____ Date _____

8F: Vocabulary Review Puzzle

For use with Chapter Review

Study Skill As you study the new words in a chapter, you may see familiar words that have unexpected new meanings when they are used mathematically. Write notes about the new mathematical meaning and compare it to the familiar one.

Use the words below to complete the crossword puzzle. For help, use the Glossary in your textbook.

domain	function	y-intercept
slope	range	relation
solution		

ACROSS

1. the second coordinates
2. an ordered pair that makes an equation true
5. the first coordinates
6. the ratio that describes the tilt of a line

DOWN

1. a set of ordered pairs
3. each member of the domain is paired with exactly one member of the range
4. the point where the line crosses the *y*-axis

Name _____ Class _____ Date _____

Practice 9-1   Introduction to Geometry: Points, Lines, and Planes

Use the figure at the right. Name each of the following.

1. Two segments that intersect $\overline{AB}$.
   _____

2. Two segments parallel to $\overline{AB}$.
   _____

3. Two segments skew to $\overline{AB}$.
   _____

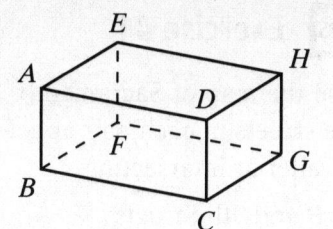

Use the figure at the right. Find each of the following.

4. all points shown
   _____

5. all segments shown
   _____

6. five different rays
   _____

7. all lines shown
   _____

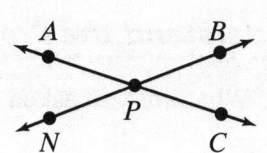

Write an equation. Then find the length of each segment.

8.

equation:
_____

$n =$ _____

$AB =$ _____ $AC =$ _____

Practice   Algebra-Readiness Lesson 9-1   **407**

Name _____ Class _____ Date _____

9-1 • Guided Problem Solving

GPS Exercise 41

Use the map of Sacramento. Tell whether the streets in each pair appear to be parallel or intersecting.

a. P and 9th Streets
b. J and 15th Streets
c. K and J Streets
d. 9th and 12th Streets
e. J and 12th Streets
f. P and 15th Streets

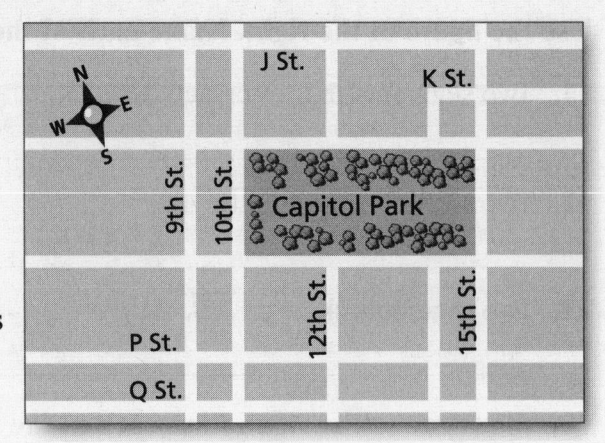

Understand the Problem

1. What are you asked to do? _____

Make and Carry Out a Plan

2. How do you know whether two lines are intersecting? _____

3. How do you know whether two lines are parallel? _____

4. Find P and 9th Streets on the map. Do they share exactly one point? _____

   Are they parallel or intersecting? _____

5. Find each pair of streets in parts (b) through (f) and tell whether they are parallel or intersecting.

   b. _____   c. _____

   d. _____   e. _____

   f. _____

Check the Answer

6. If a pair of streets do not intersect on the map, does that mean they do not intersect? Explain. _____

Solve Another Problem

7. Look at the picture of the side of a barn. Tell whether each pair of lines appears to be parallel or intersecting.

   a. 1 and 2 _____

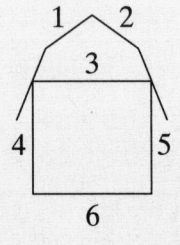

   b. 3 and 6 _____

408 Algebra-Readiness Lesson 9-1   Guided Problem Solving

Name _____ Class _____ Date _____

Practice 9-2   Angle Relationships and Parallel Lines

Find the measure of each angle in the figure at the right.

1. $m\angle 1$ _____   2. $m\angle 2$ _____

3. $m\angle 3$ _____   4. $m\angle VWR$ _____

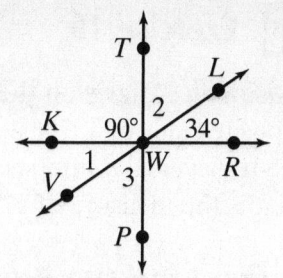

Use the figure at the right for Exercises 5-8.

5. What is the measure of $\angle ABC$? _____

6. Write an equation. _____

7. Find the value of x. _____

8. Find $m\angle DBC$. _____

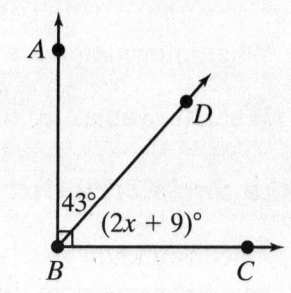

Use the figure at the right for Exercises 9-11.

9. Write an equation. _____

10. Find the value of x. _____

11. Find $m\angle MNQ$. _____

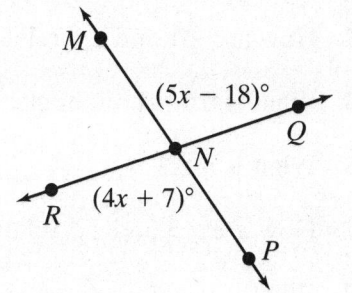

In each figure, find the measures of $\angle 1$ and $\angle 2$.

12. Given $p \parallel q$.

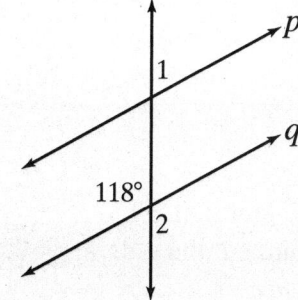

$m\angle 1 =$ _____ $m\angle 2 =$ _____

13. Given $a \parallel b$.

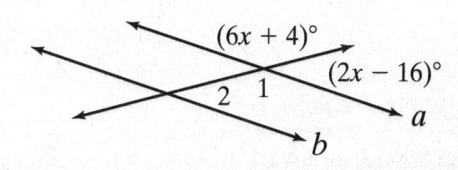

$m\angle 1 =$ _____ $m\angle 2 =$ _____

L1 Practice   Algebra-Readiness Lesson 9-2   409

Name _____ Class _____ Date _____

9-2 • Guided Problem Solving

GPS Exercise 19

Reasoning Angles on the "outside" of two lines and on opposite sides of a transversal are called **alternate exterior angles.** The transversal q intersects two parallel lines m and n. If $m\angle 1 = 84°$, what is the measure of $\angle 5$? Explain your reasoning.

Understand the Problem

1. What information are you given? _____

2. What are you asked to find? _____

Make and Carry Out a Plan

3. Since you know $m\angle 1$, can you find measures of any other angles in the diagram? _____

4. How are $\angle 1$ and $\angle 3$ related to each other? _____

5. What is true about angles that are related in this way? _____

6. What is $m\angle 3$? _____

7. How are $\angle 3$ and $\angle 5$ related to each other? _____

8. What is true about angles that are related in this way? _____

9. What is $m\angle 5$? _____

10. Based on your results, can you predict what is true about alternate exterior angles? _____

Check the Answer

To check your answer, find $m\angle 5$ in a different way. Use the fact that $\angle 1$ and $\angle 2$ are supplementary: Find $m\angle 2$. Then use the fact that $\angle 2$ and $\angle 4$ are corresponding. $\angle 4$ and $\angle 5$ are supplementary. What is $m\angle 5$?

Solve Another Problem

The transversal q intersects two parallel lines m and n. If $m\angle 4 = 98°$, what is $m\angle 7$? Explain your reasoning.

_____

410 Algebra-Readiness Lesson 9-2   Guided Problem Solving

Name _____ Class _____ Date _____

Practice 9-3

Classifying Polygons

Name all quadrilaterals that have each of the named properties.

1. four 90° angles

   _____

2. opposite sides congruent and parallel

   _____

3. at least one pair of parallel sides

   _____

   _____

Judging by appearances, classify each triangle by its sides and angles.

4.

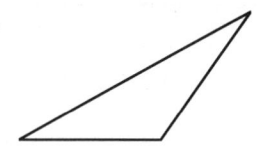

   _____

5.

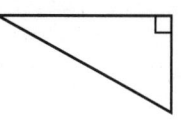

   _____

6.

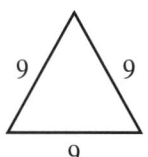

   _____

7.

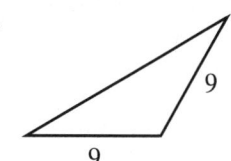

   _____

Write a formula to find the perimeter of each figure. Use the formula to find the perimeter.

8. a regular dodecagon (12-gon); one side is 5 cm

   $P =$ _____ $P =$ _____

9. a rhombus; one side is 3 yd

   $P =$ _____ $P =$ _____

10. a parallelogram; the sides are 8 m and 4 m

    $P =$ _____ $P =$ _____

L1 Practice

Algebra-Readiness Lesson 9-3

Name _____ Class _____ Date _____

9-3 • Guided Problem Solving

GPS Exercise 20

The Pentagon is a pentagon-shaped building near Washington, D.C., that is home to the United States Department of Defense. Write a formula for the perimeter of a regular pentagon in terms of the length of a side. Evaluate the formula to find the perimeter of the Pentagon, which has a side length of 921 ft.

Understand the Problem

1. What shape is the Pentagon? _____

2. What is the side length of the Pentagon? _____

3. What are you asked to do? _____

Make and Carry Out a Plan

4. How many equal sides does a regular pentagon have? _____

5. Let x equal the length of a side of a regular pentagon.
   Use x to write a formula for the perimeter of a regular pentagon. _____

6. Replace x with 921 in the formula. _____

7. What is the perimeter of the Pentagon? _____

Check the Answer

8. To check your answer, add the lengths
   of the sides of the Pentagon together. _____
   Your answer should be the same as your answer to Question 7.

Solve Another Problem

9. Maggie is digging a hexagon-shaped flower garden.
   Write a formula for the perimeter of a regular hexagon
   in terms of the length of a side. Evaluate the formula to find
   the perimeter of the flower garden, which has a side length of 8 ft. _____

Algebra-Readiness Lesson 9-3

Practice 9-4

Reasoning Strategy: Draw a Diagram

Solve by drawing a diagram.

1. How many diagonals does a quadrilateral have?
   _____

2. Which quadrilaterals always have congruent diagonals?
   _____

3. Find a formula for the number of diagonals d in a polygon with n sides. Complete the table to help you. Look for a pattern.

Figure	Number of sides	Number of vertices	Number of diagonals from each vertex	Total number of diagonals
triangle	3			
quadrilateral	4			
pentagon	5			
hexagon	6			
octagon	8			
n-gon	n			

$d = $ _____

4. A mail carrier leaves the post office at 10:00 A.M. and travels 4 miles south, then 7 miles east, then 5 miles south, then 10 miles west, and 9 miles north. At the end of her route, how far and in which direction is the mail carrier from the post office?
   _____

Name _____ Class _____ Date _____

9-4 • Guided Problem Solving

GPS Exercise 5

Solve by drawing a diagram.

There are 25 students in a math class. Ten students are in the math club. Twelve students are in the band. Five students are in both. How many students in the math class are members of neither club?

Understand the Problem

1. How many students are in the math class? _____

2. How many students are members of the math club? _____

3. How many students are in the band? _____

4. How many students are in both the math club and band? _____

5. What are you asked to find? _____

Make and Carry Out a Plan

6. The numbers 1–25 in the diagram below represent the students. Circle the numbers 1–10 to represent the students in the math club.
   1 2 3 4 5 6 7 8 9 10 11 12 13 14 15 16 17 18 19 20 21 22 23 24 25

7. Underline five of the numbers already circled to represent the students who are in both the math club and band. Then underline numbers without circles until you have a total of 12 underlined numbers, representing the 12 students in the band.

8. The numbers that are not circled or underlined represent students who belong to neither group. How many students are not members of either math club or band? _____

Check the Answer

9. To check your answer, add the numbers of students in math club and band. Next subtract the number of students who are in both. This tells you how many students are in band, math club, or both. Subtract this result from 25, the total number of students in the math class. _____ The result should be the same as your answer to Question 8.

Solve Another Problem

Solve by drawing a diagram.

10. There are 18 students in a class. Eight of the students are in soccer. Seven of the students are in the science club. Two of the students are in both. How many students in the class are not in soccer or the science club? _____

414   Algebra-Readiness Lesson 9-4   Guided Problem Solving

Name _____ Class _____ Date _____

9-5 • Guided Problem Solving

GPS Exercise 25

List the congruent corresponding parts for the pair of triangles.
Write a congruence statement (and reason) for the triangles.

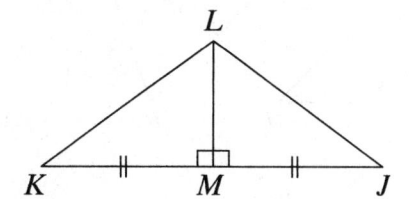

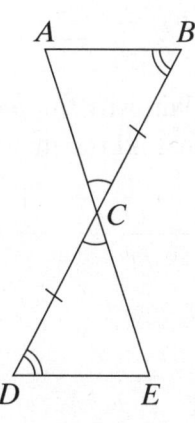

Understand the Problem

1. What are you asked to do? _____

Make and Carry Out a Plan

2. Name the corresponding congruent sides of the two triangles. _____

3. Name the corresponding congruent angles. _____

4. Write a congruence statement for the two triangles. _____

5. By which way do you know the two triangles are congruent—Side-Side-Side, Side-Angle-Side, or Angle-Side-Angle? _____

Check the Answer

6. To check your answer, look at the triangles again. Make sure you have listed the congruent corresponding parts correctly. Check your congruence statement and reason to make sure it is true of the triangles.

Solve Another Problem

7. List the congruent corresponding parts for the pair of triangles. Write a congruence statement (and reason) for the triangles.

_____

416 Algebra-Readiness Lesson 9-5   Guided Problem Solving

Practice 9-5

Congruence

Given that △GHM ≅ △RSA, complete the following.

1. $\overline{GH}$ ≅ _____
2. $\overline{AS}$ ≅ _____
3. ∠S ≅ _____
4. ∠M ≅ _____
5. $\overline{AR}$ ≅ _____
6. ∠R ≅ _____
7. m∠A = _____
8. m∠G = _____

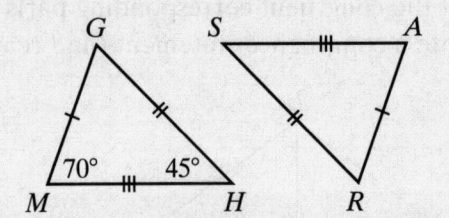

List the congruent corresponding parts of each pair of triangles. Write a congruence statement (and reason) for the triangles.

9. _____
   _____
   _____
   _____ by _____

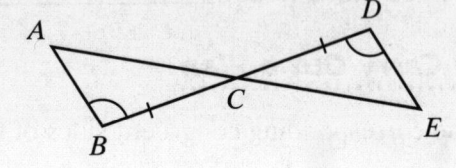

10. _____
    _____
    _____
    _____ by _____

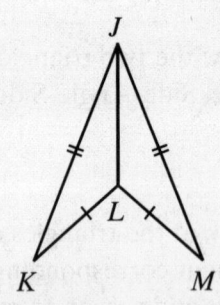

Given that HPKT ≅ BEWL, complete the following.

11. $\overline{PK}$ ≅ _____
12. ∠L ≅ _____
13. ∠KPH ≅ _____
14. $\overline{EB}$ ≅ _____

15. Explain why the pair of triangles is congruent. Then, find the missing measures.

_____

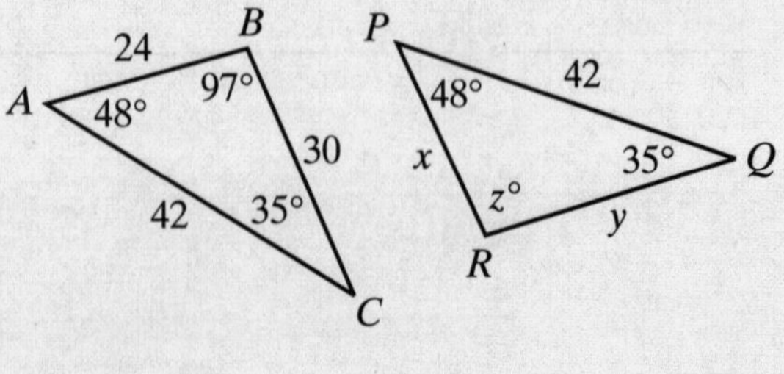

Algebra-Readiness Lesson 9-5

Name_____ Class_____ Date_____

9-6 • Guided Problem Solving

GPS Exercise 21

The data below show how a group of students travel to school each day. Make a circle graph for the data.

How Students Travel to School

Transportation	Walk	Bicycle	Bus	Car	Other
Number of Students	55	80	110	40	15

Understand the Problem

1. What do the data show? _____

2. What are you asked to do? _____

Make and Carry Out a Plan

3. Find the total number of students by adding the numbers of students in all five categories. _____

4. Write the number of students in each category as a fraction of the total number of students. _____

5. Use the fractions to write proportions to find the measure of each central angle. For example, solve $\frac{55}{300} = \frac{w}{360}$ to find w, the measure of the central angle for the number of students who walk to school.

   walk _____ bicycle _____ bus _____

   car _____ other _____

6. Use a compass to draw a circle. Draw each central angle with a protractor. Label each section with a title and the measure of the central angle.

Check the Answer

7. To check your answer, compare the data in the table and your circle graph. Do the sizes of the sections of the circle graph correspond to the data in the table? Explain. _____

Solve Another Problem

8. Alex surveyed his classmates about their favorite subjects. Draw a circle graph for the data at right.

Favorite Subjects of Students

Subject	Math	Science	Reading	History	Art
Number of Students	4	6	5	3	7

Practice 9-6

Circles

Find the measures of the central angles that you would draw to represent each percent in a circle graph. Round to the nearest degree.

	Voter Preference for Senator	Central Angle
1.	Peterson	40%
2.	Washington	30%
3.	Gomez	15%
4.	Thomson	10%
5.	Miller	5%

6. Draw a circle graph for the data on voter preference.

Voter Preference for Senator

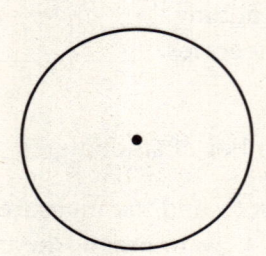

7. The total number of voters surveyed was 5,000. How many voters preferred Gomez?

_____

Find the circumference of each circle with the given radius or diameter.

8. $d = 25.8$ m

   $C = $ _____

9. $r = 9.1$ cm

   $C = $ _____

10. $r = 0.28$ km

    $C = $ _____

11. $d = 14$ ft

    $C = $ _____

L1 Practice

Algebra-Readiness Lesson 9-6

Name _____ Class _____ Date _____

Practice 9-7

Constructions

Construct each figure using the diagram at the right.

1. $\overline{MP}$ congruent to $\overline{BC}$

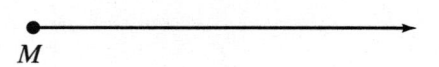

   •————————→
   M

2. $\overline{JK}$ twice as long as $\overline{BC}$

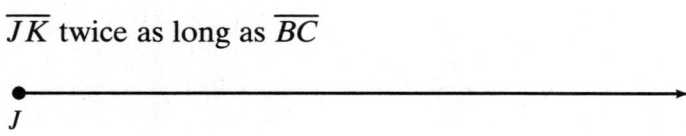

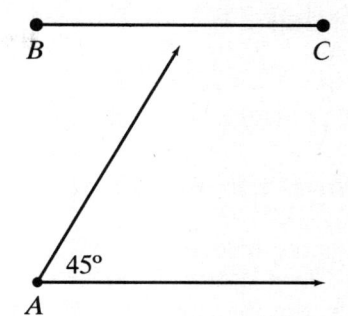

   •————————————————→
   J

3. ∠D congruent to ∠A

   •————————→
   D

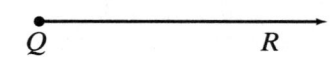

4. ∠PQR half the measure of ∠A

   •————————→
   Q   R

5. ∠STU with measure 135°

   ←————————•
                U

6. $\overline{EF}$ half as long as $\overline{BC}$

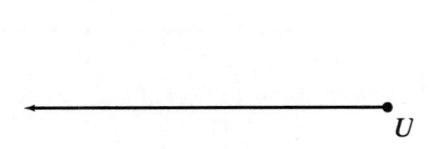

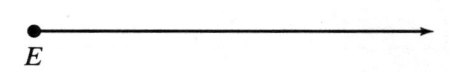

   •————————————————→
   E

7. Construct △WXY so that ∠W is congruent to ∠A, $\overline{WY}$ is congruent to $\overline{BC}$, and ∠Y is half the measure of ∠A.

   •————————————————→
   W

Practice   Algebra-Readiness Lesson 9-7   419

Name _____ Class _____ Date _____

9-7 • Guided Problem Solving

GPS Exercise 21

The bisector of ∠XYZ is $\vec{YN}$. If the measure of ∠XYN is 55°, what is the measure of ∠XYZ?

Understand the Problem

1. What is the bisector of ∠XYZ? _____

2. What is the measure of ∠XYN? _____

3. What are you asked to find? _____

Make and Carry Out a Plan

4. Sketch ∠XYZ and its bisector $\vec{YN}$ to help you visualize the problem.

5. What does an angle bisector do to an angle? _____
   _____

6. What is the measure of ∠ZYN? _____

7. Add the measures of ∠XYN and ∠ZYN to find the measure of ∠XYZ. _____

Check the Answer

8. To check your answer, subtract the measure of ∠ZYN from your answer. _____
   The result should be the measure of ∠XYN.

Solve Another Problem

9. The perpendicular bisector of $\overline{QR}$ is $\overline{ST}$. $\overline{ST}$ crosses $\overline{QR}$ at point P. If the measure of $\overline{QP}$ is 4 mm, what is the measure of $\overline{QR}$? _____

420 Algebra-Readiness Lesson 9-7   Guided Problem Solving

Practice 9-8

Translations

Write a rule to describe each translation.

1. $(x, y) \rightarrow$ _____

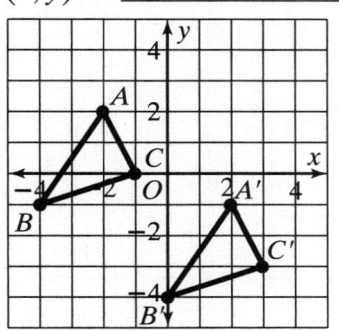

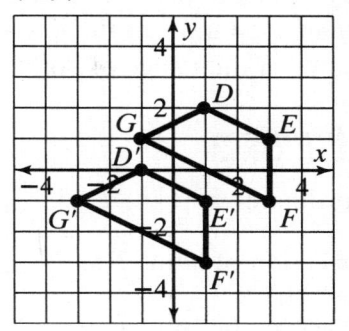

2. $(x, y) \rightarrow$ _____

3. $(x, y) \rightarrow$ _____

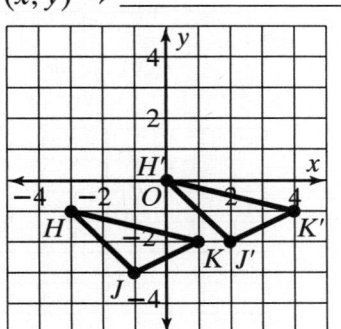

4. $(x, y) \rightarrow$ _____

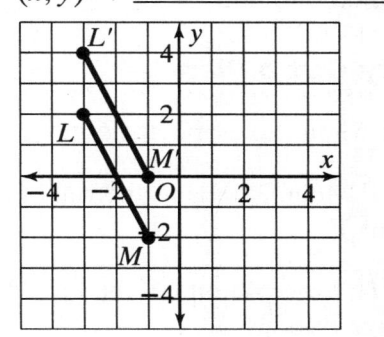

The vertices of a triangle and a translation are given. Graph each triangle and its image.

5. $G(-4, 4), H(-2, 3), J(-3, 0)$; right 5 and down 2

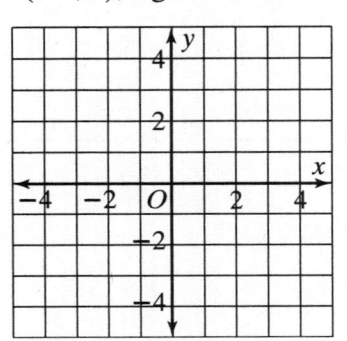

A point and its image after a translation are given. Write a rule to describe the translation.

6. $A(9, -4), A'(2, -1)$ $(x, y) \rightarrow$ _____

Practice   Algebra-Readiness Lesson 9-8   **421**

Name _____ Class _____ Date _____

9-8 • Guided Problem Solving

GPS Exercise 39

Translate point $T(2, 5)$ 2 units to the right and 6 units up.
Translate its image, point T', 4 units to the left and 1 unit down.
What are the coordinates of the image of point T'?

Understand the Problem

1. What are the coordinates of point T? _____

2. Describe the translation of point T to T'. _____

3. Describe the translation of point T' to its image. _____

4. What are you asked to find? _____

Make and Carry Out a Plan

5. Plot point $T(2, 5)$ on the graph at right.

6. Start at point T. Move 2 units to the right and 6 units up. Label this point T'.

7. Start at point T'. Move 4 units to the left and 1 unit down. This is the image of point T'.

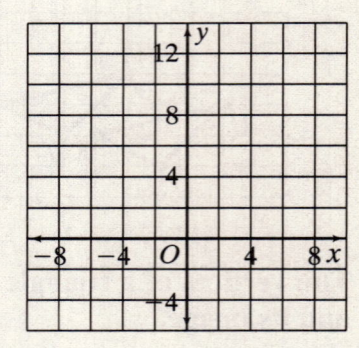

8. What are the coordinates of the image of point T'? _____

Check the Answer

9. Use mental math and combine
   (2 units right, 6 units up) with (4 units left, 1 unit down). _____

10. What is the result of translating
    $T(2, 5)$ 2 units to the left and 5 units up? _____
    The result should be the coordinates of the image of point T'.

Solve Another Problem

11. Translate point $B(4, 5)$ 3 units to the left
    and 4 units down. Translate its image,
    point B', 2 units to the right and 5 units up.
    What are the coordinates of the image of B'? _____

Practice 9-9

Symmetry and Reflections

The vertices of a polygon are listed. Graph each polygon and its image after a reflection over the given line. Name the coordinates of the image.

1. $A(1, 3), B(4, 1), C(3, -2),$
$D(2, -4); x = 0$

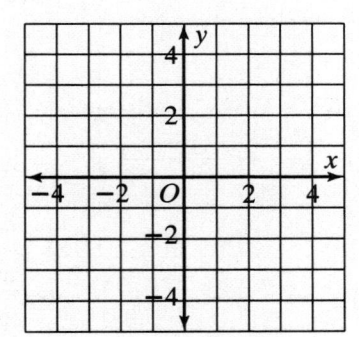

2. $J(-2, 1), K(1, 3), L(4, 2);$
$y = -1$

A' _____ B' _____

C' _____ D' _____

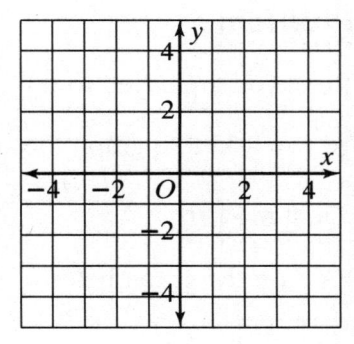

J' _____ K' _____

L' _____

Draw all the lines of symmetry for each figure.

3.

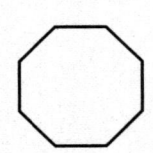

4.

Is the dashed line a line of symmetry? Write yes or no.

5. _____

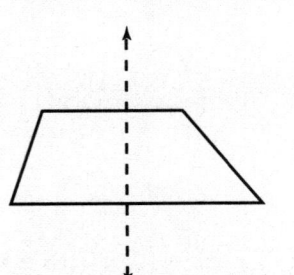

6. _____

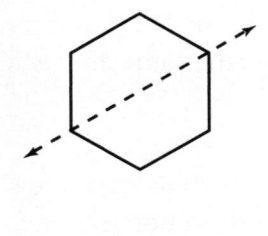

Algebra-Readiness Lesson 9-9

9-9 • Guided Problem Solving

GPS Exercise 13

△WXY has vertices W(−1, −1), X(0, 0), Y(−5, 0). Graph △WXY and its image after a reflection over the line $y = 2$.

Understand the Problem

1. What is the first thing you are asked to do? _____

2. Over what line are you asked to graph the reflection? _____

Make and Carry Out a Plan

3. Graph figure △WXY on the graph below.

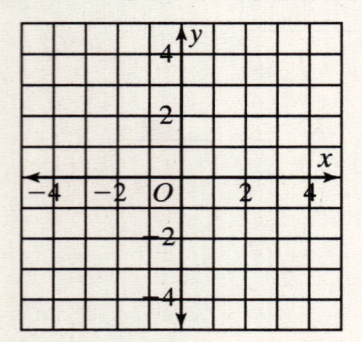

4. Draw a dashed line on the graph at $y = 2$.

5. When you reflect the triangle over the line $y = 2$, the x-coordinates of each point will remain the same. To determine the y-coordinate for each point, count the number of units to each point from $y = 2$. For example, if a point is 2 units below $y = 2$, its reflection will be 2 units above $y = 2$. Plot W′, X′, and Y′ and connect the points to form △W′X′Y′.

Check the Answer

6. To check your answer, draw the image of △W′X′Y′ after a reflection over $y = 2$. The reflected image should be the same as △WXY.

Solve Another Problem

7. △JKL has vertices J(−2, 0), K(0, 1), L(2, 0). On a separate sheet of paper, graph △JKL and its image after a reflection over $y = −2$.

Name _____ Class _____ Date _____

Practice 9-10

Rotations

Judging from appearances, does each figure have rotational symmetry? If so, what is the angle of rotation?

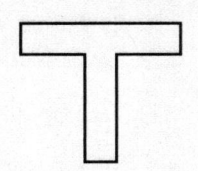

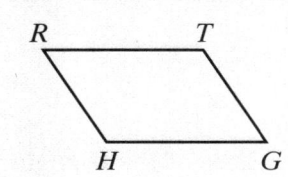

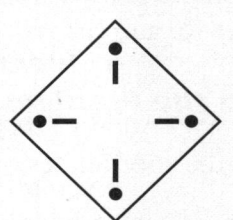

1. _____   2. _____   3. _____

The vertices of a triangle are given. Graph each triangle and its image after the given rotation about the origin. Name the coordinates of the vertices of the images.

4. $A(1, 4), B(1, 1), C(4, 2); 90°$

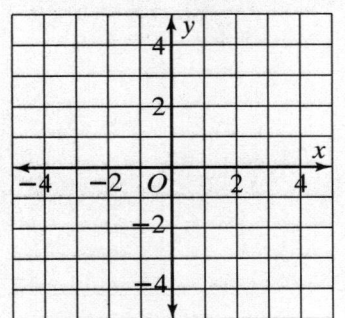

5. $S(2, 3), T(-2, 4), U(-4, 2); 180°$

A' _____   S' _____

B' _____   T' _____

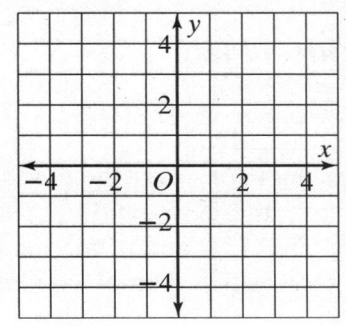

C' _____   U' _____

Name _____ Class _____ Date _____

9-10 • Guided Problem Solving

GPS Exercise 16

The vertices of a triangle are $V(0, 0)$, $W(2, 5)$, and $X(1, 5)$. On separate coordinate planes, graph the triangle and its images after rotations of (a) 90° and (b) 180° about (1, 1).

Understand the Problem

1. What are the coordinates of the three vertices of the triangle? _____

2. What is the angle of rotation in part (a)? _____

3. What is the angle of rotation in part (b)? _____

4. What is the center of rotation in parts (a) and (b)? _____

5. What are you asked to do? _____

Make and Carry Out a Plan

6. On a sheet of graph paper, draw $\triangle VWX$.

7. Place a piece of tracing paper over the graph. Trace the vertices of the triangle, the x-axis, and the y-axis. Place your pencil at the point (1, 1) and rotate the tracing paper 90° counterclockwise. How will you know you have rotated the triangle 90°? _____
_____

8. Press through the tracing paper to mark the position of each vertex of the triangle. Then remove the tracing paper and draw $\triangle V'W'X'$ on the graph.

9. On a second coordinate plane, draw $\triangle VWX$. Place the tracing paper you used to rotate the triangle 90° over $\triangle VWX$. Place your pencil at the point (1, 1) and rotate the tracing paper 180°. Press to mark the vertices, and then draw $\triangle V'W'X'$.

Check the Answer

10. To check your answers, rotate the first $\triangle V'W'X'$ 90° clockwise. Then rotate the second $\triangle V'W'X'$ 180° clockwise. The resulting triangles should be the same as $\triangle VWX$.

Solve Another Problem

11. A triangle has vertices $A(2, 0)$, $B(0, 0)$, and $C(1, 5)$. On a separate coordinate plane, graph the triangle and its image after a rotation of 90° and 180° about the origin.

426 *Algebra-Readiness* Lesson 9-10   Guided Problem Solving

Name _____ Class _____ Date _____

9A: Graphic Organizer

For use before Lesson 9-1

Study Skill When you read mathematics, have a pencil and paper ready so you can take notes and write down any questions you may have. You may want to draw diagrams or sketches to show how the math topics relate to each other.

Write your answers. Use the Table of Contents page for this chapter at the front of the book.

1. What is the title of this chapter? _____

2. Name four topics that you will study in this chapter:

   _____   _____

   _____   _____

3. What is the topic of the Reasoning Strategy lesson? _____

4. Complete the graphic organizer as you work through the chapter.
   1. Write the title of the chapter in the center oval.
   2. When you begin a lesson, write the name of the lesson in a rectangle.
   3. When you complete that lesson, write a skill or key concept from that lesson in the outer oval linked to that rectangle.
   Continue with steps 2 and 3 clockwise around the graphic organizer.

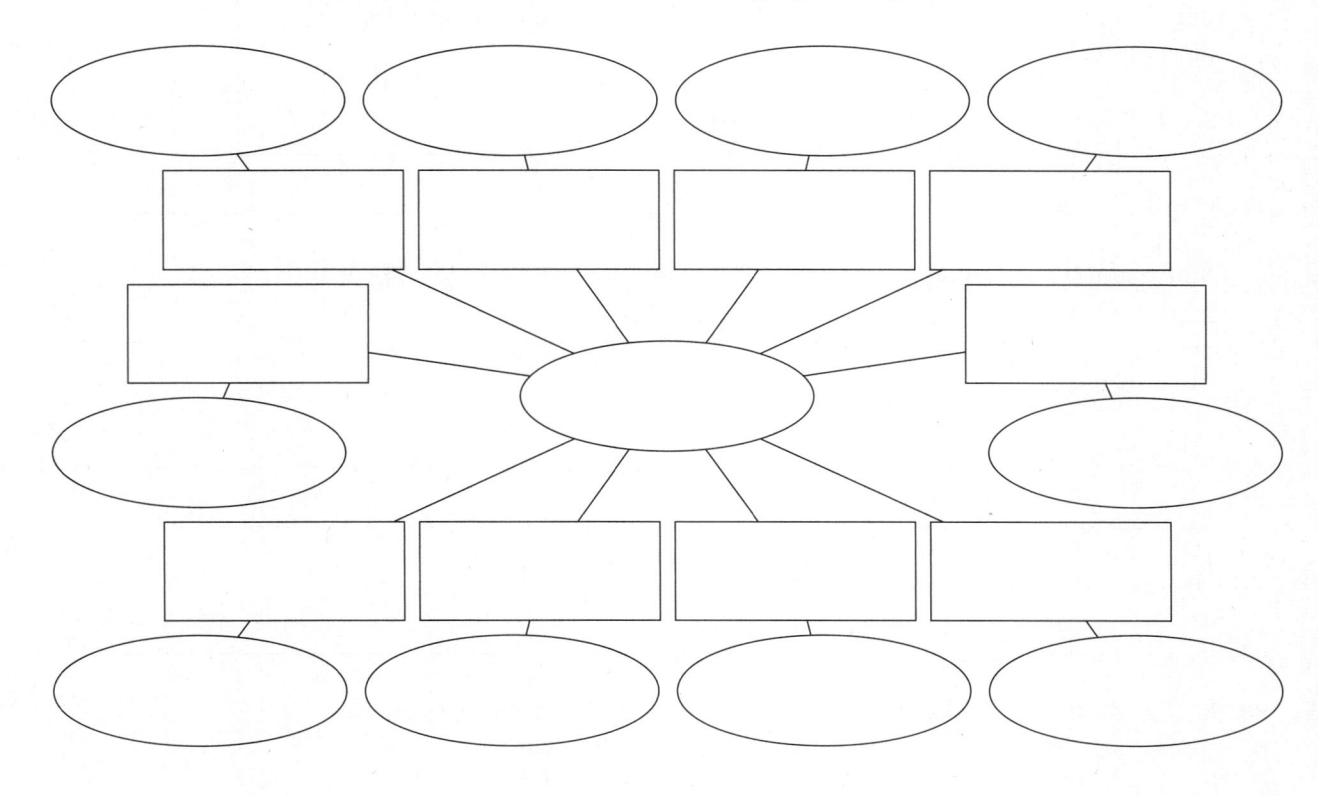

Vocabulary and Study Skills   Algebra-Readiness Chapter 9   427

Name _____ Class _____ Date _____

9B: Reading Comprehension

For use after Lesson 9-5

Study Skill After you read a long paragraph, pause and review the essential information in that paragraph. Remember that the first sentence of a paragraph often tells you the topic and the last sentence may summarize the content.

Read the passage below and answer the questions that follow.

> The word "geometry" comes from two Greek words that mean "measuring the earth." Geometry was originally concerned with practical problems that involved measuring pieces of land. In the third century B.C., the Greek mathematician Euclid wrote a logical treatise on geometry that became the model for classical geometry. Formal geometry is based on stated assumptions that consist of a set of undefined terms and a set of statements about those terms, called postulates or axioms. Then, based on these assumptions, new terms are defined and the logical process of deduction is used to prove statements, called theorems.
>
> There are many different types of geometry, some of which are listed here:
> - plane geometry, which deals with figures in a two-dimensional plane
> - solid geometry, which deals with figures in three-dimensional space
> - Euclidean geometry, both plane and solid, which is based on Euclid's postulates
> - non-Euclidean geometries, such as spherical and hyperbolic geometry, which change one or more of Euclid's postulates
> - analytic geometry, which relates algebra and geometry, using graphs and equations
> - projective geometry, which deals with the properties of figures that are unchanged by projection, like casting a shadow

1. What is the subject of this passage? _____

2. List some practical uses for geometry that are mentioned in the passage.
   _____

3. What are the characteristics of formal geometry?
   _____
   _____

4. Which types of geometry have you studied?
   _____

5. **High-Use Academic Words** What does *model* mean in the passage?
   a. simpler version used to understand something complicated
   b. example to follow

428 Algebra-Readiness Chapter 9   Vocabulary and Study Skills

Name _____ Class _____ Date _____

9C: Reading/Writing Math Symbols
For use after Lesson 9-8

Study Skill As you read your text, or other assignments, pause often to ask yourself questions such as these:

- What is this chapter about?
- What is the main topic of this paragraph?
- How does this connect to what I learned before?
- What is the most important idea here?

Answering your own questions helps you concentrate as you read so that you will remember the content.

Use symbols to write each expression.

1. Angle P is congruent to angle Q. _____

2. Triangle MAN is congruent to triangle DOG. _____

3. Side MA is congruent to side DO. _____

4. The point P with coordinates $(1, -3)$ translates to the point P' with the coordinates $(2, 1)$. _____

5. The circumference of a circle is equal to pi multiplied by the diameter. _____

Make marks or symbols on each figure to indicate the description.

6. right angle

7. isosceles triangle

8. rectangle

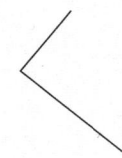

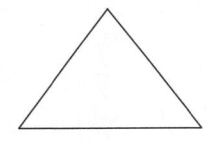

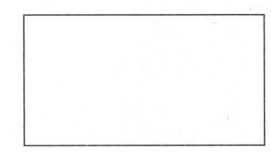

Make marks on the two figures to show each congruence.

9. $\angle T \cong \angle R$
10. $\angle A \cong \angle U$
11. $\angle C \cong \angle F$
12. $\overline{CT} \cong \overline{FR}$
13. $\overline{TA} \cong \overline{RU}$
14. $\overline{AC} \cong \overline{UF}$

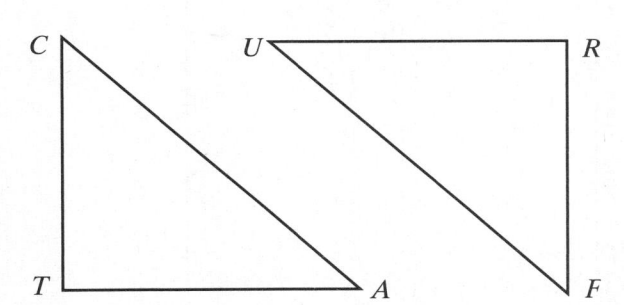

Vocabulary and Study Skills

Algebra-Readiness Chapter 9

Name _____ Class _____ Date _____

9D: Visual Vocabulary Practice
High-Use Academic Words

For use after Lesson 9-2

Study Skills Mathematics is like learning a foreign language. You have to know the vocabulary before you can speak the language correctly.

Concept List

consecutive	correlation	formula
notation	simplify	solve
strategy	table	test

Write the concept that best describes each exercise. Choose from the concept list above.

1. $I = prt$	2. Act It Out Draw a Diagram Guess, Check, Revise Look for a Pattern Work a Simpler Problem Work Backward	3. 73 and 74
4. <table><tr><td>x</td><td>y</td></tr><tr><td>−2</td><td>4</td></tr><tr><td>0</td><td>0</td></tr><tr><td>2</td><td>4</td></tr><tr><td>3</td><td>9</td></tr></table>	5. $2(c + 4) - 5c = -3c + 8$	6.
7. Not a function.	8. $2(5x - 3) = 14$ $10x - 6 = 14$ $10x = 20$ $x = 2$	9. $f(x)$ for y

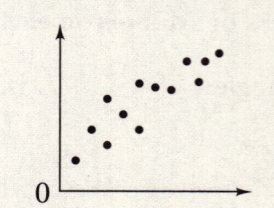

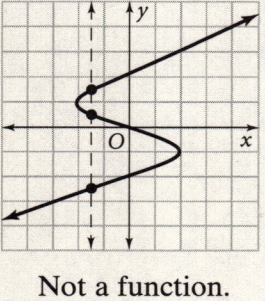

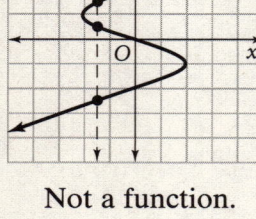

430 **Algebra-Readiness Chapter 9**   **Vocabulary and Study Skills**

Name _____ Class _____ Date _____

9E: Vocabulary Check

For use after Lesson 9-6

Study Skill Strengthen your vocabulary. Use these pages and add cues and summaries by applying the Cornell Notetaking style.

Write the definition for each word at the right. To check your work, fold the paper back along the dotted line to see the correct answers

_____

_____

_____   Circle

_____

_____

_____   Radius

_____

_____

_____   Diameter

_____

_____

_____   Circumference

_____

_____

_____   Chord

_____

_____

Vocabulary and Study Skills   Algebra-Readiness Chapter 9   **431**

Name _____ Class _____ Date _____

9E: Vocabulary Check (continued) For use after Lesson 9-6

Write the vocabulary word for each definition. To check your work, fold the paper forward along the dotted line to see the correct answers.

The set of all points in a plane that are equidistant from a given point, called the center.

_____

A segment that has one endpoint at the center of the circle and the other endpoint on the circle.

_____

A chord that passes the center of the circle.

_____

The distance around a circle.

_____

A segment whose endpoints are on the circle.

_____

432 Algebra-Readiness Chapter 9 Vocabulary and Study Skills

Name _____ Class _____ Date _____

9F: Vocabulary Review

For use with Chapter Review

Study Skill Make your own vocabulary list for each subject you are studying. Provide a formal definition with some informal notes in your own words, and an example. Review your list when you are studying for a test.

Draw an example of your own in the box provided for each term given. Include labels. Write a sentence about your example.

1. complementary angles

2. parallel lines

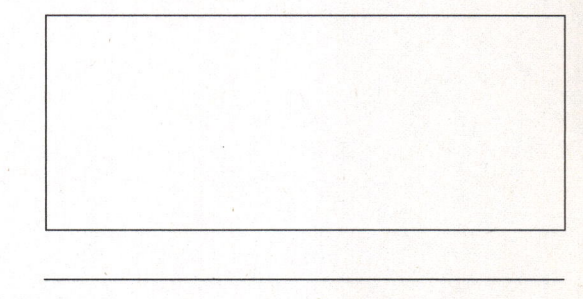

3. perpendicular lines

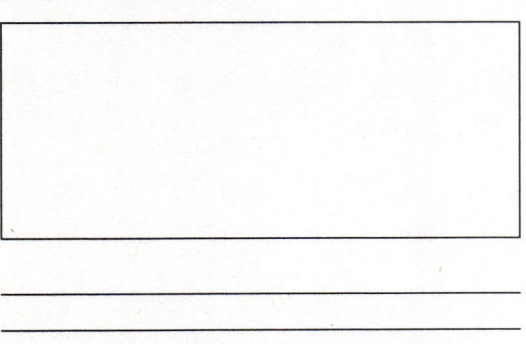

4. vertical angles

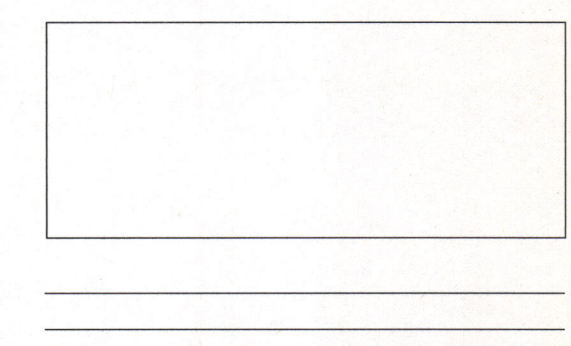

5. transversal

6. supplementary angles

Vocabulary and Study Skills — *Algebra-Readiness* Chapter 9

Practice 10-1

Area: Parallelograms

Find the area of each parallelogram.

1. (parallelogram with height 18 ft, side 19 ft, base 28 ft)

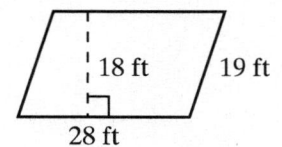

2. (parallelogram with height 9 m, base 13 m)

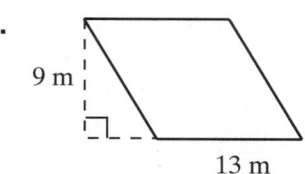

Find the area of each shaded region. Assume that all angles that appear to be right angles are right angles.

3. (shaded figure: outer 80 ft × 70 ft with inner unshaded 50 ft × 35 ft rectangle and 20 ft × 25 ft rectangle cut out)

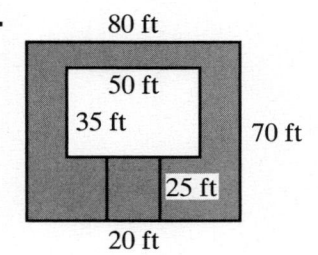

4. (shaded U-shape: outer 65 m wide, 30 m tall on sides, inner notch 45 m wide × 15 m deep, with 10 m on each bottom side)

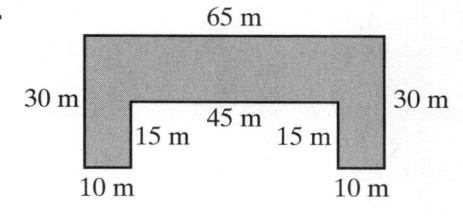

The vertices of a parallelogram are given. Draw each parallelogram. Find its area.

5. $P(1, 1), Q(3, 1), R(2, 4), S(4, 4)$

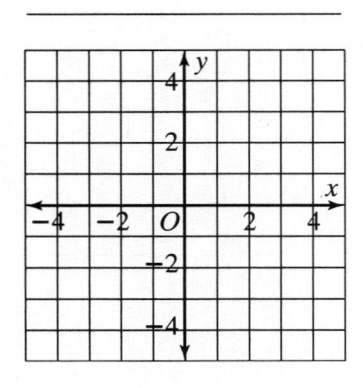

6. $J(-3, 2), K(1, 2), M(-1, -3), L(3, -3)$

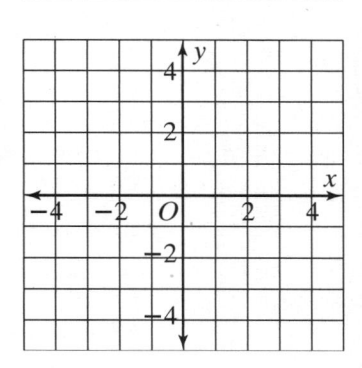

Practice — Algebra-Readiness Lesson 10-1

Name _____ Class _____ Date _____

10-1 • Guided Problem Solving

GPS Exercise 17

Find the area of the figure at the right.
Assume that all angles are right angles.

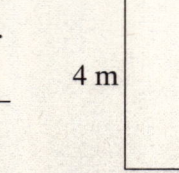

Understand the Problem

1. What are you asked to do? _____

Make and Carry Out a Plan

2. Think of the figure above as a large rectangle that has the
   missing rectangle filled in. What is the length of the large rectangle? _____

3. What is the width of the large rectangle? _____

4. What is the formula for area of a rectangle? _____

5. What is the area of the large rectangle? _____

6. What are the length and width of the small
   rectangle that has been removed from the large rectangle? _____

7. What is the area of the small rectangle? _____

8. Subtract the area of the small
   rectangle from the area of the large rectangle. _____

9. What is the area of the figure? _____

Check the Answer

10. To check your answer, find the area of the figure in another
    way. Divide the figure into three rectangles. Find the area of
    each rectangle and add them together to find the area of the figure. _____

Solve Another Problem

11. Find the area of the figure at the right.
    Assume that all angles are right angles.

    _____

436 Algebra-Readiness Lesson 10-1   Guided Problem Solving

Practice 10-2

Area: Triangles and Trapezoids

Find the area of each trapezoid.

1. 20 cm, 26 cm, 18 cm, 38 cm

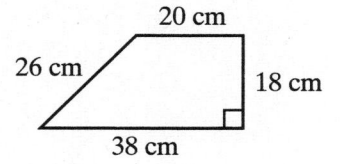

2. 55 in., 32 in., 25 in., 23 in.

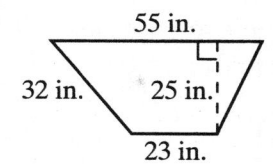

3. $base_1$ = 13 in.
   $base_2$ = 8 in.
   height = 5 in.

4. $base_1$ = 24 cm
   $base_2$ = 10 cm
   height = 15 cm

Find the area of each triangle.

5. 24 m, 42 m

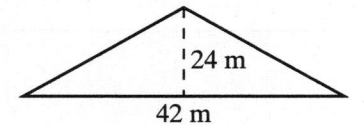

6. 21 in., 35 in., 6 in., 22 in.

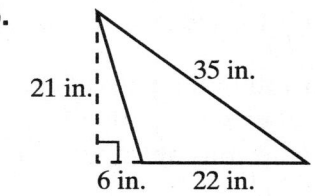

7. base = 24 in.
   height = 9 in.
   area = _____

8. height = 27 cm
   base = 34 cm
   area = _____

Find the area of each shaded region.

9. 12 ft, 12 ft, 6 ft, 12 ft, 20 ft

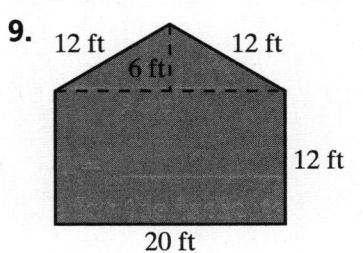

10. 18 m, 12 m, 12 m, 16 m, 22 m

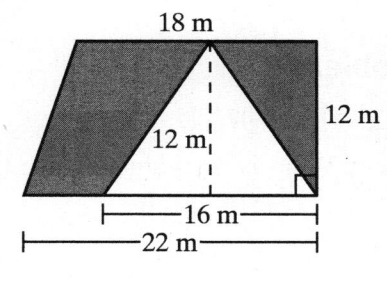

Practice — Algebra-Readiness Lesson 10-2

Name _____ Class _____ Date _____

10-2 • Guided Problem Solving

GPS Exercise 16

A trapezoid has area 50 in.² The two bases are 5 in. and 15 in.
What is the height of the trapezoid?

Understand the Problem

1. What is the area of the trapezoid? _____

2. What are the bases of the trapezoid? _____

3. What are you asked to find? _____

Make and Carry Out a Plan

4. What is the formula for area of a trapezoid? _____

5. Use the formula for area of a trapezoid.
   Replace b_1 with 5, b_2 with 15, and A with 50. _____

6. Evaluate the expression within the parentheses
   and then use the Commutative Property of
   Multiplication to gather the constants together and simplify. _____

7. By what number must you divide both sides of the equation to solve for h? _____

8. What is the height of the trapezoid? _____

Check the Answer

9. To check your answer, use the measurements of the bases
   and your answer to Question 8 to find the area of the trapezoid. _____
   The area should be the same as the area stated in the problem.

Solve Another Problem

10. The area of a trapezoid is 40 cm². The two bases
    are 8 cm and 12 cm. What is the height of the trapezoid? _____

Algebra-Readiness Lesson 10-2   Guided Problem Solving

Practice 10-3

Area: Circles

Find the area of each circle. Give an exact area and an approximate area to the nearest tenth.

1. $r = 7$ m
   A = _____
   A ≈ _____

2. $d = 18$ cm
   A = _____
   A ≈ _____

3. $r = 35$ km
   A = _____
   A ≈ _____

4. $d = 22$ cm
   A = _____
   A ≈ _____

5. $r = 25$ ft
   A = _____
   A ≈ _____

6. $d = 5$ in.
   A = _____
   A ≈ _____

Find the area of each shaded region to the nearest tenth.

7. 8 m, 8 m, 12 m

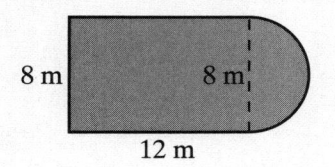

8. 3 in., 4 in.

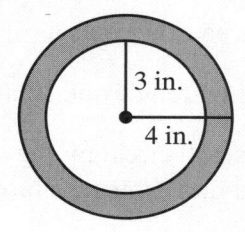

9. 10 ft, 10 ft, 5 ft

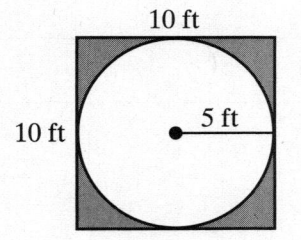

10. 7 cm, 9 cm, 12 cm

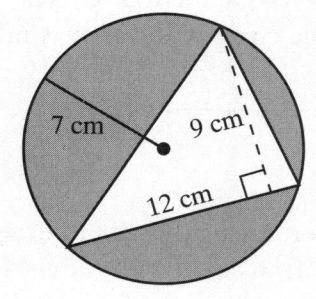

Name_____ Class_____ Date_____

10-3 • Guided Problem Solving

GPS Exercise 24

Which has a greater area, four circles, each with radius 1 m, or one circle with radius 4 m? Explain.

Understand the Problem

1. What is the radius of each of the four small circles? _____

2. What is the radius of the single larger circle? _____

3. What are you asked to do? _____

Make and Carry Out a Plan

4. What is the formula for area of a circle? _____

5. Replace r with 1 to find the area of one small circle. _____

6. Multiply the area of one small circle by the number of small circles to find their total area. _____

7. In the formula, replace r with 4 to find the area of the large circle. _____

8. Which has the greater area, the four circles with radius 1 m or the circle with radius 4 m? Explain. _____
_____

Check the Answer

9. To check your answer, use a compass to draw the large and small circles. Draw a circle with radius 4 cm to represent the large circle. Can you draw the four smaller circles so that they fit inside the large circle, without overlapping? How does the diagram support your answer to Question 8? _____
_____
_____

Solve Another Problem

10. Which has a greater area, three circles, each with radius 2 cm, or two circles, each with radius 3 cm? Explain. _____
_____
_____

Algebra-Readiness Lesson 10-3 — Guided Problem Solving

Practice 10-4

Space Figures

Name the space figure you can form from each net.

1.

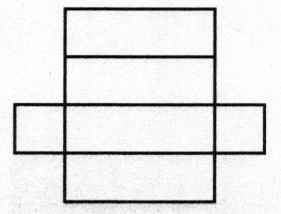

2.

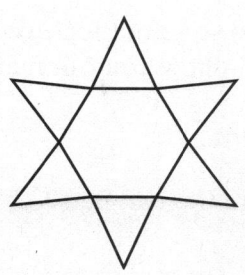

For each figure, describe the base(s) and name the figure.

3.

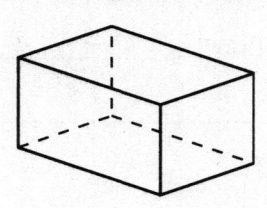

4.

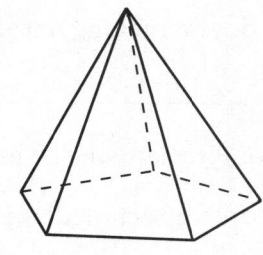

5.

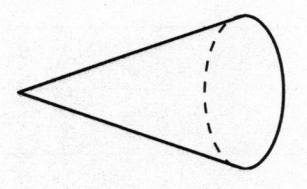

6.

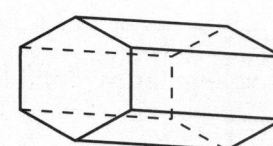

7.

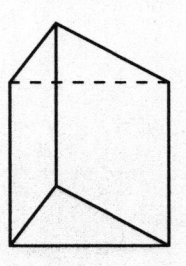

8.

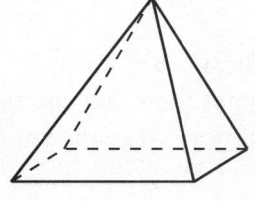

Algebra-Readiness Lesson 10-4 441

Name _____ Class _____ Date _____

10-4 • Guided Problem Solving

GPS Exercise 29

Writing in Math Suppose you see a net for a rectangular prism and a net for a rectangular pyramid. Explain how you can match each net with its name.

Understand the Problem

1. For what space figures are the two nets? _____

2. What are you asked to do? _____

Make and Carry Out a Plan

3. How many bases does a rectangular prism have? What shape are they? _____

4. How many lateral faces does a rectangular prism have? What shape are they? _____
_____

5. What shape is the base of a rectangular pyramid? _____

6. How many lateral faces does a rectangular pyramid have? What shape are they? _____
_____

7. What will the net of a rectangular prism look like? _____
_____

8. What will the net of a rectangular pyramid look like? _____
_____

9. How can you match each net with its name? _____
_____

Check the Answer

10. To check your answer, draw a net for a rectangular prism and a net for a rectangular pyramid. Do the nets support your answer to Question 9? _____

Solve Another Problem

11. Suppose you see a net for a triangular prism and a triangular pyramid. Explain how you can match each net with its name. _____
_____

442 Algebra-Readiness Lesson 10-4   Guided Problem Solving

Name _____ Class _____ Date _____

Practice 10-5

Surface Area: Prisms and Cylinders

Find the surface area of each space figure. If the answer is not a whole number, round to the nearest tenth.

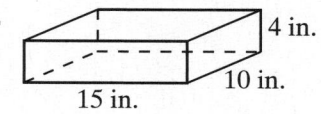

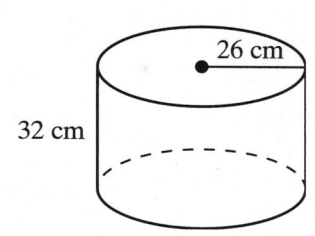

1. [rectangular prism: 15 in. × 10 in. × 4 in.]

2. [cylinder: radius 26 cm, height 32 cm]

_____   _____

Find the surface area of the space figure represented by each net to the nearest square unit.

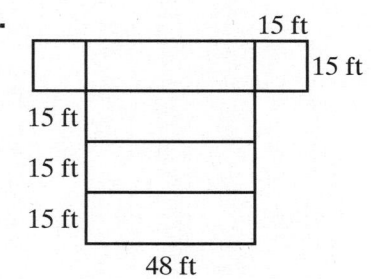

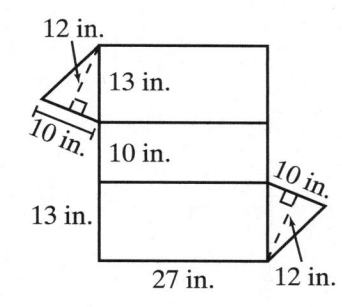

3. [net with dimensions 15 ft, 15 ft, 15 ft, 15 ft, 15 ft, 48 ft]

4. [net with dimensions 12 in., 13 in., 10 in., 10 in., 13 in., 27 in., 12 in., 10 in.]

_____   _____

5. A room is 18 ft long, 14 ft wide, and 8 ft high.

   a. Find the cost of painting the four walls with two coats of paint costing $9.50 per gallon. Each gallon covers 256 ft² with one coat.

   _____

   b. Find the cost of carpeting the floor with carpet costing $5/ft².

   _____

   c. Find the cost of covering the ceiling with acoustic tile costing $7.50/ft².

   _____

   d. Find the total cost of renovating the walls, floor, and ceiling.

   _____

L1 Practice   Algebra-Readiness Lesson 10-5   **443**

Name_____ Class_____ Date_____

10-5 • Guided Problem Solving

GPS Exercise 20

Find the area of the top and lateral surfaces of a cylindrical water tank with radius 20 ft and height 30 ft.

Understand the Problem

1. What is the radius of the water tank? _____

2. What is the height of the water tank? _____

3. What shape is the water tank? _____

4. What are you asked to find? _____

Make and Carry Out a Plan

5. Draw and label a diagram of the water tank.

6. What is the formula for lateral area of a cylinder? _____

7. Use the formula to find the lateral area
   of the water tank to the nearest square foot. _____

8. What is the formula for area of a base of a cylinder? _____

9. Use the formula to find the area of the top
   of the water tank to the nearest square foot. _____

10. Add the two areas to find the area of the
    top and lateral surfaces of the water tank. _____

Check the Answer

11. To check your answer, calculate Steps 7 and 9 in terms
    of π. Then calculate Step 10 in terms of π. Substitute 3.14
    for π and simplify to find the area of the top and lateral surface. _____
    The result should be the same as your answer to Step 10.

Solve Another Problem

12. Find the area of the top and lateral surfaces
    of a cylinder with radius 15 ft and height 40 ft. _____

444 Algebra-Readiness Lesson 10-5

Name _____ Class _____ Date _____

Practice 10-6

Surface Area: Pyramids, Cones, and Spheres

Find the surface area of each space figure to the nearest square unit.

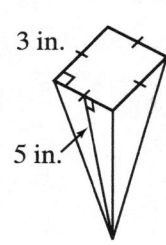

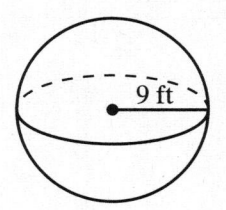

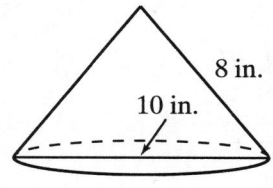

1. [rectangular prism: 15 in. × 10 in. × 4]

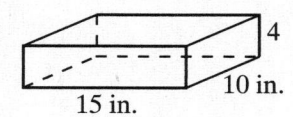

2. [pyramid with 3 in. base and 5 in. slant]

_____ _____

3. [sphere with radius 9 ft]

4. [cone with slant 8 in. and radius 10 in.]

_____ _____

5. [cylinder with cone on top: cone slant 10 ft, radius 8 ft; cylinder height 15 ft]

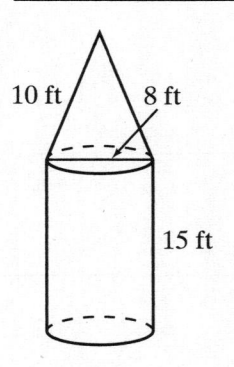

6. [rectangular prism 20 m × 20 m × 20 m with pyramid on top, slant 13 m]

_____ _____

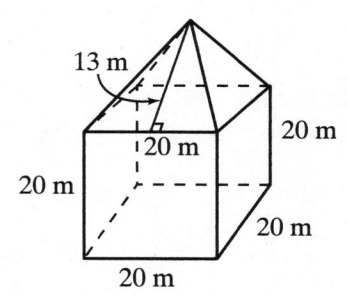

7. a hemisphere with diameter 70 cm

_____

Practice   Algebra-Readiness Lesson 10-6   445

Name_____ Class_____ Date_____

10-6 • Guided Problem Solving

GPS Exercise 14

The base of a cone has radius 3 ft. Its slant height is 8 ft. Find the surface area of the cone to the nearest square unit.

Understand the Problem

1. What is the radius of the base of the cone? _____

2. What is the slant height of the cone? _____

3. What are you asked to find? _____

Make and Carry Out a Plan

4. Draw a sketch of the cone below. Label its radius and slant height.

5. Find the lateral area of the cone. Replace r with 3 and ℓ with 8 in the formula L.A. = $\pi r \ell$. _____

6. Use 3.14 for π. What is the lateral area of the cone? _____

7. Find the base area of the cone. Replace r with 3 in the formula $B = \pi r^2$. _____

8. What is the base area of the cone? _____

9. Add the lateral area and the base area. What is the surface area of the cone? (Round to the nearest square foot.) _____

Check the Answer

10. To check your answer, find the surface area of the cone in terms of π. Then replace π with 3.14 as the final step. _____
Your answer should be the same as your answer to Question 9.

Solve Another Problem

11. The base of a cone has radius 2 m. Its slant height is 11 m. Find the surface area of the cone. _____

446 Algebra-Readiness Lesson 10-6   Guided Problem Solving

Practice 10-7

Volume: Prisms and Cylinders

Find the volume of each prism or cylinder to the nearest cubic unit.

1. cylinder: 10 m diameter, 8 m height

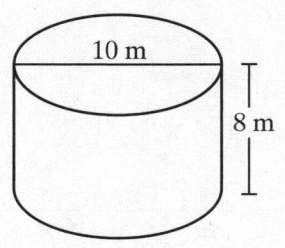

2. rectangular prism: 11 cm by 8 cm, 16 cm height

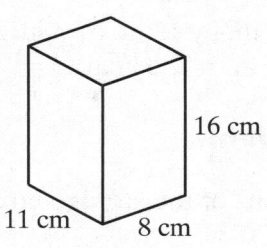

3. triangular prism: 11 in. by 11 in., 12 in. height

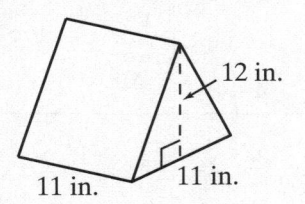

4. triangular prism: 13 ft, 12 ft, 5 ft, 16 ft

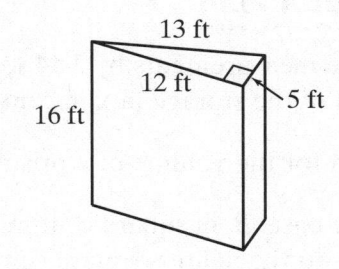

5. prism
   rectangular base:
   8 in. by 6 in.
   height: 7 in.

6. cylinder
   radius: 14 in.
   height: 18 in.

7. prism
   square base:
   3.5 ft on a side
   height: 6 ft

8. cube
   sides: 13 m

9. A water storage tank has a cylindrical shape. The base has a diameter of 18 m and the tank is 32 m high. How much water, to the nearest cubic unit, can the tank hold?

10. A tent in the shape of a triangular prism has a square base with a side of 8 feet and a height of 6 feet. What is the volume of the tent?

Name _____ Class _____ Date _____

10-7 • Guided Problem Solving

GPS Exercise 18

A storage box measures 24 in. by 12 in. by 3 in. Find its volume to the nearest cubic centimeter (1 in. = 2.54 cm).

Understand the Problem

1. What are the dimensions of the storage box? _____

2. What are you asked to find? _____

Make and Carry Out a Plan

3. Multiply each of the measurements by 2.54 to find the dimensions of the storage box in centimeters. _____

4. What is the formula for the volume of a prism? _____

5. Find the area of the base, B, in square centimeters. Round your answer to the nearest square centimeter. _____

6. Replace B with your answer to Step 5 and h with the height in centimeters in the formula for the volume of a prism. _____

7. What is the volume of the storage box to the nearest cubic centimeter? _____

Check the Answer

8. To check your answer, find the volume of the storage box in cubic inches and then convert cubic inches to cubic centimeters (1 cubic in. = 16.39 cubic cm). _____
   Your answer should be close to your answer to Question 7.

Solve Another Problem

9. A small drawer measures 16 in. by 10 in. by 4 in. Find its volume to the nearest cubic centimeter (1 in. = 2.54 cm). _____

448 Algebra-Readiness Lesson 10-7   Guided Problem Solving

Name _____ Class _____ Date _____

Practice 10-8

Reasoning Strategy: Make a Model

Solve by making a model.

1. The midpoint of a segment is the point that divides the segment into two segments of equal length. A quadrilateral with unequal sides is drawn. The midpoints of the four sides are found and connected in order.

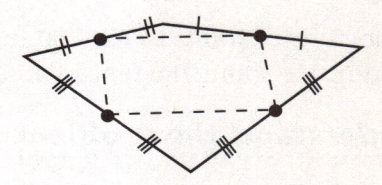

   a. Guess what kind of quadrilateral is formed.

   _____

   b. Draw four quadrilaterals with unequal sides and connect the midpoints of adjacent sides. What kind of quadrilaterals appear to have been formed?

   _____

2. A penny with Lincoln's head upright is rolled along the edge of another penny as shown in the figure.

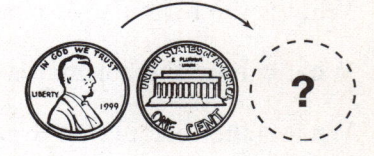

   a. At the end, do you think Lincoln will be right-side-up or upside-down?

   _____

   b. Conduct an experiment to find out. What are your results?

   _____

3. A net for an octahedron is shown. All the sides are congruent, equilateral triangles. Cut and fold on the dotted lines. Find the surface area of the octahedron. Round to the nearest square centimeter.

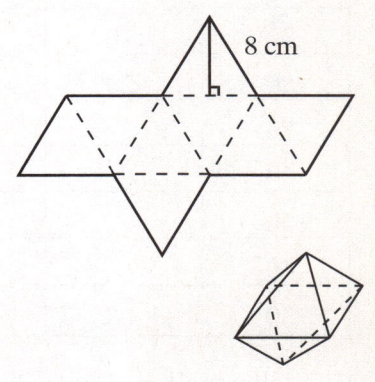

   _____

Practice — Algebra-Readiness Lesson 10-8

Name _____ Class _____ Date _____

10-8 • Guided Problem Solving

GPS Exercise 5

A dog owner wants to use 200 ft of fencing to enclose the greatest possible area for his dog. He wants the fenced area to be rectangular. What dimensions should he use?

Understand the Problem

1. How many feet of fencing does the dog owner have? _____

2. What shape does he want the fenced area to be? _____

3. What are you asked to do? _____

Make and Carry Out a Plan

4. What is the formula for perimeter of a rectangle? _____

5. What will be the perimeter of the fenced area? _____

6. What is the formula for area of a rectangle? _____

7. Look at how changing the dimensions changes the area by completing the table below.

Length	Width	Area (ft²)	Perimeter
90	10	900	200 ft
80	20		
70			
60			
50			
40			
30			

8. What dimensions should the dog owner use? _____

Check the Answer

9. Using the table, how do you know when you have found the dimensions that will give the greatest area? _____

Solve Another Problem

10. A sheep rancher wants to use 100 ft of fencing to make a rectangular feeding pen for lambs. He wants the pen to have the largest area possible. What should the dimensions of the pen be? _____

450 Algebra-Readiness Lesson 10-8

Practice 10-9

Volume: Pyramids, Cones, and Spheres

Find the volume of each figure to the nearest cubic unit. Use $\pi \approx 3.14$.

1. (sphere, 9 ft radius)

   _____

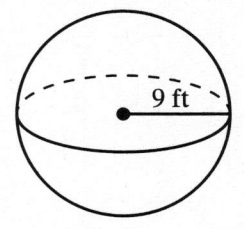

2. (cone, 15 in. height, 9 in. radius)

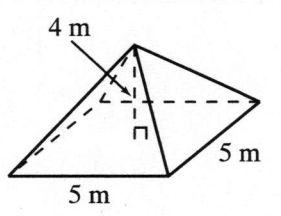

   _____

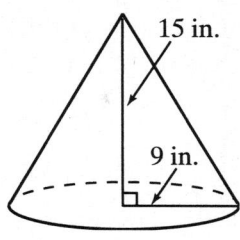

3. (pyramid, 4 m height, 5 m × 5 m base)

   _____

4. (sphere, 22 cm diameter)

   _____

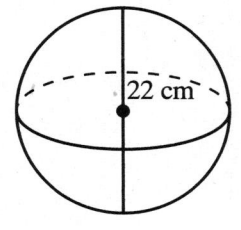

5. square-based pyramid
   $s = 9$ in.
   $h = 12$ in.

   _____

6. cone
   $r = 8$ cm
   $h = 15$ cm

   _____

7. You make a snow figure using three spheres with radii of 12 in., 10 in., and 8 in., with the biggest on the bottom and the smallest for the head. You get snow from a rectangular area that is 6 ft by 7 ft.
   Find the volume of snow in your snow figure to the nearest hundredth of a cubic inch.

   bottom: _____   middle: _____

   head: _____   total: _____

Name _____ Class _____ Date _____

10-9 • Guided Problem Solving

GPS Exercise 21

To the nearest tenth, how much frozen yogurt can you pack inside a cone that is 5 in. high with a base radius of 1.25 in.?

Understand the Problem

1. How high is the cone? _____

2. What is the radius of the base of the cone? _____

3. What are you asked to find? _____

Make and Carry Out a Plan

4. What is the formula for volume of a cone? _____

5. What is the formula for B for a cone? _____

6. In the formula, replace π with 3.14, r with 1.25, and h with 5. _____

7. Simplify. Round to the nearest tenth. _____

8. How much frozen yogurt can you pack inside the cone? _____

Check the Answer

9. Explain why the volume of the cone gives the amount of frozen yogurt that can be packed inside the cone. _____
_____

Solve Another Problem

10. To decorate a cake, a baker fills a decorating cone that is 4 in. high and has a base radius of 1.5 in. with frosting. How much frosting is in the cone? _____

Practice 10-10

Scale Factors Solids

Complete the table for each rectangular prism.

	Original Size		Doubled Dimensions		
	Dimensions (m)	S.A. (m²)	Dimensions (m)	S.A. (m²)	New S.A. ÷ Old S.A.
1.	2 × 3 × 4				
2.	5 × 5 × 9				
3.	7 × 7 × 7				
4.	8 × 12 × 15				
5.	15 × 15 × 20				
6.	32 × 32 × 32				

7. What conclusion can you draw about the relationship between the new and old surface areas?

_____

_____

8. A rectangular prism is 8 cm by 10 cm by 15 cm. What are the volume and surface area of the prism?

_____

9. In Exercise 8, if each dimension of the prism is halved, what are the new volume and surface area?

_____

Use the triangular prism shown at the right for Exercises 10 and 11.

10. Find the volume and surface area.

_____

11. If each dimension of the prism is doubled, what are the new volume and surface area?

_____

12. A rectangular prism is 8 cm long, 24 cm wide, and 43 cm high. The length is doubled, and the width is tripled. What happens to the volume?

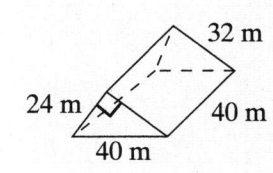

_____

Name _____ Class _____ Date _____

10-10 • Guided Problem Solving

GPS Exercise 14

Gina used 78 square feet of plywood to build a storage bin to hold her gardening supplies. How much plywood will she need to build a similar box for her hand tools if the dimensions of the box are half the dimensions of the bin?

Understand the Problem

1. What are you asked to do?
   _____
   _____

2. How many square feet of plywood did Gina use? _____

Make and Carry Out a Plan

3. What is the ratio for the surface area of similar solids? _____

4. What are the dimensions of the similar box?
   _____
   _____

5. What is the ratio of the surface areas? _____

6. Write a proportion. _____

7. Solve. _____

Check the Answer

8. How can you tell if your answer is reasonable?
   _____
   _____
   _____

Solve Another Problem

9. In pottery class, Mark made a small cylindrical bowl with a volume of 75 in.^{3} and a radius of 2 inches. He also made a larger bowl with a similar shape. It has a diameter of 8 inches. Find the volume of the larger bowl.

   _____

454 Algebra-Readiness Lesson 10-10   Guided Problem Solving

Name _____ Class _____ Date _____

10A: Graphic Organizer
For use before Lesson 10-1

Study Skill As you begin chapters toward the end of the text, take a minute to turn back through the chapters you have already studied. Think about the math you have already learned. Which chapter was your favorite? Which was your least favorite?

Write your answers. Use the Table of Contents page for this chapter at the front of the book.

1. What is the title of this chapter? _____

2. Name four topics that you will study in this chapter:
   _____   _____
   _____   _____

3. What is the topic of the Reasoning Strategy lesson? _____

4. Complete the graphic organizer as you work through the chapter.
   1. Write the title of the chapter in the center oval.
   2. When you begin a lesson, write the name of the lesson in a rectangle.
   3. When you complete that lesson, write a skill or key concept from that lesson in the outer oval linked to that rectangle.
   Continue with steps 2 and 3 clockwise around the graphic organizer.

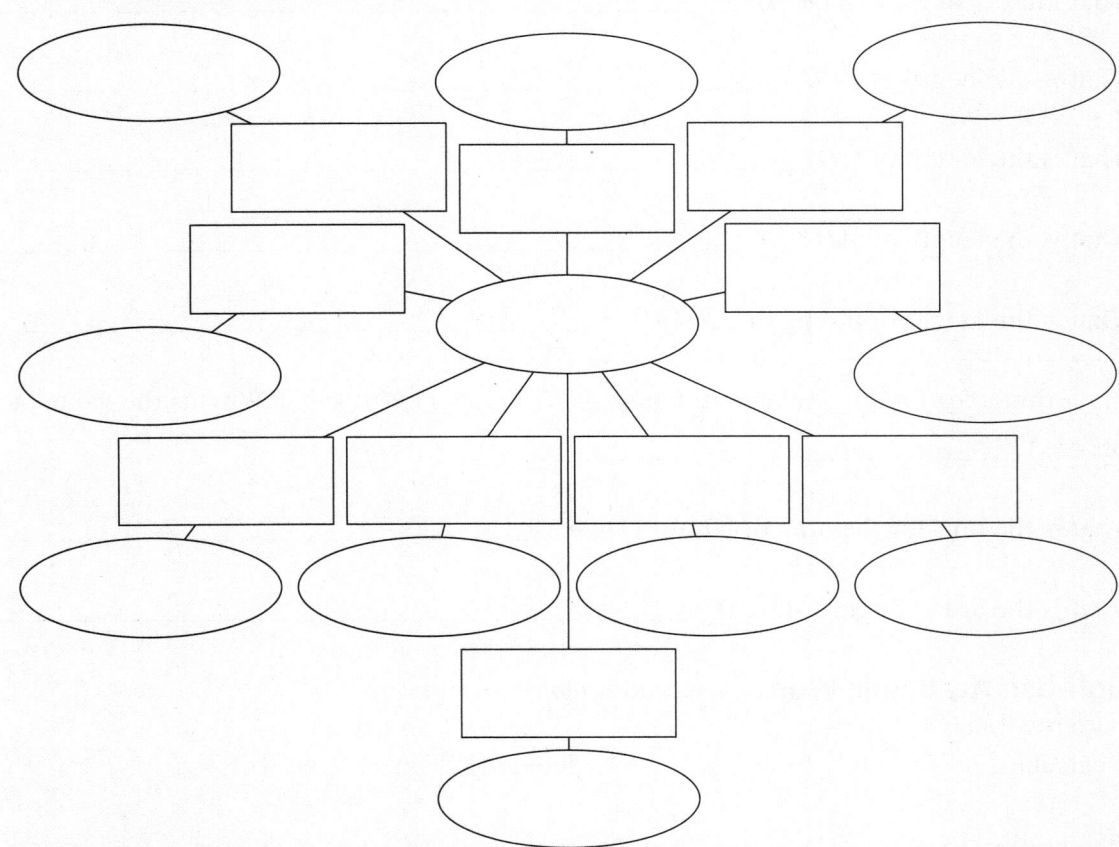

Vocabulary and Study Skills   Algebra-Readiness Chapter 10   **455**

Name _____ Class _____ Date _____

10B: Reading Comprehension
For use after Lesson 10-8

Study Skill When you first look at a paragraph, graph, or diagram, begin by taking time to read all the captions and titles. These labels tell you what this item is about and often contain important information.

Look at this geometric figure, and then answer the questions about it.

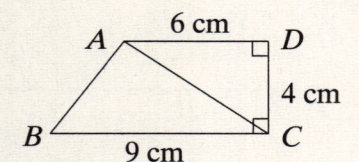

1. What is the name of the figure *ABC*? _____

2. What is the name of the figure *ADC*? _____

3. What is the name of the figure *ADCB*? _____

4. What kind of angle is ∠*ADC*? _____

5. What kind of angle is ∠*DCB*? _____

6. What is the length of $\overline{BC}$? _____

7. What is the length of $\overline{CD}$? _____

8. What is the length of $\overline{AD}$? _____

9. What is the height of the figure *ADCB*? _____

10. The formula for finding the area of figure *ADCB* is $A = \frac{1}{2}h(b_1 + b_2)$. What is the value of $(b_1 + b_2)$? _____

11. What is the unit for the area of figure *ADCB*? _____

12. What is the area of figure *ADCB*? _____

13. **High-Use Academic Words** What does *figure* mean in Exercises 1–3?

    a. calculate   **b.** geometric form

456 Algebra-Readiness Chapter 10   Vocabulary and Study Skills

Name _____ Class _____ Date _____

10C: Reading/Writing Math Symbols For use after Lesson 10-3

Study Skill When you read symbols, use the context to help you decide their meanings. Often one symbol can have more than one meaning, each depending on how it is used. Clues from the context can sometimes help you decide the meanings of symbols or terms with which you are not familiar.

Certain letters and symbols are often used with area and volume. Write the letter or symbol that is described in the blank.

1. the letter used for the area of a figure _____

2. the letter used for the base length of a figure _____

3. the letter used for the area of the base of a space figure _____

4. the abbreviation used for square feet _____

5. the expression used for the sum of the bases of a trapezoid _____

6. the letter used for the circumference of a circle _____

7. the letter used for the radius of a circle _____

8. the symbol used for ratio of the circumference of a circle to its diameter _____

Write your answers.

9. Write a brief explanation of the difference in meaning of the 2 in these expressions: b^2 $b_1 + b_2$

   _____
   _____
   _____

10. On a certain multiple choice question, you are asked to find the area of a figure. The answer choices are given below. Which ones can you immediately eliminate? Explain your reasoning.

    A. 13π ft^2 **B.** 26π ft   **C.** 36 ft^2 **D.** 42π ft^3

    _____
    _____

Vocabulary and Study Skills   Algebra-Readiness Chapter 10   **457**

Name _____ Class _____ Date _____

10D: Visual Vocabulary Practice   For use after Lesson 10-9

Study Skill Math symbols give us a way to express complex ideas in a small space.

Concept List
cylinder   prism   pyramid
surface area   sphere   surface area of a prism or cylinder
volume   volume of a cone   volume of a sphere

Write the concept that best describes each exercise. Choose from the concept list shown above.

1. L.A. + 2B	2. the amount of liquid that fills a container	3. 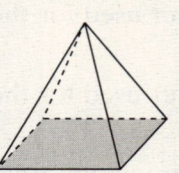
4. 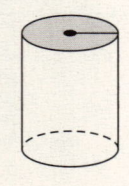	5. $\frac{1}{3}Bh$	6. 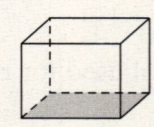
7. 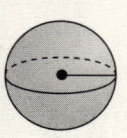	8. the amount of material needed to make a container	9. $\frac{4}{3}\pi r^3$

458 Algebra-Readiness Chapter 10   Vocabulary and Study Skills

Name _____ Class _____ Date _____

10E: Vocabulary Check

For use after Lesson 10-4

Study Skill Strengthen your vocabulary. Use these pages and add cues and summaries by applying the Cornell Notetaking style.

Write the definition for each word at the right. To check your work, fold the paper back along the dotted line to see the correct answers.

_____ Prism

_____

_____

_____ Pyramid

_____

_____

_____ Cylinder

_____

_____

_____ Cone

_____

_____

_____ Sphere

_____

_____

Vocabulary and Study Skills   Algebra-Readiness Chapter 10

10E: Vocabulary Check (continued)

For use after Lesson 10-4

Write the vocabulary word for each definition. To check your work, fold the paper forward along the dotted line to see the correct answers.

A space figure with two parallel and congruent polygonal faces, called bases, and lateral faces that are parallelograms.

_____

A space figure with triangular faces that meet at a vertex, and a base that is a polygon.

_____

A space figure with two circular, parallel, and congruent bases.

_____

A space figure with one circular base and one vertex.

_____

The set of points in space that are a given distance from a given point called the center.

_____

Name_____ Class_____ Date_____

10F: Vocabulary Review

For use with Chapter Review

Study Skill When you make a link between something visual, such as a picture, graph, or diagram, and a new vocabulary term, that link can help you to remember the meaning of the term. Make your own drawings whenever you can to picture the meaning of a new word.

Draw an example of your own in each box for each term given here. Label important parts of each figure.

1. cone

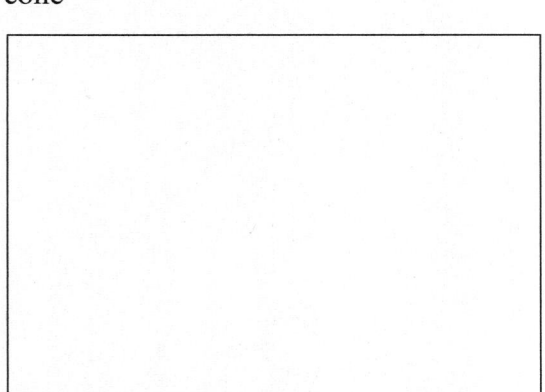

2. cylinder

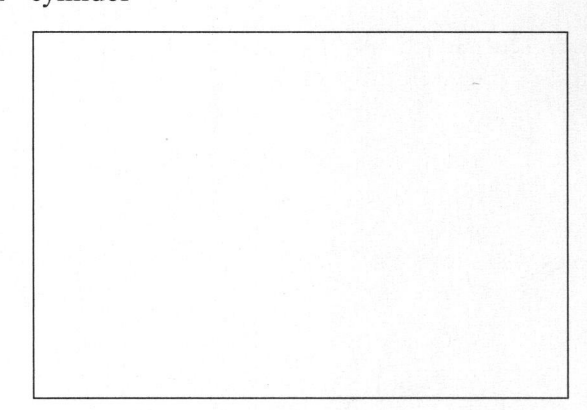

3. sphere

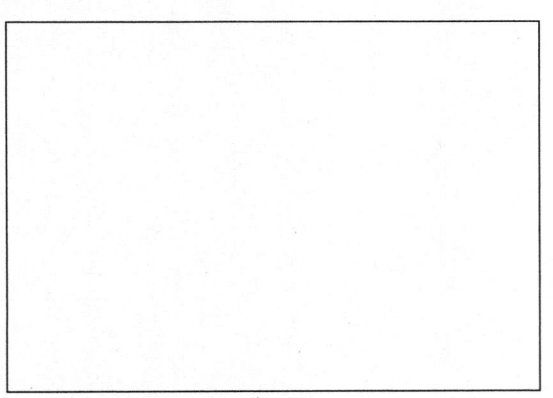

4. prism

5. pyramid

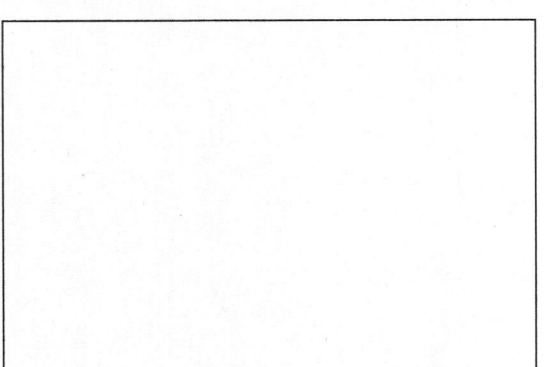

6. net for a square prism

Vocabulary and Study Skills

Algebra-Readiness Chapter 10

461

Name _____ Class _____ Date _____

Practice 11-1

Square Roots and Irrational Numbers

Estimate to the nearest integer.

1. $\sqrt{17}$ _____
2. $\sqrt{26}$ _____
3. $\sqrt{11}$ _____
4. $\sqrt{95}$ _____
5. $\sqrt{48}$ _____
6. $\sqrt{38}$ _____

Simplify each square root.

7. $\sqrt{7 + 18}$ _____
8. $\sqrt{900}$ _____
9. $-\sqrt{100}$ _____
10. $\sqrt{0.25}$ _____
11. $\sqrt{\frac{16}{81}}$ _____
12. $\sqrt{\frac{9}{25}}$ _____

Identify each number as rational or irrational.

13. 5.7777... _____
14. $\sqrt{41}$ _____
15. 0.62662... _____
16. $\sqrt{49}$ _____

Find two integers that make each equation true.

17. $x^2 = 36$ _____
18. $2m^2 = 128$ _____

Use the formula $d = \sqrt{1.5h}$ to estimate the distance to the horizon d in miles for each viewer's eye height h, in feet.

19. $h = 12$ ft
20. $h = 216$ ft

_____ _____

L1 Practice

Algebra-Readiness Lesson 11-1   463

Name _____ Class _____ Date _____

11-1 • Guided Problem Solving

GPS Exercise 50

Geometry Find the length of a side of a square with an area of 81 cm^2.

Understand the Problem

1. What is the area of the square? _____

2. What are you asked to find? _____

Make and Carry Out a Plan

3. The length of a side of a square is the square root of the area of the square. Let *s* represent the length of a side. Write an equation to show that the side of the square equals the square root of 81. _____

4. To solve for *s*, find the square root of 81. _____

5. What is the length of a side of a square with an area of 81 cm^2? _____

Check the Answer

6. To check your answer, square it. _____
   The result should be the area of the square.

Solve Another Problem

7. Find the length of a side of a square with an area of 121 cm^2. _____

464 Algebra-Readiness Lesson 11-1

Practice 11-2

The Pythagorean Theorem

Can you form a right triangle with the three lengths given? Show your work.

1. 5, 4, $\sqrt{41}$ _____

2. 8, 9, 10 _____

3. 28, 45, 53 _____

4. 6, $\sqrt{10}$, 7 _____

In each right triangle, find each missing length to the nearest tenth of a unit.

5. 5 cm, x, 13 cm

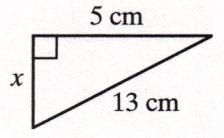

6. x, 6 ft, 8 ft

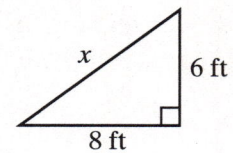

7. 9 in., x, 7 in.

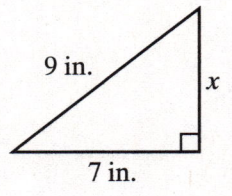

8. x, 5 m, $\sqrt{146}$ m

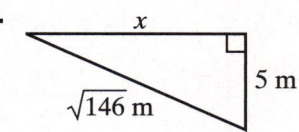

Use the triangle at the right. Find the missing length to the nearest tenth of a unit.

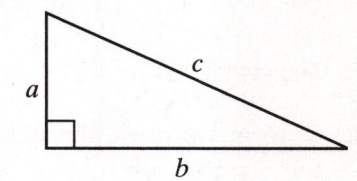

9. $a = 2$ m, $b = 4$ m
   $c \approx$ _____

10. $a = 11$ in., $c = 42$ in.
    $b \approx$ _____

11. $b = 14$ cm, $c = 22$ cm
    $a \approx$ _____

12. $a = 17$ ft, $c = 45$ ft
    $b \approx$ _____

Name _____ Class _____ Date _____

11-2 • Guided Problem Solving

GPS Exercise 13

A painter places an 11-ft ladder against a house. The base of the ladder is 3 ft from the house. How high on the house does the ladder reach?

Understand the Problem

1. How long is the ladder? What part of a right triangle does the ladder represent? _____

2. How far from the house is the base of the ladder? What part of a right triangle does this represent? _____

3. What are you asked to find? What part of a right triangle is this? _____

Make and Carry Out a Plan

4. Draw a sketch of an 11-ft ladder leaning against a house. The base of the ladder is 3 ft from the house.

5. Write the Pythagorean Theorem equation. Use a and b for the legs and c for the hypotenuse. _____

6. Replace b with 3 and c with 11. _____

7. Square 3 and 11. _____

8. Subtract from each side to solve for a^2. _____

9. Find the positive square root of each side to solve for a. Round to the nearest tenth. _____

10. How high on the house does the ladder reach? _____

Check the Answer

11. To check your answer, use the Pythagorean Theorem. Replace b with 3 and a with your answer. Find the length of the ladder, c. _____

Solve Another Problem

12. A wire from the top of a telephone pole is anchored to the ground 12 ft from the base of the pole. The pole is 16 ft tall. How long is the wire? Draw a sketch and solve the problem. _____

466 Algebra-Readiness Lesson 11-2   Guided Problem Solving

Practice 11-3

Distance and Midpoint Formulas

The table has sets of endpoints of several segments. Find the distance between each pair of points and the midpoint of each segment. Round to the nearest tenth when necessary.

	Endpoints	Distance Between (Length of Segment)	Midpoint
1.	$A(2, 6)$ and $B(4, 10)$		
2.	$C(5, -3)$ and $D(7, 2)$		
3.	$E(0, 12)$ and $F(5, 0)$		
4.	$G(4, 7)$ and $H(-2, -3)$		
5.	$J(-1, 5)$ and $K(2, 1)$		

Find the perimeter and area of each figure. Round to the nearest tenth.

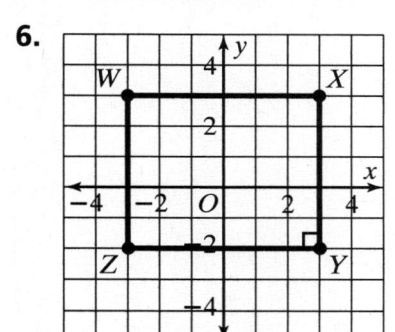

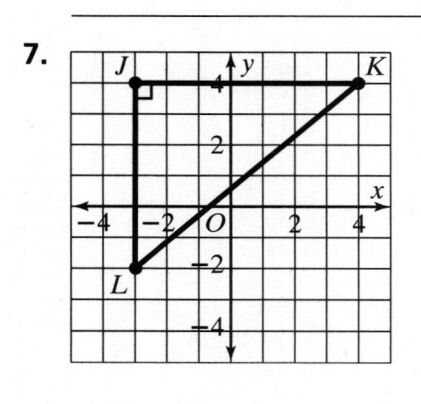

6.

7.

Algebra-Readiness Lesson 11-3

Name _____ Class _____ Date _____

11-3 • Guided Problem Solving

GPS Exercise 19

Reasoning The midpoint of $\overline{AB}$ is (3, 5). The coordinates of A are $(-6, 1)$. What are the coordinates of B?

Understand the Problem

1. What is the midpoint of $\overline{AB}$? _____

2. What are the coordinates of A? _____

3. What are you asked to find? _____

Make and Carry Out a Plan

4. Write the Midpoint Formula. _____

5. Write the formula for the x-coordinate of the midpoint. _____

6. What is the x-coordinate of the midpoint of $\overline{AB}$? _____

7. Use your answers to Steps 5 and 6 to write an equation for the x-coordinate of the midpoint. _____

8. Replace x_1 with -6 in your equation. _____

9. Solve the equation to find x_2, the x-coordinate of B. _____

10. Write the formula for the y-coordinate of the midpoint. _____

11. What is the y-coordinate of the midpoint of $\overline{AB}$? _____

12. Use your answers to Steps 10 and 11 to write an equation for the y-coordinate of the midpoint. _____

13. Replace y_1 with 1 in your equation. _____

14. Solve the equation to find y_2, the y-coordinate of B. _____

15. What are the coordinates of B? _____

Check the Answer

16. To check your answer, use the coordinates of A and the coordinates of B to find the midpoint of $\overline{AB}$. _____

Solve Another Problem

17. The midpoint of $\overline{RS}$ is (1, 6). The coordinates of R are (2, 8). What are the coordinates of S? _____

Algebra-Readiness Lesson 11-3 — Guided Problem Solving

Name _____ Class _____ Date _____

Practice 11-4

Reasoning Strategy: Write a Proportion

Write a proportion and find the value of x.

1. $\triangle KLM \sim \triangle NPQ$

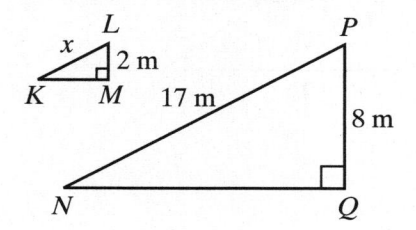

   Proportion: _____

   $x =$ _____

2. $\triangle RST \sim \triangle RPQ$

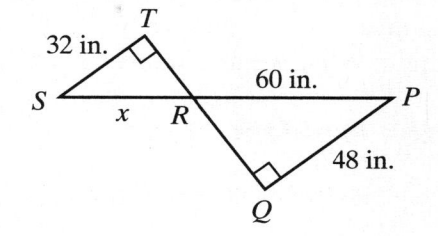

   Proportion: _____

   $x =$ _____

3. $\triangle ABC \sim \triangle ADE$

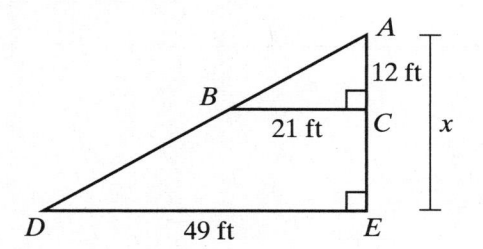

   Proportion: _____

   $x =$ _____

4. $\triangle UVW \sim \triangle UYZ$

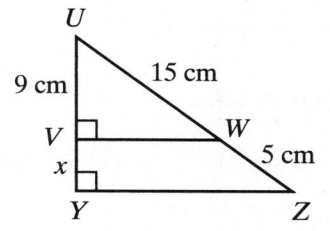

   Proportion: _____

   $x =$ _____

Solve. Show the proportion you use.

5. Three cartons of milk cost $4.77. Find the cost of 8 cartons.

   _____

Practice — Algebra-Readiness Lesson 11-4

Name _____ Class _____ Date _____

11-4 • Guided Problem Solving

GPS Exercise 4

Landscaping A landscaper needs to find the distance x across a piece of land. He estimates the distance using the similar triangles at the right. What is the distance?

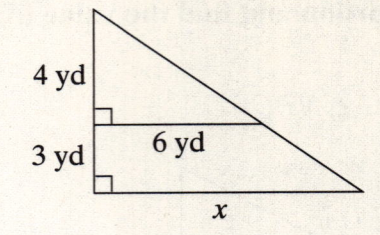

Understand the Problem

1. How many triangles are in the diagram? _____

2. What information are you given about the triangles in the problem and in the diagram? _____

3. In the smaller triangle, what are the given measurements? _____

4. In the larger triangle, what are the given measurements? _____

5. What are you asked to find? _____

Make and Carry Out a Plan

6. Write a proportion using the legs of the two triangles. _____

7. Write cross products. _____

8. By what number will you divide each side to solve for x? _____

9. What is the distance x? _____

Check the Answer

10. To check your answer, substitute your answer for x in the proportion you wrote in Step 6. Write cross products. What does the result tell you about your answer? _____

_____

Solve Another Problem

11. Jenna wants to find the distance x across a small pond. She estimates the distance using the similar triangles at the right. What is the distance?

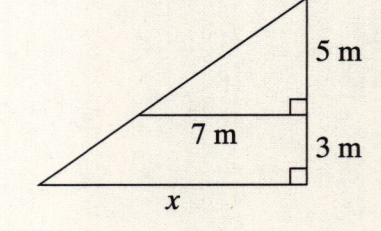

_____

470 Algebra-Readiness Lesson 11-4   Guided Problem Solving

Practice 11-5

Graphing Nonlinear Functions

For each function, complete the table for integer values of x from -2 to 2. Then graph each function.

1. $y = -2x^2$

x	$y = -2x^2$	(x, y)
-2		
-1		
0		
1		
2		

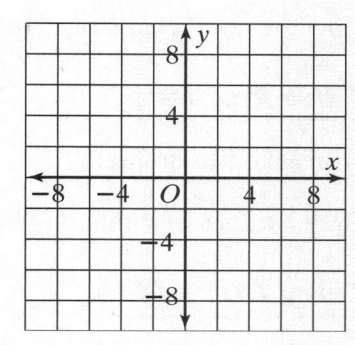

2. $y = x^2$

x	$y = x^2$	(x, y)
-2		
-1		
0		
1		
2		

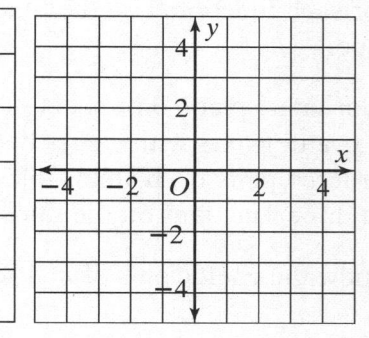

3. $y = -2x^3$

x	$y = -2x^3$	(x, y)
-2		
-1		
0		
1		
2		

4. $y = \frac{1}{2}x^3$

x	$y = \frac{1}{2}x^3$	(x, y)
-2		
-1		
0		
1		
2		

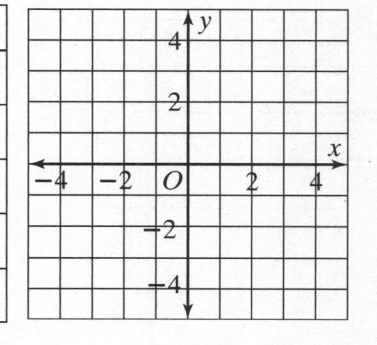

Practice

Algebra-Readiness Lesson 11-5

Name _____ Class _____ Date _____

11-5 • Guided Problem Solving

GPS Exercise 24

a. Graph $y = x^2$, $y = 2x^2$, and $y = \frac{1}{2}x^2$ on the same coordinate plane.

b. Describe how the coefficients of x^2 affect the graphs.

Understand the Problem

1. What are you asked to do first? _____

2. List the integer values of x that will be included in your table. _____

Make and Carry Out a Plan

3. Make a table like the one at right with integer values of x from -2 to 2 for each function. Use the function to find the y value for each x value.

4. Draw a coordinate plane on a sheet of graph paper. Label the x- and y-axes with values between -2 and 2. Use the ordered pairs from your tables to graph the functions. Graph the three functions on the same coordinate plane.

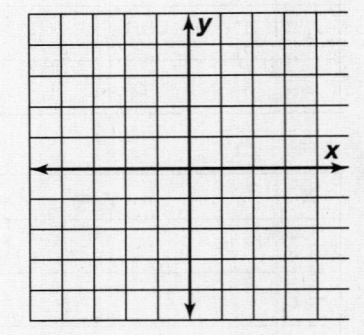

5. Describe how the coefficients of x^2 affect the graphs.

x	$y = x^2$	(x, y)
-2		
-1		
0		
1		
2		

Check the Answer

6. Compare the shape of your graphs.

Solve Another Problem

7. Graph $y = x^3$, $y = 2x^3$, and $\frac{1}{3}x^3$ on the same coordinate plane. Make a table like the one below with integer values of x from -2 to 2 for each function. Then graph the functions.

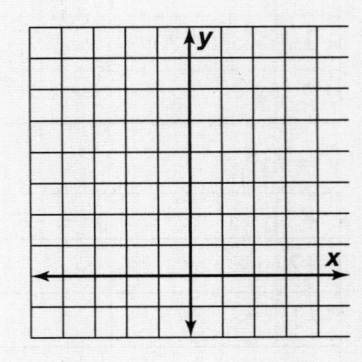

x	$y = x^3$	(x, y)
-2		
-1		
0		
1		
2		

472 *Algebra-Readiness* Lesson 11-5   Guided Problem Solving

Name _____ Class _____ Date _____

11A: Graphic Organizer

For use before Lesson 11-1

Study Skill The title for this chapter tells you what the chapter is about. Take a moment to sketch a right triangle and write some notes about what you know about these special triangles. Then skim the chapter to see what else you are going to learn from it about right triangles.

Write your answers. Use the Table of Contents page for this chapter at the front of the book.

1. What is the title of this chapter? _____

2. Name four topics that you will study in this chapter:

    _____   _____

    _____   _____

3. What is the topic of the Reasoning Strategy lesson? _____

4. Complete the graphic organizer as you work through the chapter.
    1. Write the title of the chapter in the center oval.
    2. When you begin a lesson, write the name of the lesson in a rectangle.
    3. When you complete that lesson, write a skill or key concept from that lesson in the outer oval linked to that rectangle.
    Continue with steps 2 and 3 clockwise around the graphic organizer.

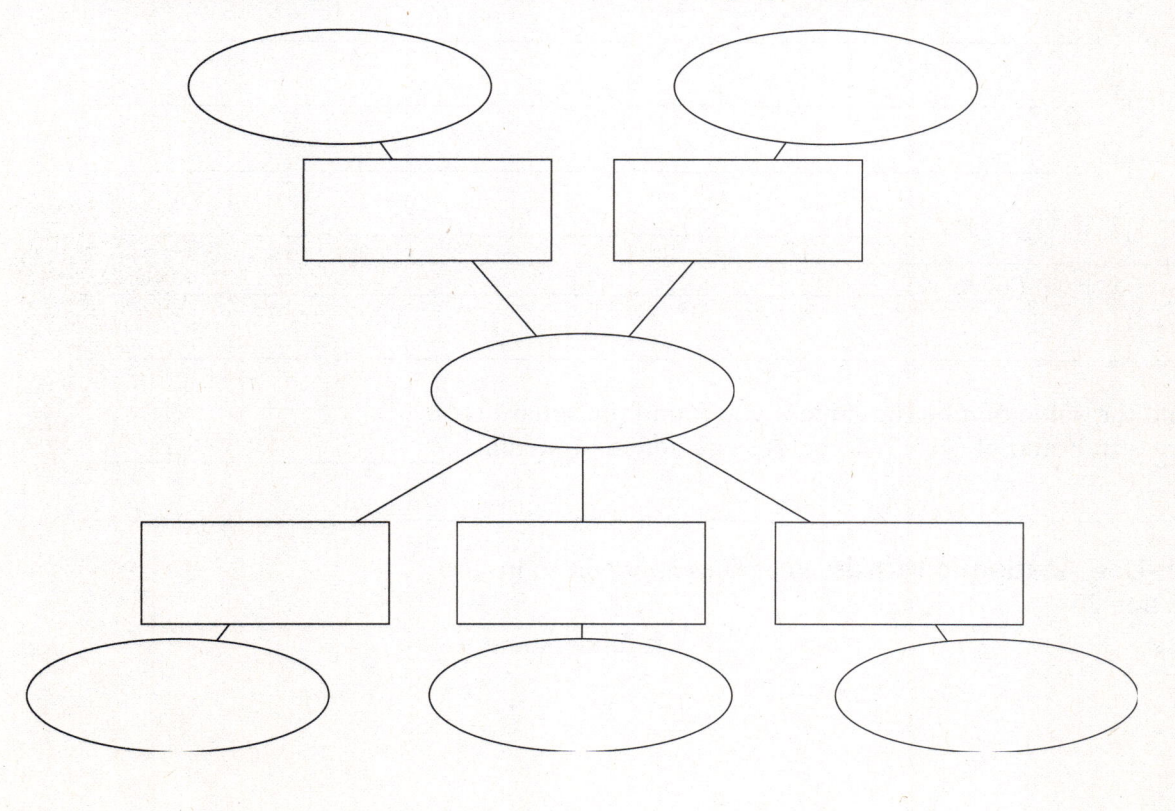

Vocabulary and Study Skills

Algebra-Readiness Chapter 11

473

Name _____ Class _____ Date _____

11B: Reading Comprehension

For use after Lesson 11-3

Study Skill When you have quite a few pages to read, take a break every two or three pages by looking up from the page, and reflecting on what you have just read.

Look at the formula. Then answer the questions that follow.

Distance Formula

$$d = \sqrt{(x_2 - x_1)^2 + (y_2 - y_1)^2}$$

1. What will this formula help you find? _____

2. In order to apply this formula to find d, what values do you have to know? _____

3. What is the difference in the meaning of the small 2 in x_2 and the small 2's that are written after the parentheses? _____

Use (1, 6) and (5, 9) as (x_1, y_1) and (x_2, y_2) and find the value of each expression.

4. $(x_2 - x_1)$ _____

5. $(y_2 - y_1)$ _____

6. $(x_2 - x_1)^2$ _____

7. $(y_2 - y_1)^2$ _____

8. $(x_2 - x_1)^2 + (y_2 - y_1)^2$ _____

9. $\sqrt{(x_2 - x_1)^2 + (y_2 - y_1)^2}$ _____

10. d _____

11. Would the value of d be the same if you found the square root of $(x_2 - x_1)^2$ and of $(y_2 - y_1)^2$ before you added? Explain. _____

12. **High-Use Academic Words** What does *apply* mean in Question 2?

    a. use   b. understand

Name _____ Class _____ Date _____

11C: Reading/Writing Math Symbols   For use after Lesson 11-2

Study Skill The position of symbols can be very important to their meaning. Learn these whenever you come across them, and add them to your personal vocabulary list.

Find the values for each set of expressions. Round final answers to the nearest tenth.

1. Find the value of each expression when $x = 3$.

   a. $-x^2$ _____   b. $(-x)^2$ _____

2. Find the value of each expression when $x = 5$.

   a. $\sqrt{x}$ _____   b. $-\sqrt{x}$ _____

3. Find the value of each expression when $x = 4$.

   a. $\sqrt{x^2}$ _____   b. $(\sqrt{x})^2$ _____

4. Find the value of each expression when $x = 2$ and $y = 3$.

   a. $(x + y)^2$ _____   b. $x + y^2$ _____

5. Find the value of each expression when $x = 1$ and $y = 5$.

   a. $\sqrt{x^2 + y^2}$ _____   b. $\sqrt{x^2} + \sqrt{y^2}$ _____

6. Although 49 has two square roots, the square root symbol means only one of them. Write the value of the expression.

   $\sqrt{49}$ = _____

7. Write a symbol in the blank that best makes a true statement.

   π _____ 3.14

Vocabulary and Study Skills   Algebra-Readiness Chapter 11   **475**

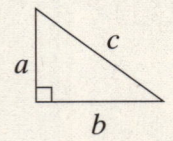

11D: Visual Vocabulary Practice

For use after Lesson 11-5

Study Skill When reading a diagram, look for any special features implied by the diagram. For instance, if the diagram is a triangle, check if it is just a 3-sided figure or a special triangle, such as a right triangle.

Concept List

cubic function	distance	hypotenuse
leg	midpoint	parabola
Pythagorean Theorem	right triangle	square root

Write the concept that best describes each exercise. Choose from the concept list above.

1. the side labeled a or b in

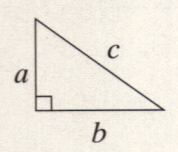

2. the side labeled c in

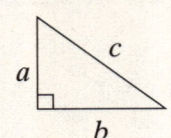

3. $a^2 + b^2 = c^2$

4. $\sqrt{(x_2 - x_1)^2 + (y_2 - y_1)^2}$

5. $\left(\dfrac{x_1 + x_2}{2}, \dfrac{y_1 + y_2}{2}\right)$

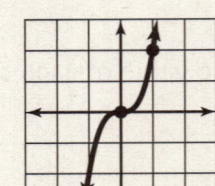

6.

7. $\sqrt{121} = 11$

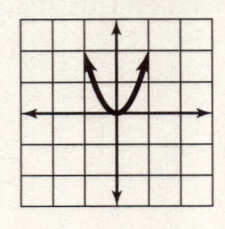

8.

9.

Name_____ Class_____ Date_____

11E: Vocabulary Check

For use after Lesson 11-5

Study Skill Strengthen your vocabulary. Use these pages and add cues and summaries by applying the Cornell Notetaking style.

Write the definition for each word at the right. To check your work, fold the paper back along the dotted line to see the correct answers.

_____

Square root

_____

Irrational number

_____

Hypotenuse

_____

Midpoint

_____

Quadratic Function

Vocabulary and Study Skills · Algebra-Readiness Chapter 11

Name _____ Class _____ Date _____

11E: Vocabulary Check (continued) For use after Lesson 11-5

Write the vocabulary word for each definition. To check your work, fold the paper forward along the dotted line to see the correct answers.

A number that when multiplied by itself equals the given number.

_____

A number whose decimal form neither terminates nor repeats.

_____

The longest side of a right triangle.

_____

The point halfway between the end points of a segment.

_____

A function where the input variable is squared.

_____

478 Algebra-Readiness Chapter 11   Vocabulary and Study Skills

Name _____ Class _____ Date _____

11F: Vocabulary Review Puzzle

For use with Chapter Review

Study Skill When you want to remember a new rule, definition, or formula, try saying it over and over to yourself. This repetition helps the new idea stay in your memory.

Unscramble the UPPERCASE letters to form a math word or phrase that completes the sentence.

1. A CEPTFER RAQUES is the square of an integer. _____

2. The longest side of a right triangle is the SOYPENTHUE. _____

3. In a right triangle, the GLES form the sides of the right angle. _____

4. Finding a RAQUES TORO is the inverse of squaring a number. _____

5. An AIRTONLARI MUBREN has a decimal form that neither terminates or repeats. _____

6. The TGEPAAHNROY EEOTMRH states that in any right triangle the sum of the squares of the lengths of the legs is equal to the square of the length of the hypotenuse. _____

7. The PITDNOIM of a segment is the point halfway between the endpoints of the segment. _____

8. Finding the QAESUR ORTO is the inverse of squaring a number. _____

9. You can use a OROTPIPNOR to solve problems involving indirect measurement. _____

10. A OOILMMAN is a real number, a variable, or a product of a real number and variables with whole-number exponents. _____

11. In a DAACRTQIU NITFCNOU, the input variable is squared. _____

12. In a BCCUI UONCFTIN, the input variable is cubed. _____

Vocabulary and Study Skills   Algebra-Readiness Chapter 11

Practice 12-1

Mean, Median, and Mode

1. There were 8 judges at a gymnastics competition. Kathleen received these scores for her performance on the uneven parallel bars:
   8.9, 8.7, 8.9, 9.2, 8.8, 8.2, 8.9, 8.8

   a. Find these statistics: mean _____ median _____ mode _____

   b. Which measure of central tendency best describes the data? Explain.

   _____

   _____

   _____

   c. Why do you think that the highest and lowest judge's scores are disregarded in tallying the total score in a gymnastics competition?

   _____

   _____

Find the mean, median, and mode. Round to the nearest tenth where necessary. Identify any outliers.

Data	Mean	Median	Mode	Outliers
2. 8, 15, 9, 7, 4, 5, 9, 11	_____	_____	_____	_____
3. 70, 61, 28, 40, 60, 72, 25, 31, 64, 63	_____	_____	_____	_____
4. 4.9, 5.7, 6.0, 5.3, 4.8, 4.9, 5.3, 4.7, 4.9, 5.6, 5.1	_____	_____	_____	_____
5. 271, 221, 234, 240, 271, 234, 213, 253, 155	_____	_____	_____	_____
6. 0, 2, 3, 3, 3, 4, 4, 5	_____	_____	_____	_____

Use the data in the table. Round to the nearest tenth where necessary.

Peak	Height (ft)
Mont Blanc	15,771
Monte Rosa	15,203
Dom	14,911
Liskamm	14,852
Weisshom	14,780

7. What is the mean height of the five highest European mountains? _____

8. What is the median height? _____

9. Are any of the heights an outlier? Explain.

_____

Practice

Algebra-Readiness Lesson 12-1   481

Name _____ Class _____ Date _____

12-1 • Guided Problem Solving

GPS Exercise 24

Find the mean, median, and mode of the data below. Which measure of central tendency best describes the data? Explain.

resting heart rate in beats per minute: 79 72 80 81 40 72

Understand the Problem

1. What values are you asked to find? _____

2. What are you asked to decide? _____

Make and Carry Out a Plan

3. How many data items are there? _____

4. Is the number of data items even or odd? _____

5. Write the data items in numerical order. _____

6. Add the data items and divide by the
   number of data items to find the mean. _____

7. Find the mean of the two middle data items to find the median. _____

8. Find the data item that occurs most often to find the mode. _____

9. Are there any outliers in the data? If so, what are they? _____

10. Compare the mean, median, and mode to the data to find which best
    describes the data. Which is the best measure of central tendency? Explain. _____
    _____

Check the Answer

11. Why does knowing whether there are any outliers in the
    data help you determine the best measure of central tendency? _____
    _____

Solve Another Problem

12. Find the mean, median, and mode. Which measure
    of central tendency best describes the data? Explain.
    scores on a quiz: 14 15 9 10 11 9 12   _____
    _____

482 Algebra-Readiness Lesson 12-1   Guided Problem Solving

Name _____ Class _____ Date _____

Practice 12-2

Frequency Tables, Line Plots, and Histograms

Display each set of data in a frequency table.

1. 5 1 4 6 2 6 4 5 1 3 2 6 4 5 4 6

Number						
Frequency						

2. 4 3 1 2 1 3 3 1 3 2 1

Number				
Frequency				

Draw a line plot and histogram for each frequency table. Find the range.

3.
Number	1	2	3	4	5	6
Frequency	2	0	4	1	2	4

range: _____

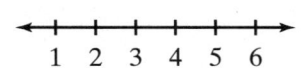

1 2 3 4 5 6

4.
Number	1	2	3	4	5	6
Frequency	4	4	0	0	3	2

range: _____

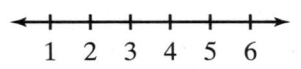

1 2 3 4 5 6

Construct a frequency table from the line plot.

5. **State Average Pupils per Teacher**

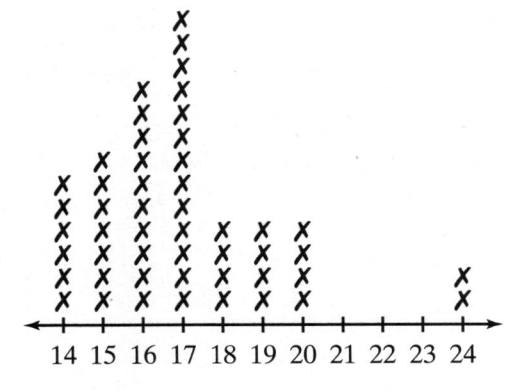

14 15 16 17 18 19 20 21 22 23 24

Pupils per Teacher											
Frequency											

6. What is the range in pupil-teacher ratios? _____

L1 Practice

Algebra-Readiness Lesson 12-2

Name _____ Class _____ Date _____

12-2 • Guided Problem Solving

GPS Exercise 11

In the World Series, the first team to win four games is the champion. Sometimes the Series lasts for seven games, but sometimes the Series ends in fewer games. Below are data for 1970–2004. Make a frequency table and use it to find the mode.
Numbers of World Series Games, 1970–2004: 5, 7, 7, 7, 5, 7, 4, 6, 6, 7, 6, 6, 7, 5, 5, 7, 7, 7, 5, 4, 4, 7, 6, 6, 0, 6, 6, 7, 4, 4, 5, 7, 7, 6, 4

Understand the Problem

1. What data are you given? _____

2. What are you asked to do? _____

Make and Carry Out a Plan

3. Look at the data. Put a tally mark in the row corresponding to the number of games played for each year.

4. When all of the tally marks have been made, count the tally marks and record the frequency for each number of games.

5. To find the mode of the data, look in the "Frequency" column. Which number of games occurred most often? _____

Number of Games	Tally	Frequency
0		
1		
2		
3		
4		
5		
6		
7		

Check the Answer

6. Check to make sure you have entered all the data in the frequency table. Use the list of World Series games played each year. Add to find the number of games played in all from 1970 to 2004. _____

Solve Another Problem

7. Angela kept track of how many hours she practiced her saxophone each week over the nine months of the school year. Make a frequency table and use it to find the mode. _____

Number of hours of practice each week: 3, 5, 5, 0, 5, 3, 2, 1, 1, 4, 2, 4, 4, 5, 3, 0, 4, 3, 4, 2, 3, 3, 0, 4, 3, 5, 5, 0, 3, 4, 5, 3, 2, 2, 1

Name _____ Class _____ Date _____

Practice 12-3

Box-and-Whisker Plots

Use the box-and-whisker plot to answer each question.

Weekly Mileage Totals, 24 Runners

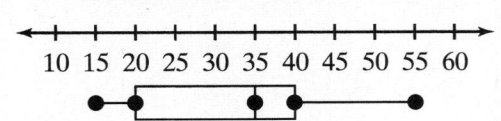

```
  10 15 20 25 30 35 40 45 50 55 60
       •——[——•——]——————•
```

1. What is the highest weekly total? _____ the lowest? _____

2. What is the median weekly total? _____

3. What percent of runners run less than 40 miles a week? _____

4. How many runners run less than 20 miles a week? _____

Make a box-and-whisker plot for each set of data.

5. 16 20 30 15 23 11 15 21 30 29 13 16

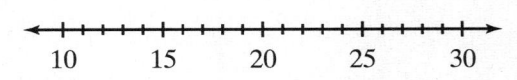

6. 9 12 10 3 2 3 9 11 5 1 10 4 7 12 3 10

7. 70 77 67 65 79 82 70 68 75 73 69 66
   70 73 89 72

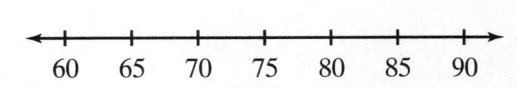

Use box-and-whisker plots to compare data sets. Use a single number line for each comparison.

8. 1st set: 7 12 25 3 1 29 30 7 15 2 5
              10 29 1 10 30 18 8 7 29
   2nd set: 37 17 14 43 27 19 32 1 8 48
              26 16 28 6 25 18

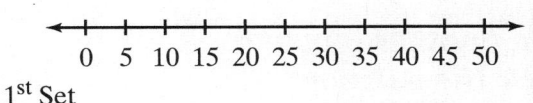

9. Area in 1,000 mi^2
   Midwestern states:
   45 36 58 97 56 65 87 82 77
   Southern states:
   52 59 48 52 42 32 54 43 70 53 66

L1 Practice

Algebra-Readiness Lesson 12-3   **485**

Name _____ Class _____ Date _____

12-3 • Guided Problem Solving

GPS Exercise 14

a. Compare the ages of male and female soccer players by making two box-and-whisker plots below one number line.

Ages of U.S. Olympic Soccer Team Players
men: 22, 21, 22, 26, 20, 26, 23, 21, 22, 22, 22, 22, 21, 22, 23, 21, 20, 22
women: 30, 27, 28, 25, 31, 24, 31, 24, 21, 23, 27, 18, 19, 24, 23, 20

b. Compare the two box-and-whisker plots. What can you conclude? _____

Understand the Problem

1. What data are you given? _____

2. What are you asked to do in part (a)? _____

3. What are you asked to do in part (b)? _____

Make and Carry Out a Plan

4. Arrange the ages of the men in order from least to greatest. Find the median of the data. Find the lower quartile and upper quartile, which are the medians of the lower and upper halves of the data. _____

5. Arrange the ages of the women in order from least to greatest. Find the median of the data. Find the lower quartile and upper quartile of the data. _____

6. On a separate sheet of paper, draw a number line that includes all of the ages of both the men and women soccer players.

7. Using the data you found in Step 4, draw a box-and-whisker plot for the data on the men's ages. (*Hint:* Since the upper quartile and the median are the same value, make only one mark.)

8. Below the first box-and-whisker plot, draw a box-and-whisker plot for the data on the women's ages.

9. How are the two box-and-whisker plots different? _____

Check the Answer

10. What information can you find from the two box-and-whisker plots due to the fact that they use the same number line? _____

Solve Another Problem

11. a. Use the data below to make two box-and-whisker plots on one number line.

Ages of Members of the Varsity Swim Team
boys: 16, 15, 15, 16, 17, 18, 17, 18, 17, 18, 14, 15, 15, 18, 17, 16, 18, 17
girls: 12, 15, 15, 14, 17, 18, 18, 17, 14, 15, 14, 14, 16, 14, 13, 15

b. Compare the two box-and-whisker plots. What can you conclude? _____

486 Algebra-Readiness Lesson 12-3   Guided Problem Solving

Practice 12-4

Stem-and-Leaf Plots

The stem-and-leaf plot at the right shows the bowling scores for 20 bowlers. Use the plot for Exercises 1–3.

```
10 | 0 2 2 4 4 4
11 | 1 3 5 5 5 9
12 | 4 5 9 9
13 | 0 6 8 8
```
Key: 13 | 8 means 138.

1. What numbers make up the stems?

   _____

2. What are the leaves for the stem 12?

   _____

3. Find the median and mode.

   _____

Make a stem-and-leaf plot for each set of data. Then find the median and mode.

4. 8 19 27 36 35 24 6 15 16 24 38 23 20

   _____

5. 8.6 9.1 7.4 6.3 8.2 9.0 7.5 7.9 6.3 8.1 7.1 8.2 7.0 9.6 9.9

   _____

6. 436 521 470 586 692 634 417 675 526 719 817

   _____

The back-to-back stem-and-leaf plot at the right shows the high and low temperatures for a week in a certain city. Use this plot for Exercises 7–9.

7. Find the mean for the high temperatures.

   _____

8. Find the median for the low temperatures.

   _____

9. Find the mode for the high temperatures.

   _____

```
  Low    |   | High
   8 7   | 5 |
   4 3   | 6 | 5 9 9
 2 1 0   | 7 | 2 5 6
         | 8 | 0
```
63 ← 3 | 6 | 5 → 65

Name _____ Class _____ Date _____

12-4 • Guided Problem Solving

GPS **Exercise 6:**

Make a stem-and-leaf plot for the data below. Find the median and the mode.

124 129 131 116 138 107 105 116 122 137 138 134

Understand

1. What are you being asked to do?
   _____

2. What are you being asked to find?
   _____

Plan and Carry Out

3. What are the least and greatest values in the set of data?
   _____

4. What will the stems be? _____

5. Make a stem-and-leaf plot for the data. Include a key.

6. How many data values are there? _____

7. Average the two middle values to find the median.
   _____

8. Find the mode(s) by looking at the stem-and-leaf plot.

Check

9. Order the numbers to find the median. Is your answer correct?
   _____

Solve Another Problem

10. The Cougars' practice times, in minutes, for the past two weeks are listed below. Make a stem-and-leaf plot of the data. Then find the median and the mode.
    51 69 65 66 78 79 65 56 59 79 66 79 71 67

488 Algebra-Readiness Lesson 12-4   Guided Problem Solving

Name _____ Class _____ Date _____

Practice 12-5

Scatter Plots

Use the data in the table.

1. Make a (year, units of CD's) scatter plot.

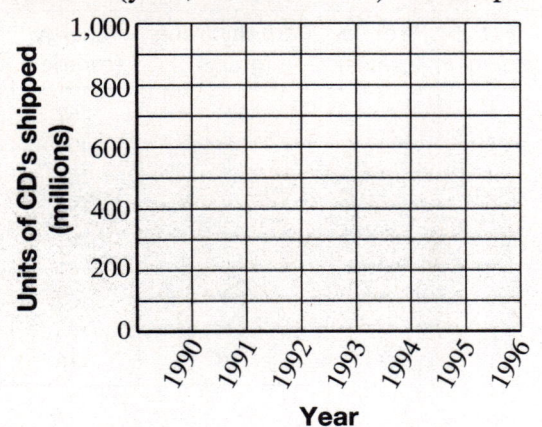

Sales of Recorded Music			
Year	Millions of Units Shipped		
	CD's	Cassettes	LP's
1990	287	442	12
1991	333	360	5
1992	408	366	2
1993	495	340	1
1994	662	345	2
1995	723	273	2
1996	779	225	3

2. Make a (year, units of cassettes) scatter plot.

3. Make a (year, units of LP's) scatter plot.

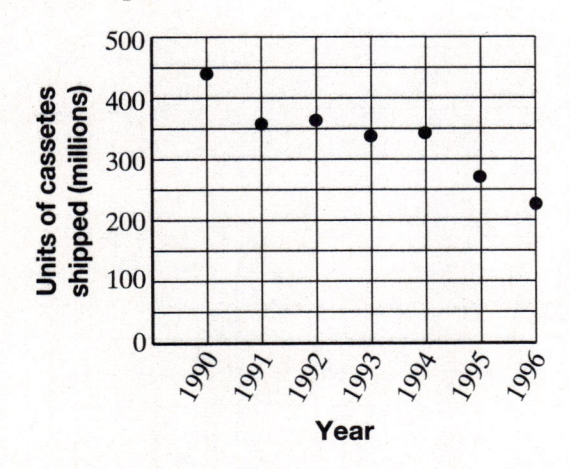

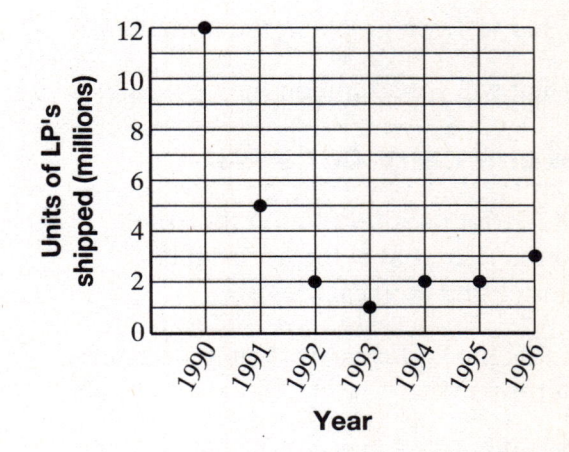

Is there a *positive correlation*, a *negative correlation*, or *no correlation* between the data sets in each scatter plot?

4. (year, units of CD's) scatter plot _____

5. (year, units of cassettes) scatter plot _____

6. (year, units of LP's) scatter plot _____

Practice

Algebra-Readiness Lesson 12-5

Name _____ Class _____ Date _____

12-5 • Guided Problem Solving

GPS Exercise 8

Use the table at right. Make a scatter plot for calories and grams of protein. Graph calories on the horizontal axis.

Nutritional Values for 100 Grams of Food

Food	Fat (grams)	Protein (grams)	Carbohydrates (grams)	Energy (calories)
Bread	4	8	50	267
Cheese	33	25	1	403
Chicken	4	31	0	165
Eggs	11	13	1	155
Ground beef	19	27	0	292
Milk	3	3	5	61
Peanuts	49	26	16	567
Pizza	5	12	33	223
Tuna	1	26	0	116

Understand the Problem

1. What are you asked to do? _____

2. What will you graph on the horizontal axis? _____

3. What will you graph on the vertical axis? _____

Make and Carry Out a Plan

4. Make your scatter plot on the graph to the right. Label the horizontal axis (1 unit = 50 calories).

5. Label the vertical axis (1 unit = 5 grams of protein).

6. Plot the data for each food on the scatter plot. Find the number of calories for each food on the horizontal axis and its corresponding number of grams of protein on the vertical axis. Make a dot for each (calories, grams) ordered pair.

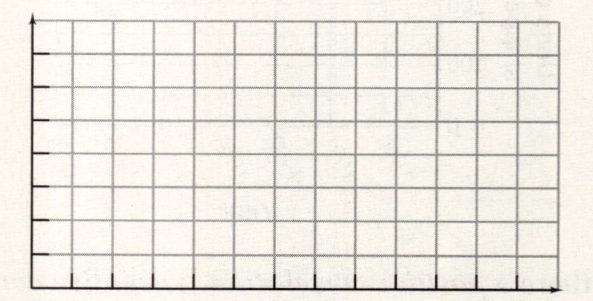

Check the Answer

7. To make sure you have plotted the graph correctly, check each point to make sure its location corresponds to its coordinates in the data table.

Solve Another Problem

8. Make a scatter plot for the data.

Minutes Studied	28	38	15	75	46	55	87	28
Score on Test	65	70	58	86	70	72	97	55

490 Algebra-Readiness Lesson 12-5 Guided Problem Solving

Name _____ Class _____ Date _____

Practice 12-6
Reasoning Strategy: Solve by Graphing

A giraffe was 1 ft tall at birth, 7 ft tall at the age of 4, and $11\frac{1}{2}$ ft tall at the age of 7.

1. Use the data to make a (age, height) scatter plot.
2. Draw a trend line.
3. Write an equation for your trend line in slope-intercept form.

   _____

4. Use your equation to find the following information.
   a. the giraffe's height at the age of 5

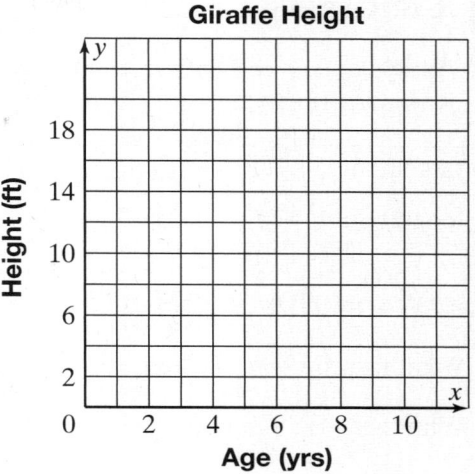

   _____

   b. the age at which the giraffe was 16 ft tall

   _____

Giraffe Height

A hippopotamus weighed 700 lb at the age of 1 and 1,900 lb at the age of 3, and 2,500 lb at the age of 4.

5. Use the data to make a (age, weight) scatter plot.
6. Draw a trend line.
7. Write an equation for your trend line.

   _____

8. Use the equation to predict the following information.
   a. the hippo's weight at the age of 8

   _____

   b. the age at which the hippo weighed 7,900 lb

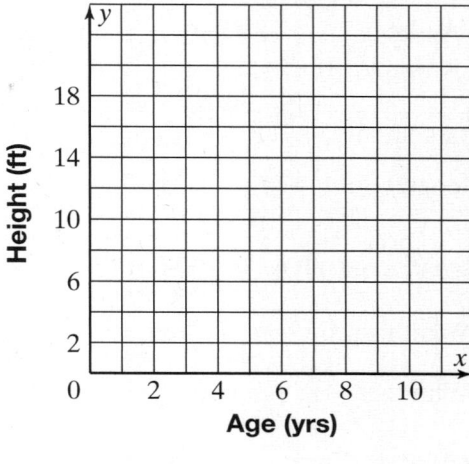

   _____

9. Can this equation be used to predict the hippo's weight at any age? Explain.

   _____

   _____

Hippopotamus Weight

L1 Practice

Algebra-Readiness Lesson 12-6 **491**

Name _____ Class _____ Date _____

12-6 • Guided Problem Solving

GPS Exercise 3

Data Analysis Use the data in the table below. Predict the number of gallons bought for $15.

Dollars Spent	12	14	11	12	10	6	10	8
Gallons Bought	7.3	8.0	5.9	6.5	5.7	3.5	5.1	4.4

Understand the Problem

1. What are the two variables? _____

2. What are you asked to predict? _____

Make and Carry Out a Plan

3. Graph the data in a scatter plot. Use the horizontal axis for dollars spent and the vertical axis for gallons bought. Then graph the (dollars, gallons) ordered pairs.

4. Sketch a trend line. Remember that the line should be as close as possible to each data point, and there should be about as many points above the line as there are below.

5. Find the point on your trend line that corresponds to 15 on the horizontal axis. To what value does this point correspond on the vertical axis? _____

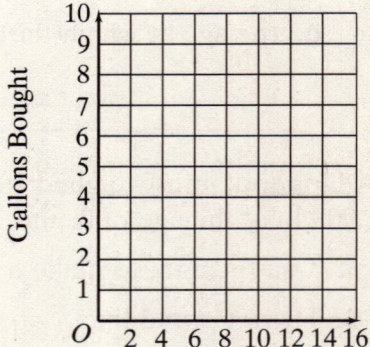

6. About how many gallons can be bought for $15? _____

Check the Answer

7. To check your answer, solve the proportion $\frac{11}{5.9} = \frac{15}{x}$. _____

   This should be close to the answer you got for Step 6.

Solve Another Problem

8. Use the data in the table below.
   Predict the cost of making a 25-minute call. _____

Length of Phone Call (min)	2	4.5	20	13.25	8	4.5	17.75	10.5
Cost of Phone Call	$0.18	$0.25	$1.01	$0.76	$0.40	$0.23	$0.96	$0.60

Algebra-Readiness Lesson 12-6

Name _____ Class _____ Date _____

12A: Graphic Organizer
For use before Lesson 12-1

Study Skill The title for this chapter tells you what the chapter is about. Take a moment to sketch a right triangle and write some notes about what you know about these special triangles. Then skim the chapter to see what else you are going to learn from it about right triangles.

Write your answers. Use the Table of Contents page for this chapter at the front of the book.

1. What is the title of this chapter? _____

2. Name four topics that you will study in this chapter:

   _____   _____

   _____   _____

3. What is the topic of the Reasoning Strategy lesson? _____

4. Complete the graphic organizer as you work through the chapter.
   1. Write the title of the chapter in the center oval.
   2. When you begin a lesson, write the name of the lesson in a rectangle.
   3. When you complete that lesson, write a skill or key concept from that lesson in the outer oval linked to that rectangle.
   Continue with steps 2 and 3 clockwise around the graphic organizer.

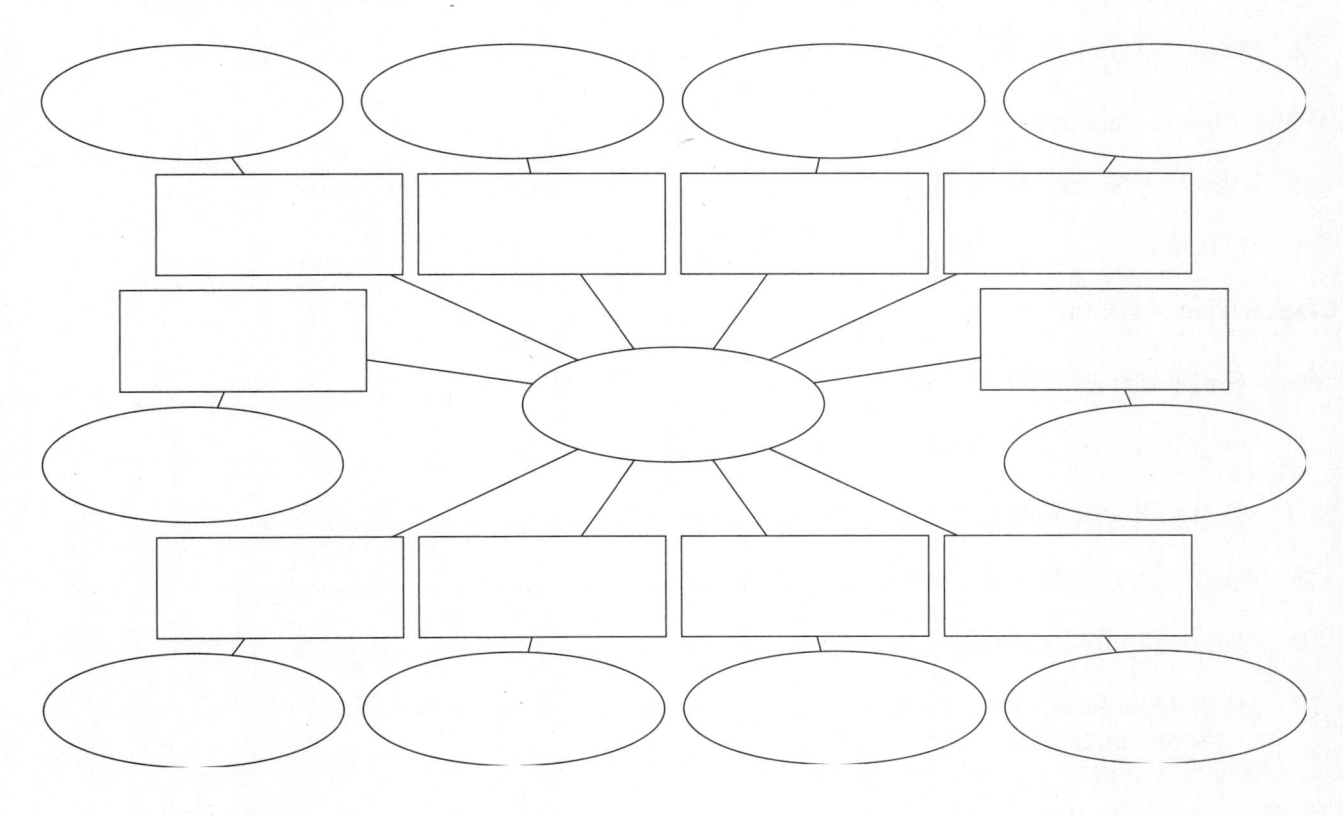

Vocabulary and Study Skills   Algebra-Readiness Chapter 12   493

Name _____ Class _____ Date _____

12B: Reading Comprehension

For use after Lesson 12-6

Study Skill If you will be answering questions about a passage, read the questions before you read the passage and have a notebook handy so that you can write brief notes as you read.

Read the passage below and answer the questions that follow.

The data used in statistics can be either discrete or continuous. The number of hits by a baseball player and the number of students in a class are examples of discrete data, because the data can have only certain values. Discrete data are often in the form of whole numbers—the results of counting. However, discrete data sometimes have fractional values. For example, a hat size might be 7 or $7\frac{1}{4}$ or $7\frac{1}{2}$, but there are no hat sizes between those values.

On the other hand, heights and temperatures are examples of continuous data, because these measurements can have any values, including fractional and even irrational values. A door might be 79.75 inches tall, or 79.754 inches tall (if a measuring instrument that is precise enough is used); the temperature of a liquid might be 99.8 degrees, or 99.8032 degrees, or anywhere in between. Continuous data are often the results of measurements. Continuous data are often grouped into discrete sets for the purpose of organization. For example, heights might be measured to the nearest inch or nearest half inch.

1. What is the subject of this passage? _____

2. What are the two kinds of statistical data described? _____

Which kind of data are the following?

3. basketball scores _____

4. shoe sizes _____

5. weights of coins _____

Write your answer.

6. What kind of data usually result from counting? _____

7. What kind of data usually result from measurement? _____

8. Can discrete data ever have fractional values? _____

9. Can continuous data have whole number values? _____

10. **High-Use Academic Words** What does *purpose* mean in the second to the last sentence in the passage?
    a. goal   **b.** comparison

494 *Algebra-Readiness* Chapter 12   Vocabulary and Study Skills

Name_____ Class_____ Date_____

12C: Reading/Writing Math Symbols For use after Lesson 12-3

Study Skill Diagrams can be very useful tools if they are complete. When making a diagram, be sure it contains all the key information even if this information has been given in the text that goes with the diagram.

Use this box-and-whisker plot to answer the questions about the data set it represents.

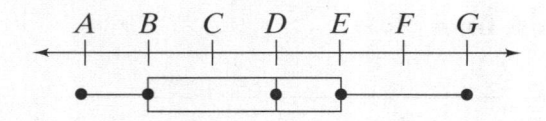

What does each dot show?

1. A _____

2. G _____

3. B _____

4. D _____

5. E _____

What fraction represents each of the following?

6. data contained in the box from B to E _____

7. data contained in the box from B to D _____

8. data contained in the box from D to E _____

9. data shown by the whisker from A to B _____

10. data shown by the whisker from E to G _____

11. What can you say about the number of data points from B to D, compared to the number from D to E? _____

Vocabulary and Study Skills   Algebra-Readiness Chapter 12

Name _____ Class _____ Date _____

12D: Visual Vocabulary Practice For use after Lesson 12-6

Study Skill Mathematic skills are easier to understand and remember if you can apply them to your own life.

Concept List
- bar graph
- box-and-whisker plot
- circle graph
- frequency table
- histogram
- line graph
- line plot
- stem-and-leaf plot
- tree diagram

Write the concept that best describes each exercise. Choose from the concept list above.

1. (frequency table with Number/Frequency columns)

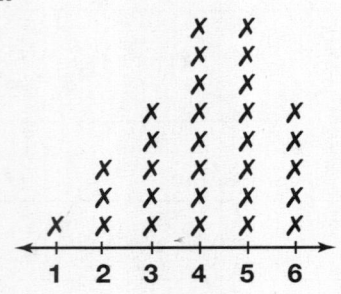

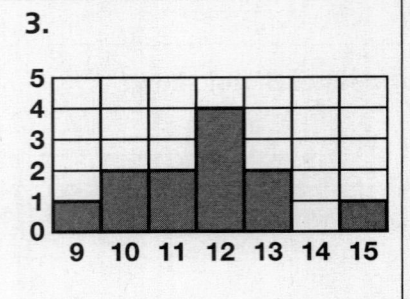

2. (line plot with x's over 1–6)

3. (histogram with bars over 9–15)

4. (box-and-whisker plot: Olympic Basketball Players' Heights, Men/Women)

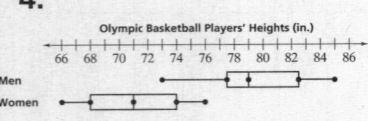

5. (stem-and-leaf plot; 7 | 5 means 75)

6. (bar graph: Surface area, California vs Texas)

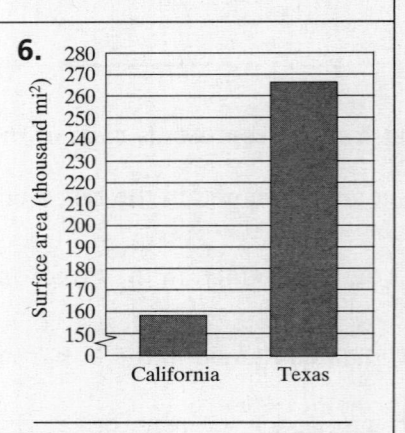

7. (line graph: Fish Caught, 1993–1996)

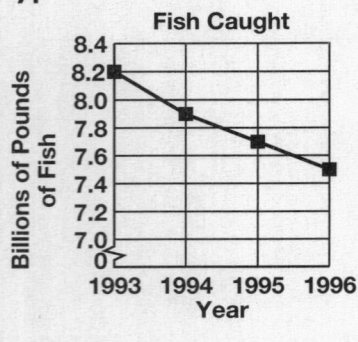

8. (circle graph: Selected Students' Favorite Sports)

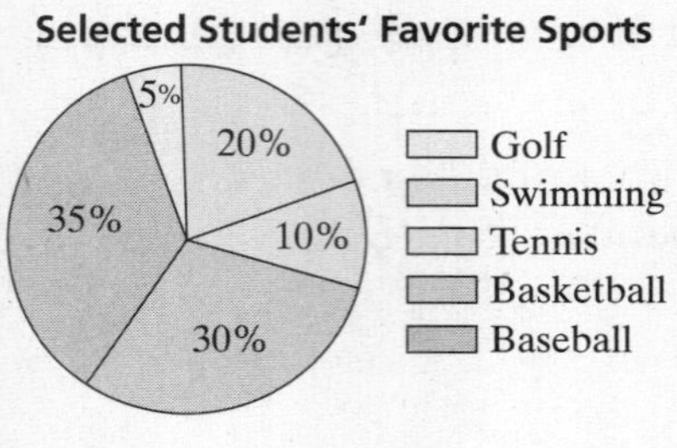

9. (tree diagram: blue/white/black → child/adult → cotton/polyester)

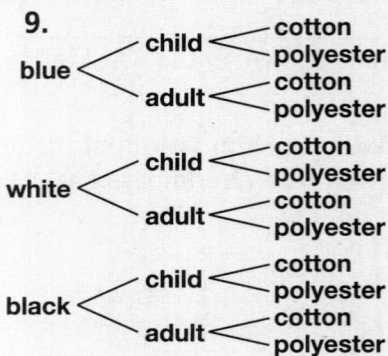

496 Algebra-Readiness Chapter 12   Vocabulary and Study Skills

12E: Vocabulary Check

For use after Lesson 12-2

Study Skill Strengthen your vocabulary. Use these pages and add cues and summaries by applying the Cornell Notetaking style.

Write the definition for each word or term at the right. To check your work, fold the paper back along the dotted line to see the correct answers.

_____ central angle

_____ mode

_____ mean

_____ negative trend

_____ outlier

Vocabulary and Study Skills

Algebra-Readiness Chapter 12

Name _____ Class _____ Date _____

12E: Vocabulary Check (continued) — For use after Lesson 12-2

Write the vocabulary word or term for each definition. To check your work, fold the paper forward along the dotted line to see the correct answers.

an angle whose vertex is the center of a circle   _____

the item in a data set that occurs with the greatest frequency   _____

the sum of the data divided by the number of data items   _____

when one set of values tends to increase while the other set tends to decrease   _____

an item in a data set that is much higher or much lower than the other items in a data set   _____

498 Algebra-Readiness Chapter 12   Vocabulary and Study Skills

Name_____ Class_____ Date_____

12F: Vocabulary Review Puzzle

For use with Chapter Review

Study Skill When reviewing a chapter, use the Chapter Review materials that have been provided in the text. Verify that you know the definition of each word or phrase in the Vocabulary Review.

Write the words that match the descriptions below and then circle the letters that form each word in the puzzle. Remember that a word may go right to left, left to right, or it may go up as well as down.

1. difference between greatest and least values _____
2. the number of times a data item occurs _____
3. divides the data into four equal parts _____
4. a model used to find experimental probability _____
5. a part of the population used to make estimates _____
6. a group about which you want information _____
7. one member is as likely to be chosen as any other _____
8. events in which the first event does affect the second event _____

E	D	E	P	E	N	D	E	N	T	F	U	N
P	O	P	U	L	A	T	I	O	N	R	M	O
E	E	N	P	O	Q	R	S	U	P	E	O	I
A	T	U	N	P	U	A	U	I	E	Q	S	T
N	U	M	D	E	A	N	L	D	U	U	D	A
S	U	D	L	L	R	G	N	M	M	E	T	L
N	A	N	A	G	T	E	N	E	A	N	I	U
M	T	O	E	O	I	P	Q	U	I	C	E	M
N	A	P	O	E	L	U	E	R	L	Y	O	I
E	T	S	F	E	E	R	A	N	D	O	M	S
N	L	N	D	S	A	M	P	L	E	P	U	D

Vocabulary and Study Skills

Algebra-Readiness Chapter 12

499